The Albanian Question

The Albanian Question

Reshaping the Balkans

James Pettifer and Miranda Vickers

I.B. TAURIS

LONDON · NEW YORK

Published in 2007 by I.B.Tauris & Co Ltd
6 Salem Road, London W2 4BU
175 Fifth Avenue, New York NY 10010
www.ibtauris.com

In the United States of America and Canada
distributed by Palgrave Macmillan, a division of St. Martin's Press
175 Fifth Avenue, New York NY 10010

ISBN 978 1 86064 974 5

A full CIP record for this book is available from the British Library
A full CIP record is available from the Library of Congress

Library of Congress Catalog Card Number: available

Typeset in Adobe Garamond Pro by Sara Millington, Editorial and Design Services
Printed and bound in Great Britain by T.J. International Ltd, Padstow, Cornwall

This book is dedicated to
John Maguire and Sue Comely

Contents

List of Illustrations and Maps

List of Abbreviations

AACL	Albanian American Civic League
ATA	Albanian Telegraphic Agency
BBC	British Broadcasting Corporation
CIA	Central Intelligence Agency
CNN	Cable News Network
CSRC	Conflict Studies Research Centre
DP	Democratic Party (in Albania)
DPA	Democratic Party of Albanians (in Macedonia)
EU	European Union
FARK	National Army of Kosova
FBI	Federal Bureau of Investigation
FYROM	Former Yugoslav Republic of Macedonia
GDP	Gross domestic product
GMT	Greenwich mean time
HQ	Headquarters
IMF	International Monetary Fund
IMRO	Internal Macedonian Revolutionary Organisation
INGO	International non-governmental organisation
IWPR	Institute of War and Peace Reporting
JNA	Yugoslav People's Army
KFOR	Kosovo Force (NATO peacekeeping mission)
KLA	Kosova Liberation Army
KPC	Kosova Protection Corps
LDK	Kosova Democratic League
LKCK	National League for the Liberation of Kosova
LPK	Kosova People's League

LPRK	Popular League for the Republic of Kosova
MP	Member of Parliament
NAAC	National Albanian-American Council
NAPS	New economic space comprising western Macedonia, Kosova and Albania
NATO	North Atlantic Treaty Organisation
NGO	Non-governmental organisation
NLA	National Liberation Army of Albanians (in Macedonia)
OSCE	Organization for Security and Cooperation in Europe
PASOK	Pan-Hellenic Socialist Movement
PDK	Democratic Party of Kosova
PLA	Albanian Party of Labour
PM	Prime Minister
SHIK	Albanian Intelligence Service
SP	Socialist Party (in Albania)
SPS	Socialist Party of Serbia
UCPMB	Liberation Army of Preshevo, Medvedja and Bujanovac
UDB-a	Yugoslav Secret Intelligence Service
UfD	Union for Democracy
UN	United Nations
UNHCR	United Nations High Commission for Refugees
UNMIK	United Nations Mission in Kosova
USAF	United States Air Force
WEU	Western European Union

Chronology of Events

June 1998	NATO air operation 'Determined Falcon' over region
Summer 1998	Refugee crisis develops in Albania and Macedonia
September 1998	Assassination of Azem Hajdari and attempted coup d'état in Albania
October 1998	Deployment of the Kosova Verification Mission
November 1998	Democratic Party of Albanians joins the Macedonian government
January 1999	Racak massacre in Kosova
February 1999	Rambouillet conference in Paris
March 1999	NATO bombing of Yugoslavia begins
April 1999	Kosova Provisional Government formed by Hashim Thaci
April–May 1999	Major refugee emergency in Albania and Macedonia
June 1999	NATO forces enter Kosova
July 1999	Refugee return
September 1999	Demobilisation of the KLA
December 1999	Agreement signed on the Joint Kosova Administrative Structure
February 2000	20,000 march to Mitrovica to demand reunification of the city
March 2000	Fighting in Kosova Lindore/Preshevo forces 5000 to flee to Kosova
May 2000	Assassination of ex-KLA commander Eqrem Rexha, 'Captain Drini' in Prizren
August 2000	Kosova electoral law adopted
October 2000	Local elections in Albania
November 2000	Local elections in Kosova
February 2001	Onset of armed conflict in Macedonia
August 2001	Ohrid Accords end the Macedonian conflict
November 2001	National elections in Albania

Language and Terminology

In the text we use standard Anglicised forms of Albanian place names. Within Albania itself, Greek, a dialect of Slav-Macedonian and Rom are also spoken and are sometimes used in place names. In Kosova there have always been two main languages in use: Albanian, the language of the 95 per cent majority; and Serbian, with smaller minorities speaking other languages such as Turkish, Croatian and Rom. Other Slavic minorities such as the Gorani, Torbesh and Bosniacs use their own dialects; some are closer to Macedonian, others to Serbian. Albanian is spoken in the northern Gheg dialect but is generally written using the standard Albanian literary language, which is based on the southern Tosk dialect. The Albanian language also retains many Turkish words, particularly in rural areas and small towns in eastern Kosova.

We have used the verbal forms most common in daily usage as we encountered them. Most Kosova place names have an Albanian and Serbian form (i.e. Vucitern/Vushtrri). In this book we have used, in the main, the Albanian majority community language conventions, terminology and spelling; for example, Kosova, not Kosovo, although the latter Serbian form is still more common in some sections of the international community. In some cases, though, we have not been entirely consistent as language usage varies from place to place (thus the book keeps the Serbian form Podujevo, rather than Albanian Besian, but uses the Albanian form Peje rather than the Serbian Pec). In both cases this is the adoption of the most common current usage practised by the international community in Kosova, and this also represents a personal view on common usage in the Albanian majority community. Thus, Serbian Urosevac has been generally displaced by Albanian Ferizaj, but Besian has yet to displace Podujevo. The UN Humanitarian Information Office in Prishtina publishes a very useful *Atlas of Kosovo/a*, which reflects current usage.

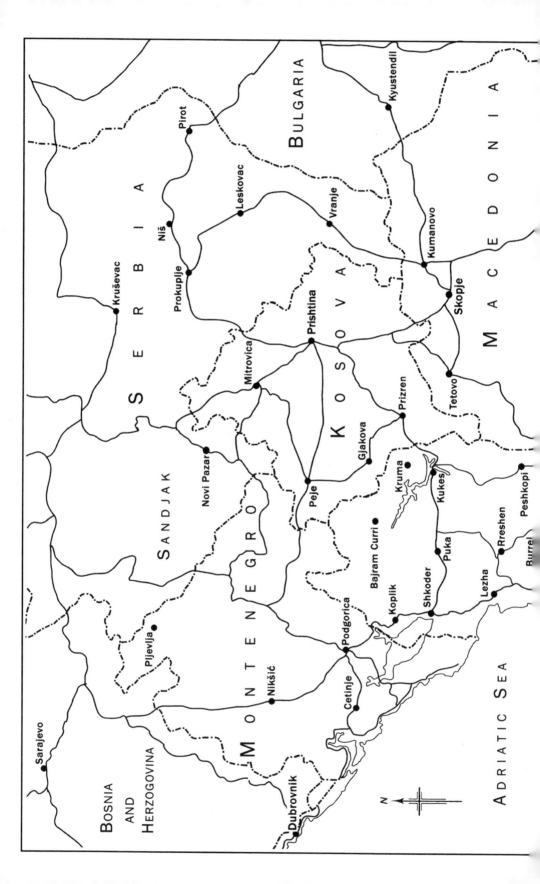

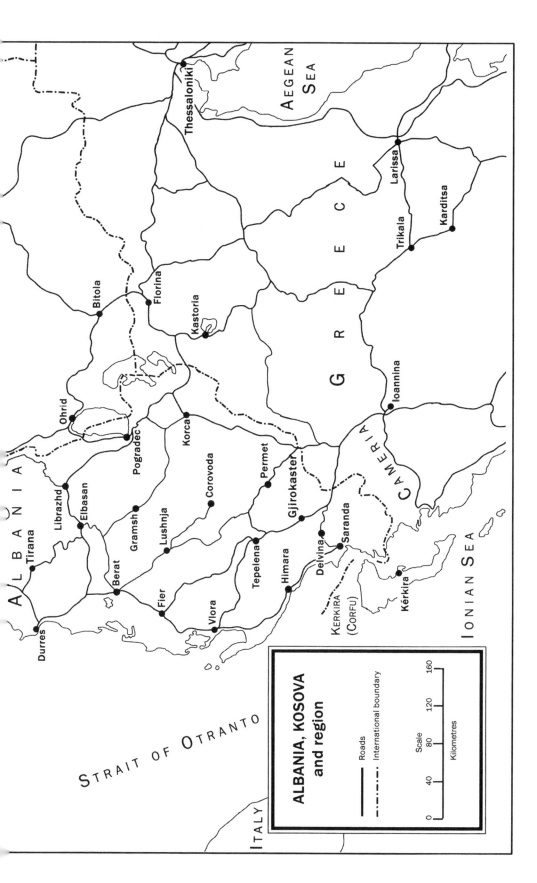

Preface

In our first book on post-communist Albania, *Albania – From Anarchy to a Balkan Identity*,[1] we traced the history of the final crisis of the one-party state after the death of Enver Hoxha in 1985 and the subsequent process of democratisation and personal freedom in Albania after 1990. That book concluded with a description of events in the autumn of 1996, and alluded to the developing problems affecting the future of the government of Dr Sali Berisha. This volume in essence takes up the story from that point, and traces the dramatic and turbulent events during the turmoil of 1997 and the onset of the Kosova and Macedonian crises during the following five years.[2]

It does so in the context of the emergence of the Albanian 'national question' in a new form during this period.[3] The serious concerns that we alluded to at the end of our first book grew very quickly to assume the dimensions of a threat to the foundations of the Albanian state itself, and thus the centre of gravity of our story is in the Albanian capital Tirana. The period from the collapse of the Berisha government and the armed uprising in the spring of 1997 through to the relative stabilisation of the country under the Socialist-led government, elected in June 1997, and the renewal of regional conflict constitutes one of the most dramatic periods in the history of the Albanian people.

Albania entered the post-communist world in an impoverished and broken state. Although some progress was made under the Democratic Party government after 1992, many underlying problems were not addressed. A highly overvalued currency developed as émigré remittances came to dominate economic life. Most local production, other than subsistence agriculture, totally collapsed. Despite efforts by the international community to build democratic institutions and assist economic development, these processes were hindered by the entrenched and bitter rivalries within Albania's political class. The international community did not fully appreciate the extent of the deeply rooted antagonisms between the left and right of Albanian politics, and as a result was largely taken by surprise by the events of 1997. The national question did not appear to be a significant issue until the conflict in Kosova posed a major threat to the region's stability.

Since the onset of the ground war in Kosova in 1998, the national question has become increasingly important in pan-Albanian politics.[4] It continues to remain central to the future stability of the southern Balkans. The Communist-period borders surrounding Albania and their movement restrictions have collapsed, and the Kosova refugee crisis played a central role in this. We have thus given a good deal of space to the events of the summer of 1998 in Tirana, as the massive refugee movement from Kosova began to take place.[5]

In our view the roots of the new national question lie in that period. The Kosova war posed the issue for the international community in a concrete form, something that was repeated in 2001 with the conflict in Macedonia. This opened the historic 'Macedonian Question' in a new context, with the Albanian minority actively participanting in addition to the traditional Greek–Bulgarian dichotomy.[6] Some regional spectators, principally Serbia and its allies, have claimed that these developments indicate the emergence of a so-called 'Greater Albania' as a threat to peace in the region. It is part of our argument that this is not the case. What appears to be developing is an extra-national pan-Albanian consciousness, which is growing within the modern European norms of the opening and abolition of national borders.

In 1999 Albania gained unprecedented world attention as NATO waged its first war to remove the Yugoslav police and security apparatus from Kosova. After a year of comparative tranquillity in 2000, with the apparent settlement of the Preshevo Valley disturbances, the spring of 2001 saw the outbreak of widespread violence, in what was then the Former Yugoslav Republic of Macedonia (FYROM), between the Albanian minority and the Slav majority. Human rights campaigns also developed to reassert the rights of the Albanian population in the Albanian-majority region of south-west Montenegro and in the disputed Chameria region of north-west Greece. The Chameria lands of Greece had a substantial ethnic Albanian population in Ottoman times, which was drastically reduced by Greek ethnic cleansing in the twentieth century, culminating in the massacres of the 1943–4 period.[7] The Chameria issue played a significant part in the fall from power of the Nano-led Socialist government in 2005.

Since 1998, the Albanian National Question has become increasingly important in the politics of Tirana as a result of the liberation of Kosova and changes in the geopolitical priorities of the USA and NATO in the region. Traditional rivalries for influence between Greece and Italy over Albania also resurfaced during this time, after being obscured for most of the Cold War period.[8] Such events are discussed in some detail, as the inherited structures from communist Albania and Milosevic's Yugoslavia broke down under the pressure of events after the 1997 Albanian uprising.

In the aftermath of the Kosova conflict, cultural and economic links were re-established between the Albanian peoples that previously had been limited or totally prevented by artificial communist borders for more than two generations. A new Albanian political, cultural and economic space subsequently came into existence, and it continues to develop a growing regional economic influence. In the large Albanian diaspora there has been a cultural and political revival, which provided key humanitarian and other assistance to the war efforts in Kosova, Preshevo and Macedonia, and continues to support pan-Albanian national development through various fundraising and lobbying activities.

Despite almost a decade of violent conflict the Albanian nation has been able to make substantial progress in recent years, with a dynamic economy and one of the highest rates of economic growth in the region. However, despite a substantial rise in national income and the general standard of living for the more privileged groups, many Albanians still live in grinding poverty amidst derelict social infrastructure.

In this book we have endeavoured to set out the main current of events as far as they have affected Albania itself. Thus, this is not a recent history of the wider Albanian world in the Balkans. The Kosova liberation struggle was of a scale and magnitude that reopened the entire national issue, and brought about a fundamental reorientation in the world of Tirana politics. In some instances, particularly concerning the refugee crisis and the coup attempt in the summer of 1998 in Tirana, the central event was precisely and exactly determined by events in Kosova, and the two stories merge, while on other matters (such as the economy and the armed uprising in 1997) the story is largely contained within the borders of Albania itself.

Albania's international relations during this period have been of considerable complexity and involve many countries, including its Balkan neighbours and major external actors such as the USA and the European Union (EU). Whilst we have made every possible effort to depict fully the course of events, it is inevitable that more information will become available as government archives are opened and individual participants publish their memoirs. We have not, on the whole, spent much time on the activities of secondary international organisations and their initiatives, such as the South East Europe Stability Pact, as we have found that the effects of their activity on local events and political and economic developments have been much less significant than could have been expected in the aftermath of the Dayton Accords in 1995.

The book also contains less material on cultural and religious life than our predecessor volume, as the last five years have been totally dominated by political, economic and military developments. The post-communist cultural and religious transition that we outlined in our earlier book up to autumn 1996 has in general followed the same pattern of development in succeeding years. Churches and mosques have continued to be rebuilt and have growing observant congregations, but to date religion has been a moderate and sensible aspect of Albanian and Kosovar life and has not entered the political arena as a determinant factor. Cultural life has continued to develop in conditions of freedom, if often with some economic difficulty, as elsewhere in the world. The cultural and political differences between the northern Gheg Albanians and the southern Tosk groups have been discussed insofar as they have affected events – in the main to a much smaller degree than many external commentators on Albania had anticipated.[9]

The proliferation of contemporary source material has meant that we have been in a much more fortunate position to attribute views than was the case with our previous volume. The last restrictions on freedom of speech theoretically disappeared with the demise of the one-party state in 1990 but in practice, however, some negative traditions continued in the later Berisha years and this atmosphere affected our previous volume. These constraints finally disappeared in 1997 and since then complete freedom of publication has prevailed, and Albania has become a model for many other south-east European countries in this respect.

As employees of international research organisations, newspapers and universities, we have had the benefit of personal eyewitness participation in most of the major events described in this book. Miranda Vickers has mainly followed Tirana and the central issues of Albanian governance throughout the period covered, while James Pettifer was present in southern Albania in March 1997 and for much of the time at intervals in Kosova and Macedonia since.

In only a few cases have we not been able to disclose the identity of our sources as a result of security problems. These are in the main connected with the development of events in the summer of 1998, following the death of Azem Hajdari and the attempted coup. Both in Tirana and Prishtina numerous political leaders, journalists and military leaders have been most generous with their time and recollections in discussing this momentous time in Albanian history with us. We owe particular thanks to Arian Starova, Neritan Ceka, Hashim Thaci, Ramush Haradinaj, Adem Demaci, Remzi Lani, Gani Geci, Sami Lushtaku and the staff of Dukagjini Enterprises. The same applies to a number of members of staff of diplomatic missions who were posted in Albania and Kosova in this period, particularly Geert Ahrens, Stephen Nash, Daan Everts, Louis Sell and Shaun Byrnes.

In the main the specifically military and media aspects of the Kosova war are not covered in this book, and readers should refer to James Pettifer's companion volume, *Kosova Express*[10] for more material on that subject. We owe particular thanks to the following individuals: Iradj Bagherzade and Liz Friend-Smith at our publisher I.B.Tauris, Sara Millington, Russell Townsend, Alexander Pettifer, Robert Curis, John Phillips, Melanie Friend, Richard Owen, colleagues at the Conflict Studies Research Centre at the Defence Academy in Britain, and the International Crisis Group (www.crisisweb.org), for whom Miranda Vickers has worked as Tirana analyst for the period covered by this book.

In the UK Bob Churcher, Julia Pettifer, Charles Dick, Colonel C. Dennison Lane and Professor Dame Averil Cameron have been kind enough to read and comment on parts of the draft text. Donald J. Smith and Primrose Peacock have provided very useful material on the crisis of summer 1997 in Tirana. In Washington Ambassador William Ryerson provided helpful and penetrating comment on our first book, which has enabled us to modify our earlier judgments of some events.[11] We have also benefited from reading a memoir document by Scott N. Carlson recording his eyewitness experience of the 1998 coup period.[12] In the USA we are grateful for the ever-generous support of Eqrem and Donika Bardha and the staff of Bardha Enterprises in Michigan and Tirana in marketing our work, Gani Perolli and family in New Jersey and Greg Kay, Henry Kelley and Antonia Young. We would also like to express our thanks to the journalists of *Illyria* newspaper in New York City, particularly Sokol Rama, Vehbi Bajrami, Ruben Avxhiu and Dalip Greca, and to Stacy Sullivan of the Institute for War and Peace Research.

Thanks are also due to Paul Stoddart and John Labercombe for much useful factual elucidation of the role of the Royal Air Force in the conflict.

All errors and judgments are our sole responsibility.

James Pettifer
Miranda Vickers

Ealing–Bath–Prishtina–Tirana

PART

I

1997

THE CRISIS OF POST-COMMUNIST ALBANIA

1

The Pyramid Banking Crisis and the Democratic Party Government

In the aftermath of the 1998–9 Kosova conflict, the Preshevo Valley violence in 2000 and the conflict in Macedonia in 2001, it is often difficult to recall accurately the very different climate in the Balkans in 1996. To most observers then it appeared that the Dayton Accords signed in October 1995 had brought peace to the region, and that the commitment of the USA that Dayton embodied would bring an end to the Yugoslav wars of secession. Slobodan Milosevic, later on trial for genocide at the Hague tribunal, was then seen as a force for peace, a man to do business with, capable of constructive compromise.

There were high hopes for the creation of a successful multi-ethnic Bosnia. It was thought that the Kosova problem would be solved by reform within Yugoslavia and the return to political autonomy for Kosova and a revival of the 1974 constitution. The pacifist leadership of the Kosovar Albanians under Dr Ibrahim Rugova seemed unchallenged.[1] President Kiro Gligorov was the widely respected leader of a new Macedonian Republic, and the signing of the 'small package' agreement in the autumn of 1995 appeared to have resolved the most outstanding problems with Greece.[2] The existence of an estimated 25 per cent Albanian minority within Macedonia was generally unknown. Albania itself was seen as one of the most successful countries in the post-communist transition, with a widely respected President, Sali Berisha, who had pushed through essential economic reforms, which had helped alleviate the misery and poverty of the immediate post-1990 period of chaos in the country. The days of rioting and ship seizures by desperate asylum seekers appeared to be over.

Although there had been acrimonious arguments over the spring 1996 election, much of the international community dismissed the overwhelming evidence that the election had been rigged as being politically motivated by leftist troublemakers. The theory was still current in many quarters that 'strong Presidents' were the answer to the problems of the region, and Dr Berisha was seen as a representative example. It was not clear then that the extent of the apparent prosperity was based almost entirely on political, and particularly economic and fiscal, illusions.

In the autumn of 1996 an atmosphere of uncertainty was beginning to spread through the political elite in Tirana but the majority of the population, however, were unaware of the storm that was to come. The International Monetary Fund (IMF) had issued a statement, on 5 October 1996, expressing concern about the growth of the so-called pyramid banking schemes after meetings with senior officials in the finance ministry. The banking system that Albania had inherited from communism had not been privatised and was deeply dysfunctional and inadequate for coping with the new inrush of hard currency from émigré remittances after 1990. In a post-mortem report on the causes of the turmoil in 1997, the World Bank observed that:

> Few countries have experienced such a rapid development of pyramid schemes and certainly none have experienced such a catastrophic breakdown in civil order verging on civil war following the demise of these schemes. The first such schemes emerged after the fall of the communist government in 1990. The number of pyramid schemes and investment funds grew to over 20 by 1996. Not all schemes started as pure, fraudulent pyramids. Some were more legitimate investment funds with commercial and trading activities that took on the characteristics of pyramid schemes somewhat later because of cavalier management and changes in the business environment (for example the end of UN sanctions against Federal Republic of Yugoslavia in 1995) … it is unlikely that any legitimate bank could have offered deposit rates that would have forestalled the flow of funds into these schemes.[3]

As a consequence, new finance companies were started, to soak up this liquidity. In Albania, however, there were few avenues for investment in the 'real economy'. The pyramids flourished and were able to offer very high rates of interest with new inflows of money financing the high returns paid to existing depositors.[4] Some Tirana citizens also had pleasant memories of the money made through the '2K' high-interest scheme in the early 1990s, run by Koco Kokedhima.[5] Soon rates of 30 per cent or more were becoming the norm.[6] Outside observers joked that people in Tirana had stopped doing any work at all, given the very high daily rates of interest payable by the banks – over 60 per cent on some accounts. Albanians returning from a summer of work in Greece hurried to place funds on deposit as soon as possible, and then paid for long holidays on the beach with the proceeds. It was a time of Weimar-like optimism, but the dance was on the edge of the cliff. The government did not have any adequate financial authority capable of regulating the pyramids, even if it had wished to do so.

The administration of President Sali Berisha did not heed the warnings of the IMF office in Tirana in October 1996.[7] The pyramid banks continued as before, with hitherto little-known figures such as ex-army sergeant Vehbi Alimucaj catapulted to public celebrity as the manager of the VEFA banking and retail group with a multi-million pound turnover. VEFA had many close links with the Democratic Party and the government.

The IMF had already observed the effects of this form of banking system in the pyramid crises in Romania, Serbia and Russia earlier in the decade, and felt the same risks might be reappearing in Albania. But the only practical effect of the IMF warning was that companies further increased interest rates in order to attract new deposit money. Alimucaj attacked the IMF in *Albania* newspaper, claiming that, 'The IMF wants to sabotage investment in Albania. I feel sorry to see that the IMF, an experienced organisation, identifies the business with usury.'[8]

Gradually, as winter approached, a minority of intelligent depositors in the main urban centres began to feel that it might be time to take out their profits. Consequently, some of the smaller and weaker schemes began to be affected by withdrawals of cash. Tirana was not the centre of some of the largest and best-financed pyramid banks; this distinction was held by towns like Vlora, with the Gjallica scheme, and Berat with the Kamberi bank. It was therefore natural that the first bank failures should be in Tirana as the run on these banks, with their weak capital base, began.

The little Sudja bank was closed in December 1996, as angry protestors crowded outside its offices. The London *Independent* noted:

> Albania has been in the grip of investment fever, with companies borrowing money from people and paying them extraordinarily high interest rates … the schemes are a powerful magnet, providing a glimmer of hope in a country with an average wage of only $55 and high unemployment.[9]

The exact amount of money invested in the pyramid banks is unknown but international financial authorities estimate that over $2 billion was involved, a huge sum for a small country like Albania.

The economic development of Albania between 1992 and 1996 had been based upon many illusory premises, but in fact it had rested on the rapid accumulation of hard currency from émigré remittances, which resulted in an overvalued currency. This coincided with the near total collapse in production in most of the old state-owned industries, and transition problems in much of the agricultural sector. Émigré workers were accused of irresponsibility and naivety in backing the pyramid schemes, but for most people there were few legitimate outlets for investment of money in real economy businesses. This created a very strange economy, where fiscal and economic life hardly connected. From the point of view of the foreigner observing superficially there had been considerable progress under the Berisha government, but in fact nearly all real economic value was being created by émigré workers outside Albania.

Once a crisis or 'run' on the banks began, there was little real economy available to prevent a major collapse affecting the entire foundation of society. The mechanisms of the Albanian state were too weak to prevent the government from being able to control popular street protest effectively. This was to emerge as particularly true in southern Albania where apart from a few towns such as Kavaja and Elbasan, where there was a tradition of active support for the Democratic Party (DP), the people were able to take control of their localities without difficulty.

At the same time, the Berisha government was encountering increasing unpopularity as human rights issues proliferated, and some key international backers in the USA and elsewhere began to withdraw their support. After several controversies following the 1996 election (in particular the expulsion of judge Zef Brozi and the exile of former Berisha henchman Gramoz Pashko[10] to Washington), widespread concern began to spread in some parts of the US government apparatus about the real democratic content of the Berisha administration and its increasingly authoritarian tendencies. The influential Greek lobby in and around the State Department saw Berisha as an aggressive nationalist. The Pentagon, however, remained more sympathetic to the Democratic Party regime.

In Europe, the Conservative government of John Major in London remained strongly supportive of Berisha, as did the governments of Italy and France. European intelligence agencies such as MI6 in Britain were aware of the 'hidden wiring' linking supporters of the Democratic Party in the European nations with pro-Serb forces, and were anxious to keep Berisha in power.[11] The Albanian diaspora in the USA exerted very different influences. Although traditionally very right wing and dominated by rich Kosovar families, there had been a trickle of important refugees from Tirana after 1991, such as ex-Foreign Minister Muhammed Kapallani, and a number of leading officers who had been purged from the armed forces by Berisha. They had begun to

1. President Sali Berisha addresses a meeting, 1 September 2005

affect opinion within the US diaspora, which in any event was growing more militant and better organised as a result of the emerging Kosova crisis.

On the issue of Kosova, the Berisha government was seen within the US diaspora as ineffectual and weak. In London, Albania was perceived as needing 'strong government' in the aftermath of communism. The government of John Major did not appear to see, or wish to see, that many of the political habits of the communist past carried on in the leadership of the Democratic Party.[12] The British government appeared unconcerned that Albania did not have adequate institutional or democratic development to restrain the President from excessive behaviour or extremist policies, or to protect him from the popular movement in the streets as it evolved in early 1997.[13] In regard to the growing disquiet in Kosova, the Europeans also seemed unaware of the significant new factor in 1996 of the emergence of the Kosova Liberation Army (KLA) as a paramilitary force, following attacks on Serb military and police installations in May 1996.[14] In reality, the omission of the Kosova question from the Dayton Accords had fatally weakened the leadership of the Kosova Democratic League (LDK) and Ibrahim Rugova.

Meanwhile, the crisis in Tirana began to intensify after Christmas 1996, with larger and larger crowds on the streets outside the offices of the pyramid companies as rumours spread about their waning financial health. On 3

January, the London *Independent* reported that 'huge losses in Albanian savings fraud'[15] were causing many families to face financial ruin as a result of their involvement in the investment schemes. In the centre of Tirana the offices of VEFA Holdings, the largest and most powerful of the investment schemes 'shot laser beams of white light over the city rooftops. It was a symbol of the brash new capitalism pervading Albania's post-communist society.'[16] The previous day, Finance Minister Ridvan Bode had warned that catastrophe faced Albania if the schemes collapsed, and made the first attempt by a member of the government to come to terms with the looming financial disaster.[17] The statement rebounded on the government when several pyramid operators increased their interest rates in response, as a move to reassure worried depositors, so that one competitor of VEFA was offering 32 per cent interest for just 55 days of deposit period. VEFA produced a new slogan for its supermarket advertisements on television: 'VEFA Holdings – always near you', an ironic commentary on later events.

The pyramid operators were more aware of the severity of the financial crisis than the majority of the government, and the following week *Albania* reported that $130 million had been taken out of Albania on a speedboat going to Italy.[18] It was also reported in Tirana that money was being taken from Albania to buy gold to deposit in Swiss and Austrian banks. In the capital itself, money poured into real estate, and *Voice of America* statistics showed that although in the poorest country in Europe, Tirana was the second most expensive capital in the whole of ex-communist Eastern Europe. Flats that could be bought for a few thousand dollars in 1990 were fetching ten times that amount in 1996.[19]

Some more informed people were returning their money to ordinary banks from the pyramid schemes, usually in foreign currency, and thereby increasing the strains on the pyramid operator's finances. But many pyramid banks continued to distribute largesse to their local communities; in an extreme example, the Lushnja-based pyramid operator Xhaferi paid for the local soccer club to have Brazilian and Nigerian soccer players imported. Although the glass bubble of prosperity seemed secure in Tirana, in other parts of the Albanian world, in the forests and fields far away to the north-east, the military struggle of the Kosovar Albanians against Serbia was intensifying. But in those days Kosova was far from the concerns of Tirana.

On 16 January the crisis deepened in the captial when the Sudja pyramid declared itself bankrupt, and a crowd of angry depositors besieged the headquarters. There were also angry demonstrations in the southern town of Vlora over the same issues.[20] Although the Sudja operation was a small scheme, it had attracted many depositors who were residents of central

Tirana. The colourful personality of Mrs Sudja, an extrovert Roma woman who had started life as a washerwoman, made much media coverage. She had claimed to be able to foretell the financial future and the level of interest rates by consulting her crystal ball.[21]

The angry Tirana depositors converged on the Sudja offices and rioted after buckets of dirty water and urine were poured over them. In an ominous sign for the Berisha administration, the police stood by and did not attempt to prevent the demonstrators venting their anger on the Sudja premises. The demonstrators shouted 'O Sali, o fajdexhi', 'Sali, you usurer', abusing the President. Around 500 demonstrators broke away from the main demonstration and marched on the central Skanderbeg Square, where police eventually acted to prevent them attacking government offices. Given that the Sudja scheme had stopped making payments to depositors as long ago as mid-November 1996, it was perhaps surprising that street protest had taken as long to materialise as it did.

Immediately, the Socialist Party sought to capitalise on the situation, and called for nationwide street protests against the government. For some, though, their position was compromised by close links between a small minority of prominent Socialists in the south and some of the pyramid operators. A few of the more intelligent among them, such as the Silva scheme management, were now lowering interest rates to as little as 5 per cent a month, and the Gjallica organisation attempted to placate worried depositors by forming a creditors' committee to represent its 200,000 account holders after it had reported problems in repaying depositors funds. The Populli scheme also ran out of liquid funds in the week of 16 January and its director, Bashkim Driza, blamed the government for the crisis as it tried to limit daily account liquidations to a maximum level of 30 million Albanian lek (about $300,000).

The Berisha government, seeing the situation worsening, attempted to consolidate support for the key pyramids close to the Democratic Party, VEFA and Kamberi, by giving them the status of banks. VEFA boss Vehbi Alimucaj later told a foreign reporter he had many non-banking assets, such as the 30 supermarkets he owned all over the country, and claimed that VEFA was in a stable condition.[22] It was certainly true that VEFA had worthwhile industrial and agricultural assets, unlike many of the pyramid organisations, but most of them were incapable of generating anything like the enormous amounts of cash to underwrite the liabilities of the pyramid banking parts of VEFA. According to the Central Bank of Albania, funds deposited in the secondary banks had increased in 1996 by $290 million compared to 1995. Prime Minister Alexander Meksi said that the government would compile a law to close down the pyramid schemes, saying that 'all Albanians deserved equal compensation from the division of the properties of these companies'.[23]

During this critical week, although three operators had been closed down, the government took no action to stem the flow of funds out of the remaining schemes, and it was not until 21 January that an order was issued by the finance ministry to freeze hundreds of thousands of accounts. The government appears to have hesitated to act, as closure of the schemes would have dented the Berisha government's reputation as an architect of popular capitalism. The closure decision was taken after a large and angry Tirana demonstration the previous day but only led to a growth in militancy elsewhere in Albania, particularly in the Adriatic coastal city of Vlora. Vlora people had been some of the most active participants in the pyramid schemes, and the tough and poverty-stricken city has a strong nationalist and popular political tradition. Under communism, Vlora had been the power base of leading politicians such as Enver Hoxha's Foreign Minister Hysni Kapo. The town had also housed numerous Albanian refugees from Greece, known as Chams, in the post-Second World War period, and was a febrile mixture of intense political loyalties.[24] Additionally, a significant number of army officers who had been purged from the army by the Democratic Party government Defence Ministers came from Vlora.

Aware of the risks to its future, VEFA Holdings republished its public relations booklet, entitled 'Our aim is to create as many jobs as possible', and stated that the centre of its business was in Vlora, where it managed 45 enterprises ranging from battery chicken farms and macaroni factories to brickworks and other construction material enterprises. The publication went on to claim that VEFA had established 'the ABC of capitalism in Albania'.[25] Cynics might claim that, in view of later events, it would have been helpful if popular knowledge had extended nearer to the end of the alphabet. Before long, the political agenda of the demonstrations became clear, with demonstrators in Tirana fighting a pitched battle with the police in central city streets on 22 January, shouting slogans such as 'down with the Berisha dictatorship' and 'we want our money'. Much of the growing turmoil went unreported in the international media, which with its characteristic Serbo-centric preoccupations was still concentrating on the foundering middle-class street demonstrations in Belgrade against the Milosevic regime.

Although the Tirana demonstrations were violent, the government did not start to lose control of a locality until two days later, when in Lushnja thousands of demonstrators blockaded the town and cut off the railway line linking the town with the capital. A police truck was set alight and barricades were hastily built of wrecked cars, heavy rocks and railway sleepers, and the government radio reported that the crowd had set fire to the town hall and wrecked a cinema. The boss of the dominant local pyramid scheme, Rrapush Xhaferi, had been arrested the previous week and the depositors believed that the Berisha government had stolen all their money.[26] Xhaferi (known as 'The General' locally) was, like many of the pyramid operators, from an ex-military background. Lushnja crowds beat up visiting Democratic Party Foreign Minister Tritan Shehu, and elsewhere in the south demonstrators attacked town halls and public buildings.

In the closure of the Xhaferi pyramid scheme, the Berisha government was acting on the orders of foreign diplomats and international officials, who knew (which the Albanian people did not) that this scheme contained substantial funds belonging to the people of Kosova, deposited there by the Kosova 'government in exile'. The organised crime lobby within the international community saw this as a way to strike a blow against the nascent KLA, and as a way to weaken the Albanian cause in Serbia generally. But by doing so, the Berisha government alienated a key constituency of support in the coming struggle for power. Kosova money in Albania was concentrated in Lushnja, Kavaja and nearby Shijak, and officials may have been right to see some criminal involvement, but the action was profoundly destabilising for Berisha.

Meanwhile, back in Tirana, the government began to deploy soldiers in the capital to protect government offices, and President Berisha himself assumed emergency powers on 27 January. The move followed an ominous sign for his government, as normally staunch northern Democratic Party supporters began to join in the street demonstrations. An emergency session of parliament enabled the President to rule by decree on public order issues and to use the military to clear the roads and protect security. In the north-western city of Shkoder an estimated 40,000 demonstrators took to the streets against Berisha, while Prime Minister Alexander Meksi accused the opposition Socialists of orchestrating the demonstrations in a bid to keep power, as water cannons were used to prevent demonstrators storming public buildings.

This day's events marked the first time that the word 'anarchy' was used in foreign press reports, along with sententious observations about the nature of the Berisha regime. The London *Guardian* noted that Berisha 'earned Western tolerance by his resistance to any pan-Albanian tendency which might add to the problems in Serbian Kosovo and in western Macedonia'.[27] The material that was being released by the CIA to selected journalists in London and elsewhere also contributed to the process of destabilisation, as it was hard for even very pro-Berisha governments to maintain their support for a government that seemed to be so entwined with organised crime.

The vision of army trucks on the streets provided only a temporary respite for the government, as it was becoming clear to many Albanians (and to foreign reporters) that the very structure of the state was now under threat, and a struggle for power and control was beginning between the Democratic Party government and the demonstrators. It had not been long since the violent and chaotic days of the end of the one-party state in 1990 and 1991, and intelligent people had every good reason to fear what might materialise. However, despite the alarmist tone of much of the reporting of events there was little international diplomatic activity, with most diplomats seeing the crisis as a teething stage in the development towards capitalism and the Albanian transition, akin to the Serbian and Romanian pyramid crises of 1992–3. In an Olympian editorial, *The Times* observed that capitalism was not going to give the Albanians a free lunch.[28]

For many opposition activists and protest leaders, the key issue during the ensuing days was not whether they would receive a free lunch from the government, but whether they would remain free at all. The feared SHIK (Albanian Intelligence Service) secret police swung into action in an effort to arrest the leaders of the actions in the southern towns, and on 31 January the Interior Ministry said that about 250 opposition activists had been detained.[29] Dr Berisha appeared on television in late January and promised that during the next week the government would begin repaying lost deposits through funds seized from the closed-down schemes. This produced enormous popular anger, as people saw their money being transferred primarily to save the key VEFA pyramid organisation that was generally believed to be very close to the Democratic Party.

In a political response to the crisis on the streets, and prompted by the American embassy, the seven opposition parties, including the Association of Political Prisoners from the former communist era, announced that they had formed the 'Forum for Democracy' to make an alliance against the ruling Democrats. In retrospect this could be seen as too little, too late to affect the popular movement. If the initiative had been undertaken in autumn 1996, it is possible it could have defused the crisis into parliamentary channels, but by the time it actually occurred the crowds had little interest in the doings of the political elite in Tirana and their foreign associates. The financial reality affecting them and determining their outlook was that after a government refusal of direct financial aid on 30 January, VEFA was doomed and the rest of the pyramid banks with it. In a surreal move, the VEFA management claimed to the august audience of the *Financial Times* that they were not a pyramid scheme, and that the company was ' rhythmically forging ahead', with 'subsidiaries in the USA and most world countries'.[30] There was now a complete divorce from reality in the Albanian fiscal world. The value of the lek plunged by nearly 10 per cent that last day of January as people tried to turn their savings into foreign currency.

President Berisha and the government were now awakening to the magnitude of the crisis. Public order seemed to be the main priority, in the absence of capacity to halt the run on the banking system. The mobilisation of the army held the line for the government during the next week, as a precarious equilibrium developed between the government and the people, and fear of arrest drove some opposition leaders into hiding or even into temporary exile.

The government writ did not, however, run in the port town of Vlora, where over the first week in February there was a collapse of the local state and a takeover of the town by the opposition. At this stage, the Berisha inner circle did not appear to have had a survival strategy, or any clear grasp of what needed to be done. As a northerner, Berisha saw Vlora as an opposition heartland and he may have felt that it was better to leave it alone militarily until the anger subsided. But he could not afford to see a total loss of government control spread from the town all over southern Albania.

Within the next month, however, this was exactly what was to happen. The special police units were sent southwards to open up blocked roads and stop demonstrators from cutting off links between Vlora and Tirana. On 10 February 1997, heavily armed forces fired on demonstrators, killing two people, while another citizen died of a heart attack.[31] More than 1000 riot police tried to drive demonstrators out of the main square, which they had been peacefully occupying for five days. A large number of people marching from the neighboring industrial town of Fier tried to come across towards Vlora from the east, but were held back by troops. Local journalists linked the violence to the final collapse of the Gjallica pyramid scheme, which was based locally and had been the recipient of most people's savings.

The funerals of the dead were held in Vlora on 11 February and marked another stage in the acceleration of the crisis. About 30,000 people attended the funeral of Artur Rustemi, aged 33, who had been shot dead by the police two days before, and families looked down from their balconies as the enormous crowd wound through the streets. The headquarters of the Democratic Party was burnt down as the funeral progressed; an action for which the timing may indicate the entry of more planning and media-savvy leadership into the ranks of the demonstrators. Vlora had been a strong communist town, and old secret police and party networks undoubtedly played a part in providing local leadership for the mass movement. On the government side, although the security forces kept well away from the funeral, troop reinforcements were sent to Sazan Island, in the Bay of Vlora, which residents saw as a prelude to the power struggle for the town.

Meanwhile, in Tirana Parliament was debating whether to introduce a state of emergency in the Vlora area. The plan of Prime Minister Meksi to put Vlora under martial law had not materialised, with some Democratic Party leaders fearful that it might lead to a bloodbath and civil war. In London and Washington the focus turned to the Major government and its relations with the Berisha regime, with media allegations that John Major himself, Foreign Minister Douglas Hurd and other members of the government had received presents from President Berisha whilst on a visit to London that were illegally looted from Albanian state museums. These allegations were a revival of the claims that were prevented by MI6 and/or Foreign Office pressure from appearing in *The Cook Report* on British television in November 1995, and were an uncomfortable reminder of the close links between the Democratic Party, the British government and the London Foreign Office.

Following a raid by armed police on the home of opposition leader Neritan Ceka, many members of the Tirana elite were beginning to see themselves drawn into the maelstrom that was centred on Vlora and the south. They would have difficult and complex decisions to make in the coming weeks. In the light of documentation that has surfaced since 1997 their fears were justified, with the revelation that a list existed of many prominent political figures that the government wanted to arrest.[32] Yet their position was not straightforward. Although nearly all feared and despised Berisha and wished to see new elections, most were closely integrated into the traditional Tirana political elite formed under the communist system, and instinctively distrusted popular political initiatives. Many who had recently been senior communist officials regarded the majority of the population with open distaste, particularly peasants and the urban poor. Those with knowledge of northern Albania had no illusions about the depth of unresolved revenge instincts there, and the possibility of a national schism over the pyramid crisis. Unlike in Kosova, whose Albanians had built strong trades unions, in Albania there were no rank-and-file organisations commanding the loyalty of ordinary people or with leaders that might act as mediators between popular anger and a sensible governmental response.

The political elite in Tirana were a small, often socially isolated group and although no longer communist, they remained in many ways prisoners of the modus operandi of the Enverist political world, or even, some might claim, aspects of the narrow world of inherited political traditions of pre-Second World War Tirana. This isolation and the seriousness of the crisis meant that from the point of view of most leaders, a priority was to stay in Tirana and attempt to curry favour with key international community and diplomatic figures, in the hope of becoming part of a post-Berisha political settlement.

It was also a factor in their oppositional psychology that with Tirana government authority itself under threat, a responsible course was to stay in the capital and try to reinforce government authority and prevent civil conflict.

However understandable all these motives may have been, it meant in practice that the crowds of angry depositors in the provinces were either leaderless, or open to influence from old political networks surviving from the communist period. There were no obvious 'moderate' leaders who might try to control the movement and open negotiations with the government. In that sense, the development of the crisis is part of the wider crisis of political elite development in Albania after the end of the one-party state in 1991. The foreign diplomats trying to control the crisis in many cases rarely left Tirana, and consequently had little knowledge of provincial life.

In the British case, ambassadors in the Balkan region were dependent for intelligence on MI6 officials, many of whom were imbued with strong pro-Serb sympathies and an uncritical, almost religious admiration for Berisha. In contrast, the USA's CIA was making more objective material available to journalists, such as detail on the London government gifts scandal, but did not have a significant presence in Albania outside of Tirana. Italy, with Germany, the main international backer of the Berisha government, was preoccupied with population movement issues, and feared the return of the days of ship seizures and the mass emigration attempts of the 1991–2 period, and lacked the diplomatic presence in Tirana to influence events. France had a number of prominent experts on Albania, but most of them were close to the old ex-communists and were often of an elitist personal culture and unaware of developments on the streets.

The week beginning 17 February 1997 was one of some success for Berisha on the public order front, and may have accounted for the obduracy he showed later in the crisis. It appeared from the centre of Tirana that his public order measures might be working. Although demonstrations of several thousand people took to the streets every day in Fier, Vlora, Patos and other southern towns, the anti-government movement seemed to be contained there, and the police and security apparatus were able to prevent mass action on the streets of the capital. At this point President Berisha was beginning to attract some media support from conservative figures who saw the whole crisis as one of 'anarchy and criminality'. Prominent apologists for the Berisha government were able to write in major international newspapers on the government's behalf claiming that the whole issue was one of organised crime and the mafia.[33] *The Times* correspondent Richard Owen interviewed Berisha on 14 February and found him confident of survival, and noted that the protests 'lacked direction'.[34] In Tirana, some small amounts of money began to be repaid by the government to some favoured investors, which may have taken some of the heat out of the protests.

Yet in terms of international opinion, the January and early February protests had delivered a potentially fatal blow to the government. The *Financial Times* wrote on 19 February that the hopes of the past were in tatters, and money continued to flood out of the country and the value of the lek currency reduced further.[35] Although the rebel-controlled area of the south was not growing in size, being comprised essentially of Vlora, Patos, Lushnja and Fier with some smaller adjacent centres, there was no sign of the government having the capacity to retake control of them.

The power of SHIK was now being tested to the full, with random arrests and imprisonment of suspected militants, and a free hand being given against suspect foreigners, particularly British journalists (such as Joanna Robertson of the *Guardian*, one of several foreign reporters beaten up by SHIK outside parliament in Tirana on 28 February). In the capital the reign of SHIK terror seemed to be succeeding, but the position in the provinces was less clear. While in the south the rebellion continued, in the north the prospect of acting as storm troopers for an anti-Berisha movement clearly did not appeal to many who might otherwise have joined the protest movement.

The divergence between American and European policy on how to contain the crisis continued to grow. The USA was concerned for the future of Albanian democracy and its Tirana Embassy issued a strong statement on 27 February calling for early elections and a new constitution. The British and European missions, however, remained silent, clearly hoping that Berisha would gain a public order victory and that the protest movement would collapse. In practice, it appeared that the Europeans were prepared to see a period of martial law in Albania and the complete suspension of democratic rights as Berisha established a de facto dictatorship.

Faced with this prospect, militancy grew in the Greek-speaking areas of the south. Relations between Greece and the administration of President Berisha had been very poor since the 'Omonia' human rights trial in autumn 1995. Greece also had close links with many Socialist leaders, a significant number of whom had been in exile in Greece during the Berisha period. Southern coastal towns such as Saranda and Himara had always been some of the most prosperous places in Albania, with their good climate and prosperous agriculture based on olive and fruit cultivation, together with some tourist income. Under communism, links with Greece had grown since the 1976 agreement on trade between the two countries, and some humanitarian and medical exchanges (with Ioannina) were permitted to citizens of whom the Albanian Party of Labour (PLA) did not disapprove. The Greek-speaking population laid claim to large sections of the old Ottoman *ciflik* estates that dominated agriculture in the interior river vallies, although many of these restitution claims have been questioned in the post-privatisation period. During the 1992–5 land privatisation they had been favourably treated on this basis by Berisha. A surprising number of communist leaders originating from the deep south had Ottoman Muslim Bey family roots and Berisha had no wish to reward his political opponents in the privatisation process.

Thus the Democratic Party land reform and privatisation policy, however understandable from the point of view of the short-term interests of the Democratic Party, was highly divisive, and produced dissatisfaction on all sides. In Tirana few people realised the explosive nature of the crisis that was developing in the south, with most of the elite and virtually all foreigners seeing the north as the traditional place of violence and insecurity. The Greek-speaking community had large land holdings but no way of farming them satisfactorily and were leaving in ever-greater numbers each year to work in Greece, whilst the mostly Muslim Albanian majority felt a sense of grievance with the DP over the land issue, in addition to widespread cultural alienation from the northerner-dominated government in general. Some Kosova refugees and economic migrants from the north were beginning to move south, and contributing further to the land shortage among the non-minority population.

In the meantime the Athens government exacerbated the economic crisis by giving preference to Orthodox applicants in the work permit application process; so Muslim villages like Vrina, south of Butrint, sank into deeper and deeper poverty. The large-scale communist-period agricultural collectives such as the Lukova terraces, which had been very productive, collapsed due to lack of workers and disputes about who owned the land. The Greek Orthodox Church, under the nationalist extremist the late Metropolitan Sevastianos of Drinoupolis, had started to use the newly reviving church for northern Epirot propaganda.[36] Right-wing émigrés from Greece, particularly Corfu, were beginning to move back to restituted land going back to the pre-1939 period, particularly in Himara and Gjirokaster. Pro-Berisha and Hellenophobic enclaves, such as the maverick village of Llazarati near Gjirokaster, moved into confrontational relationships with their neighbours. The recently purged army and ex-secret police and border control officials formed a coherent and bitterly angry anti-Berisha group, who saw the patriotic achievements of the Hoxha period at risk from both the DP government and Greek interference.

There was a plentiful supply of small arms in the numerous magazines in towns and villages that had been organised so that, according to Hoxhaist military theory, the population could repel a Greek invasion. Heavier weapons were available in the army bases in Gjirokaster and Saranda. Southern Albania was a potent mixture of different social groups with an intense suspicion of each other and numerous economic grievances that caused savage social tensions. This provides the background for the extraordinary speed with which violence spread throughout south-west Albania in the spring of 1997.

The roots of the crisis lay in many misplaced policies that the international community had followed towards Albania in a politically motivated attempt to secure the long-term future of the Berisha government. As the World Bank pointed out in 1998:

> Albania in 1992 was an unusual country. The State was in an advanced state of disintegration, and yet the strategy treated Albania as a more conventional transition economy with sector and policy deficiencies that could be remedied by a swift inflow of resources, liberalization, regulatory reform, and traditional financial instruments. The strategy did not adequately recognize that the existing State/Society nexus was extremely fragile, demanding a very strong emphasis on governance issues and a prioritization of key institutional and sector reforms.[37]

In an odd way, the policy behind Berisha mirrored the voluntarism, to use the technical Marxist–Leninist term, of the Enver Hoxha period. In his key article in the *The Times* comparing Berisha to Enver Hoxha, Richard Owen encapsulated this fact, although the article infuriated Berisha's London coterie of support.[38] Then the Albanian people were expected to disregard 'objective difficulties' in agricultural and mining development based on forced labour in order to achieve preset norms of production. The international community neglected the objective difficulties facing the country in the transition and put forward a perspective for Berisha of capitalist voluntarism, where a market economy and institutions could be built by neglect of real problems.

The failure of this policy was to prove very expensive, in every sense, for its progenitors, as the events of February and March in the country were to demonstrate – as the reality of events punctured international illusions and those of Sali Berisha himself. The looming prospect of disorder and chaos was on many minds in Albania in this period, but few people could have anticipated the scale of the deluge that was to come, bringing the country to the brink of civil war within a matter of weeks and ending in the deaths of over two thousand people.

2

The March Uprising

The nature of the coming struggle for power in Albania was becoming clear to local observers by the middle of February 1997. At that point the rebellion in the south was still confined to a number of small areas, mainly the city of Vlora and the town of Lushnja. As yet there was no sign of disorder spreading to the capital: an important factor in a small, highly centralised country. The partial success of the public order crackdown in late February had encouraged President Berisha and his few close advisers to press on in the same policy direction. After a period of stasis in the last few days of February, with neither side strong enough to shake the resolve of the other, the government declared a 'General State of Emergency' on 3 March, which was done within the framework of communist-period legislation designed to mobilise the country against foreign military attack.

The Emergency Laws gave the government draconian powers to rule by decree, and to use the army against internal opposition. There was to be complete government control of the media. This emergency decision was taken as a response to the incapacity of SHIK and the police to effectively crush the uprising and as Berisha and Prime Minister Alexander Meksi began to see the seriousness of the challenge to their authority. Reports were reaching the government of random militant actions, often small-scale, against public property, particularly police stations, the offices of pyramid organisations and the Democratic Party. A key factor in raising their alarm was the involvement of the Greek-speaking areas in the south. Berisha insisted upon a shoot-to-kill policy against the rioters, which was authorised for southern Albania, in conjunction with a dusk-to-dawn curfew, censorship of the media, and roadblocks and car searches on all main roads.[1]

Dr Berisha was now struggling to maintain his hold on power as the final struggle for the future of post-communist Albania under his government began. In the south, old Socialist Party and Sigurimi[2] networks spread the power of rank-and-file workers and peasants into new localities, some coming under the control of 'People's Committees' (also referred to as 'Salvation Committees'). These committees were generally based on local Socialist Party organisations, which saw them as the only way to preserve Albanian democracy against the prospect of military rule or open dictatorship. Some, as in Korca, called themselves 'pluralism committees' to express their priority of defending democracy in Albania from one-man rule. Ex-military figures that had been purged from the army by Berisha were often prominent, such as the self-styled 'General Gozhita' in Gjirokaster. These people often had direct links with the Partisan Army traditions dating from the Second World War. Particular features of the Partisan military tradition were soon to emerge in the rising.

The Berisha government, however, saw the Salvation Committees as reviving the old communist-period local town and village party committees, thereby embodying the threat of a return to communist rule. The stage was thus set for a final, inevitably violent confrontation.[3] The supply of weapons was to become a major issue. As long as SHIK, the army and the police held a monopoly of small arms, Democratic Party power would be secure. In an ominous development, on 3 March in Vlora, crowds broke open military and police arsenals and began to form local militias. The scene was set for a potential north–south civil conflict. It is unclear whether the emergency measures passed by the government were taken as a response to these developments in Vlora, or whether the committees themselves acted to open military magazines and loot police stations as a response to the government crackdown. The exact sequence of events on 2–3 March is less important than the fact that both sides moved the power struggle onto a military footing.

By now the international media was becoming critical of Berisha and began reflecting the views of many Berisha critics in Tirana who felt the way was being paved for a new dictatorship.[4] In a television broadcast, Berisha called the events 'a communist rebellion backed by foreign intelligence agencies'.[5] The President's rage turned onto his old inner circle. For several days, Prime Minister Meksi had been uneasy about the implications of the more extreme measures, and the recourse to military confrontation.[6] As an intellectual and a renowned scholar from a Tirana family that had held senior positions under King Zog, he had a less confrontational character than the President, with his northern Tropoja background.

In a fury, Berisha dismissed Meksi's government on 2 March, using the Prime Minister very much as a scapegoat, and assumed personal rule himself. This was a legitimate tactic, but as the government tried to mobilise the army against the rebels, the army as the chosen instrument of state repression began to fragment and head for collapse. In the crisis, Meksi may have had a more realistic view of the incapacity of the army than Berisha. Many soldiers were deserting their posts and the officer class was split into several political factions. In Tirana Berisha clashed with his army generals, and the following day General Shemi Kosova was sacked as chief of staff and replaced by Berisha's military adviser, Adem Copani.[7] This was a result of Berisha's anger at the failure of the country's military leaders to take effective control of the situation, but in reality the army had been run down for a long period and by the spring of 1997 was in a state of decay, if not collapse.

Questions relating to individual officers' leadership and their capacity, or lack of it, were irrelevant. The Officer Corps had been repeatedly purged to remove those whom Berisha saw (sometimes justifiably) as pro-communist, and overall resource and organisational neglect was universal. The top US military adviser Colonel Dennison Lane had been removed from his post in autumn 1996, after being declared unwelcome in Albania. He had reported to the Pentagon on the real decline and disintegration of the Albanian forces that was taking place in the field and in the barracks, and had clashed with pro-Berisha generals. This crisis within the military was largely unknown to the outside world, even among those generally well informed about Albania, and many European foreign ministries and defence experts assumed that Berisha could win the power struggle using military methods. The idea of a successful popular uprising in mainland Europe in the late twentieth century was beyond diplomatic comprehension. In reality the army was as alienated from the government as the rest of the population, particularly in the south, and in practice Berisha could count on the loyalty only of the SHIK secret police.[8]

General Kosova was blamed for the reluctance of the army to open fire on civilians, but the armed forces were barely capable of physical deployment in many places. On the ground in the south, the capacity of Tirana politicians to influence events was proving fruitless. Their calls for people to stay calm within their homes were met with further angry demonstrations, often fuelled by the growing realisation that the collapse of the pyramid banks was final and their savings had definitely been lost. In Vlora, the undisputed heart of the rising, deafening volleys of gunfire filled the streets. On 4 March in Tirana, pro-Berisha thugs ransacked and burnt down the office of *Koha Jone*, in those days the main opposition newspaper, as Parliament, surrounded by scruffy troops with automatic weapons, re-elected President Berisha for another five-year term. SHIK operatives in black leather jackets toured the capital at night, ready to fire on anyone found breaking the curfew. But although the rebellion had developed into a major crisis in the past three weeks, the area controlled by the rebels had still hardly changed.

The key features of the first week in March were the rising militancy in the rebel areas and the incapacity of the government to prevent the transfer of looted small arms to the wider population. The Berisha government policy was in essence based upon an appraisal of the situation that suggested the uprising could be confined to the deep south-west and gradually crushed. The insurgents, however, depended on being able to spread their movement like a bushfire north towards Tirana for victory. The Communist Partisan military tactics of the Second World War closely influenced this perspective. The stand-off was unstable, and in practice, once paramilitary organisations had been formed in Vlora and elsewhere, there was little to prevent the spread of street power to the Greek-influenced areas around Saranda and Gjirokaster.

Saranda saw the streets full of angry demonstrators, and an attempt by an army detachment to move into the town was defeated after a pitched battle along the Saranda-Delvina mountain road, in which rebels seized a government tank. The Saranda army commander resigned his post on 4 March and ordered his men to desert and go home. The next day the army base at the little coastal town of Himara, with its Greek-speaking element, was looted, a barracks at Fier was overrun, and the local army commander was captured and had to be rescued by police. These events and other evidence of the 'virtual' and desultory nature of the Tirana military 'crackdown' were a catalyst for the beginning of a general uprising.

Italy began evacuating foreigners from Albania, and mobilised the border police and Italian coastguard in anticipation of mass migration attempts along the lines of those in 1991. The Roman Catholic Archbishop of Tirana, Rrok Miredita, called for direct Italian intervention to stabilise the situation; an indication of the connections between the Catholic Church and sections of the Democratic Party. The EU echoed calls made by the USA for a new government of national unity to be formed.

This weak response from the international community fell on deaf ears, as more reports came in to Tirana of the looting of military barracks in the south, and an Albanian Air Force pilot flew his MIG fighter to Italy and asked for political asylum[9]. Foreign Minister Tritan Shehu said on television that the south of the country was ' completely out of control', and German Foreign Minister Klaus Kinkel said he was 'extremely concerned' and called for an Organization for Security and Cooperation in Europe (OSCE) delegation to visit Tirana immediately.[10]

Southern villages near the Greek border quickly continued to come under the control of armed groups, while in Tirana long queues formed for bread and other basic commodities. Roadblocks around the capital were reinforced with special police units, while people anxiously gathered in the maze of new cafés in the central park and tried to get accurate news of developments in the south. During the course of this week, the doors of the last functioning pyramid operators closed and angry depositors surrounded the buildings, although VEFA supermarkets and other businesses continued to operate normally.

When on 7 March in the Greek-influenced town of Saranda the people's committee declared itself the local government authority, it was an auspicious harbinger of developments over the next two weeks. Later there were allegations that the Greek secret police and right wing extremist 'Northern Epirus' organisations had played a part in this decision in Saranda. It does not, however, seem likely that this is the case, as the then Greek government was fearful of the growing disorder spreading southwards into Greece, as the mobilisation of the Greek Army infantry forces to Ioannina during the next week showed.[11] If any secret services were involved deeply in the south, it was the old pro-Socialist Sigurimi networks. Those in charge in Saranda were an indigenous mixture of traditional Socialists and mainstream Greek-speaking political leaders, whom by background and experience since 1992 were profoundly alienated from the government of Dr Berisha.

Media controversy spread in foreign countries where the Albanian lobby was influential, but was often bitterly divided into pro- and anti-Berisha groupings. US State Department spokesman Nicholas Burns had condemned the state of emergency legislation in strong terms, saying 'We're very concerned the state of emergency declared by Parliament is being used to stifle free expression.'[12] In the London *Guardian* on 5 March, Miranda Vickers had called for Europe to rethink its hitherto unconditional support for Berisha, and a cartoon showed Berisha standing on a crushed ballot box. The pro-Democratic Party Oxford Helsinki Human Rights Group replied in kind in other publications. The Vickers article enraged the President and worsened the atmosphere between the government and the foreign media.[13] In *The Times*, James Pettifer wrote that it was doubtful whether the army could maintain discipline if there was a prolonged occupation of the southern towns.[14]

In retrospect, this was already an over-optimistic evaluation of the capacity of the army. The soldiers only held two major southern towns, Gjirokaster and Korca, and soon the power struggle would move to these centres with little prospect of the survival of DP government control. In London, NATO General Secretary Javier Solana ruled out any NATO military operation in support of Berisha, a decision which seemed to come as a surprise to the President, and which demoralised some of his associates considerably. Solana did, though, leave open the possibility of a future peacekeeping mission, of an unspecified character.[15] In neighbouring Macedonia the army was mobilised to defend the western border, and in Greece the dingy small hotels in the regional capital of Ioannina were suddenly filled with uniformed army officers.

In military terms by 7 March a de facto front line had formed right across south-west Albania: along the Vjoses River, from Vlora on the coast, then following the main road south via Ballsh and Memaliaj to Tepelena, and then eastwards towards Permet. South-west of the line of the river Tirana's authority had ceased to exist, except on or near some main roads. Pro-Berisha forces had a monopoly of heavy vehicles and armour, but the basic situation closely resembled the Partisan warfare of the Second World War, where these vehicles were very vulnerable to attack in the steep mountain gorges and tough local terrain. The insurgents often used donkeys and other pack animals rather than any kind of motorised vehicle and usually moved north on foot if they ventured into the hills. Most of the time, however, they remained holed up in pro-Socialist urban centres with a supportive population.

The key industrial city of Fier remained ostensibly neutral at this stage, although the small SHIK force controlling the town hall was greatly outnumbered by oppositionists milling around in the streets. The government writ did not run in the countryside within this zone, and rebel groups which had taken on a paramilitary character were pushing northwards towards key towns such as Lushnja that were known to be sympathetic to the rebellion. Lushnja was also the strategic gateway to Tirana itself along the lowland north–south main road artery. Armed formations from Tepelena – by 5 March firmly in hard-line rebel hands – had fought a pitched battle at Memaliaj to prevent Berisha trying to gain control of the road north.[16] This action involved dynamiting of an important bridge over the Vjoses River.

Although when the crisis was viewed from Tirana the government seemed to be holding a territorial front line, in reality in the countryside on both sides of the 'front' the army was suffering a continual erosion of control and loss of personnel through desertion. The Tirana government did, however, control most of the southern perimeter towns, such as Permet; the result of a reign of terror by the firmly loyal SHIK secret police. This was also the case in the key armament manufacturing towns of Gramsch and Poliçan, south of the strategically vital town of Elbasan, where SHIK operatives held trades-union and political activists prisoner in local police stations.

As a result of the rudimentary nature of the transport network and the uncertainty about who actually controlled the roads, it was not possible at this stage for towns like Vlora (where there was a large surplus of armed militants) to bring much assistance to the insurgents in the Osumit Valley to the east. In order for this to happen, the key city of Gjirokaster would have to pass into rebel hands. The terror tactics of SHIK in Permet lasted three days, on 5–8 March, and led to clandestine meetings of local opposition and people's committee leaders from other southern towns and villages. Here old political networks and groups of angry ex-army officers were activated to coordinate activities to attack SHIK operatives and seize control of the remaining towns in the south-west not under rebel control.

News of this must have reached Tirana through SHIK spies or friendly foreign intelligence agencies, or both, and Berisha and Copani made military plans for a final showdown with the south. Special forces units in helicopters were prepared between 5 and 8 March, with a view to a 'final assault' on the rebels and Berisha denounced Socialist Party leaders on television, accusing them of organising an armed rebellion 'to overturn the constitutional order and Albanian democracy'. This had the effect of driving hitherto passive Socialist Party figures into active support for the rebellion, as they feared that Berisha would not hesitate to take on dictatorial powers against their party in the event of a victory over the rebels. Rumours swept through the circles of the Tirana elite that the government had prepared a long list of people it wished to arrest, a rumour that later turned out to be correct.

On the morning of 6 March tanks on transporters rumbled southwards, and the security operation began throughout southern Albania. A MIG plane bombed the small south-western town of Delvina.[17] Four hundred armed and hooded men surrounded Saranda as cars brought looted anti-tank weapons and explosives into the town. In Vlora, armed men were stationed on the roofs of buildings. At last, sensing the depth of the crisis, the Major government in London began to modify its hitherto ardently pro-Berisha line, and in a limp gesture Foreign Secretary Malcolm Rifkind threatened to cut off foreign aid as a protest against Berisha's dictatorial behaviour. An important factor in this policy change was the cogent position put forward to the Foreign Office by ex-SOE[18] officer and leading diplomat Sir Reginald Hibbert, who exposed the secret links between the Democratic Party and key members of the right-wing and generally pro-Serb political establishment in Britain.

Back in southern Albania, there was a mass mobilisation of rebel forces, with the Fier–Tepelena road finally falling to armed groups and lorry loads of armed civilians taking up positions in the hills above the road to protect their new strategic asset. Berisha's soldiers fled north to a secure area in hills near the oil refinery town of Ballsh.[19] In the chaos, the already weak command and communications structure of the army in the south was rapidly breaking down. Groups of soldiers remaining loyal to the government were often without radio communications, money and food. Many simply deserted, fading into the countryside and going home. In the next critical week, as in many previous Balkan conflicts, control of the roads was central, and the new link-up between the Vlora and Tepelena militants isolated Berisha-controlled Gjirokaster. This ancient and famous town admired by Lord Byron occupies a dramatic site above the Vjoses Valley, and secures control of the main road route down to Greece and across to Korca, the main town of the south-east. It held a massive military magazine, with tens of thousands of weapons. If Gjirokaster fell to the rebels, Berisha would soon lose control of all of southern Albania.

The military odds were moving against the President as every day passed. In Vlora an estimated 15,000 men were now under arms and the military initiative moved back to the rebels again, after the previous two weeks had seen a relative stabilisation in favour of the government. In a desperate bid to contain the rebel assault the government concentrated soldiers north of the Vjoses estuary to try to hold the road but were attacked and driven away by a Vlora insurgent force under the leadership of Zani Caushi, a local paramilitary leader from a well-known Vlora criminal family resident in the Cole district of the town.[20]

The President was in essence relying on the power of heavy armour and tanks to subdue the rebels. But in the severe southern mountainous terrain, armour is of limited value, and the low operational capacity of the army handicapped its effectiveness. As General Colin Powell, the US Army Chief of Staff had commented in another Balkan context, 'we don't do mountains', but in effect that was what the Berisha forces had to try to do, with an army in a state of advanced disintegration. Although in theory the army had about 55,000 men in uniform and hundreds of armoured vehicles, only a few were in good condition, and in an ominous development for Berisha a tank had been seized by rebels on the Saranda road almost as soon as it had been deployed there. The military post on the Muzines Pass road finally fell to the rebels after a long firefight on the morning of 7 March. In classic insurgency style, barricades were built across the roads outside rebel-held towns; a product of the compulsory military training in Hoxhaist-period education, when Albanians were taught how to improvise defence against foreign invaders.

This training was an important background factor in the sweep of the rebellion northwards; most Albanians did not need to be instructed on methods of popular community defence, as it had been rammed into them in the civilian population military education process for decades in the Hoxha period. The same applied to the use of weapons; virtually the entire population knew how to use small arms and AK-47s. Military Chief of Staff Adem Copani and his military team in Tirana had increasingly few options to clamp down on the insurgency. In an effort to disrupt the rebels by attacking their communications, telephone lines were cut between Tirana and the south. Mobile phone networks did not exist in Albania at this time, and the government believed that this would have a major impact but this analysis neglected to acknowledge the power of the informal networks of personal communication in the southern communities, and the power of the Partisan popular military tradition where everyone knew how to improvise basic military techniques.

By the morning of 7 March it was clear that the government offensive had largely failed and Berisha was forced to change tack, offering a truce if the rebel leaders handed over their weapons. In Tirana, Alliance Party leader Neritan Ceka had assembled a 'Forum for Democracy' of centrist politicians, and this was strongly supported by Tirana's diplomatic community. Round-table talks were held between the President, the Forum, and those members of the opposition who could be pressured by foreign ambassadors to join them. Almost immediately, however, the talks between the Forum and Berisha broke down in acrimony.[21]

An important factor during these volatile days appears to have been the relative success of the SHIK in terrorising the north of the country, where opposition protests remained muted. The President seemed to have believed, even at this late stage, that his coercive tactics would still be equally effective in the south. But in reality the southern rebellion continued to gain ground, with the demolition of the main bridge on the Gjirokaster–Saranda road on 8 March cutting off the key government-held base in Gjirokaster from the coast. On the same day, hundreds of armed men paraded through Tepelena after they had driven the last holed-up SHIK operatives from the town. In Saranda, former army officers took command of the militias and began the construction of defensive positions around the town.

The international community began to see the emergence of the feared civil war, with the north remaining loyal to Berisha and the south passing out of government control. In Tepelena a Revolutionary Council was formed, consisting of 15 local politicians and ex-army officers, drawing on the area's rich traditions from the Second World War Partisan period. Berisha's soldiers withdrew into the hills to the north of Tepelena while different militia groups began to take control of the perimeter roads. In a desperate attempt to secure Gjirokaster on 8 March the government sent in special forces in helicopters to disarm the town, but the local police chief led an attack on his own police station and then army magazines were opened and the jubilant population was armed. The special forces troops were forced to retreat to their helicopters and to withdraw northwards.

2. The fall of Gjirokaster, 10 March 1997

Gjirokaster and virtually the entire south-west of the country was now fully under rebel control. In scenes more reminiscent of the Paris Commune than twentieth-century Europe, the armed citizens of the city beat off the military assault and drove the SHIK operatives from the town hall. Many of the last 200 regular soldiers of the original 1000-strong garrison fled into the countryside as crowds flooded into the magazines, seizing a plethora of weapons. Anti-aircraft guns and artillery pieces were set up in the town, and mortars were positioned below the ancient citadel. A hail of fire was directed across the Vjoses Valley into the few remaining government-held villages on the side of the valley near the Glina mineral water factory.

Amid the chaos, groups of army deserters marched north towards Ballsh to set up a formal front line, across the Ballsh-Zulaj road, in the hope of securing the road routes north to Tirana. A few small pockets of support for the government remained in traditional rightist villages such as Llazarati, south of Gjirokaster, but in general between noon on 8 March and evening on 9 March, government authority had ceased to exist over a wide area in and around Gjirokaster, and the foreign media began to describe southern Albania as being in a 'state of anarchy'. This was a dramatic and major setback for Berisha, particularly because most of the international media were in Gjirokaster so the rebellion story there broke straight onto most front pages. It made it very difficult for Berisha to continue to claim to his foreign friends and the international community generally that he had any realistic chance of a military victory over the rebels.

In practice, although central government authority certainly had collapsed, and criminals and socially marginal people were given full scope to indulge in robbery and attacks on state buildings, a new local form of authority soon sprung up. In most towns a senior ex-military officer, such as 'General' Agim Gozhita in Gjirokaster, acted as spokesman for a local people's committee. In Korca, a 'pluralism committee' took over the government of the town, meeting in the old communist party offices, and it was able to provide a modicum of social authority that enabled the town to avoid much serious violence. The traditionally radical villages near Korca were in the hands of militant armed insurgents who drove out any police in the vicinity and ruled the little communities through revolutionary committees.

A key issue for the insurgents was to determine how to spread the anti-government movement northwards towards Tirana. It is not clear how far conscious decisions were actually taken by a political leadership, but in practice a strategy soon evolved. When a town on the road north fell to the rebels the pro-Berisha elements in the urban state apparatus would leave, and the poorer and always more radical country people would then quickly evict the secret police from their rural localities. The Socialist Party had always retained considerable support in the southern countryside throughout the Berisha period, and even though peasants may not have participated in the pyramid banking schemes as much as town dwellers, they had many grievances against the new aggressive market economy and many dissatisfactions with the government. In particular the often mediocre but universal and free medical and educational systems of the communist period had completely collapsed, and rural people found they had few sources of income in the new economy.

On 9 March, after the fall of Gjirokaster, pack animals loaded with weapons and ammunition were made ready to bring in military supplies to Permet, the town that dominated the next branch of the Vjoses Valley, 30 miles to the east of Gjirokaster. Tepelena was fortified with miliary heavy artillery from the Gjirokaster barracks and rebels began marching north in informal groups towards Tirana.[22] Berisha's soldiers and SHIK men still held the key crossroads at Kelcyre, ten miles north of Permet, and pack roads across the mountains were used to make ready the assault on them.[23] In Gjirokaster on 10 March, wild crowds celebrated their victory by firing thousands of rounds of ammunition into the air all night. The Greek consulate, with the only functioning telephone in the town, was full of journalists sleeping on the floor like sardines in a tin. Berisha appeared on television and made a worried appeal for 'Partisan' activity to stop. In Vlora Commander Skender Sera, one of the insurgent leaders, said that the insurgent victory in Gjirokaster was ' a celebration with Kalishnikovs and Berisha is giving up step by step'.[24]

The rebellion was certainly spreading up the southern valleys, much as the anti-Axis resistance had after 1943, and unless it was stopped it would only be a matter of time before Tirana was threatened. As a result, on the evening of 10 March, Berisha ordered his forces to make a stand at Permet. Vicious fighting went on for over 48 hours, resulting in the destruction of several public buildings by fire.

A pitched battle was then fought along the road between Permet and Kelcyre resulting in several deaths. Kelcyre was the old Ottoman capital of the region, and was still a Muslim and pro-Democratic Party town. The local mosque had just been rebuilt with funds from Democratic Party leader Azem Hajdari, who was to be murdered in the summer of 1998.[25] Permet was one of the few cities in Albania where there had been overwhelming popular support for communism, and the town had become the regional capital in communist times. There was little love lost between the two towns, and a de facto front line in the conflict formed across the main road to the north of Permet. On 11 March, the traditionally Enverist stronghold of Berat began to become more involved, with skirmishes on both the roads to the north and to the south of the town. Soldiers loyal to Berisha were dug in north of the little town of Ura Vajgurore, seven miles north of Berat. This had been both an Ottoman and a Zogist garrison, and its strategic importance on the river crossing led to its role in the 1997 rising.

At the same time there was an acceleration of foreign diplomatic activity. The USA still held to its principled position that new elections were urgently needed and a broad-based government of national unity should be formed, but in Europe the focus was much more exclusively on public order issues, led by Italy, who would bear the brunt of any refugee influx.[26] Greek attitudes were more ambiguous. Italy always had close links with the Albanian Right in the post-communist DP government period, but Greece had given political asylum to many Albanian political oppositionists, purged soldiers and secret policemen who had fallen foul of the Berisha government. Some of these people had then started businesses, both legal and illegal, and so economic interests were also involved.

For whatever reason, the southern insurgents began to receive favourable coverage on Greek television. One reason may have been that many southern insurgents, from whatever ethnic background, could often explain themselves to the media in quite reasonable Greek – a much less common skill among Berisha supporters. In the background, religion was also a factor. Many Greek Orthodox clergy privately relished the downfall of the northern, predominantly Muslim government. As always in Balkan conflicts, religion is a major factor under the surface and there is no doubt that the Greek Orthodox Church was very privately happy to see the departure of the DP government. It was also clear to Athenian politicians that if they gave a certain amount of tacit diplomatic help to the rebellion, they could expect a post-conflict government in Tirana that was likely to be much more sympathetic to Greece and its regional priorities than the Berisha administration.

The downfall of Berisha's power in the south and the crumbling of the Albanian state itself were now causing alarm bells to ring in European and other foreign ministries. It had been assumed for several weeks that the unrest would subside and that the Albanian army and security forces would be capable of quelling the 'anarchy', actually the popular uprising. These were both ill-founded ideas, and indicate a major intelligence failure by the EU nations.[27] By the end of the last week in March, however, politicians and officials believed they might be seeing the beginning of the end of the Albanian state.

The local committees that were growing up in all localities were composed of people who had often been in positions of authority for many years until 1992,[28] and saw themselves as agents for the restoration of democracy. In such a small country there were numerous family and community links they could draw upon, and the popular movement grew in confidence as one government military failure followed another. The effect of the widespread acquisition of guns and munitions on popular confidence cannot be overestimated, as the government and the state lost its previous monopoly of armed force.

Thus, at a key stage there was disunity between Italy and Greece, the two NATO and EU members most closely involved in the crisis. It is also worth bearing in mind that by spring 1997, the full costs and difficulties of the post-Dayton period in Bosnia were becoming clear, and this had blunted the appetite for further Balkan intervention with some international political actors. There was no international community representation in provincial Albania at that time. Therefore, had the insurgents in remote places such as the 'no man's land' south of Saranda or in the high mountains of the Acroceraunian Alps wished to follow the international community leaders' advice, they had no means of knowing what it was other than through the BBC World Service or the *Voice of America*. The former had for a long time had a difficult relationship with the Tirana government over human rights abuses, and its objective reporting made it a major news source throughout Albania.[29]

The collapse of government authority in the south ended the geographical isolation of Vlora and relieved the intense pressure that had been on the town for several weeks. Militants from Vlora moved down the Adriatic coast towards Saranda, with some bitter clashes in Himara en route, where traditional rivalries and the influence of organised crime links with Italy was a factor. In Himara numerous buildings that had been constructed illegally by speculators who had profited from the pyramid banks were attacked with bulldozers, and a significant proportion of the population left the town during the violent chaos. Most villages along the coast, such as Vuno and Pigeras, that had traditional socialist and communist orientations supported the rebels with enthusiasm, but some pro-Democratic Party villages nearby, like Borsch, were still loyal to the government.

During the following weeks, the entire coast was racked by random violence, until it became clear that the Berisha government was finished in the south and local score-settling had run its course. Pro-Socialist militias wrecked the British ecotourist project at Qeparo, which was locally believed to be a cover for British intelligence activities. A British Council teacher living there had to be evacuated from his house by helicopter. Local people have since claimed that two helicopters were needed to remove all the technical equipment from the site.[30] An Australian tourist company official, Wilma Goudapple, was shot in the stomach in Saranda ten days later.[31]

Over the next few days, the focus of events moved to Berat and the surrounding towns. Berat investors had lost heavily in the pyramid schemes, and were generally strong leftists, but some inhabitants also blamed the socialist elite and leadership there from profiting from the pyramids. During the nights of 11–12 March Poliçan, south of Berat, came under rebel control. Berat and the military airport at nearby Kuçova followed the next day, although SHIK forces still held Gramsh, the armaments manufacturing town near Poliçan, and the town was closed off. The effectiveness of the SHIK forces was limited by the fact that most of them were northerners, or certainly not from the locality. They lacked detailed local knowledge of the packhorse roads that were used to move insurgents and weapons by mule and donkey, usually under cover of darkness, and beyond a few prominent socialist leaders in a locality often had little idea of whom to arrest in order to halt the spread of rebellion.

The fall of Berat was a key event from the point of view of military supply, as it was a favoured military town and 'Hero City' under communism, and had a very large barracks and arsenal. To the east of Berat lay Lake Ohrid and the numerous mountain passes to Macedonia, and during these tumultuous days Pogradec and the surrounding villages were the scene of fierce battles between pro- and anti-government forces. Some of the villages near Pogradec had a strongly rightist tradition, while the town itself had been one of the last bastions of communist control during the fall of the one-party state in 1991–2.[32]

By the evening of 13 March, the only significant concentration of government forces in the south was between Fier and Lushnja, protecting the main road to Tirana. At the same time, the land south of Gjirokaster finally passed from government control down to the Greek border post at Kakavia, and Albanian border and customs officials fled. The small military post at the border was overrun and looted by insurgents from Vlora, leaving the building stripped apart from pathetic heaps of conscripts' possessions abandoned, as they fled into Greece or north back to their homes and families. The disintegration of the Albanian Army in the south was now complete, and with it went the last vestiges of state authority. On 14 March Defence Minister Safet Zhulali fled the country to Italy, and then to Turkey.[33]

Meanwhile, in rebel-controlled Gjirokaster, the de facto capital of the liberated areas, food was in short supply and there were long queues outside bread shops as families stockpiled food as best they could. Most fuel was seized for military use. In marked contrast, in the north the authority of the government held on, with officials going to work in towns such as Shkoder under armed guard. The international community could by now see the depth of the crisis but there was little sense of any agreement on how to deal with it. In a way this was not surprising, as the rebellion was turning into an armed uprising of the people against a repressive government along lines that had not been seen in Europe since the nineteenth century.

Although the Yugoslav wars of secession had been a serious shock to the transnational leadership pretensions of the EU, the popular movement in Albania seemed a new and dangerous contagion that could affect the simmering Kosova crisis. It was an event that was certainly not supposed to happen in a unified and tranquil post-communist Europe. As many of its features seemed to represent the development in practice of classical Marxist revolutionary tenets, it was not long before right-wing commentators started to look for conspiring groups who were seeking to replace Berisha with a neo-communist regime.[34] These concerns were misplaced, with the exception of the aspects of Greek influence alluded to elsewhere.

Few foreigners understood much of the real nature of the Albanian state as it had evolved under Enver Hoxha's brand of communism. This state had been rigidly enforced for over 50 years and parts of it remained in operation in 1997. As the Enverist state as a whole was widely, and correctly, seen as dictatorial, it was assumed by foreigners that there was no internal democracy or organisations that gave popular empowerment at any level. They neglected the damage done to the party institutions by the ideological zigzags of the Hoxha years. Most of all, few understood the regional nature of communist support.

In southern Albania almost everywhere there was some active support for communism and, in a few places, genuine majority popular support as late as 1997 for at least some aspects of the old regime. Within the Enverist system, there was the mass organisation of the Democratic Front, to which almost everybody had to belong. Local Party committees were not always able to centrally control it very effectively, and the experience of the link with China in the Cultural Revolution period had bred a younger generation who were suspicious of authority in the party, and of bureaucracy and its structures. From an ideological point of view, suspicion of the bureaucracy had been legitimised by the opposition of Enver Hoxha to revisionist Yugoslav communism where the 'New Class' based in Belgrade had so exploited and misled people, with the results that have been seen post-1990. In terms of state legitimacy, the Albanian political elite in Tirana had been losing ground for many years, long before the crisis of 1997.

In the south, and a few places elsewhere like Kukes and Peshkopi in the north-east where the Communist Party was well supported and the leadership did not feel threatened, there was a significant degree of local autonomy and partial but genuine democracy in decision-making. To these people, in areas that had done much better than the north under the one-party state, knowing the Berisha 'biographi'[35] and his modus operandi, aspects of the Democratic Party government seemed to embody the return of centralism and government by diktat, with foreigners forming a new bureaucratic class. The DP government seemed to them to have all the disadvantages of Enverist leadership, with none of its more positive features. The early stages of the uprising devolved power back to the traditional local leaderships, who had been at best bypassed and often vilified and even put under arrest by the DP. In the capital and in much of the north, the Socialist Party leadership lost legitimacy as a political force as much as the Democratic Party. This was due in part to the fact that Tirana did not have such effective popular structures, a key fact in the events that were to develop in the ensuing weeks.

In the perceptions of foreigners, all this was subsumed under the banner of 'anarchy', whereas in fact what was being worked out was an advanced stage in the conflict between two traditions formed under communism: the 'Enverist', with its emphasis on revolution and popular empowerment, which could also incorporate aspects of Albanian nationalism; and the 'economist and technocratic', represented by President Berisha and his government. 'Enverism' did, in its way, embody a genuinely revolutionary content that had taken deep roots in popular political consciousness – perhaps not surprising given the brainwashing the people had been subjected to in their education. Few foreigners realised, either, the degree to which the remnants of an extreme egalitarian ideology from the rigid communist system still affected the national consciousness, and it took little for the revolt against the excesses and corruption of the pyramid bank operators to become a revolt of poverty-stricken rebels against the practice of capitalism itself. Many ordinary Albanian people had been seriously impoverished during the transition period, and the crisis of the spring of 1997 was offering them an undreamed of and unanticipated opportunity for revenge against those who had grown rich so quickly.

3

Political Crisis and Government Transition

Within the international community the direction of events in southern Albania was seen with increasing alarm, particularly among Albania's immediate neighbours. The traditional fear of a mass population exodus was the main policy determinant. On 4 March an Italian warship moved to the Adriatic coast of Albania, and the following week the Italian Ambassador to Albania, Paolo Foresti, attempted to broker talks between Tirana's political leaders aboard the ship[1]. The people he assembled, however, were unrepresentative of the non-Democratic Party national leadership, as many Socialist and other opposition leaders were in hiding. Leaders of the insurgents in Vlora who were present promised to try to persuade their followers to lay down their arms, but this had little effect in the city. Italian Foreign Minister Lamberto Dini flew to Tirana to discuss the outcome with Berisha, but participants in the talks felt they would have no real useful outcome.[2]

In a separate initiative Alliance Party leader Arben Imami travelled to Saranda via Corfu to try to start political negotiations with local leaders. This Greek-backed initiative was more fruitful, and led to the rapid emergence of Bashkim Fino, the Mayor of Gjirokaster, as a new national leader. The diminutive, sharply dressed Socialist with a liking for long blue overcoats was appointed Alexander Meksi's successor as Prime Minister on 12 March. Very few Albanians knew anything whatsoever about him, except that he was part of the increasingly prosperous southern Socialist entourage. His old Party boss, Fatos Nano, had been incarcerated by President Berisha in Tepelena high-security jail two years before. The doors of the jail had been opened on 9 March, during the period of rebel takeover in Tepelena, but

Nano had refused to leave until he received a pardon from the government.[3] Nano was the real power behind Fino, and would become the architect of Berisha's exit from office a few weeks hence.[4]

In an ironic development, just as diplomacy moved to try to pacify the south by Fino's appointment, the crisis was now beginning to involve the north. The army base at Kukes was in violent chaos, with rebels taking over the barracks in Bajram Curri, in Berisha's home region of Tropoja, and seizing massive quantities of weapons.[5] On the streets the price of an AK-47 dropped to as little as $5, with ammunition free.

As the Italian government feared, refugee movement had already begun on a significant scale during the first week in March. Hundreds of destitute people, including members of President Berisha's family, arrived on a ferry at the port of Bari. Although the Italian government claimed it was going to repatriate all refugees, in practice it did not do so. Three Albanian Air Force helicopters landed at Brindisi and their crews asked for political asylum.

On 11 March, the last pro-Berisha forces withdrew from Fier, and rebels with enormous supplies of guns and munitions began to move towards the Adriatic port of Durres, only 25 miles from Tirana (the stronghold on the Albanian coast that according to Albanian historiography is said to have changed hands 33 times in its long history). Trucks loaded with weapons were also reported to be moving through the capital into northern Albania. A British journalist visiting Shkoder on 9 March had found the city restive and unwilling to form a militia under the leadership of the Mayor, Hamdi Ura, with the aim of protecting the President.[6] Durres was soon to change hands again, while the government and Opposition met for long hours in Tirana and tried to form a national government.

This meant little in towns like Vlora, which were without water and where food was running short. Dynamite looted from garrisons was used to stun fish in the harbour, and people boiled pasta as the bread supply ran out. Although there was substantial Democratic Party support in Durres and links through trade with Italy (Berisha's main diplomatic backer), in the event there was little resistance to the rebels, as many Durres people had lost large sums of money in the pyramid schemes. The local town administration collapsed as rebels and local people helped themselves to weapons from police stations and magazines. Endless volleys of automatic fire rang out in the streets around the ancient Roman amphitheatre. Kosovar Albanian arms dealers converged on Durres as an open-air weapons market developed on the quayside.

News of the impending humanitarian crisis in Vlora and elsewhere was a powerful incentive to foreign nations to become more involved, as the old fear of mass Albanian population movement into Western Europe was never far below the surface in EU members' foreign policy calculations concerning the country. So far refugee numbers remained small, compared to the time of ship seizures in 1991, but there was a strong feeling in European capitals that panic could seize the country and society could collapse at any moment. In the background was the possibility that the chaos could finally destabilise Kosova and prompt the Milosevic regime to drive out the Albanian population.[7] The wider international political context was not encouraging for interventionist arguments. On the other hand, a total collapse of Albania was too much for the international community to risk, although this prospect was exaggerated as foreigners were unaware of the effective local power structures based on the people's committees. Weariness of the Balkans in the aftermath of the problems of the Bosnian peace settlement at Dayton was overcome as it became clear that regional stability itself was threatened.

Traditional interpretations of regional and international politics also began to appear, with some Kosovars afraid that the nation was going to be divided between Serbia and Greece as their protector, Sali Berisha, fell from power. This was a very shortsighted view, given the limitations and weaknesses of Berisha's Kosova policy, but it had some rational basis in past history. The Serbs had invaded northern Albania twice before in the twentieth century. Many ordinary Kosovars had seen Berisha as 'their' President, and were fearful of what southerners in government might bring. Some foreign observers also feared that the increasing role of Greece in the background was linked to long-term plans to annexe the Greek-speaking areas in the south.

Meanwhile, within Albania the conflict was now spreading rapidly to Tirana and the north, as the government's hitherto reasonably effective control there began to collapse. On 13 March armed gangs took over the magazine of the Military Academy in central Tirana. In many places, large and small, protests were developing against the Berisha government, and in response on 12 March gunmen broke into the magazines in Berisha's home town of Tropoja and began to form a new paramilitary force, swearing to defend their President. This was a group of fanatical loyalists to Berisha, and the nucleus of what was later to become the FARK (National Army of Kosova) paramilitary organisation during the Kosova conflict.[8] But other Kosovars saw things differently. For them this was a major opportunity to pick up weapons and move them into their undefended Kosova villages.[9]

Back in Tirana the transition of power to non-Democratic Party politicians had begun, after the appointment of Bashkim Fino as Prime Minister. Fino looked plausible and was bright, articulate and in touch with the new southern political forces. He was of the younger generation of Socialist politicians who had not occupied prominent national-level positions in the old communist PLA. He was someone who appealed – at least in terms of image – to the European component of the international community.

His Greek links propelled Athens to a central role in government life. Greece had worked closely during the previous week in the development of ex-Austrian Chancellor Franz Vranitsky's OSCE peacekeeping delegation, which was to play a key role in events in Albania in April and May. Athens Foreign Ministry officials were openly critical of the failures of Italian diplomacy to control the situation.[10] The political incapacity and internal divisions in the EU over the crisis had led to the OSCE taking on a leading conflict resolution role. Greek Foreign Minister Pangalos had some Albanian blood in his background and unlike some of his blinkered associates in Athens, who were only concerned about the security of the Greek-speaking community, he saw how Greece could dramatically increase its hegemonic role in Albania as a result of the crisis. It is likely that in this period, the claims of the Berisha lobby about Greek secret intelligence activity in Albania had more substance than in previous weeks.

The scenario of the uprising as something planned and plotted months beforehand by the ex-communists and Greek-speaking community has always been little more than a conspiracy theory. There is, however, more convincing anecdotal evidence about the Greek role once the mid-March period had been reached. Within the country, the appointment of Fino as Nano's de facto 'Trojan Horse' within the government started a process of 'reform from the top', pushed by well-meaning internationals, that was to determine international community policy during the next month or so. It did not have much effect on the practical capacity of the government to affect events. It did, though, serve to do two things: to legitimise the protest movement in the south and to provide an impression of government existence and continuity, even if the 'government' was largely an empty, powerless charade. Crucially, it enabled Greece to advance nationalist and Orthodox clerical political agendas through the new government under the cloak of 'European' moderation and 'conflict resolution'.

In the eyes of many Democratic Party supporters, it seemed as though the foreigners were taking the side of the street rebels against the legally elected parliament, while to the protestors it was a first victory in terms of ending Democratic Party power, and an encouragement to militancy. Fino was a mildly charismatic figure with close links to Greece. He had a reputation for financial acumen, was involved in many southern business projects and had a wide network of contacts. The Tirana ambassadors clearly hoped that he might be able to calm the insurrection in the south. This was a rational policy but it did not in itself give him legitimacy, as no one had elected him to his job, and many Albanians had hardly heard of him or even knew who he was.[11]

The Fino deal could indeed be said to have begun to draw people into the conflict in Tirana itself, as the militants saw the emptiness of the authority of the government and felt they had nothing to gain by compromise and much to gain by further street militancy. At the same time, paramilitary groups were being formed in the capital of militants loyal to the President, particularly in the Kamza shantytown of northern migrants who had moved south to the capital during the Berisha era and who still held onto fierce traditional northern political loyalties.

There was a definite change in the tone of the rebellion in this 48-hour period between 13 and 15 March. Until now, in most places, the rebellion had swept north without meeting significant resistance, as old Enverist state structures were destroyed and replaced by people's committees. In Tirana, as a large and socially fragmented city, this was not possible. The civil war and state collapse scenario, which so many feared, had more credibility when based on the capital and associated lowlands region.

The social character and class structure of Tirana needs to be borne in mind when analysing this stage of the insurgency. Although on the surface it is a city of a homogenous character, with a universally poor population and few ethnic minorities, in fact the city is divided by history and tradition into many defined but informal and invisible quarters. For example, the area to the east of the Parliament is the traditional home of Chams; Mount Daiti and the Dibra road area is for the prosperous business elite; and the railway station and prison vicinity is the home of the Roma and the poorest people. The advent of the post-1990 rightist northern immigration had only added further complexities. Although the city contained as many disaffected people and pyramid bank creditors as anywhere else, it also had a deeply conservative core with many Democratic Party supporters, often survivors from the old Zogist middle class ruined by communism.[12] If a final showdown were to occur in Tirana, it would be complex and bloody.

As the rising approached the capital from the south, social tension rose to breaking point. This and other signs of an approaching confrontation prompted the British and other foreign embassies to urge all their citizens to leave the country. In the far north-east, insurgents raided the big military base at Bajram Curri and carted away truckloads of weapons and ammunition. This was an auspicious development for neighbouring Kosova, the KLA, and for the FARK militia. The nascent KLA was developing in the political underground over the border, and there would be a ready outlet for the weapons.

3. Local insurgents, Drinos Valley, March 1997

A short time later the insurgency hit the capital, with another daring raid on the arsenal of a barracks, right in the centre of town. Tirana's Mayor Albert Brojka appealed for calm, saying that the people of the capital 'should have cool heads, to protect their city from any kind of provocation or rumour'.[13] At the same time, the rebels in the south announced the formation of a shadowy 'Committee for National Salvation': perhaps a response to new Prime Minister Bashkim Fino's call for negotiations with the rebels. The new Prime Minister had stated on television that ' this is not a time to issue orders on either side, but for dialogue.'[14] This process was encouraged by the action of the EU in giving open support to the OSCE mediation mission, led by former Austrian Chancellor Franz Vranitsky.

A basic problem was, though, that nobody had elected the rebel commanders in the south to their posts. In Tirana and the north, and in Europe, nobody really knew who they were. Some were shadowy figures operating under false names or nicknames. The diplomatic community had no obvious way to involve them in the dialogue, even if they wished to take part. There was also the drawback that although they might control a particular southern locality, they had no influence over the spreading popular movements on the streets in the contested areas nearer Tirana.

In this sense, analysed using traditional theories of revolutionary change, the Albanian movement had much more in common with the theories of revolutionary syndicalism and the world of peasant uprisings than orthodox Marxism. This is linked to the extreme backwardness of Albanian economic development that even under Hoxha had preserved features of pre-capitalist economic formations, particularly those connected with rural life and agriculture.[15] It is often forgotten that in 1997 over two-thirds of the nation lived as rural poor, and their rebellion arose from bases of economic and social life that were in many aspects pre-capitalist. The organised working class, always small, had seen much of its basis for life destroyed in the de-industrialisation that followed 1990 and the end of communism.

On 14 March both Korca and Elbasan passed out of government control. Most foreign missionaries and aid workers fled from Korca over the nearby border to the Greek town of Kastoria.[16] In a serious setback for the army and police, the rebels took control of Elbasan, a strategically vital town dominating the Shkumbini Valley. Nearby Librazhd, always a town with a notably rebellious tradition, had accumulated a vast arsenal from the nearby armaments factories, and rebels controlled all traffic on the main road to Macedonia. The Elbasan garrison commander was reported to be in tears as the population entered his magazines and removed a huge haul of weapons, with boys as young as eight carrying rifles onto the street. Roma street traders stripped clean the barracks of the nearby Labinot tank depot of all furniture and fittings. By now perhaps 200,000 Kalishnikovs were in the hands of the population, as the fall of towns like Berat and Elbasan and the armament towns of Poliçan and Gramsh to the rebels had released massive quantities of munitions from the big central armouries.

In Vlora a witch hunt started to find and execute members of the hated SHIK secret police, which was only halted, with difficulty, by General Skender Sera, the rebel commander in the town, who put SHIK suspects under arrest in safe custody. The numerous Western missionaries and aid operations were faced with either fleeing the country, as did the Missionaries of Charity in Korca, or recruiting a private militia to protect their local assets. The new Coca Cola factory on the outskirts of Tirana was protected by a family of five brothers and their heavily armed friends, and thus managed to survive the next few weeks without mishap. It was now clear that there were enough weapons in circulation for a civil war to take place, something that was perhaps doubtful until the fall of the central Albanian and Shkumbini Valley towns during this week in March.

The final demise of the army also took place during the course of the same week, and Robert Fox of the London *Daily Telegraph* noted on 13 March that the road from Durres to Tirana was only guarded by two tanks with no ammunition. A naval mutiny at Pasha Limani base in the Bay of

Vlora resulted in the handover to the rebels of a submarine and two coastal patrol ships, and in Tirana public buildings guards were the only visible sign of a military presence, surly conscript youths in badly fitting uniforms. Mass desertions were taking place all over the country, as conscripts stole weapons to sell or to defend their families. The few generals who were still loyal to Berisha and Adem Copani, his military chief, were sitting at their desks in Tirana and issuing commands to regional commanders yet had no idea whether their orders were reaching their intended recipients or if they were willing, or capable, of taking any action on them.

On 12 March, the Pentagon's military liaison team abandoned their desks in the Defence Ministry and left the country after meeting President Berisha and telling him that he could no longer rely on the army to keep him in power. This was a belated and long overdue recognition of reality, and an indication that after Colonel Lane's departure four months before, the quality of intelligence reaching the Pentagon about the actual military situation in Albania had been low.[17] All Western electronic intelligence collection in the Balkans at that time was still focused on Serbia, Croatia and Bosnia, and expensive and time-consuming collection exercises and technical changes like reorientating satellites could not be attempted easily. Western intelligence chiefs were being berated for the lack of warning to their governments of the uprising, and still had little hard information on events.

European governments were less interested in details of the survival prospects of Dr Berisha than the evacuation of their own nationals, none more so than the British. Years of uncritical obeisance to Berisha and his circle had left the embassy ill-prepared for any emergency. The immediate priority was the evacuation of British citizens in Albania. At the end of the first week in March, two Royal Navy destroyers were sent from the central Mediterranean towards the Albanian coast, HMS *Birmingham* and HMS *Exeter*. About 120 British nationals were trapped in Albania. The Foreign Office's organised evacuation operation collapsed into chaos on 13 March, as a large convoy of vehicles crashed into each other outside Durres harbour gates. Hapless British aid workers were left without shelter to survive the night on the beach as armed gangs roamed the city.

In Tirana, similar gangs controlled the night, in scenes compared by correspondents to Saigon at the end of the Vietnam War. On the previous day, the Italian navy had evacuated about 400 foreigners from Durres. The new Fino government had no practical capacity to control the ports or airports. A British Foreign Office official commented that 'It is extremely difficult to get anything in by air. There are people running around the airport with weapons. There is a great deal of indiscriminate firing and chaos.'[18] In these circumstances, Berisha had to consider whether to flee the country or to remain and face the wrath of the people. Within the country, the loss of government control was more or less complete, with the exception of rural Tropoja and the far north-east. The northern mining town of Fushe Arrez fell to the rebels the same week, as Democratic Party power began to disintegrate in Miredita and in Dibra, adjoining the Macedonian border. In these regions it has been claimed that much of the damage done to public buildings, as in the main town of Peshkopi, was organised by local Democratic parties who hoped the international community would be provoked to intervene on their behalf against 'communism' – a vain hope as events turned out.[19]

By the evening of 14 March, Berisha was becoming increasingly marginalised, with the Vranitsky mission[20] holding talks with Prime Minister Fino on board a ship at Durres whilst Berisha languished alone in his Presidential palace in Tirana. In another sign for the future, an envoy arrived from the OSCE in Vienna to discuss whether the international community might undertake some sort of internal policing operation to collect the weapons. But this was far off at that point.

In the localities, particularly in politically mixed areas, the arrival of the foreign warships was often misinterpreted and rightist supporters thought that there was going to be international intervention on behalf of the Democratic Party government, despite what leading international community figures like Javier Solana had said on this issue over a week before. This produced more looting and violence in some areas that up until now had remained largely free of it. Gangs of Democratic Party supporters trashed public buildings and facilities, in the hope that the rebels and the opposition would be blamed by the internationals and intervention on their behalf would follow. This was a foolish and naive assumption; international officials had no way of knowing what was going on in these communities, and no means whatsoever of affecting or influencing them.

Aid agencies were preparing an emergency food supply operation. It was, though, far from clear how such operations might work, given that nearly all UN and other international organisation staff had left the country. In outlying areas of Tirana, people were simply hanging about in the streets and waiting for the full force of the rebellion to arrive in the capital. They did not have to wait long. By the morning of 15 March it came, with the intermittent gunfire of previous days turning into a dangerous hail of bullets falling from the sky as weapons from Durres and the south spread through the population. By mid-morning the hospitals had received eleven dead bodies and over 150 wounded. London *Observer* journalist John Sweeney described the sky in Tirana on 16 March as 'raining bullets', and a roadblock 'manned by plainclothes toughs from the new civil police, who looked remarkably like the old secret police, the SHIK. They had the same strut.'[21]

Against this genuinely anarchic background, new political actors were to appear on the scene. The EU at last began to move into some kind of action, as a delegation of 11 senior diplomats and military advisers arrived in Tirana on 18 March. Commentators in the British and US press had criticised EU inaction.[22] There was now no doubt the international community would have to make a serious long-term commitment to help Albania escape its past and become a relatively 'normal' European country. It was, however, as yet unclear whether the political will was available to make this commitment. In most EU capitals, with the exception of Italy and Austria, nations still seemed unwilling to engage with the full gravity of the crisis.

In Germany Chancellor Helmut Kohl said that Albania's problems were internal and that sending in an outside force to pacify the situation was not realistic. British Foreign Office minister Nicholas Bonsor, rejecting pro-interventionist arguments in the British liberal press, saying that 'it was unrealistic to expect the international community to establish such a force', echoed this view.[23] The British Tory government was on its last legs, just before a General Election, and was in no mood for international entanglements. Berisha's friends in the British Conservative government did not in the end turn out to be very reliable allies, putting their non-interventionist principles before the survival of the Albanian President. They were about to lose power to Tony Blair's new Labour administration. The Tory Balkan strategy of keeping Albania weak under Berisha while collaborating with Milosevic's Serbian expansionism was in ruins.

As in the field of the economy, in the diplomatic field the Democratic Party's much vaunted achievements seemed to be built on shaky foundations. In response to the fighting in Tirana, EU emissary Vranitsky continued to call for the establishment of an international peace operation.[24] In response, Premier Bashkim Fino called for a new volunteer militia force to be formed, and hundreds of young men gathered outside Tirana police stations, attempting to join it. However, many of those taken on only stayed in the force until they obtained a gun, and then deserted. In many European eyes the failed-state scenario had come about and an inquest started as to the causes of it.

A major intelligence failure had taken place. On a small scale, and in an 'unimportant' country, it exposed many of the same failings as the later Iraq war intelligence debacle. In particular, there was a lack of real human input on the ground, and in the British case, an over-reliance on a backscratching coterie of Berisha admirers who distorted the real situation and smeared those with contrary views in order to protect their stranglehold over the policy process. The unfortunate Geoff Briggs, MI6 resident in the Tirana embassy during the rising, was made a scapegoat for many deeper problems.[25] The USA was heavily reliant on Albanian émigrés who often had their own political agendas, sometimes based on the reality of Albania many years ago rather than the present.

Some groups and organisations on the international scene seemed more culpable than others. The IMF could claim the cleanest record, in that it had made explicit and public warnings to Berisha on the pyramid operations as early as October 1996. The World Bank stayed closer to the Berisha project much longer, and did not make its views public until a very advanced stage of the crisis. With regard to the USA, the Defence Intelligence staff in the Pentagon could claim some credit, as a result of the reports from Colonel Dennison Lane and his subsequent forced departure from the country, although the Pentagon and NATO higher bureaucracy do not always seem to have absorbed clearly what was said. The CIA and the State Department had seen the dangers to democracy well before many others, although it could be argued that the State Department had kept a somewhat Olympian stance throughout.

In Britain the pro-Serb stance of the Major government and the powerful right wing lobby of Zogist émigrés and the Anglo-Albanian Association had seen the most determined and ideological support for Berisha anywhere in the world. Scandinavian countries generally had only modest contact with Albania, with their local lobbies dominated by Kosovar refugees, and watched events unfold with amazement. In France the Albanian scene had a strongly left-wing flavour, with it being the European country that was the only EU nation to be favoured with relatively normal trade and diplomatic relations during the Hoxha period, and with a centre of Albanian studies at Lyons University. Although Berisha had his friends in Paris government circles and friendly relations with the French intelligence services, and had been indoctrinated into Freemasonry in France, the vast majority of French Balkanist opinion was anti-Berisha.[26] In Germany, his government had strong support on the Right, and in some Catholic circles, but many opponents on the Left and among the very large and often radical Kosovar émigré community who had become increasingly disillusioned about his failure to take a stronger line against Serbia.

Some US State Department opinion saw Albania as inevitably a 'dependent state' given its poverty and economic backwardness, and as a result saw it as being subject to an inevitable power struggle between Italy and Greece during the spring 1997 crisis. As both were NATO allies, it was not at this time of strategic concern to the USA as to which country became dominant.[27]

This may partly account for the distance kept by Washington from the social conflict. Although the Bosnian intervention two years previously had provided a successful example of peacekeeping using US forces in the region, there were (and always had been) many voices in the US power elite who opposed further Balkan involvements and wished to find an exit strategy in Bosnia as quickly as possible. Television pictures on CNN and elsewhere gave ordinary Americans the impression of a Kalishnikov-toting nation gone mad and US casualties seemed inevitable if any intervention was to be attempted, so the 'body bags' factor played a major part in decision-making. A minority of US experts who knew the region well saw the Berisha government as inevitably doomed and felt intervention was a lost cause in any event.[28]

Religion may also have been a background factor in external power calculations. Italy has always been the main protector of Albania's Roman Catholics, centred in the north-west around Shkoder, and the overwhelming majority of them vote for the Democratic Party. Islam as a political factor did not emerge at all throughout the crisis, even though most of the Berisha government was nominally Muslim. The presence of prominent northern Catholics such as Pjeter Arbnori, as Speaker of the Parliament and someone close to the government, assisted this perception while on the rebel side Orthodox links with Greece were certainly useful. Greek–Albanian relations had been poor since 1994, with the imprisonment of Greek human rights activists by the Berisha government, and the Greek Orthodox Church had harboured major expansionist plans in Albania for many years, long pre-dating the fall of communism; local priests openly welcomed the demise of the Berisha government.

In Belgrade the Milosevic regime watched the events unfold with a mixture of horror and smug admiration. A central factor in the Serb police-state mechanisms in Kosova was the control of small arms, and the news of Kosovars buying large quantities of arms and ammunition in cities such as Durres sent a chill down government spines.[29] On the other hand, Berisha was seen in Belgrade, largely wrongly, as a militant northerner with a Montenegrin-Albanian wife who had allied himself closely with Dr Ibrahim Rugova's Democratic League in Prishtina, and was interested in Kosova affairs. So the release of Fatos Nano from prison in March was openly welcomed. Nano had many Belgrade connections going back to his time as a Communist Party official in the 'thaw' in relations with Yugoslavia in the 1980s, and his authoritarian socialist technocratic approach found many kindred spirits in Milosevic's Socialist Party of Serbia (SPS).

Nano's views on Kosova in this period were assumed to be representative of the Albanian Socialist Party as a whole. This was not the case. The Belgrade government did not understand the complexity of the patriotic tradition within the ex-Party of Labour cadres, who were ideologically close to some of the Kosova underground groups stemming from the Hoxhaist political outlook, and their capacity to organise support for the KLA. The simplistic and misleading equations (northern = Gheg = pro-Kosovar; and southern = Tosk = anti-Kosovar) was widely believed. But also, at popular level, there was a spark of admiration for the Albanian rebels among Albania's Balkan neighbours, and not only in Serbia.

The Albanian rebellion of 1997 was the inheritor of a tradition of rebellion shared by groups such as the Serbian *haiduks*, Kosovar *kakacs*, the Greek *klephts* and *andartes*, and the Bulgarian *comitajis*, some of whom had actively collaborated together against the Ottoman Empire. There were also some links, if often complex and contentious, from the Second World War Partisan period, the foundation of all post-1945 Balkan Communist regimes. Whatever analysis is made of the causes of the March overthrow of the government, it was a very Balkan affair, with ordinary men and women changing history with guns in their hands. The man in the Balkan street in most countries in the region suffered profound alienation from governments often dominated by either ex-Communist bureaucrats, or Mafioso people mixed up with organised crime and sinister apparatniks, all operating in a general atmosphere of corruption.

It was not surprising that a covert or open admiration for the Albanian rebels was common in many places. The March rebellion was a vast outburst of suppressed energy and frustration among the Albanian people, and as such mirrored the frustrations of many other regional peoples. But they did not have the benefit – or nightmare, depending on point of view – of the Enverist/Partisan approach to national defence, with its educational value for those planning basic street fighting and use of small arms on a mass scale. It was difficult for foreigners to understand the intense emphasis put on the Partisan tradition as a nation-building force by the Communist leadership, and the consequent ease with which it re-entered the political landscape in 1997.

The analysis of the events put forward by the 'organised crime' theorists of the rebellion, that it was basically a Mafia-inspired phenomenon, quite misses the point.[30] This analysis depoliticises a profoundly political situation. Local criminals certainly benefited from the breakdown of the state and the Berisha government, as they would anywhere, and in towns like Vlora there was a very developed criminal subculture. However, the reason the state broke down was not because of the Mafia, or even the pyramid crisis. The difference between what could have been just a local series of riots in the south and an uprising that broke the government was caused by the fact that southerners who hated the government were able to draw upon long-established Partisan models of insurgency and respected leadership figures with a Partisan-trained military education, with basic military skills spread throughout the adult population. This was also coupled with the liberating effect of recovering the right to bear arms, in an Albanian culture where locally held weapons were a historically important defence capacity for communities under threat from unrepresentative governments and hostile neighbours such as Greece and Serbia.

The reactions to this development in the Kosovar Albanian and Macedonian Albanian communities are instructive. The leaders of both communities, such as Arben Xhaferi in Tetovo in Macedonia and Ibrahim Rugova in Prishtina, were both seen as representative of pro-Berisha opinion in the wider Albanian world, although the very astute Tetovo politicians had seen the weaknesses of Berisha on the national question early on and expected little in the way of practical help from the Democratic Party government.[31] The southern insurgents' implied links with Greece was a hindrance to Nano and his associates, and his vulnerability to Greek pressure to appease Serbia was a handicap his future government was never going to escape. The vision of these politicians and many people in Kosova was of a developing and strong rightist government in Albania that would gain the favour of the USA and the Europeans, who in turn would help Kosova to become democratic and independent and to improve the human rights of the Macedonian Albanians. It was in many ways a utopian vision, as events turned out, and assumed a degree of order both in the region on the ground and in the international system that did not exist. Most of all it presupposed the perpetuity of Serbian hegemony in the region from Belgrade.

If European governments were prisoners of a massive intelligence and policy failure over the March events, the same could be said of the wider perspectives of many of the Albanian leaders themselves. They assumed the communist and Titoist worlds could evolve seamlessly into the New World Order, rather than the actual New World Disorder that has come to dominate south-east Europe for so long. The same mixture of voluntarism, self-delusion, intellectual dishonesty and wishful thinking, which had been articulated so long and so pointlessly to try to persuade the Albanian people about the 'benefits' of communism, was now applied to belief in the post-1989 settlement, where capitalism and globalisation were supposed to offer solutions to many long-standing problems.

The New World Order was seen as a salvation for the Balkans; in fact it could offer some much better perspectives, but only if the USA became sufficiently involved. The Clinton administration, though, remained suspicious of further involvement, something the Tirana elite never clearly understood in 1997.[32] Instead leadership had to contend with the actual reality of European politicians, and the vast gulf between their perceptions of how the Balkans should be and what they actually were.

In Kosova and Western Macedonia, both at the heart of the crisis of Yugoslavia, the Albanian leaderships (with the exception of Ibrahim Rugova) saw things differently. The majority adopted a more activist perspective on the national question, and this dialectic, between Tirana-based optimism about the role of the international community and local Albanian self-reliance (particularly the development of military capacity), would determine the background to the escalating crisis over the exactly two years between the fall of the Berisha government and the beginning of NATO's campaign against Serbia in March 1999. In the meantime, the dysfunctional reality of globalisation and the internationalisation of the crisis were soon to make itself felt to the average Albanian in the form of the soldiers of the 'Operation Alba' international intervention force.

PART

II

THE STRUGGLE FOR POWER

4

The Crisis in Northern Albania

By mid-March the authorities remained in nominal control only of Tirana, whilst informal networks of old Socialist Party activists had become the only meaningful political authority in the south of Albania (and in many places elsewhere). Most of the country had been comprehensively ransacked, with almost every industrial or manufacturing plant having been looted and destroyed. The same applied to many schools and hospitals. Gangland shootings and random violence were on the increase as rival gangs roamed around intercepting anyone who moved across their 'territory'. Bridges and roads were being dynamited regularly, and the price of a Kalashnikov had dropped to just $4.00. The streets of the cities and towns were strewn with months of uncleared rubbish, whilst the shells of burnt out cars continued to form barricades across side roads.

A few loyalists continued to guard the SHIK headquarters, with six tanks, and soldiers massed outside the Presidential palace, but any sense of a functional government was fast disappearing. Groups of heavily armed men in official and unofficial vehicles drove around the streets firing guns from car windows as the world of Mad Max films came to Tirana. Shopkeepers emptied their shops and put their goods into storage as armed gangs wearing balaclava helmets systematically looted all state and public property.

Throughout this period, Parliament did not convene: a sign of the fragility of the institution and the heritage from communist times when it was merely a rubber stamp for Party of Labour decisions, often those of the Politburo alone. The social breakdown of Tirana had become apparent as the anarchy of the south began to embrace the capital. Civil servants, teachers and doctors were no longer being paid. The city's prisons were emptied and volleys of gunfire echoed throughout the nights as the presidential guard imposed a climate of fear by firing its weapons at the start of the dusk-to-dawn curfew. The Albanian government appealed to the EU for urgent financial aid, saying the country was facing serious food shortages after government grain stocks were ransacked. In the recent past, food supplies to the towns had been drastically reduced because so many farmers had sold their land and livestock in order to invest in the disastrous pyramid savings schemes.

The Albanian army was in a catastrophic state, with soldiers being sent home because there was no money to pay them. The interim government of Bashkim Fino faced the daunting task of rebuilding the army with no money and giving it a sense of purpose to prevent it falling apart again. Indoctrinated during the communist period to see enemies in all of Albania's neighbours, the armed forces were forced to do an about-face after communism's collapse. But although Marxist doctrine was purged, the troops were given no new values to defend, and nothing had prepared them for the bitter political divisions that now threatened to tear their country apart. Like Albanians in general, officers and soldiers were split in their loyalties to Berisha, and were acutely aware of the key role in the uprising being played by men who until recently had been their respected colleagues. The President's former Defence Minister, Safet Zhulali, had already fled the country on a refugee boat to Italy, leaving behind the growing insurrection and charges that he had been running guns to Yugoslavia.[1]

There were now four pseudo-centres of power: President Berisha's armed supporters – mostly northerners, and with the officially disbanded SHIK security service forming the backbone; Prime Minister Bashkim Fino's residual state police force; the rebel 'salvation committees' throughout the south; and the emerging armed warlords. The opposition and many of the wider population believed that President Berisha was in command of his own illegal army and was preparing to divide the country and rule from the north. According to one report, Berisha was aiming to create the impression that the south was against the north and against democracy in the country.[2] However, the anti-Berisha 'salvation committees' did not control the south any more than government forces controlled the northern half of the country, whilst northern officials and policemen, appointed by Tirana, had either fled or were forced out by heavily armed local militia gangs.

The political class was totally without authority, as President Berisha remained holed up in the presidential office in Tirana, accusing communists and foreign agents of being behind the disorder. As the fighting spread into the capital, the flood of Albanians fleeing across the Adriatic to southern

Italy had reached 10,000, causing widespread alarm amongst Italians, who feared their country was facing an influx of illegal immigrants and criminals rather than a refugee crisis. This was not an irrational fear, as many of the recently escaped criminals from the opened jails had not lingered in Albania but had immediately fled to Italy on the Adriatic ferries while the going was good. The Italian authorities were wholly unprepared to cope with such numbers.

As European foreign ministers met in the Netherlands on 17 March to discuss plans for possible intervention in Albania, many of the country's diplomatic personnel and other foreigners joined fleeing Albanians on the beaches of Durres. The Western powers faced a specific military dilemma as Albania began to fragment into mutually antagonistic communities. The major powers such as the USA, Italy and Britain had ships nearby, but only very limited infantry forces were on them and they had no wish to become involved in the Albanian mayhem. Thus most evacuations proved difficult. The USA had to suspend its evacuation operation after helicopters were fired upon near the airport. Most of the 1600 US citizens in the country were in the north, often visiting families, and were not thought to be in serious danger. German soldiers fired to defend their country's mission, in what was the first time that shots had been fired in anger abroad by the German army since 1945. The forces used to back even the evacuation plans were inadequate, let alone to influence the internal development of the power struggle.

As the scale of protest increased, leaders of the rebel 'salvation committees' refused to negotiate any issue until Sali Berisha was removed from power. The President, however, intended to hold onto power by whatever means necessary, predicting that further destabilisation would follow if he were forced to step down. Berisha claimed that adhering to the constitutional order was important, and therefore he could not step down until he was voted out of office. He thus ordered government troops to seal off much of central Tirana, and to surround the headquarters of the Socialist Party – a move that was widely interpreted as heralding the introduction of a formal dictatorship by Berisha. Although the 'government of national reconciliation' had been formed under a Socialist prime minister, Berisha had not surrendered control of the key Interior Ministry, and his Democratic Party still held other powerful positions.

By now, all of Albania's land borders, ports and airports were closed and the country found itself back in familiar isolation. The government had lost control of the airport and the port of Durres. Although the police still held control over the centre of Tirana, the state had been left fragmented into well-armed fiefdoms of conflicting loyalty. Criminal gangs equipped with tanks, machine guns and missiles operated their own 'no-go areas' inside each of the respective zones.

The spread of uncontrolled violence to the capital came against mounting claims that at least some of the arming of civilians in Tirana had been organised by President Berisha and his loyalists. Berisha was indeed in the process of raising and arming his own personal army from local DP thugs and former SHIK members. He was also mobilising police units from the north of the country. A group nicknamed 'the Chechens' held one Tirana suburb. Originally from the Tropoja district in northern Albania, birthplace of Berisha, the heavily armed men were hard core Berisha loyalists who vowed to fight any attempt to remove him with force. 'If he resigns, it's war', one of the group's commanders told a journalist. 'We don't care about the Government, but we'll fight to protect our President.'[3]

Although the 'salvation committees' had a measure of erratic control in the south of the country, the groups had little in common politically beyond a desire to get rid of Berisha. The uprising had no leaders, and no philosophy or strategy – its sole coherent objective was the removal of Sali Berisha from the presidential palace. A typical committee commander was Xhevat Kociu, the insurgent leader in Saranda. A swaggering graduate of Tirana's military intelligence academy, he had served for more than 20 years until he was demobilised in 1993 as a brigadier general. The once proud officer was reduced to working as a security guard. Other dismissed military leaders were selling bananas. When the opportunity arose, they seized their chance to regain some sort of power, and indeed self-respect.

The collapse of the pyramid schemes had been merely the catalyst for the people's bitter frustration at not being able to dislodge the deeply unpopular administration of President Berisha through the parliamentary process. Following the previous year's election fiasco, Albania's slow drive towards democracy had been put into sharp reverse. By then Berisha was in firm control of parliament, and corruption had moved to the very heart of the state machine. During his period in office, he had tried to consolidate support for himself by appointing people from his native town of Tropoja and other parts of the north to powerful positions, particularly in the security forces. Thus, most of the police were from the north. This was one reason why the waves of hatred spread more rapidly in the south.[4]

Western diplomats, however, remained strongly supportive of Berisha's administration on the grounds of the alleged 'economic miracle' and social transformation achieved since the Democratic Party came to power in 1992. Many also saw Berisha, quite absurdly, as a leader untainted by past communist associations.⁵ In reality, the whole evolution of the Democratic Party had been profoundly linked to that political tradition.

The response from the international community to the crisis of the spring of 1997 had been initially feeble in the extreme. Europe, weary of its Bosnian responsibilities, was reluctant to commit troops to Albania, but still willing to continue throwing money at it rather than address the most important issue – ensuring genuine democratic governance. But Albania had already received the highest per capita level of EU aid of any Eastern European state, obtaining £520 million over the previous five years. Yet apart from obvious improvements in telecommunications, there was little to show for it.

Major financial support from the outside world, such as the $500 million of debt restructuring negotiated in July 1995, meant little to ordinary Albanians. In an attempt to escape unemployment, poverty and increasing bloody feuds over land ownership – in 1997 there were an estimated 75,000 people actively involved in feuds throughout northern Albania – thousands of northerners had migrated south, leaving many mountain communities abandoned. Shantytowns were growing up around Tirana and other lowland towns. It was from these marginalised and dispossessed northerners that Berisha recruited his dubious support base in the capital. These same people would later be paid a few precious dollars per head to take part in anti-Socialist street demonstrations.

By the end of March armed gangs were beginning to define their areas of control, making movement around the country increasingly difficult. The rebel committees were now in the process of transformation themselves, and could be better described as a collection of bandit-insurgent families rather than a coherent political force. Typical of such families was that led by Zani Caushi, which was strongly linked to the criminal fraternity in Vlora. Prior to the spring of 1997, Zani Caushi had been a minor criminal. But in March 1997, when Berisha's government troops were massing north of the Vojses River estuary in preparation for an assault on Vlora, Caushi formed paramilitary groups to defend the city. He then led attacks on local arms magazines and distributed Kalashnikovs to the population. Zani was able to amass a large arsenal himself in the process, and subsequently enjoyed wide admiration throughout southern and central Albania for his successful obstruction of the regime's plans for the military suppression of the south.⁶

As March drew to a close, both President Berisha and the opposition admitted that the country was beyond their control and made a united plea to the EU for an international intervention force. Fino's government was a government in name only. Berisha was now hanging onto power by a thread, and Albania's Balkan neighbours were battening down the hatches and preparing for the worst. Reports of Kosovar Albanians buying up large quantities of weapons had sent chills down many spines in the region. But controlling small arms transfers along Albania's wild and remote borders was a near impossibility. Tirana had neither the military forces nor the political consensus or willpower necessary to monitor the border effectively. The extremely remote terrain near the Black Drin Valley was particularly problematic. The security vacuum inside Albania had given the KLA a relatively free hand to smuggle light weapons and ammunition across on remote mountain paths to resupply its growing guerrilla movement.

As well as the possibility of the spread of conflict to Kosova, weapons were also being smuggled into Macedonia, where at the time it was widely believed that the risk of the spread of conflict was greatest. The 25 per cent ethnic Albanian minority living along the western border with Albania were growing increasingly dissatisfied with their second-class status. They had elected a tough new leadership in the de facto Albanian capital, Tetovo, and were determined to voice their anger at their perceived human rights abuses through mass street demonstrations.[7] Macedonia's aged President Gligorov presided over a country dominated by hard-line nationalists and ex-communists, whose main loyalty was to Serbia. Most real power in Skopje was in the hands of the Interior Ministry, which at the time had close informal links with the Milosevic regime's security apparatus in Belgrade.

To the south, Greece was equally alarmed by the anarchic and violent events in Albania, although the concern was less to do with arms than with population movement. Apart from the normal refugee flow, thousands more Albanians crossed illegally into Greece through the great wilderness forests north of Korca and Kastoria. To counter this unwelcome traffic, the nationalist right in Athens was watching the Simitis government closely for any signs of neglect of the estimated 50,000 ethnic Greeks in southern Albania. The far right in Greece were pushing for the establishment of a 'zone of influence' in southern Albania. However, the Greek government under Premier Simitis, unlike his predecessors, was firmly against stirring up any form of nationalist trouble, especially since Greece had formally repudiated its previous claims on southern Albania. In reality, the ethnic Greeks in Albania had played little in the way of a leadership role in the uprising. The ethnic Greeks' organisation in Albania, Omonia, did not in fact take part at all. Neither did the local ethnic Greek political party, the Union of Human Rights Party.

The number of ethnic Greeks crossing from Albania into Greece had risen dramatically since the start of the March. Two ethnic Greek villages,

Tsiouka and Vryssera, in the districts of Saranda and Gjirokaster respectively, had been abandoned completely by their inhabitants, following attacks by criminal gangs. The Greek consulate in Gjirokaster had been attacked half a dozen times and was severely pockmarked with bullet holes. The exodus of ethnic Greeks, like their Albanian neighbours, was also fuelled by the climate of uncertainty resulting from the social and political upheaval, and the dire economic situation in the country as a whole. The relatively few men who had not migrated to Greece earlier stayed to defend their villages against marauding gangs and Berisha's SHIK agents.

On 26 March, Albania's outgoing head of the secret service, Bashkim Gazidede, told the Albanian parliament that Greek nationalist groups had been plotting to 'liberate' southern Albania, and that these groups were also behind the insurrection in the south of the country. Gazidede accused Greek nationalists of orchestrating the uprising with the aim of dividing the country and then appropriating southern Albania to northern Greece. Such claims were to be heard from Democratic Party supporters and other right-wing groups across Albania.

This was indicative of the fact that no one on the right was prepared to acknowledge the real level of hatred towards the Berisha administration that had built up over the previous five years, and the indignation at the 'stolen' elections of May 1996. In other words, no outside elements were needed to instigate the rebellion, which was quite simply a homegrown affair. The Greek Foreign Ministry dismissed the allegations, saying such claims were not even worthy of denial. As it was, Greece appeared to be doing everything in its power to help normalise the situation in Albania by providing emergency financial, technical and diplomatic assistance, as well as offering a Greek contingent as part of the UN-mandated multinational force, which would shortly begin operations in Albania. None of Albania's neighbours had any desire to cross over the Albanian border to try and restore order, let alone annex portions of territory. Instead, the overwhelming impulse was to try and hermetically seal the country; an ironic echo of Enver Hoxha's policies.

In fact, Greece was so alarmed at the deteriorating situation that the country went into a diplomatic spin. Foreign Minister Theodoros Pangalos paid a hurried visit to Skopje and Belgrade at the beginning of April, and Prime Minister Costas Simitis called a crisis meeting in Athens with the heads of the EU, the OSCE and Albanian Premier Bashkim Fino. Following the meeting, OSCE special envoy for Albania, Franz Vranitsky, outlined the three areas of action planned by the international community, namely: the distribution of humanitarian and economic aid; the establishment of democracy and human rights, which included parliamentary elections to be held in June; and the co-ordination of an international peace force, to be undertaken by Italy.

Mr Vranitsky stressed that the international community in no way wanted to direct Albania from abroad but to offer it the help to stand on its own feet. The international effort was to be made up of three main 'pillars': the OSCE, the EU and the Multinational Protection Force (named Operation Alba). The main goals of this institutional effort were to strengthen the all-party Government of National Reconciliation, to restore public order, to provide humanitarian and other emergency relief, and to assist in the preparation of free and fair elections.

In mid-April the OSCE took over the overall coordination of the international operation and formally established a 'presence' in Albania. The Italian-led expedition to Albania began in earnest on 15 April, when over 1000 Italian, French and Spanish troops landed in the port of Durres. Within days some 2700 troops (of the proposed 6000) from the multinational force had been deployed in Albania as Operation Alba began extending its control beyond the first bridgeheads in Durres and Tirana.[8]

Italy, however, was deeply divided over its plans for military intervention. With no clear mandate, no chain of command, no properly defined military tasks and no exit strategy, Operation Alba's humanitarian mission risked becoming bogged down in the political chaos of Albania, with its troops left at the mercy of thieves, gangsters and opportunists. Nevertheless, the Italian government was so alarmed at the prospect of yet another uncontrolled wave of Albanian refugees spreading throughout Italy that it was deemed absolutely necessary to try and halt the flow of refugees by using Operation Alba to try and improve conditions in Albania itself.

By the end of April it had become apparent that there would be no open rebellion in the capital or the north, and the tragedy of a civil war had been averted. Consequently, there were signs of a gradual return to normality in some parts of the country. Schools and markets were reopening, and the start of the nightly curfew was changed by two hours from 18.00 to 20.00. In several districts police had begun collecting weapons from civilians, and nightly shootings were becoming less frequent. However, the situation in the capital remained tense as gangs continued to roam the streets and robberies were being committed using ever more sophisticated weaponry. Schools in Tirana only reopened after strict guarantees of police protection.

With the arrival of the multinational force and the gradual calming of the situation, the OSCE brokered debate amongst the Albanian political leadership on the need to hold parliamentary elections as soon as possible. Surprisingly, it proved easier than expected to reach a consensus on this controversial issue. Thus, on 20 April the Albanian political parties and President Berisha reached an agreement to hold new parliamentary elections on 29 June 1997. Whist agreeing on the necessity of holding elections, the right-wing parties were nevertheless deeply unhappy with the Fino government's continuing cooperation with the southern rebel committees. They stressed the importance of immediately disbanding the committees, which undermined the establishment of local government authority and severely restricted the campaigning possibilities of the right-wing political parties.

Others wondered if it was possible to hold elections at all whilst so many of the population remained heavily armed, which would seriously hinder the free and unrestricted movement of people throughout the country. The lack of dialogue with the rebel committees, largely because of Berisha's intransigence, suggested that elections in the south would be particularly fraught. Nevertheless, the advantage of early elections, however chaotic, was that the Democratic Party would be ousted from the parliament, which would then be able to move against Berisha. Berisha, and his implicit threat of an armed response from his followers, were the biggest hurdles in the way of restoring order.

In order to prepare for the elections there were calls from the international community, and those on the right and centre of Albanian politics, for the Socialist Party to abandon its continuing support for the southern rebels. The independent daily *Koha Jone* argued that:

> Albanian society would become safer with the removal of those forces that had destabilised the south, who had turned Vlora, Gjirokaster, Himara and Tepelena into an arena of conflict for gangs and hoodlums, and a test-case for the exercises of the secret services of our neighbours.[9]

This was a reference to a number of alleged activities orchestrated by the Greek secret service. These ranged from organising the raising of the Greek flag and other nationalist activities in Himara, with its influences from local Greek-speakers, to the release of Albanian criminals from Greek prisons, who were then encouraged to return to Vlora, Gjirokaster and Tepelena to cause further unrest.

In an effort to convince the leaders of the salvation committees that the government was dealing with the 'enemies of the state' and that perhaps it was time to re-evaluate the need for the committees, Prime Minister Fino visited the rebel-held bastions in the south for the first time since the insurgents had seized the region. Fino told the rebel leaders that Berisha's dreaded SHIK secret police had been disbanded, and its head had fled the country. This news, however, failed to impress, as most southerners believed the 'government' was incapable of dismantling a traffic jam, let alone Berisha's own personal militia, which was how they interpreted SHIK.

Although Fino had some popular support, he had no means of implementing any government directive. The armed hold-up of Fino's motorcade near the northern city of Shkoder on 5 April was indicative of the state's impotence. It appears the committees felt they still had a valuable role to play in assisting the authorities' attempts to stabilise the country. Fehmi Telegraphi, chairman of the Berat citizens' committee, told journalists of the committee's support for Fino's government:

> Our mission is a broad political and social one, to help the Fino government to carry out the onerous and difficult duties it has undertaken, to carry the country towards free and fair elections, and to neutralise and eliminate the rule of Berisha, who is resorting to cunning and duplicity to obstruct the Fino government in its mission.[10]

In the meantime, another volatile element was thrown into the already heady cocktail of Albanian politics. Leka Zog, the 6ft 8in pretender to the Albanian throne, returned to Albania having spent all but two days of his 58 years in exile.[11] The self-proclaimed king had made just one previous, extremely brief and uninvited visit to his birthplace in November 1993. Then Leka had flown to Tirana on a private jet lent by his friend King Hussein.[12] Upon his arrival, he was asked to leave immediately because his passport gave his occupation as 'King of the Albanians'. He was bluntly told that he would only be re-admitted if he were in possession of an ordinary citizen's passport. Meeting with both President Berisha and Prime Minister Fino, Leka explained that he hoped his presence would help fill a void in the national psyche of the Albanian people, who he believed were seeking a symbol for their identity during these difficult times for the nation. He also hoped his presence would be 'a factor of peace and unity in the country'.[13]

Although there was a slim possibility that Leka might have provided a stabilising factor amidst the political vacuum in Albania, his subsequent advocacy of a unified Albanian nation caused concern amongst Albania's neighbours and in international circles. Although on the Albanian streets little was actually known about the history of the Albanian monarchy, it was widely known that Leka's father, Ahmet Zog, had crowned himself King of all the Albanians, not just those living in Albania. In an interview, Leka was asked what his thoughts were on the Albanians living as minorities in Macedonia, Serbia and Greece. He replied, 'I have always supported ethnic Albanians, and I think that an Albanian nation-state is necessary for peace in the Balkans, because a nation cannot remain divided.' Leka said that his support for an 'ethnic Albania' was based on the universal right of people to self-determination.[14]

Having set these alarm bells ringing, Leka then began a tour of Albania, stopping first at his father's birthplace in the village of Burgajet in the central district of Mat.[15] The king and his cortege travelled in a selection of old, black Mercedes and were given a tremendous welcome by Zog family loyalists living along the route. Leka's father was born in Mat in 1895 and it was here amongst Zog clan loyalists that Leka hoped to build a new power base amidst the political chaos.

This first leg of the tour to an area of strong monarchist support boosted Leka's morale, but left him unprepared for the fierce opposition he was to face at his next port of call in Vlora. As his motley entourage arrived in the ravaged and bitter town, a large, hostile, stone-throwing crowd greeted Leka. Despite tight security from Italian troops, at one point he was kicked by youths. To restore his confidence, he was hastily rushed back to the more welcoming north. In the traditionally right-wing city of Shkoder, he was greeted by an enthusiastic crowd and by the mayor of the city, Bahri Borici, and other notable citizens. Despite pockets of monarchist support in the south of Albania, the north of the country has historically been more receptive to the notion of the monarchy.

As Leka continued his tour of the country, his monarchist party activists began earnestly preparing for the referendum on the monarchy, which was to follow the parliamentary election on 29 June. The rest of the country's political parties were also preparing their campaigns. As levels of spontaneous violence subsided, it became apparent that there was virtually no danger of outright civil war, nor was there a distinct Gheg–Tosk conflict. With the disintegration of the army, Berisha could no longer call on the troops. In fact, as the forthcoming elections were to prove, Berisha was as unpopular in large parts of the north as he was in the south.

Despite all efforts to mobilise them, the overwhelming majority of north-erners had failed to come to the aid of the beleaguered President, and his much trumpeted support base there proved to be non-existent. Apart from his home district of Tropoja, and those who had migrated to Tirana and other central areas from Tropoja, Berisha found himself increasingly isolated from both north and south. The dictator Enver Hohxa had been sufficiently shrewd to gather around himself representatives of different Albanian towns and regions. Even his chosen successor, Ramiz Alia, came from Shkoder. Berisha, however, did not possess such foresight, and the lack of representa-tion of the south in his government removed any influence he might have had there.[16]

The key to resolving the crisis in Albania could only be genuine democratic political consensus. Yet Berisha, who had been re-elected unopposed by parliament on 3 March 1997 to a new five-year term, had no intention of relinquishing power. The President had continued to be regarded with excessive indulgence until long past his personal point of no return. His new 'coalition' government had come far too late, following days of stubborn negotiations whilst the south of the country fell apart. As Sir Reginald Hibbert pointed out, the severe political crisis afflicting Albania was largely due to 'one side trying to exclude the other'.[17] Enver Hoxha did it for some 40 years; Berisha, from a much weaker power base, had been trying to do it for five. The Albanian people needed and deserved a political framework designed to include rather than exclude. This was what they were demanding from their President.

His refusal to concede it and his insistence on branding all those who demanded it as Marxists, communists and traitors had been leading day by day to greater disaster. The international community consistently ignored the warning signs of the inevitable unrest in Albania. As Enver Hoxha's concrete bunkers slipped gradually from sight, covered by grass and foliage, his political heritage was becoming harder to overome.

5

Operation Alba

Even today, nearly a decade after the 1997 events, it is easy to forget the sense of disorientation and shock that the Albanian uprising caused within the international community. After the 1995 Bosnian settlement at Dayton, it was assumed that any major problems in South-East Europe were over. It was assumed Slobodan Milosevic would evolve into a tolerable partner in the international community, the commitment of the USA was secure, and a period of general recuperation from the northern Balkan wars was needed. This would then be followed by general reconstruction leading to eventual integration into the European Union.

This over-sanguine view was tempered in some informed minds by the existence of major problems still outstanding, such as the unresolved status of Kosova. There was, however, no warning whatsoever of the turmoil that was to engulf Albania. In these circumstances it was not surprising that the prospect of international intervention there was unwelcome and controversial. There were considerable difficulties in the international community in agreeing both what should be done, and how it should be done, and – even more problematic – who should do it.[1]

It was also clear that as the Bosnian crisis was the most apparently relevant experience for the international community, the 'Bosnian model' of intervention would be central to international community thinking, as later also proved to be the case in Kosovo in 1999 and in Macedonia in 2001. This was the situation even though the UN was to play little role in the crisis. In that sense, the Albanian intervention was an early example of a 'coalition of the willing' outside of formal UN structures (an early model of the later operations in Afghanistan and Iraq), and an indication of the damage done to the UN in the Balkans by the failures and tragedies in Croatia and Bosnia.

Yet it was equally apparent to those with even a superficial understanding of the Albanian situation that the only common factor between this and the Bosnian crisis was regional geography, and that the uprising of the Albanian people against the Berisha government was very different from the prolonged ethnically based war against Bosnia led by the Bosnian Serbs. The Bosnian model of intervention has been much discussed but in essence it involved the imposition of martial law through NATO, the construction of a civil authority that was under UN auspices, and a consequent attempt to rebuild the central state institutions in Sarajevo.[2] This involved in practice the construction of a 'new' state but by using existing institutions as its basis, given the absence of agreement in the past and the destruction of Sarajevo government authority in the wartime period.

In Albania there was a legal and still partly functional state, with sovereign authority, but the army and police had collapsed as effective social control mechanisms. There was no doubt, though, that sovereignty still resided in the Tirana government institutions, however dysfunctional, and thus the international community could not seek to impose an external military authority with legal sovereignty, however attractive this might be in private to some anti-Albanian forces in the international community.[3] To his great credit this was recognised by NATO General Secretary Javier Solana at the outset when military intervention to save the Berisha government was refused, as it could have led to NATO soldiers being involved on one side in the conflict and could have led to the civil war it was designed to prevent. The UN played little part in the crisis of Albania in 1997 in any shape or form.

In practice the language of intervention harked back to the earlier stages of the Bosnian crisis, where troops were to be deployed to protect humanitarian aid, and to enable the forthcoming elections to be held under reasonably peaceful conditions. The mission did not stress police capacity, only the ability to dissuade local groups and factions from armed conflict. As such, in some ways it was a preventative peacekeeping operation and also built on the experiences of the UN force that had been deployed on the borders of Former Yugoslav Macedonia since 1993, and had been seen in the international community as a general success.[4] It did not involve coercive peace enforcement. This raised the question in some Albanian minds as to whether Operation Alba was really needed. The operation has been much studied and discussed in the international security community and by 2005 there were over 26,000 World Wide Web entries for the subject.

The essence of the argument against intervention and Operation Alba has been that the scale of the disaster in Albania was exaggerated by the news media, and as a result the international community was persuaded to intervene when it was unnecessary to do so.[5] This has been a familiar theme in all recent debates in the international community about the practice of what Noam Chomsky has called 'the new military humanism'. Other aspects of the debate have been repeated over successive years in respect of the Rwanda, Kosova, Afghanistan and Iraq operations, with critics of action noting that the heavily armed military presence with a draconian mandate was not adequate to deal with local political opposition and violent disorder in failing states, and an extensive police mission would have been much better able to control disorder and prevent a descent into anarchy.

At the heart of Operation Alba there was division in international community thinking as to whether the priority was really to protect humanitarian aid, or to restore public order, or to prevent mass refugee movements, or really to protect the government of Dr Berisha and stop a successful uprising, or to protect the electoral process and oversee an orderly end of the Democratic Party government. In reality, unlike the Bosnian operation in wartime, humanitarian aid was ultimately not an important aspect of Operation Alba's work, despite what was said at the time. Food supplies were adequate over all of the country except for local shortages (often caused by panic buying) for very limited periods of time, as in the Vlora bread crisis in March 1997.

In conception and leadership Operation Alba was very much an Italian creation.[6] Italy already had relevant experience after the 1991 'Operation Pelican' in Albania, which had certainly made a major contribution to the relief of the humanitarian crisis, and had good local knowledge of at least some parts of Albania, mainly the Mediterranean coast and associated lowlands and the Catholic north-west around the city of Shkoder.[7] Italy and Greece were the countries within the EU and NATO most directly threatened by a mass influx of destitute, possibly armed people.

Italy had harmonious relations with the Berisha government, and a few Democratic Party leaders, such as Pjeter Arbnori, were Catholics with close Italian and Vatican links. As a result Italian leadership of the mission was a natural development. Italian politicians had totally failed to influence political developments to preserve the Democratic Party government in February and March, and the Alba mission gave them an opportunity to restore some Italian credibility through the military. The total number of troops in the mission was about 6300, of which 2800 were Italian, with other nations inside and outside NATO contributing very small numbers (such as Denmark with 59 soldiers, Austria with 110 and Spain with 340).

The 'Anglo-Saxon' big players in NATO, like Canada, the USA and Britain, did not send any soldiers at all. The only detachments to approach the Italian commitment were those of Greece (with 760 men) and France (with 950).

The deployment itself was almost exclusively based in the southern and central lowlands, with major force concentrations in the towns of Lezha, Durres and Elbasan. It is impossible to avoid the impression that whatever was said at the time by NATO officials about humanitarian aid and overseeing peaceful elections, the dominant thread in Alba military planning was for the troops to act as a barrier between the Socialist-held south and the generally pro-Berisha north, and thus prevent the chaos from developing into a civil war. Local politicians in Tirana were soon aware of this, and it was clear to the Socialists that effective control of polling stations in an election would be highly unlikely. This aided their push for power through the ballot box in June, sometimes by unethical means.

Alba troops were able to quickly take control of the key roads linking central Albania with the north and north-east, which was an important insurance policy against any possibility, however remote, that the violence could spread towards the border with Kosova and so risk the involvement of the Yugoslavs in the crisis. Thus, in outline, Alba turned out to be a 'trial run' for the later NATO 'Operation Allied Harbour' deployment in Albania in 1998 in the Kosova war crisis, and many of the same military bases and planning parameters were used in both operations. Conspiracy theorists on the Albanian side could allege that the real purpose of the Operation Alba exercise in some NATO minds was to protect Kosova and the Milosevic regime from the 'contagion' of the Albanian uprising. This may seem a far-fetched theory but it has some rational basis, with the emergence of an armed underground organisation, the KLA, in Kosova in 1996 and regular attacks on the Yugoslav army and police units there.

Although Kosova militants were not involved in the initial stages of the uprising, they were quick to take advantage of the possibilities the uprising presented by buying up large quantities of weapons. At an informal level, some of the patriotic ex-army officers who led the rebellion in the south were sympathetic to the Kosova military struggle, seeing it within the paradigm of Enverist nationalism and the Partisan tradition. However, as in Serbia and Croatia, few diplomats in the years of the ex-Yugoslav wars really understood the force that the Partisan and resistance tradition derived from the anti-Axis struggles of the Second World War still had in popular Balkan life and political perceptions.

The Italian government saw the problems of the entire Balkan region as highly interdependent. Speaking after the 1997 events, Foreign Minister

Lamberto Dini told a NATO ministerial meeting in 2000 that ' the security and stabilisation of the whole of southeastern Europe must be pursued on a regional and integrated basis'. As Operation Alba was being deployed, the Italians still continued to provide a large force in Bosnia and smaller forces elsewhere in the world in peacekeeping operations, something that led UN Secretary General Kofi Annan to describe Italy as 'an ideal UN member'.[8]

In contrast, it was difficult for the most uncritical international backers of the Democratic Party government, such as the British in London and the Republican Right in the USA, to acknowledge that the nature of the crisis was part of the bitter legacy of Albanian communism, and that the Berisha government had made only very limited progress in escaping from this heritage. Some US diplomats went further and saw the Berisha government as having residual elements of an authoritarian regime in its modus operandi.[9] American involvement was also limited by force protection considerations, coupled with a knowledge that the close links that were being formed between the Pentagon and some senior Albanian officials sufficed to provide the USA with the influence it needed in Albania, whatever the outcome of the spring 1997 power struggle. The wider issue of US influence needs to be borne in mind; however, although the USA was very dominant over the government in the 1992–6 period, that was not the case in 1997.[10]

It is becoming clear that the 'coalition of the willing' model of force organisation was not an ideal but in fact was a last resort, forced upon Italy and Greece as immediate neighbours threatened by refugee movement. In the early weeks of the crisis the Italian and French governments had put pressure on the EU and NATO to organise military intervention on Berisha's behalf, but they had not been able to do so. Speaking in February 1998, Italian Foreign Ministry Balkan Director Stefanni said that, 'We, Italy, fell back on it because of the lack of response from the established institutions that should have had primary responsibility, NATO, EU, UN, WEU, OSCE, you name it.'[11] The fact that Operation Alba was a relative success was, in these circumstances, to leave an important legacy that would influence international opinion in a pro-interventionist direction in the 1998–9 Kosova crisis.

The question has been raised as to why the KLA was able to secure international tacit approval in a way that previous Balkan liberation movements such as the Internal Macedonian Revolutionary Organisation (IMRO) had been denied. Part of the answer lies in the fact that the 1997 crisis was contained without massive external refugee flows, and one should never underestimate the extent to which policies of international actors towards the Balkans are determined by fears of population movements. It was also the case that a UN resolution was passed justifying the operation and the OSCE did eventually provide an organisational 'umbrella' at a political level.

A difficulty for the international community in all these considerations was the Helsinki Final Act, which ruled out border changes in post-communist Europe. Although in the Balkans Croatia and Slovenia had already successfully circumvented it, and Bosnia less so, there was still an important opinion constituency in the international community seeking to prevent any more border changes in the region. A key factor in the relative success of Alba was the timing of the operation, which secured local approval for the deployment and a general welcome to the soldiers when they arrived. The first Italian naval ships set sail from Brindisi on 3 March, but they did not make any impression on the country with troop deployments until the following week, and many soldiers did not arrive anywhere at all in provincial Albania until the second wave of deployment in mid-March. The official Italian military history of Operation Alba dates full deployment as having been achieved by 18–22 March, a realistic estimate. By this time the fate of the Berisha government had been sealed, during the key period beginning 9 March in Gjirokaster, and such a relatively small force could not conceivably be seen by anti-government Albanians as likely to prevent a change of government.

The fact of physical deployment did not mean that actual peacekeeping operations in the localities had necessarily begun. The poor condition of many Albanian military facilities that the Alba troops found on arrival, and the general civil chaos meant that the soldiers had to spend vital time on menial tasks such as making their barracks habitable and secure rather than making any impression on Albania and its problems. A typical problem was that the arriving forces depended upon rations that required refrigeration (a vital factor with the hot Albanian summer coming) and ample supplies of electricity. Yet they found empty kitchens, few or no refrigerators and frequent power cuts. A far higher percentage of the soldiers' time and energy was taken up by logistics and communications activity than the Rome military planners had originally envisaged.

An additional problem was that once the troops were deployed, although under a central HQ command structure, they were subject to various influences from the other international organisations concerned with managing the crisis. The OSCE election mandate meant that many local deployments were designed primarily to secure and protect polling stations rather than intervene in the political conflict, and for a long time local clashes between different groups continued. In practice, in some towns, let alone the countryside, Alba forces were not in action on patrol until well into the first week in April, by which time the fate of the DP government was definitely sealed.

If the purpose of Operation Alba was really to save the DP government, it never came remotely near the possibility of success. The most militant and heavily armed towns, such as Tepelena and Librazhd, were largely unaffected by Alba forces for several weeks. Very few Alba soldiers ever ventured into northern and north-east Albania at all, with a small deployment to Kukes only being achieved late in the crisis. Nevertheless, in the central lowlands and elsewhere the troops were seen as a positive element in national security by most of the population, who were fearful for the future of their country when civil war had seemed a possibility, and the soldiers were a stabilising element in the transition to a new government.

It is of course an open question as to what the real intentions of some members of the Italian government were, with some ministers strongly pro-Berisha while other political forces in Italy, such as the communist Left, were very close to the Albanian Socialist Party.[12] It is possible that they may have seen Alba as a way to prevent the overthrow of the Democratic Party government, but if so the deployment was overtaken by the speed of events on the ground in Albania. Until Rome government archives are open, these questions are likely to remain unanswered.

The Alba force organisation seems to have been planned with considerable sophistication and some knowledge of local political loyalties, so that the Greek contingent was kept well away from the Greek-speaking areas in the south, although there was a joint headquarters with the Italians in the key city of Vlora. The French were prominent in the capital Tirana, an expression of commitment by a major EU nation that was outside the historic problematic of Italian–Greek rivalry for influence over the Albanian government.

One of the most important achievements of the Alba mission was securing the election facilities and making sure that voting could take place in the polling stations for the national parliamentary elections and monarchy referendum on 29 June. In the north-east and Dibra and some other Berisha-controlled heartland areas, a substantial part of the damage to public installations and property had been caused by militants within the Democratic Party itself, who were keen to promote chaos with a view to encouraging NATO intervention on the side of the DP government.[13] In the June election, to the surprise of many observers, the Left polled quite well in many of these places, so that sitting DP members lost seats in Dibra and elsewhere.

This fact has, of course, been seized upon by those opposed to the principle of the operation, believing that Alba was unnecessary. With the benefit of hindsight this is an easy point to make, but it is worth noting that many of those making these criticisms have been traditional Tirana-based intellectuals whose knowledge and experience of other parts of the country, the wilder parts of the north in particular, was often limited. It is very doubtful if the election could have been held at all in many of these areas without the Alba security presence, and the whole controversy illustrates the weaknesses of the Tirana-centric viewpoint of some critics of the Alba intervention (with the background of the Hoxhaist psychological heritage of blaming anything that was wrong in Albania on the foreign media or foreign interference).

In addition to the military forces under the Alba flag, there was also a deployment of the Carabineri, the Italian paramilitary police, and small numbers of similar policemen from other countries. In practice the Carabineri came under the central military command and performed the same basic security tasks as the army, but their presence set an important precedent in that foreign police have had a continuous presence in the country ever since: first as part of a Western European Union (WEU) police mission in the 1998–2000 period, and then as an element in the EU police training mission that has followed it. It is far from clear what these organisations have actually achieved but March 1997 saw their arrival on the Albanian landscape. Carabineri were soon responsible for some of the easier security deployments, such as port and harbour security in Durres after the initial Alba military presence had restored order, and patrols on main roads. The training of these paramilitary forces often means that they are more suited to some public order and security tasks than soldiers.

Another main current of criticism of the Alba operation has been bound up with consideration of the role of the OSCE in the Albanian crisis. The standard account of OSCE operations in Albania in this period sees it as a 'time of lost opportunity'.[14] The OSCE lost the initiative in the diplomatic sphere very early on in the crisis to the EU, and later, when military intervention was under discussion, to NATO. It is not widely realised that the first request for military intervention from the Berisha government to an outside party came direct to the EU, requesting a WEU force to back the Albanian army against the insurgents in the south. The Dutch Presidency of the EU was approached on about 10 March with a request for the deployment of a Rapid Reaction Force.[15]

It is significant in showing the degree of alienation of the Berisha government from the USA that this took place at all, as on the face of it NATO with its US leadership would have been a more logical choice. The

USA was beginning to assume its current role as protector of Albanian aspirations and national security, linked to the strong influence in US politics of powerful diaspora organisations and the Albanian lobby on Capitol Hill in Washington.[16] But ever since the summer of 1996 and the acerbic exchanges about the validity of the 1996 election,[17] distance between the Democratic Party government and the US State Department had been growing rapidly. In late summer 1996 Germany had started discussions with Berisha on taking over various military aid and training programmes that previously had been run by the USA.[18]

When this request to the WEU for a Rapid Reaction Force came to nothing, owing to the lack of capacity of the WEU to organise and lead such a force, the Italian government received a request to lead a force that would not be mandated to enforce peace, but to resupply the Albanian army with munitions and armaments and to secure the storage of these commodities. In essence this would have probably meant that Italian forces could have come under Albanian command, or at least joint command; something that was quite unacceptable to the Italian army and government.

The fact that the request was made at all, though, does indicate the closeness of identity with Italy seen in regional politics by the Democratic Party leadership, and may also indicate foreknowledge of the 'Greek factor' in the southern uprising. The reaction of the Rome government to this request was to leave open the possibility of an OSCE-mandated force, but it also wanted a UN Security Council resolution. This immediately undermined the OSCE, however understandable the decision was from an Italian point of view. The whole process also took up valuable time when every day the practical authority of the DP government was in decline.

In the event, on 21 March the Security Council adopted Resolution 1101 authorising the countries participating in the multinational force to conduct an operation on the basis of Chapter VII of the UN charter.[19] On the key issue of the rules of engagement the exact language of the Bosnian operation was reproduced, giving the right to use force to accomplish the mission, and 'the right to position' defence. This could be interpreted as providing the framework for a peace 'enforcement' operation, although in practice fighting between different groups was subsiding in most localities outside the 'difficult' cities such as Vlora and Gjirokaster by the time of second-wave deployment in late March.

In practice, very little peace enforcement at all of a direct kind was ever undertaken by the Alba force, if this is to be defined as cracking down on local armed groups, counter-insurgency and patrolling in the manner that the British Army has used in Ulster and elsewhere. The vast majority of the 1700-plus operations undertaken by Alba forces between deployment days and the withdrawal in August 1997 were low-key operations to secure roads and property, particularly state buildings, and to prevent looting and arson. No less than 674 missions were carried out to protect OSCE election observers. No attempt was made to collect looted small arms unless a favourable opportunity presented itself, which meant that virtually none were collected, and very few people were ever arrested by Alba soldiers. In Tirana, the vast majority of the effort of the French forces' time was taken up by driving around the streets in heavily armoured vehicles in a symbolic role, but at night the city was still full of the sound of random small arms fire.

The Alba operation focused attention within NATO on Albania (even if NATO initially rejected a lead role in the intervention process) and on the unclear and ambiguous policy options. In the post-Cold War era NATO's mandate was widening, as the Bosnian intervention showed, and Albania was actually the first ex-communist East European state to apply for full NATO membership. The Pentagon and the CIA had considered Albania a key ally during the Bosnian operations due to its strategic position on the Adriatic seaboard, its strategic airspace, its strongly pro-American population (unique in the region) and its general geostrategic position. The airport near Lezha was the main Balkan base for unmanned surveillance drones to fly over Serbia and the Bosnian warzone. The late 1990s were a period of the growth in projection of the USA as a seapower, something that has benefited Albania considerably in recent years. However, in the 1997 crisis US commitment was limited by the lack of enthusiasm for the Berisha government, and what one US commentator has described as a 'half-hearted' approach to the problem of Kosova that was to soon loom over the region in 1998.[20]

The very powerful Albanian lobby in the USA was in practice mainly dominated by Albanians from Kosova, who had little sympathy with the re-emergence of the Socialists as the governing force, which was almost universally seen in the US Albanian world as a backward step. Fatos Nano was almost unknown in America, compared to Sali Berisha, who had made frequent vists there and enjoyed the support of the Albanian-American media and many intellectuals coming from rightist Ballist and Royalist families who had emigrated there after the Second World War. The Presidential style and ethos of the early Berisha government was strongly influenced by US models, and appealed to the traditionalist lower-middle-class and working-class people who make up the vast majority of the 'poor white' US-based Albanian diaspora community. The US administration was blamed by some Europeans for not doing enough to prevent the anarchy in Albania but it should be remembered that the US Albanian community itself was very divided in its response to the events, and was thus unable to give the same clear lead to the administration as it would do over Kosova in 1998–9.

An additional factor was the generally vacillating attitude of the Clinton administration on many foreign policy issues and the legacy of Holbrooke-type Balkan diplomacy, with its focus on set-piece, highly organised negotiations. These methods were very unsuited to the Albanian chaos in 1997. Also, the US Serbian community had some influence in the Democratic Party in parts of the USA, such as Chicago and the Midwest, which certainly did not encourage involvement in Albanian affairs. At the back of many military, security and intelligence minds in the USA, if not in Europe, was the medium-term prospect of NATO action in a future Kosova crisis. If that was to be successful, NATO needed united support in Albania for intervention, and that might not have been forthcoming if there was a NATO deployment on the ground in 1997, which would have risked associating the alliance with one side or the other in the Tirana power struggle. Neither side was very attractive as a possible leadership to the more orthodox sections of opinion in Washington: the Democratic Party because of human rights violations and the move towards an authoritarian regime, and the Socialists who seemed to be much too close to the Marxist-Leninist Albanian Party of Labour from which they had so recently emerged.

Although these were all negative considerations for NATO, as a US-led alliance, in its relations with Albania, a new relationship did begin to develop as a result of the spring 1997 crisis, and both sides stumbled into a de facto close relationship that was largely unseen by the world in general but became a major background factor in the 1998–9 Kosova intervention. It became clear to US and NATO strategic and military planners that there was an unavoidable link between the stabilisation of Albania and the development of its democratic institutions, and the stability of the region as a whole – linked in turn to the platform that a stable Albania would provide to try to resolve the future of Kosova peacefully. In the background was the silent but vital interest of the USA in oil transport from the Middle East and the Caspian, the strategic importance for the US navy of the Albanian Adriatic coast and new geopolitical priorities linked to protection of the oil and gas pipelines. US military planning works on very long lead times; the current chaos in Albania was not an obstacle to its playing a full role in US regional planning. Although small and weak, Albania was seen as strongly pro-Western, whereas Serbia was always seen as partly linked to Russia.

Slobodan Milosevic and the Serb leadership, and pro-Serb countries such as Greece and Russia, seem in retrospect to have been very slow to appreciate what was happening, and to realise the nature of the unspoken compact between Tirana and Washington – otherwise Milosevic might have chosen different policy options in the run-up to the Kosova crisis. NATO itself also appears to have been slow to see the increasing focus in the USA on the projection of US naval power as central to its global role, in which Albania could play a minor but regionally critical part in South-East Europe. Whatever its weaknesses in other ways as a governing class, the Albanian elite was well aware of growing superpower interest in the region, and in the light of previous experience of dealing with Russian and Chinese superpower partners under communism they were adept at influencing US policy in the desired direction.

The Democratic Party government in March 1997 was quite naively unaware of most aspects of these geopolitical complexities affecting the fate of Albania, and saw its survival as synonomous with the survival of democracy itself. In turn this was intimately linked to the personality of the leader, with Dr Berisha seeing his own role, and that of his party, in strictly black-and-white terms. This was not the case with the Socialist Party leadership, who saw events in a more sophisticated way. When he escaped from prison near Tepelena in March, Fatos Nano knew that his fragile new government could only survive with powerful friends, and at the time this meant Greece, and in the background, Britain. The new Labour government in London was anxious to distance itself from the Balkan policies of its Tory predecessor, where ministers had come close to support for Serbian violations of international law and war crimes.[21]

The international community was, however, misled over the relative success of Operation Alba. The fact that civil war had been prevented, a rough but probably fair election held and the threat of mass emigration and social collapse stalled did not mean that the new Socialist-led coalition inherited a country with a normal or functioning state machine, a functional army or police force, or with the capacity to enforce its will over the whole country. The crisis in spring 1997 had bred bitter enmities, and ever since then there has always been a hard core of pro-Berisha support that has seen the international community as accomplices to what was in essence a communist return to power.

Individual international community leaders in Albania at the time, like Dutch ex-Foreign Minister Daan Everts, the head of the Albania OSCE mission from 1996 to 1998, have been vilified by these people in Albania for their role in the transfer of power in June 1997, and this has led to a problem of legitimacy in the post-1997 settlement. In turn this fundamentally affected the capacity of the Tirana government to control the looming Kosova crisis, as calls for the control of the KLA and similar paramilitary groups meant little in the northern regions, where hardly anyone respected the legitimacy of the Fatos Nano administration, let alone acted on its policies. Therefore, at one level the weak or failed state scenario had been avoided, but only partly so.

As such the dynamic of the next stage of the crisis moved from southern to northern Albania, where the state had never had much legitimacy (ever since independence in November 1912), where the most poverty and dissatisfaction with Tirana was always concentrated, and where cultural traditions were imbued with notions of revenge. Although following the elections the international community believed the question of state power had been resolved in the early summer of 1997, many supporters of Dr Berisha did not agree, and these forces were mostly concentrated in his northern heartland. Their initiatives to reopen the question of power would be further complicated by the onset of war in neighbouring Kosova where many families, including that of Dr Berisha, had close family and historical links. Thus this period marks the opening of the national question in a new and broader dimension.

The UPRISING in SOUTHERN ALBANIA
6–11 March 1997

ADRIATIC SEA

Divjaka

Lushnja

•Deshiran

•Gramsh

Pogradec•

Government
forces
concentrated
here
9-11/3

Kuçova ← Fell to rebels
10/3

Ura
Vajgurore

Fier

Berat ← Fell to rebels
10/3
*Magazines
opened*

North of
Vlora, no
overall
control

Patos ← Held by
government

Poliçan ← Fell to rebels
10/3

Ballsh ← Held by
government

Vlora

Corovoda | *Situation
confused
9-10/3*

Road blocked
by government
forces

Bridge
dynamited
7/3

Boundary of
rebel control
pm8/3

Fell to
rebellion
10/3
*some buildings
on fire*

STRAIT OF OTRANTO

Orikum

•Memaliaj

Rebel forward
stronghold
guns moved to
Permet 9-10/3 → **Tepelena**

Kelcyra

Permet

DP
Terror in Permet
6-8/3

Leskovik•

N

Government
road block
(defunct by
9/3)

Himara

Rebel-held coast Saranda to Vlora

Gjirokaster ← Fell to rebellion
8/3

Libohova•

IONIAN SEA

Govt tank
positions
(3 tanks)

Greek 8th
Army Division

Rebel HQ
Delvina

•Finiq

Government
held until
8/3 pm

Kakavia
(to rebels
10/3)

Rebel
supply route

Saranda
•Cuka

KERKIRA
(CORFU)

Xarra

No-man's land
8 to 9/3

GREECE

•Konispol

•Kérkira (Corfu)

Legend

——— Roads

—·—·—· Greek–Albanian border

/////// Extent of rebel held coastal
area

Scale

0   5   15   20   25   30

Kilometres

6

The Revival of Socialist Power and the Royalist Challenge

As spring edged towards summer the anarchy subsided, to be replaced by an uneasy stand-off between the rebel forces in the south and a beleaguered President Berisha holed up in the capital. Premier Bashkim Fino's weak and ineffective government had failed to provide a guarantee against further conflict, as a weary population hurried through their daily tasks before retreating fearfully behind locked doors at the start of the nightly curfew. As soon as Operation Alba's troops withdrew from the streets at dusk, the gangs would begin to settle their scores to the sound of gunfire and grenades. It was clear that new elections would be needed before there was any prospect of a government with real legitimacy.

At the end of May 1997, Albania's politicians finally agreed to go ahead with a general election on 29 June, thus ending a stand-off between President Berisha and his Democratic Party, who had pushed their own electoral law through parliament. In theory, parliament was supposed to approve an electoral law only after the government had negotiated a decision on it. But Berisha was in no mood for conciliation, and used his constitutional powers to the full.[1] He chose then to make a provocative trip to the southern town of Fier, one of the most virulent centres of revolt against his rule, to boast that the DP was going to win 75 per cent of the vote on 29 June. This was widely interpreted as a threat that his Democratic Party intended to hang on to absolute power by whatever means it could. The international community appeared uncertain as to what to do next, except to keep pressing for dialogue between the two parties. A referendum on the future of the monarchy was to be held in tandem with the parliamentary elections.

The OSCE was once more preparing to oversee the two-round election. Following the May 1996 elections the OSCE had produced a highly critical election report, which catalogued a range of serious polling irregularities, including incomplete electoral registers, ballot-stuffing and voter intimidation.[2] This time, however, due to the poor security situation, it was going to prove impossible for the OSCE to provided anything but the most rudimentary monitoring outside the capital. The organisation warned that only those of a 'strong mental and physical disposition' need apply for the 500 monitoring posts. Although foreign analysts admitted the election would be imperfect, they argued that something had to be done in order to avoid the possibility of civil war and that holding an election was better than doing nothing.

On 30 May, nine right and centre-right political parties and 23 political/cultural associations signed a social pact proposed by the Democratic Party that would contest the elections under the political umbrella of the 'Union for Democracy' (UfD). The most pressing concern for the right-wing parties remained the unresolved issue of the rebel committees, which the UfD correctly pointed out prevented the normal activity of political parties in the southern areas, making it very difficult to conduct an effective electoral campaign. The UfD called on Premier Fino to officially dissolve the committees as soon as possible. Although the government had done little to curtail the activities of the committees, it too was concerned that they were undermining attempts to reimpose state control over the south of the country. Premier Fino claimed that although the committees had been useful when they were first established, in areas where the police and local authorities were now functioning properly the salvation committees should be abandoned.[3]

The build-up to the election witnessed the nightly ritual of violent clashes in the centre of the main towns, as Berisha's own militia provoked exchanges of gunfire. This maintained a climate of fear in order to justify extending the state of emergency in which police had been ordered to shoot to kill. In doing so Berisha and his supporters hoped to delay and possibly postpone the elections by making it impossible to organise any effective campaigning. Berisha was also keeping a tight reign on the Interior Ministry, which gave him control over the police as well as what was left of the armed forces.

To enhance the tense atmosphere, a series of violent incidents marred the election campaign. On 1 June the pro-DP newspaper *Albania* announced that a café in the centre of Tirana, owned by the Deputy Interior Minister and Socialist Party member Lush Perpali, was going to be blown up. The next day the café was duly destroyed by a bomb, with 20 people injured. The same day a bridge on the Muzina-Saranda road was also blown up, and another bomb exploded near the Socialist Party headquarters in the centre of Tirana. A few hours later a bridge near the southern town of Saranda was blown up. On 9 June an explosion damaged the Kiri Bridge near Shkoder, making it impassable. After seven bombs in five days in the capital, there were calls for the mandate of Operation Alba to be extended to allow it to offer more protection to campaigning politicians. At this stage, more than 1700 people had been killed since the beginning of the uprising in March. The previous year only the police had Kalashnikovs; now virtually the entire population was armed.

Amidst the violence, an assassination attempt was made on President Berisha when a hand grenade was hurled at him as he addressed supporters at a rally in the village of Shkallnuer near Durres. From then on Berisha travelled under heavy guard only to towns he could safely reach, holding carefully orchestrated rallies that were shown on state TV. Bashkim Fino's election convoy was fired upon as he approached the northern city of Shkoder, a DP bastion. An armed gang turned Socialist Party leader Fatos Nano back from the northern town of Rreshen, whilst the citizens of Vlora made it abundantly clear that Berisha would not survive a visit to the town. However, to complicate matters, this did not translate into a clear north–south split. The DP was managing to campaign in some southern districts, whilst Fatos Nano successfully visited the northern town of Kukes. In an embarrassing moment during his campaign visit to Vlora, Nano fell to his knees and wept before the crowds, promising to return the millions of pounds Albanians had lost in the pyramid collapse. The crowd applauded saying they would vote for anyone who would get rid of Berisha and return their lost savings. The Vlora population had lost a great deal in the pyramid schemes and they blamed Berisha. 'He stole our elections (1996) and then he stole our money', they shouted.

As tensions increased, many UfD candidates were increasingly fearful of being attacked and refused to campaign beyond the security of their immediate neighbourhoods. As a result, the electorate had very little idea of what policies, if any, the 30 or so political parties were offering. In all but a few districts the DP was finding it very hard to run an effective election campaign in the south, where Socialist Party intimidation kept many Democratic Party members from serving on electoral commissions. In Vlora some two-thirds of them did not show up. The 6000-strong multinational force was nowhere to be seen in the eastern town of Korca, which was still held by the government (the DP having won all six parliamentary seats in the May 1996 election). Yet the party, whose headquarters had been burnt down, was virtually unable to campaign anywhere outside the city. Rebels supporting the Socialist Party dominated the surrounding countryside.

Meanwhile, the self-proclaimed king Leka Zog had been travelling the country with his royal entourage in a valiant attempt to drum up support for the referendum on the monarchy, which was considered by many to be merely a sideshow to the main elections. Although they believed that the two main parties would try to manipulate the result of the referendum, Leka's supporters expected between 55 and 60 per cent of the electorate to cast their vote in favour of the monarchy. However, throughout much of Albania there was still strong opposition to the return of the king and much of Leka's audiences attended the monarchist rallies mainly out of sheer curiosity. On 2 June Leka was refused entry to the southern town of Saranda, and two days later a roadblock of 40 heavily armed men barred his entry to the central town of Cerrik, demanding that he turn back. The return of Leka, who liked to portray himself as a source of stability, only served to further inflame Albania's volatile politics.[4] He and his entourage's obsession with guns just added another lethal element to the Albanian political cocktail, which comprised President Berisha's semi-loyal presidential guard, the Socialists with their special police units and now Leka Zog with his own private army.

Some light-hearted relief from the rigours of the electoral campaign was provided by the curious background to the knifing of British diplomat Geoffrey Briggs in Tirana. On the 8–9 June, Briggs, 33, a second secretary, was apparently stabbed in the stomach after a quarrel with his Albanian girlfriend, who worked as a waitress in the Rogner Hotel.[5] He underwent emergency treatment in Italy before being squirrelled back to Britain to recover from what the Foreign Office described as a 'purely domestic affair'. The incident did little to improve the image of the British embassy, which was still trying to recover from the humiliating evacuation fiasco in March when British nationals trying to flee the country were trapped in Durres as rebels stole most of the embassy's cars.

On the election day itself, violence claimed several victims with gunmen pressurising people to vote for either the Socialists or the UfD coalition. Reports of intimidation around the country abounded. In the northern town of Lezha, voting was halted in four polling stations because groups of young men seized the ballots and marked them for the candidate of the pro-monarchy Legality Party. Nevertheless, there were a number of improvements over the voting procedure of the previous year. These included the use of indelible ink on people's thumbs to prevent double voting and better compliance with the requirement that representatives of at least three parties attend each polling station to confirm the count.

The elections resulted in a landslide victory for the Socialists, who won 52 per cent to the Democrats' 26 per cent. The Monarchist's Legality Movement Party gained only 3.66 per cent. Following constitutional court rulings on disputes and some changing of alliances, the Socialists and their coalition allies emerged with 118 seats in the 155-seat parliament, whilst the Democrats had 24. An OSCE statement admitted that: 'despite some minor flaws in many areas and some very serious problems in a few areas, the vote had shown the Albanians' true desire for a democratic future'.[6] It went on to conclude that about 80 per cent of the 1000 electoral reports considered the voting procedure to be 'good or very good'. Despite the OSCE claim that the elections were 'acceptable', several international observers expressed their disquiet at the way the OSCE was seen to use its authority to validate whatever result it believed to be politically desirable. According to one report, a British parliamentarian had admitted that the election was not democratic but it was a 'necessary process to get a new government in Albania'.[7] The Democratic Party issued an immediate protest against the election results, and accused the Socialists of using violence and terror against DP representatives.

There is no denying that the whole conduct of the elections was highly irregular. Several districts were without any international monitoring at all and representatives of the Democratic Party were unable to campaign in large areas of the south. If the key issue was restoring the people's faith in a free vote, then it clearly failed to achieve its objective. Nevertheless, had the elections not taken place and the country had descended into further anarchy, there was a very real possibility of Kosova being drawn into the conflict. This was too great a risk for the international community to take. The elections were therefore deemed 'acceptable' as the lesser of two evils. Given the equally undemocratic nature of the previous year's elections, it could be argued that the scores were now even for both the Democrats and the Socialists in terms of achieving victory status in Tirana. Thus, in the hope of re-establishing stability and the rule of law in Albania, whilst at the same time trying to keep Kosova from being dragged into events in Albania, the international community decided to ignore major discrepancies in the electoral process and call it 'acceptable'.

The question of whether the monarchy should be restored was resolved by the referendum held simultaneously with the parliamentary elections. Despite the optimism of the monarchists, the electorate voted decisively in favour of continued republicanism with a majority of 66.74 per cent, whilst

33.26 per cent voted in favour of a monarchy. The monarchists were predictably unhappy with this result, considering it invalid due to tampering by the Socialist Party. According to representatives of the 'royal court', preliminary reports showed that in the majority of the northern districts of Albania voting in the referendum had been in favour of restoring a constitutional monarchy. The 'royal court' minister, Abedin Mulosmani, told a news conference 'the results of the referendum have exceeded 60 per cent.' He then called on 'Albanians to defend their vote as they would defend the lives of their children.'[8] Mr Mulosmani directly blamed the Socialist Party leader Fatos Nano and the political force he represented, for the 'fraudulent' result. Monarchists in Shkoder were particularly angry at the alleged manipulation of the results. Leka attended a monarchist rally in the town where he criticised the Socialists 'for manipulating the victory of the referendum', and called on the citizens of Shkoder to protect their vote.[9]

On 3 July Leka, dressed in military fatigues with a grenade and a pistol strapped to his leg, greeted around 2000 monarchist supporters gathered in Tirana's central Skanderbeg Square to further protest claims of vote-rigging by the Socialist Party. Chanting, 'the Albanians will defend their vote – down with the communists – we want a king', the crowd led by Leka marched down Tirana's central boulevard. Suddenly bursts of gunfire erupted, which were followed by a powerful and long volley of shots. The crowd fled in panic in all directions as one man was killed and two more injured. The monarchists blamed police acting under the orders of Premier Fino for the shooting, whilst the Socialist Party accused President Berisha as well as the monarchists of provoking confrontation and destabilisation.[10] In a statement the Socialist Party claimed that:

> In desperation and panic, Berisha was seeking to include Leka Zog and his followers, along with his own gangs and mercenaries, in a confrontation with the government. The SP believes that all the recent acts of destabilisation by Leka Zog and his followers have the full co-operation of Berisha in order to keep the country in the grip of chaos.[11]

In an inflammatory response, the pro-Berisha daily *Albania* claimed that the Socialist leader was ordering tanks to be deployed against the north. The article entitled: 'Nano – tanks towards the North', reported that the Defence Minister, Shaqir Vukaj, was ordering tanks towards the north in order to crush demonstrations by monarchist supporters.[12] The government denied such accusations as 'inventions of fantasy', which were intended to incite conflict between the people and the army.

Leka and his 'royal court' minister, Abedin Mulosmani, failed to respond to the request from the prosecutor's office to appear in court for questioning about the violence on 3 July. On 12 July a humiliated Leka Zog and his entourage once again fled Albania and headed back home to Johannesburg. Apart from the traditional monarchist bastions, the presence of the self-proclaimed king had singularly failed to impress the majority of Albanians. Being surrounded by a heavily armed, uneducated and sometimes distinctly violent entourage had given the 'royal' delegation an aura of dangerous unpredictability. Given the uncertain and violent conditions that surrounded their daily lives, this was not appreciated by ordinary Albanians. If Leka had been a person of substance and charisma, and his entourage had had a measure of education and civility, the monarchy could conceivably have been voted back into existence.

With the departure of the king, a deflated and despondent President Berisha contested the legitimacy of the elections and only half-heartedly accepted the verdict as a 'political solution' to the crisis. Having promised to resign if his party lost the election, he conceded defeat and duly resigned on 23 July – shortly before the first meeting of the new parliament dominated by his Socialist opponents. Berisha once again became chairman of the DP following the resignation of Tritan Shehu. In a letter to the legislature, Berisha said he was stepping down to take a seat as an opposition deputy for his Democratic Party: 'I declare today my irrevocable resignation from the post of head of state to continue political life supporting the values and the alternative I believe in.' He stressed that his decision to step down had been taken on a 'moral plane' since there was no constitutional obligation for him to resign.[13] The news was greeted with celebratory gunshots in Tirana and with wild jubilation in the streets of anti-Berisha strongholds such as Berat, Permet and Vlora. The independent daily *Koha Jone*'s front page had a photograph of a wild-eyed Berisha giving a stiff-armed Hitler salute to a rally with the headline 'July 23, 1997 – the end of the dictatorship'.

Berisha's resignation brought to a close five years of deeply controversial government. The fraudulent election of May 1996 had set the stage for his dramatic downfall. Following the international criticism of the fraudulent 1996 elections and their violent aftermath, US diplomats had stayed away from the opening session of Albania's new parliament. Nevertheless, virtually all the rest of Tirana's diplomatic corps attended the ceremony in a demonstration of continuing European subservience to the Berisha regime. Instead, the international community should have begun a total reappraisal of its relationship with Albania (support for which was conditioned by the fact that Berisha represented a bastion of stability in an otherwise unstable region). By the spring of 1997 however, he had become a dangerously unpredictable element, in his political isolation. In view of the deepening crisis in Kosova, the role of Albania as a factor of stability in the southern Balkans had been dramatically increased. For some in the international community it had seemed worth running the risk of civil war in Albania as a legitimate price to pay for peace in Kosova.

The charismatic heart surgeon, who was swept into power on a wave of popularity, had squandered his support by autocratic rule. His tendency to covet power and to delegate only to trusted cronies led to a crackdown on his political opponents that mirrored in some eyes the actions of Enver Hoxha. He was a victim of the autocratic powers inherited from Ramiz Alia in 1991–2. Berisha's lack of tolerance of dissent within his own party, and use of the courts and secret police to intimidate and imprison political opponents, cost him dearly. Corruption in his own government also undermined his position in the eyes of many, who, eager to escape decades of poverty and restriction under Hoxha, saw in Berisha (rightly or wrongly) just another one-party ruler.[14] Berisha equated democracy with anti-communism, and he survived in power for so long largely because there was no political figure to challenge him. Fatos Nano's release from prison had gone a long way to towards filling that vacuum.[15] The re-election in 1997 of Berisha as leader of the DP and of the man he had imprisoned, Fatos Nano, as Prime Minister ensured that Albanian politics would remain repetitiously divisive and confrontational for some years to come.

On 24 July, the day after his resignation, Berisha was succeeded as President by Rexhep Meidani (60), who immediately appointed Fatos Nano as Prime Minister. Meidani, a mathematician and physics lecturer from Tirana University, was the Socialist Party Secretary General. He was a moderate politician who had been a key figure in the SP's internal battle to espouse a social democratic line while ditching the dogma that had until recently branded the SP as neo-communist. Unlike Nano or Berisha, Meidani had never been a member of the Communist Party under Enver Hohxa, although he was appointed in 1991 to the Presidential Council under President Ramiz Alia, shortly before the collapse of the communist regime. Meidani only joined the SP a few days before being made Party Secretary in August 1996 when the conservative old guard of the party, led by Servet Pellumbi, was ousted.[16] His elevation to the Presidency was a sign of the increasing British role in the Tirana crisis. Meidani had studied in Britain, spoke good English and had a background that meant he could be relied upon to consider carefully advice from the British Foreign Office on policy issues.

4. Fatos Nano, the new Socialist Prime Minister, June 1997

Fatos Nano's administration was to be based, in theory, on an executive premiership, with the President having only an honorary role. The new coalition government was primarily technocratic in nature. Of the 21 cabinet members, 14 were from the dominant Socialist Party, four from the small Democratic Alliance, two from the Social Democratic Party, and one each from the Agrarian Party and the Union of Human Rights Party. The three main posts of the state – the President, Prime Minister and the parliamentary Speaker – were to be shared between the Socialists and Social Democrats. The major shortcoming of the new cabinet was that only one minister – Shakir Vukaj, trade and tourism minister – was from the north of the country. This fact was immediately criticised by the opposition and showed how far the country's political structures still had to go in order to bridge the deep gulf between north and south.

The new assembly was immediately dubbed the 'parliament of the Kalashnikovs' by pro-Berisha newspapers and the 'parliament of hope' by the pro-Socialist dailies. Predictably, the Democrats said they would boycott the new parliamentary session to protest against the conduct of the election. They complained that the polls had been held in a climate of terror and that they had been unable to campaign in the south. However, their losses in Tirana, which unlike the rest of the country were very heavily monitored, put paid to any serious claims that the Democratic Party could have gained a significantly higher share of the vote. With the elections over, the defeated Democrats and snubbed Monarchists dissolved into warring factions.

The first tasks of the new assembly were to restore law and order and to resolve the economic chaos left by the collapse of the pyramid schemes. Addressing parliament for the first time, Nano painted a bleak economic picture. He pledged a campaign to halt further erosion of gross domestic product (GDP) as well as soaring inflation, which had then reached 50 per cent. Having implied so publicly in Vlora that in the event of a Socialist victory the people would get their money back, Nano was duty-bound to address the issue of the lost pyramid funds as quickly as possible. He therefore announced, 'the government would undertake a serious audit of the pyramid firms' activities and immediately suspend the activity of any other business related in any way to money-lending pyramid companies.'[17] He went on to claim that, in cooperation with the IMF and the World Bank, the new government would force 'whoever stole, misused or transferred abroad the Albanian's deposits ... to pay it back according to a state based upon the rule of law'.[18] This is what the people wanted to hear, and for the time being they were prepared to believe that somehow, with international assistance, the new government would return to them their lost savings.

With the departure of Berisha, the Socialists set about removing the state ministries of Berisha loyalists. In an effort to weed out corrupt and inefficient state officials, one of the first acts of the new administration was to replace all top central departmental executives.[19] Naturally the Democrats protested strongly at these changes, which were justified by the Socialists by arguing that the election results indicated the population's wish to see not only a change of top cabinet personnel but the removal of the key players throughout the country's civil administration. The whirlwind of changes that were expected created a tense climate of anxiety amongst the large army of directors and employees of the various ministerial departments. It would not be an exaggeration to say that an element of panic set in, as civil servants hurriedly tried to make new friends and contacts with Socialist Party leaders. In an effort to appear busy, they kept making phone calls and tried to pass along the Socialist Party corridors as often as possible, or have coffee in a nearby café, hoping to strike up an acquaintance with some prominent Socialist.

Meanwhile, although the security situation had improved from the heady days of March, the roads leading to the south were for the most part still under the control of armed gangs. These were mainly splinter groups acting independently of the committees, and many were involved in smuggling networks and other criminal activities. Policemen still loyal to Berisha who feared for their jobs under the new administration were attempting to undermine the government's attempts to stabilise the country by contributing to the continued shootings in towns up and down the country.[20] In response the government set up a rapid deployment unit to try to deal with local warlords in the south as well as Berisha loyalists. However, the police and new Special Forces units had little capability for sustained operations. The integrity of the SHIK security service was so compromised under Berisha's regime that it was clearly in no position to provide intelligence back-up or reliable operational assistance. Many SHIK staff had fled the country in fear of their lives. The appointment of a new SHIK director, Fatos Klosi, would have little discernible effect until the intelligence service had been thoroughly cleansed of employees of the former administration.

The new government's toughest portfolio fell to Interior Minister Neritan Ceka, a prominent archaeologist, chairman of the Democratic Alliance and a forthright critic of the corruption that had pervaded the DP regime. Dr Ceka was initially anxious to regain state control over the south, before concentrating on mopping up the remaining pockets of opposition from Berisha loyalists in the north. He explained that the first task of the police was to wrest back control of the southern highways from gangsters and to crack down on criminals using some southern towns as personal fiefdoms. This would inevitably bring the authorities into conflict with the rebel committees, which had little reason to continue operating now that Berisha had resigned. The opposition press was linking the Socialists with the 'criminal mafia' activities of the committees, claiming that the committees wanted to make the new government their 'puppet'.[21]

In the meantime the last Italian soldiers from Operation Alba pulled out of Albania on 11 August, one day before the end of their mandate, but some Greek troops remained behind. These were no longer part of the multinational force but a result of a separate agreement between the Albanian and Greek governments. This was a key sign of Greek ambitions to make a de facto protectorate of the country under Nano. Both Italy and Greece had pledged to help restructure Albania's police and armed forces, as the two countries vied for influence over the country. Both countries have historic ties to Albania and have played out their regional rivalry through it. However, during the summer of 1997, their foremost concern was in keeping the number of Albanian migrants down, as they struggled to cope with increasing numbers of illegal Albanian immigrants.

As the rebel committees continued their campaign for the return of lost savings in the pyramid schemes there were simultaneous discussions on the future of the committees. According to the chairman of the Vlora committee, Luftar Petroshati, several alternatives regarding the committee's future were being discussed. He told reporters: 'We will decide whether the committee will become a civil action committee, a depositor's commission, or whether it will be transformed into a reconciliation and national unity committee.'[22] Other southern committees were holding similar discussions. In many respects, however, the government was initially forced to cooperate with the committees in order to ensure the safe passage of traffic on at least the main route south to the Greek border. The leader of the rebel authorities in Tepelena, Gjoleke Malaj, said the new Interior Minister wanted to cooperate with him to protect roads in the south and that Ceka had promised him that if he continued to protect the roads, the police would also assist him.[23]

Nevertheless, with or without the assistance of the salvation committees, the government faced an uphill struggle to restore order in the south. The withdrawal of Italian and Greek troops from Vlora had left the town at the mercy of rival gangs. Whilst the Operation Alba troops were present the gangs had only fought each other at night, but as soon as the Alba mission had departed they began fighting in broad daylight. They had in fact become organised armies. Perhaps the most violent town in the country during this period was the southern city of Berat. Here on one day – 14 July – six people were murdered in a 24-hour period following shootouts between rival gangs. The entire town was then controlled by two gangs, which repeatedly fought each other and then forced doctors to treat their friends but to refuse to treat their opponents. Between March and June in Berat, 204 people were killed and more than 1200 injured, and hundreds of families had fled the town and their homes were then looted.[24]

During this period Albania increased its importance as a transit centre for hard drugs coming into Western Europe, as local warlords established their own authority over well-defined areas of the country. For several years in Albania the lack of a conventional economy, the deficiencies of the government of Sali Berisha and the highly corrupt bureaucracy had provided ideal conditions for the cultivation and trafficking of drugs. The ruling Democratic Party had been immersed in illegal activities since the beginning of the Bosnian War, trading weapons, fuel and drugs through a front company, Sqiponja, until the lifting of UN sanctions on Yugoslavia at the end of 1995. Then part of the business was transferred to a private company, VEFA Holdings, which also ran the largest pyramid fund.[25] Until the uprising in March, drugs had been brought into Albania through several established routes, with the complicity or direct involvement of the Albanian security service, the SHIK. Arguably the biggest route was from northern Greece through the eastern town of Korca, although the other main route from western Macedonia remained important, along with the cross-Balkan route from Bulgaria through Macedonia to the Adriatic.

Aside from the restoration of law and order and the dissolution of the rebel committees, one of the toughest challenges the new government had to face was the fierce opposition of its adversaries, led by Berisha. The former President, who was counting the days before he was back in office, was well aware that the success of Nano's government depended solely upon international aid, and that the essential condition for this aid was the restoration of stability in the country.[26] Bearing this in mind, he set about utilising all the remaining structures in his power, including those within SHIK and other armed groups, to hold the country firmly in the grip of instability. Thus, the real battle that was now to be waged between the government and the opposition was that over the country's stability. In an ominous prediction of events yet to come, Neritan Ceka warned of further trouble from elements within SHIK still loyal to Berisha and his administration. He feared they would try to stir up unrest in northern Albania, and that the police could not rely on SHIK for information because its intelligence network had disintegrated.[27] As a result of these fears, and amidst growing concerns about anti-government activities in the north, a programme of arms seizures began in the northern town of Shkoder in an effort to reclaim some of the weapons seized from army depots in the spring.

As the summer progressed, top DP officials continued to abandon their party and flee the country. As the extent of their electoral defeat became apparent, the haemorrhage from the topmost echelons of the DP gathered momentum. After the large-scale abandonment in March other big names, such as Agim Shehu (the controversial Tirana police chief) and Xhait Xhaferi (the commander of the presidential guard) joined the rush to Rinas, Tirana's airport. Berisha's Interior Minister, Belul Celo, left for Greece as other Interior Ministry officials found refuge abroad. The former head of SHIK, Bashkim Gazidede, had already fled to Turkey.

As the disintegration of the Democratic Party coincided with rising tensions in Kosova, anti-government elements decided it was time to play the national card. The Socialist-led government now came under attack for its 'anti-Albanian, pro-Slav attitude'. In response to a comment by the new Foreign Minister Paskal Milo, who allegedly referred to the Albanians of Macedonia as a minority, the pro-Berisha daily *Albania* claimed that:

> to treat Albanians living in Macedonia as a minority when they constitute over 40 per cent of the population, means becoming an advocate of the filthiest Slavic chauvinist theories. This man clearly shows what a danger he will pose for the Albanian national cause. His attitude mirrors the anti-Albanian attitude that thrives amongst left-wing parties in Albania, which are traditionally linked to Albania's national enemies.[28]

Milo, head of the Social Democratic Party, who although of pure Albanian ethnicity himself comes from Himara, with its Greek-speaking community, was held by the right to have pro-Greek sympathies along with the entire leadership of the Socialist Party.[29] Thus, the tone was set for the forthcoming year of bitter polemics between right and left, which would once again bring Albania to the brink of disaster.

The wider struggle for power had been clearly resolved in favour of the Socialists, which in turn would release radical political forces into the arena that would enable the KLA to obtain real practical support for the first time in Albania, and the next stage of the reopening of the national question was inextricably linked to the crisis and developing conflict in Kosova.

PART

III

THE KOSOVA DIMENSION OF
THE NATIONAL QUESTION

7

Tirana, the Crisis in Kosova and the Origins of the KLA

While turmoil persisted on the hot midsummer streets of Albania, little attention was being paid by the international media to developments in Kosova. There was, however, much private concern in chancelleries and the offices of international organisations that the Albanian crisis might spread there. A minority of better-informed international diplomats were familiar with the ferment in the Albanian diaspora and the growing criticism of the pacifist policies of the LDK.[1] Pro-Serb nations such as Britain and France, which had close collaborationist links between their intelligence services and those of Yugoslavia, were receiving disturbing reports from Belgrade about the renewal of the Albanian armed underground.[2] Before the popular uprising overwhelmed the Tirana government in January 1997, the Berisha administration had passed on its concerns to the diplomatic community about the worsening situation in Kosova. At the end of that month, Prime Minister Alexander Meksi issued a joint statement with Kosova 'Prime Minister' Bujar Bukoshi condemning the policies of the Milosevic government and pledging Albania's support for 'peaceful resistance in Kosova and the legitimate right of the people of Kosova to self-determination'.[3]

Although on the surface this was a reasonable response to the situation, the evasion represented in the wording of the statement (that omitted support for the KLA, or even recognition of its existence) is exemplified by the fact that the following week 16 Albanians were to be prosecuted in Prishtina District Court for belonging to the KLA. In reality the time for peaceful solutions was passing away, and the gap between the Berisha government and the LDK collaborationist leadership on the one hand and the realities of Kosova on the other was growing daily. Even the old barriers between the 'pacifist' and 'militant' wings of the national movement were breaking down. In the wealthy and powerful Swiss diaspora community, the Kosovar-owned and LDK-controlled Albanian/Swiss newspaper *Rilindja* reprinted an article from the hardline National League for the Liberation of Kosova (LKCK) periodical *Çlimiri* on 23 January 1997, setting out the case for war. It was a key sign that the hitherto docile LDK press was no longer prepared to accept the LDK leadership line.[4]

Meanwhile on the ground, among the fields and woods of Kosova, the conflict intensified. North-east Kosova was one of the strongest nationalist regions, and the Serb security apparatus had been driven from many areas as early as autumn 1996.[5] On the last day of January the Serb police ambushed and shot dead three key KLA leaders from the north-east – Zahir Pajaziti, Edmond Hoxha and Hakif Zejnullah – on a bridge near the town of Vushtrri.[6] By now, in the international press, some stories were beginning to appear about Kosovar arms purchases in Albania. A period of political flux began in the Tirana–Prishtina relationship, which exposed all Tirana and international political actors to manifold and complex uncertainties for the next year or more. This was caused by two factors: the breakdown in the Berisha–Rugova relationship that had totally dominated political discourse about Kosova in Tirana since 1992, consequent on Berisha's loss of power, and the emergence of the KLA as a local military force with a modus operandi in both Albania and Kosova.[7]

In turn this produced a crisis in the international community's diplomatic relationship with the Kosova question, which hitherto had relied upon the Berisha–Rugova link to mediate the Kosova issue in the Albanian world in a moderate manner. In practice this meant that, from the time Berisha took power in 1991–2 to the DP government collapse in 1997, all official discourse and action in Tirana about Kosova was confined to the diplomatic arena, and military action by the Kosovar Albanians against the Serbian occupation was ruled out. After the spring of 1997, however, many such levers that could be pulled by NATO and the EU to propel particular political actors in a set direction either disappeared altogether or lost their previous effectiveness. The war to end Serbian control of Kosova and the popular uprising to end Berisha's control of Albania were proceeding in one sense separately, yet in another sense parallel to the reopening of the national question. The beginnings of a pan-Albanian consciousness were growing in many unconnected quarters. Berisha's pro-Serb backers in Britain were horrified, as their worst fears of the beginning of a serious military struggle to free Kosova from Serbian rule were coming to life. As in Albania, politics in Kosova was leaving the domain of the political elite – or at least that part of it seen in the West as responsible – and taking to the urban streets and the hilly countryside.

This passivity on the part of the elite had never been the complete picture of the Kosovar activity in Albania, of course, and for many years there had been Serbian allegations that a secret underground army was being formed in Albania to invade and Albanianise Kosova. This army was said to be the inheritor of the Drenica region uprising against the Titoist revisionist apparat after the Second World War. Then, the whole of central Kosova had become a general battleground for four years as the Albanian community fought against Belgrade-imposed 'communism'. [8] Organisations like the *Levizjes Kombetares per Clirimin e Kosoves* (the National League for the Liberation of Kosova, or LKCK and the *Levizjes Popullore te Kosoves* (the Kosova People's League, or LPK) – the latter founded as long ago as 1982, following the 1981 student riots in Prishtina – were growing in the political underground. They saw Albania as a free society, even under Enver Hoxha, compared to the national repression in Kosova. In the turbulent period in Kosova from 1985 to 1990, when Milosevic used Kosova as a platform to seize power,[9] the existing collaborationist Albanian leadership of the Communist Party under Azem Vlasi was overthrown, and Ibrahim Rugova and the LDK filled the political vacuum.

Rugova had always claimed to have overwhelming support from all Kosovar Albanians for his pacifist political approach, but this was never the case. Those in Kosova and those elsewhere with close knowledge of Kosova were aware that it was an approach dictated to him by circumstances after the massive defeats of the Trepca miners in 1988–9.[10] There were also always principled nationalists in the LDK who saw in private the need for a Kosovar military force. Kosova 'Prime Minister' Bujar Bukoshi had formed a 'Defence Ministry' within the so-called 'government-in-exile' in 1991, and for a time sought to oppose the complete pacifism and organisational incapacity of Rugova. Bukoshi wished the shadow 'Defence Ministry' to be free from political control and to use the talents of the numerous competent Kosovar Albanian ex-soldiers from the old Yugoslav People's Army. But this was never possible, as the LDK leadership overruled him, and Rugova's views prevailed.[11] A few other LDK leaders, like party vice-chairman Fehmi Agani, were in touch with Drenica KLA leaders like Adem Jashari.

Outside the party, throughout Kosovar Albanian society, some militants had never agreed with the political basis of the LDK, and developed the inheritance of small underground groups with faith in the armed struggle.

These stemmed from the era of imprisoned national hero Adem Demaci and began to coalesce after 1992 into the nascent KLA. Small groups of committed individuals were in military training and securing arms throughout this period.[12] There were also principled nationalists within the LDK who disagreed with the strategy of the leadership and did what they could at local level to help develop military capacity. In the aftermath of the war in Croatia, some Kosovar Albanian conscripts were deserting from the Yugoslav Army and beginning military training in Albania to form a new military force.[13]

At this stage only a very few people were actively involved, and the names of future leaders like Hashim Thaci, Ramush Haradinaj, Agim Ceku and Adem Jashari were totally unknown. They existed in small organisations with obscure names, of which the *Levizja Popullore e Kosoves* (LPK), the LKCK and the *Levizja Popullore e Republikes se Kosoves* (Popular League for the Republic of Kosova, or LPRK) were the most influential.[14] In turn their roots lay deep in recent Kosova history: from 1949 onwards Enver Hoxha had sought to set up underground groups in Kosova led by legendary figures such as Zhelajdin Qira to prepare the ground for struggle against Belgrade control. These had mostly failed and been broken up by the Titoist police.[15] From the military standpoint, Albania presented important possibilities for the Kosova radicals, in that it would provide a safe base area where training and logistics activity could be conducted. Early steps in this direction had been taken in 1991 when a group of 54 Kosovars began military training in the military academy in Tirana. As soon as intelligence on these developments reached Western capitals, the Democratic Party government was put under immense pressure, particularly from the British government, to close down training camps and arrest key personnel. It could be argued that the Democratic Party government betrayed the nation by giving way to these pressures and moving against the nascent KLA.

The DP government did not respect the human rights of the Kososvar activists when in power. KLA founding father Adem Jashari, who was to die a violent death in March 1998 in Prekaz, Drenica (in central Kosova), and whose family was to become a legend in the early days of the Kosova war was arrested and jailed in Tirana in 1993. KLA political spokesman Hashim Thaci was jailed in 1996, and later in Tirana narrowly escaped with his life when his flatmate, journalist Hysni Vulaj, was murdered by a hit squad.[16] Zahir Pajaziti, the charismatic leader of the Llap group who was murdered by Serb police in 1997, was arrested by Berisha's government in 1995.

In general the Albanian Army (or at least a minority of activist and patriotic officers) were the salvation of these Kosova militants, and secured their release from jail. Senior soldier and later Berisha's military adviser Adem Copani played a key role in the release of many Kosovar activists, particularly that of Hashim Thaci. In turn this led to international (particularly British) pressure on Berisha from the Major government to purge the army of alleged communists and extremists of Enverist outlook, who were believed to be behind rumoured military training of Kosovars using official government facilities.

In practice many of those purged were neither, but were merely strong patriots who saw the DP government as attacking the army as an institution. This was the beginning of a terminal crisis for the Albanian Army, which culminated in the chaos and humiliations of 1997.[17] It was an irony that Western pressure against the army to try to curb Kosovar nationalism and 'communism' ended up destroying the one force that four years later, in 1997, might have had the capacity to save the Berisha government. At the same time, the officer corps had been decimated by repeated purges of those believed to be sympathetic to communism in the 1992–4 period, and it had disintegrated as a serious force. This left some more nationalist officers with a legacy of resentment against the DP government; they saw Berisha as having done little or nothing to defend the interests of fellow-Albanians in Kosova against Serbia and to have left Albania in general unable to defend itself. From these perceptions, it was but a short step to getting involved in the various underground support movements for the KLA that were forming in Albania. Money was also a factor, with soldiers able to supplement their meagre salaries by small arms dealing.

During the summer of 1997 a series of major strategic decisions were taken by the KLA leadership, mostly through the LPK, in association with diaspora and Macedonian-Albanian community leaders, that were to set the main mechanism of the war into motion. These involved prioritising small arms purchases in Albania and abroad, and infiltrating men and supplies into Kosova through Albania, Macedonia and Montenegro. In the main this leadership group was made up of a central core of people with long backgrounds in the LPK, LPRK and other similar organisations. These included Xhavit Haliti, a veteran of the Haxhiu group that had been organising in north-east Kosova in the 1980s; Ali Ahmeti and Fazli Veliu, both later to become leaders of the National Liberation Army (NLA) in the 2001 conflict in Macedonia; and Hashim Thaci, future KLA political spokesman and afterwards leader of the PDK in post-1999 Kosova. Other key figures were Thaci's uncle, the formidable Azem Syla (for a period the KLA Chief of Staff), intelligence chief Rexhep Selimi ('the Sultan'), and the Jashari family and their associates in northern Drenica. A financial support organisation was set up, the 'Homeland Calling' fund, run from Denmark and Switzerland by Jashar Salihu, a tough LPK veteran who had been jailed for nationalist activities by Tito. But unknown to the European part of the international community, who depended largely on Rugova's characterisations of the little groups as isolated Marxist cells, or on Serbian allegations that they were fronts for drug dealing, the key military leadership group of the insurgent movement was closely in touch with the non-LDK political leadership and media figures such as Veton Surroi,[18] as well as recently retired CIA operatives and Kosovar and Albanian diaspora leaders.

The underground KLA leadership and associated political organisations possessed people of great political astuteness, imagination, organisational flair and ruthless dedication to the national ideal – something that was totally unknown to the international community. Father figure and national icon Adem Demaci was believed, wrongly, to be a spent political force. The younger generation were quite unknown except to a few American and British intelligence officers who were in spasmodic touch with them from about 1994.[19] The beneficial effects of life in Swiss and German culture and/or in American universities on the KLA leaders' organisational capacity were also not understood. This applied not only to intellectuals like Thaci but also to the less educated rank-and-file 'Gastarbeiter' – where a period of work in a Basle, Hamburg or Michigan factory, for example, was an education in practical modern organisational efficiency at shop-floor level that could spill over into politics. In exile, a whole generation from the students' and workers' struggles of 1981 and 1989 learned to break with the mentality of Yugoslav communism and absorb a Western outlook. Some exiles had lived almost 20 years in Germany or Switzerland by 1990, and had cut their teeth on episodes such as the murder of the heroic Gervalla brothers in Germany as early as 1982. (They were involved in organising a Kosova army and were betrayed by a Serb police informer and shot near Stuttgart.)

In Western eyes Serb intelligence seemed to be complete and all-powerful, and always likely to remain so, but gradually the LPK and LPRK in particular learned to set up tight cell structures that were secure. In the USA this was generally not necessary, as Serb intelligence was weak and the favourable US legal climate gave specific rights for anti-communist exile organisations. The official Western view of the diaspora was not based on accurate information. In Switzerland, Germany and the USA Kosovars had access to the excellent education opportunities, and no longer conformed to the popular image of destitute migrants seizing ships to escape Albania. In cities such as Zurich, Berlin, Hamburg, Lucerne and Berne there were hundreds of Albanian businesses of all kinds, from travel to construction to catering. The Swiss diaspora is particularly characterised by its efficiency and financial resources, and the US diaspora by vast energy and nationalist commitment – in a way imitating the national stereotypes of the host nations. None of this was known either in the European diplomatic community or in Tirana political circles.

Many Tirana diplomats simply did not believe that Albanians would be capable of the complex patterns of covert organisation needed to take on the Milosevic system. They did not understand the cultural advances in the diaspora that would transform the nature of Kosovar Albanian politics. The Serb communist stereotypes of crime and drugs were a profound obstruction to understanding the coming conflict. It was always assumed that the LDK would be 'the leadership' of the Kosovars, and this view was not significantly affected by the evidence of events (such as the 150,000-strong mass demonstration against repression that was organised in Prishtina by the LKCK and LPK on 13 March 1997).

The Serb propaganda machine, internationally, and the key Greek embassy in Tirana, under the command of Ambassador Alexandros Mallias, spent much time and money trying to present the view that the Kosovar struggle was a danger to Albania, and that harbouring the KLA could bring a north–south conflict to the country – something that in practice was actually an object of their own aggressive and revanchist diplomacy and the use of political and paramilitary underground against the Kosovars. For the confused and disoriented EU diplomats, spending too much time in Belgrade (and Tirana) deprived the international community of the capacity to analyse and understand events on the ground; the gradual spread of the KLA into northern Albania and along the border with Kosova was unseen. Their Yugocentric ideology and political assumptions prevented them getting to grips with the reality of Kosova. New technology also played its part: mobile phones that were difficult for government phone interception technology to control were coming into general use. Most KLA leaders kept in touch using Swisscom mobiles throughout the wartime period. After the experience of the Bosnian war, it was clear to the KLA leadership that the impending Kosova conflict would be fought in the media as well as on the ground, and the Albanians' understanding of the media and the Internet was far in advance of that of the Milosevic regime in Belgrade. Internet capacity had grown rapidly in the Albanian world as a result of the need to keep in touch with an often far-flung diaspora.

Nevertheless, the KLA leadership remained very isolated from Fatos Nano and the new Socialist-led coalition in Tirana. Although the open betrayals, murders and arrests during the early DP period had clearly come to an end, the Kosovars could not rely on the new Socialist government for direct help either, however much the chaotic conditions of 1997 were a clear aid to underground political and military organisation. Fatos Nano himself had developed many contacts with Yugoslavia in the 1980s when he was a rising star in the Institute of Marxist-Leninism in Tirana. Relations with Belgrade at that time were quite fruitful, and as a southern Albanian who grew up in a village only 20 miles from the Greek border, Nano saw the Socialist-led government in Greece as a positive force in the way it had stood up to pressure from Berisha over the Greek-speaking community issue in the 'Omonia' crisis in 1995. As a personality Nano had little instinctive rapport with the Kosovars, unlike his predecessor in the Socialist leadership, Ramiz Alia, a northerner from Shkoder who had been in Kosova for a short time in the Second World War as a young man.[20] Alia had encouraged the early military training contacts that Kosovars had had in the late 1980s in the military academy in Tirana, and in the mid- and late 1980s had refocused Party of Labour attention on Kosova, with a clear understanding of the threat that the Greater Serbia project represented to the wider region as well as to the Kosova Albanians.[21]

Another danger to the Kosova movement in Albania was the ever-present factor of recently sacked splinter groups of DP militants, who were armed and formed into informal small paramilitary groups. The Greeks, the Serbs and the most extreme anti-KLA elements in the counter-insurgency agencies in Western countries were also beginning to be alert to the possibility of a wider war in Kosova. They saw the nascent KLA as a legitimate target for their operations; death squads began to operate in Tirana and elsewhere. While social conditions in Albania were improving very gradually, with the retreat from the outright anarchy of the spring months, a dirty and secret Greek-led war against the Kosovar Albanians was in the offing, that would last well beyond the time of the NATO intervention of 1999, and would claim the lives of outstanding patriots like Ilir Konuscevci in 1998. The anarchic social conditions provided a suitable cover for this, as it meant that murders of KLA militants could be ascribed to family or clan rivalries – blood feuds.[22] All the traditional sub-political and sub-historical vocabulary of obsolete anthropological conceptions about the Albanian world came into play. This factor was to play a great role in the events leading up the murder of Azem Hajdari, a keynote death in the underground war in 1998.

In essence, as Albania itself gradually became relatively more stable and calm during the autumn of 1997, the political and military impetus of the national liberation movement moved north towards Kosova, with more frequent and effective attacks on the Serbian police and military apparatus and the opening of significant tracts of forest and countryside to de facto Albanian control. Apart from daytime forays on the main roads by the Serb army and police, there was a sense of imminent conflict spread throughout Kosova. Kosovar activity accelerated in the important arms market in Macedonia and key figures that had been in exile in Switzerland and Germany for many years began to move to addresses in Albania, where certain Tirana cafés became havens for militants to meet and locate new recruits. The departure of most internationals and virtually all diplomats and intelligence officers from Albania during the spring events had been a great boost to the Kosova organisers, who for the first time ever in their political lives were able to work in a generally sympathetic political environment without massive intelligence and/or military surveillance. In the north, where the writ of Tirana did not run at all, towns like Bajram Curri were becoming dominated by small arms dealing, with Kosovars playing a leading part.

The Nano government was not fully aware of these developments during the summer and autumn of 1997, having only a patchy and incomplete knowledge of events. The propaganda spread by pro-Serb Greek diplomats in Tirana against the Kosovars' cause was a key factor, along with the generous Greek slush fund. Greece was a powerful influence in Tirana in the summer of 1997, and the new head of the intelligence service, Fatos Klosi, was widely believed to have had contacts with the Greek intelligence operators who had helped Nano escape from Tirana jail in March 1997.[23] The British security apparatus also worked closely with Greece, and key Pan-Hellenic Socialist Movement (PASOK) foreign policy advisers in Athens, such as the Anglo-Greek Alex Rondos, had London intelligence links.[24] In the USA the head of the CIA, George Tenet, was a first-generation immigrant from a Greek-speaking community background near Himara.[25] In Albania, the new government was predominantly southern. The first post-Berisha Prime Minister, Bashkim Fino, was from Gjirokaster and most of the 'new men' in the Tirana leadership were Orthodox. Consequently, the Kosova crisis was far from their background or experience, and few of them had ever set foot there. The visits of Rugova to Tirana during the Berisha period were a depressing and repetitive image of Kosovar practical military incapacity, and outside the well-informed CIA orbit most felt that the Kosovars would never be capable of throwing off the Serbian yoke.

However, this was not a universal view in the south of Albania. Some of the most pro-Kosova figures in the country were ex-soldiers involved in the salvation committees who had been central to the uprising, and by late summer many of them had been by-passed and were no longer in touch with their military commanders in Tirana. They felt free to get involved in the Kosova issue if they wished. The government itself only governed Tirana and the surrounding district, even in the sense that it was unsafe for the ministers to travel outside these areas, and there was nothing to stop small arms trading or paramilitary activity. The cultural gap between the Tirana elite ex-PLA leadership group around Prime Minister Nano and the often working-class Kosovar activists, many from rural backgrounds, should not be underestimated. The ethos of the old Party of Labour leadership among the Tirana elite was full of contempt for 'peasants', whether from Kosova or Albania. Many Foreign Ministry personnel were still imbued with the residual ideology of the period of late communism. They saw the Kosova conflict as a danger to Albania, not an opportunity, and failed to understand that Yugoslavia was a state with no future. The key post of Interior Minister was held after June 1997 by archaeologist Neritan Ceka, who had close British links but only a limited knowledge of Kosova (and was compromised by his previous contacts with Belgrade and Milosevic regime members over the issue in the Berisha period). The police and intelligence service were in chaos, and were not able to provide systematic information on Kosovar activity, or to do much to control or influence it.

An important factor at this stage was the element in US policy that sought to keep Kosova part of Serbia as a way of protecting the Dayton settlement. In April 1997, newly appointed US Assistant Secretary of State responsible for the region John Kornblum stated after a meeting with Dr Rugova in Prishtina that: 'the future of Kosova was possible within Serbia and that would be a major contribution to peace in the region.'[26] These and similar statements were deeply undermining to Rugova, as it appeared that for all his fealty to the USA, the central LDK demand for independence by peaceful exit from Serbia with US help was being ruled out.

Although NATO had an office and some activity in Albania, the telephone system (if and when it worked) was still independent and the extensive phone-tapping and eavesdropping apparatus of the later Kosova war period, when Mount Daiti was bristling with high technology aerials and satellite disks, did not exist.[27] The generally pro-Serb internationals had no method of providing reliable local intelligence to the Nano government on what was happening, let alone influencing it. The Greek link in the intelligence chain was adept at propaganda and could pay for assassinations of political militants, but was not effective in northern Albania. Meanwhile, the Serbs had upped their military pressure on the growing KLA activity in the cross-border region, with the murder in Has on 6 May of Luan Haradinaj, the brother of future KLA commander General Ramush Haradinaj. This was a vital battle for the Serbs, as the Haradinaj-controlled supply line through the Kosare corridor was, for a time that summer, the main small arms and munitions supply route into Kosova from Albania.[28]

Yet as the summer wore on, the more informed elements within the international community began to foresee a situation where the chaos and instability in Albania could spread to Kosova, and where the KLA was about to emerge as a fully-fledged insurgent force on the international stage. Tirana was dominated by an atmosphere of looming crisis. The death of Mother Teresa on 11 September once more focused international attention on Albania, and the nation went into deep mourning. After the immediate domestic priorities of the restoration of order and economic revival began to be achieved, the subject of Kosova rose up the diplomatic agenda, both domestic and international. In the absence of the Rugova–Berisha axis, a new polarity of 'moderation' began to be sought, and in the absence of any alternative the Europeans, through the traditional regional bag carrier and stool pigeon, Greece, began to pressurise Nano into entering open talks with the Serbs. Nano, still insecure and craving international respectability, grasped the poisoned chalice sent from Athens, and drank deeply from it, as if it was full of his favourite Chivas Regal whisky.

To the anger and astonishment of the Kosovar Albanians, and indeed every Albanian with a shred of patriotism, Fatos Nano agreed to meet Serbian President Slobodan Milosevic for talks on the Greek island of Crete. It was a gross political misjudgement of the national mood. Tirana newspapers that appeared during the Crete meeting carried cartoons of a blood-spattered Nano seeking a job in the Serbian leader's butcher's shop, or similar insults. It had therefore not taken long for the new Tirana Prime Minister to fall foul of the Kosova issue, and for the next five years it would be a persistent irritant to his ambitions and lead to him losing political jobs and on one occasion, in the September 1998 coup, almost losing his life. Like a recurrent cancer, the hand of Athens bearing gold for Tirana politicians to betray Kosova was sliced off only to grow again immediately and reinfect the Albanian body politic. The Crete meeting was a further blow to Rugova and the LDK. On 9 November 1997 Rugova put out a strong statement condemning Nano and reminding him that Albania had recognised the Kosovar Republic. To all intents and purposes any common approach had ended between Tirana and the LDK, something that was to allow a new political space for the KLA spokesmen to develop in Tirana in the course of time.[29]

For the as yet unknown military leaders of the Kosovar cause, like Ramush Haradinaj from near Decani, these or similar Tirana intrigues in the stinking midden of international diplomacy were more or less totally irrelevant. Haradinaj's visits to Albania were not focused on Tirana, or even Bajram

Curri, but the endless dense dwarf-oak and beech forest, running often 20 or 30 miles deep, straddling the border with Yugoslavia.[30] As early as the summer of 1993, fresh from Swiss exile, Haradinaj spent weeks in the forests studying and analysing the border. It ran hundreds of miles from the White Drin Valley in the south northwards over the Has hills, then into the Gjakova mountains, and finally up to the wilds of Tropoja and the approaches to Montenegro. In some places, like the Prushi Pass near Gjakova, it ran over open moorland and was easy to mine and to police; in others there was impenetrable forest where a companion a few yards away was invisible. There was no border fence anywhere.

The Serbs seemed to have the capacity to control this vast wilderness in a few areas, but in general they relied upon the remote terrain to do their work for them. Many Serb border units were short of manpower due to the damage the wars in the north had done to their resources. Morale was low, with food often poor, and problems with spare parts for army and police equipment and vehicles were common. The lack of road development and maintenance in many hilly areas under years of Yugoslav and Tirana neglect meant that vehicle movement became almost impossible in the deep winter snow. In contrast, the harsh ground conditions favoured the Albanian insurgents, who moved on foot. As was so often the case in Albania's twentieth-century history, the perspective for the national cause looked very different and more positive the greater the distance of the onlooker from Tirana. There were no Serb villages at all along the border zone, anywhere in the hundreds of miles of its length, that might provide local intelligence against the KLA insurgents. The Serb soldiers were an isolated, lonely and undermanned force; fish in a hostile sea.

In some key regions, like the Has hills to the west of Prizren and the Kosovar–Montenegrin borderlands west of Peje, the population was closely linked by culture and tradition and still seethed against the Great Powers' division of the Albanian nation in 1913. Their diaspora leaders in the USA, like Gani Perolli in New Jersey and Eqrem Bardha in Michigan, were men of exceptional political capacity. These villages were aware of the new underground army and were a source of both recruits and logistic support, and provided an ideal military operating environment for an insurgent force. The forest around them was to be a green blanket of concealment and a friend of the insurgents. Without the Drenica and Dukagjini forests, the KLA could not have survived early reverses or the critical days of the 'First Offensive' period of spring 1998.[31]

Few of the Tirana political elite had ever been to these wild forests, except those working in the chrome mines or hydroelectricity industry, or as soldiers or policemen on border duty. Although few in number this latter group of men were to play a decisive role in the war, and their local knowledge (many came from Tropoja or Dibra, both traditional areas of army careerdom and traditional patriotism) was invaluable to the KLA. To those schooled in the Enverist theories of Partisan warfare the importance of the border was obvious, but to the limp and defeatist Tirana political elite, obsessed with petty intriguing for favour with the foreigners, it was merely the wild and backward north, where Yugoslav power would probably prevail.

As the war developed it was clear to the KLA leadership that ways would have to be found to open 'corridors' through the border forests so that substantial quantities of men and munitions could be moved into Kosova. The Serbs would always be able to control the asphalt roads leading into Kosova, like the Morina Pass road from Kukes to Prizren, by the use of heavy armour, as the KLA had no airpower. The Albanians would have to use horses and donkeys to move men and supplies through the forests and over the mountains. To Ramush Haradinaj and KLA Political Spokesman Hashim Thaci and their colleagues, this would be a permanent preoccupation, just as border security and the deployment of an international force against the KLA would preoccupy the mind of Yugophiles in the international community. In the same way, for NATO the question of possible air strikes in support of the KLA was an early item on the agenda, with the origin of the famous phrase of the anti-interventionists that 'NATO would not become the KLA's airforce' occurring during this period.[32] The most important choice that Haradinaj made was to focus operations on the Koshare Valley corridor, leading from the village of Balushe near Junik up through dense forest into Albania. The battles to control the corridor were to be one of the most epic episodes for the KLA in the whole war.[33]

However, in 1997 all this lay ahead: in Albania and Kosova disparate military and political forces that were not controlled by the international community were still assembling, but were from different backgrounds and with great variations in their personal, political and military experience. It would take time for their individual contributions to coalesce. In some aspects of military activity they never did; the KLA was a mixture of village defence force and insurgent army, where some basic military problems were never solved until the end of the war, such as adequate weapons and ammunition supply, and clear and functional command structures.[34] Some soldiers who volunteered were primarily loyal to the commanders who recruited them, or to their political organisations, or to the senior men in their local village or town. This was both the KLA's great strength and also its weakness; it was never possible for the Serbs to succeed in designating the KLA a terrorist force in a clear-cut, convincing way. So many of its members were not professional soldiers, possessed little or no training, and were involved primarily in the self-defence of their local communities. But this political victory for the KLA had a military cost; when the pressure of the 'First Offensive' period was applied, the Serbs were able to recover much of the ground that they had lost in the winter of 1997–8 in central Kosova. To hold the ground would have required a different kind of army, with sophisticated weapons and advanced organisation, which the Albanians did not have.

At the heart of the international community's policy dilemma in the late summer and autumn of 1997 was the failure to distance itself from Belgrade-centric conceptions and Belgrade-sourced intelligence data and military information. It was widely assumed that once the allegedly tightly knit group at the top of the command, like Hashim Thaci and his colleagues, were either killed or arrested, the KLA would collapse and the Milosevic forces would 'pacify' Kosova and 'normality' would be restored. This was a major misconception, based on the use of poor-quality intelligence and Cold War analytical tools, where the KLA was seen as an essentially Marxist-Leninist creation and where a small group of politically motivated men and women were seen as manipulating 'innocent' followers in Kosova. In reality, in militant parts of Kosova like Llap, Drenica and Dukagjini there was no gap between the political views of the majority and of the leadership, based on decades of nationalist struggle. It is indeed arguable that sometimes the local people were more militant against the Serbs than their leaderships. The fierce, bitter rank-and-file struggles in the mining trades unions in the giant Trepce complex at Mitrovica had bred a popular political culture in many places where distrust of even the most militant and committed leaders was endemic. In the past they had been bought off by the revisionists in Belgrade, and compromise was a dirty word. In rural areas in the west people had borne the brunt of the Serb and Yugoslav police apparatus for generations and the police were seen as a universal enemy, where violence against them brought praise and status rather than condemnation.

The ideological influence of organisations like the LKCK and LPRK was exerted largely through their newspapers, which circulated illegally in the community, advocating confrontation and the armed struggle. The actual organisation of the KLA leadership was far more sophisticated than anyone outside it realised, with a parallel leadership in existence at all times in case people like Thaci, Selimi and Haliti were arrested. Although northern Kosova looked a poor, beautiful and conventional part of Yugoslavia to outsiders on their occasional visits, in reality it has an extraordinarily tough and resilient oppositional working class, with an intellectual and peasant political culture, akin to the Ruhr miners' desperate struggles against fascism in Germany, the peasants of the Midi in the French Resistance in the Second World War or the world of the Russian working class before 1917.

Although individual intelligence officers with professional integrity in Britain sometimes tried to input contrary and more rational assessments into the system, often in Britain, the USA and Europe the whole intelligence assessment machine was run by pro-Serb figures. They were tasked by policy-makers who had little interest in seeing their traditional preconceptions disturbed. The Bosnian war years had introduced profound distortions into the British system, with a whole strata of civil servants and military officers involved who saw the British interest in the region as inextricably linked to support for Belgrade and defending Serbian interests in the region. The new reality of Kosova was disturbing to them. In mythological terms, there was a new monster in the forests and they did not wish to see that it was there. The reliance on collaboration with the Yugoslavs over the years in the 'humint' intelligence field had meant that Western agencies had very few good agents on the ground in Kosova once the conflict started. It would have been difficult to place them, in any event.[35]

The long years of Yugoslav repression had taught the Kosova Albanians skills in developing and securing underground organisations that had not been seen in mainland Europe since the Second World War and the various anti-Nazi Resistance movements. Some local-level LDK leaders were privately strongly supportive of the creation of an army for Kosova, and could and did contribute something valuable to the development of the movement, despite what Rugova was saying in Prishtina. Smugglers and socially marginal people involved in the economic/criminal underground had a strong motivation to work with the new force as a source of rich profits from munitions supply. The tightly knit structure of extended Kosovar families was an additional barrier against secret police penetration. Crucially, there was a developing and significant proportion of young men and women in the Kosova world who felt that there was no alternative to fighting, and were prepared to die for Kosova if necessary. The reasons for the Serb's apparently irrational, random and brutal attacks on villages and families, which appalled the international community in late 1997 and early 1998, seem obscure until the facts of the situation from the Belgrade viewpoint are understood.

Although for public consumption the Milosevic government pushed the 'drug dealers and terrorists' line about the nature of the KLA, the more intelligent officers in the Yugoslav army and internal security apparatus un-derstood perfectly well the force they were up against – a potentially formidable opponent – and that local terror was one of the few weapons they had available to try to intimidate those communities who supported the KLA. In that sense, the Kosova conflict developed in the 'phoney war' stage as a classic Balkan conflict, with parallel discourses in play: that of the 'official' understanding of events, where an army represented a sovereign state that was under threat from a terror campaign run by Marxist militants, and the actual war, where local rural communities were trying to free themselves from a terrible and genocidal regime. However, as in all wars, it took time for the local and international media to develop a better popular understanding of what was actually happening. By the summer of 1998 the parameters of the conflict were set and unlikely to change until the war had run its course. The media is frequently blamed for exacerbating conflicts but in Kosova in the late 1990s the problem was that there was too little media activity (until it was too late) for the understanding that good reporting engendered to affect policy.[36]

The exact timing of decision-making that led to the decision of the KLA to accelerate the war is not yet clear, but at about the same time as the Nano–Milosevic meeting in Crete took place, the KLA made a more concerted effort to appear as an open force in central Drenica, and further communiqués about their activities were sent to the BBC and other major international news organisations from Switzerland.[37] The desperate efforts of the international community to shore up the power of the Milosevic regime in Kosova had caused the movement towards major conflict to now become unstoppable.

8

The Kosova War: The First Offensive

In the years since the summer of 1999 there have been many arguments about exactly when the Kosova war began. In terms of international media attention this is an easy question to answer, in that systematic coverage started in the November and December of 1997 and accelerated steadily thereafter. By the first week of March 1998 it had achieved the status of a major foreign story. In British media terms there is an exact date (28 November 1997), when the media covered the funeral of Halit Geci, a teacher killed by Serb forces in the little village of Llausha, near Klina, where the KLA made their first official and ceremonial public appearance as an organisation.[1] However, the foundation of the KLA goes back to 1993 and significant armed actions were starting then, with many more taking place by spring 1996[2] and continuing largely unreported. Virtually all the main KLA leaders had a family background of involvement in the anti-communist resistance after 1944. The grandfather of Hashim Thaci fought with legendary resistance leader Sadik Rama against the Bulgarian occupiers of eastern Kosova and then narrowly escaped the Titoist bloodbath of the Albanian Partisans at Tivat in Montenegro in 1945.[3] But memory of these leaders had become eclipsed in the Western minds by the fog of sentimental admiration for the Titoist revisionist regime.

To use the colloquial phrase, nobody except a tiny handful of specialists knew where the KLA was 'coming from'.[4] It was also very difficult for the 'establishment' coterie of military theorists, defence experts, military historians and soldiers to imagine that an underground paramilitary insurgency like the KLA could have any validity in post-communist modern Europe. It was an easy transition from this incomprehension to a variety of conspiracy theories, of which the Enverist/Russian-supported plot against 'democractic Yugoslavia' was the most popular in the pro-Serb strata in Britain.[5]

This crisis in understanding the KLA relates closely to the projection of the nature of war in the modern media. The Kosova war was an early postmodern war. Media perceptions of it were as important as the military reality itself.[6] In reality, a war only becomes a significant 'war' in terms of the international community when casualty numbers are significant in a country that is taken seriously as an international 'player'. This rules out numerous conflicts from ever becoming proper 'wars', such as those current in many parts of Africa and the ethnic, religious and tribal conflicts on the Indian sub-continent and many other places. It took time for the Kosova war to transcend these factors. The KLA decided to announce itself to the world.[7] It was a propitious time to do so.

By the end of 1997, as greater calm descended upon Albania, the parameters of the Kosova conflict were soon set. Local KLA groups in Drenica cleared the villages of Serb security forces, and the breakdown continued of what remained of normal economic and social activity there. The Yugoslav army began to plan for a long counter-insurgency campaign. They brought in additional heavy armour to Kosova from the big garrison supply depots at Niš and Vranje to reinforce the Prishtina Corps. Little of this was revealed to the Serbian public in the media at this stage, as the Milosevic regime wished to conceal, as far as possible, the reality of another impending war from its war-weary public. In the Serb villages, small arms capacity was being hastily built up. In Prishtina and large towns, however, life carried on much as usual, with the Serb media portraying Serb operations as normal police actions against a familiar but minor terrorist threat. Abroad, though, concerns were mounting that the conflict amounted to much more. Soon foreign war correspondents were coming to Kosova. Work focused on visiting the liberated areas and interviewing families of the bereaved.[8] As yet, however, it still remained a local conflict and it was not until late February 1998, after the visit of US envoy Robert Gelbard, when in a controversial press conference he seemed to sanction a Milosevic crackdown, that the conflict accelerated.

On 3 and 4 March the Milosevic security forces attacked the farm of the Jashari family in the little village of Prekaz, in northern Drenica, and massacred over 50 people, destroying virtually an extended family. The Jashari's had been a core founding family of the KLA, and Adem Jashari had been a close associate of the young Hashim Thaci in his early KLA recruitment and military activities. Adem Jashari had been among the groups who had undergone military training in Albania, and had been arrested by the Berisha government in 1993 and imprisoned for a time. The family were a living symbol of the resistance, and the massacre changed the whole character and atmosphere of the conflict. A mass funereal attended by over 40,000 people was held a day or so later on a hillside near Prekaz, and the entire Kosovar Albanian community was subsequently thrown into crisis.

5. The Jashari brothers – founding fathers of the KLA

The ordinary Kosovar Albanian public could identify readily with the Jashari family, who had never left Kosova and lived hard-working smallholders' lives with their cows on their family farm. Their public image was quite different from the shadowy intellectuals in the diaspora underground, with their false names and covert modus operandi. Some LPK leaders had been living in Switzerland for nearly 15 years, and were little known to the public in general and seemed remote from their origins. This did not, though, apply to the younger generation of the exiled leadership – men like Thaci and Haradinaj – who had only been in Switzerland for a year or two and returned covertly to Albania and Kosova on numerous occasions. This is an important background reason for their rapid emergence in top positions after summer 1999, and their sustained popularity. During March the KLA-controlled area of Kosova spread rapidly, as sleeper groups were activated by the leadership and formed armed formations in village communities, which began killing Serbian police and army personnel.

Across the border in Albania widespread unrest was still endemic, and in the last week of February 1998 the northern town of Shkoder had descended into chaos, with gangs supporting Sali Berisha taking over the town after a DP rally on 22 February, looting and damaging buildings and setting fire to the University. In the eyes of some Tirana observers, the Democratic Party appeared to be exploiting the Kosovar crisis, with the holding of frequent rallies and militant demonstrations of oppositionists in the capital itself. From the viewpoint of the Nano government, everywhere north and north-east of the Mati River, for hundreds of miles, was a region of uncertainty and posed chaotic threats to the 'order' they were trying to impose. The Albanian Army command issued a statement calling for calm and emphasising its capacity to control the borders, but also noting that the Serbs were moving special units into Kosova and that attacks on the civilian population were accelerating. It was widely believed in Tirana that Berisha stood for the formation of a new 'technical' government, which his critics saw as a framework for his potential return to power.

In reality the political machinations in Tirana at this stage were largely irrelevant to developments on the ground in Kosova. The KLA-controlled region spread south from northern Drenica down through central Drenica, and westwards towards the Peje–Gjakova–Prizren road, and in essence this remained the military situation for several weeks. There was no open KLA activity in Prishtina or any other large city. In the early stages it was a war without a front, or fronts. A KLA group might occupy ground for a time, only to retreat when superior Serb forces arrived on the scene and then reoccupy it when the Serbs left. It was a rural and village uprising, and the largest town in the liberated area, Malishevo, only had a population of a few thousand people. An improvised KLA press centre was set up here, and ex-schoolteacher Jakup Krasniqi became the KLA's first public spokesman. The rural insurgency was also developing strongly in the far west of Kosova but largely out of the public eye, as reporters found it much easier to work in Drenica than in the remote and dangerous border areas near Albania. This was particularly the case west of Peje, Decani and Gjakova. Here the war had a different character. The Dukagjini groups were led by some very tough and effective commanders, of which Ramush Haradinaj is only the most prominent and best known.

Other important commanders were from the Lladrovci, Ramadani, Krasniqi and Rama families, and from traditionally militant nationalist villages such as Jabllanica where in practice it had not been safe for the Serb police to go for several years before 1998. Here the battle was not simply to liberate territory but to open the border with Albania, and as a result it had an additional military and politically symbolic dimension that was not present elsewhere. This resulted in a Serb offensive against the Dukagjini hill villages of great severity before the war had spread elsewhere in Kosova. Houses were shelled or burnt down by rockets launched from lorries with mounted fixed artillery pieces, which were driven along the main roads and fired into the villages from the woods above them. The importance of the KLA here was reflected in post-1999 politics in Kosova, with survivors like Fehmi Lladrovci becoming commander of the Kosova Protection Corps (KPC) Rapid Reaction Force and Ramush Haradinaj, after losing two of his brothers in the war, becoming a party leader and Kosovar Prime Minister in 2004.

There was as yet no open KLA activity in south-east Kosova at all, but in the north-east in the wooded Llap hills near Mitrovica KLA brigades under the command of Rrustem Mustafa (Captain Remi) were making serious inroads into the Serbs' capacity to control the roads and the strategic town of Podujevo (Besian in Albanian usage). Podujevo was an Albanian-majority town with a strong national consciousness, only ten miles from the border with Serbia. Consequently the Serbs could not afford to lose control of the Podujevo–Niš road there, as it was one of the two main arterial routes on wide asphalt roads into Kosova, and a direct link to the main Prishtina Corps garrison centre at Niš. This town was to be a key theatre of the conflict for the next 18 months, along with nearby Vushtrri, an old Ottoman centre that had been overshadowed by the growth of the nineteenth-century mining town of Mitrovica.[9]

In the meantime the government in Tirana observed the escalating violence in Kosova with a mixture of anxiety and private satisfaction. Despite the difficulties many of the elite had in dealing with the Kosovars, they were in the end all Albanians and war in Kosova had long been prophesied. The neglect of Kosova at Dayton was widely felt, on the DP side of politics, as having fatally undermined Rugova. This view was shared in the small but influential Republican Party in Albania. The general inferiority complex of the Tirana elite on the international stage had not blinded them to the special treatment often given to Serbia and the Milosevic government, especially by Europeans, and the lack of respect shown towards Tirana in comparison. The moderate positions on Kosova put forward by Tirana politicians had received little international support, and many leaders felt that they were being patronised over the Kosova issue.

In the recent past, Albania's foreign ambassadors had been full of reassurance that the international community could and would control the situation, and that the Tirana government had nothing to worry about. The relative success of the Daan Everts/Vranitsky activity by the EU/OSCE in Tirana gave them the confidence to feel that Kosova might enjoy similar conflict management. Now that this illusory perspective had disappeared, the war did at least give Albania's politicians and policy-makers a somewhat

greater importance in the world and a certain sense of *Schadenfreude* over the
'I told you so' factor. The fact that the crisis had finally exploded in Kosova
benefited Tirana in terms of international attention. Some areas of the
Tirana government, particularly the military, were soon receiving a stream of
visiting NATO and other officials. Aid flows increased and ties with the USA
and NATO grew. Activity also accelerated at Albanian military facilities that
had been used by NATO during the Bosnian war.

This positive development was not reflected in the official Albanian media,
which as late as March 1998 was often only referring to the 'violence', and
describing Kosova villages as 'claiming' they were under police siege.[10] It was
of course more or less impossible for Albanian journalists to obtain a visa
to work in Kosova, and editors in Tirana often had a narrow outlook, did
not instinctively trust foreigners reporting in the Western media and were
bogged down in obsolete conceptions. Like the political leadership few had
ever visited Kosova, at least since the relatively benign days of the 1970s and
early 1980s, and had no clear vision of the repression under Milosevic.

The political crisis over the national question remained acute, although
it was not articulated in the normal political discourse of the government.
Issues emerged into the open in a few vital days at the end of April that were
to determine the terms of the development of the debate until the September
coup attempt, and the departure of Nano from the post of Prime Minister.
The events of March after the death of the Jashari family had made clear to
everybody in Tirana that the national question was reopening, something
that the Greeks in Tirana were determined to resist. However, the Greek
embassy had no control over the development of the military realities, much
as they could control the Tirana elite. On 24 April Fatos Nano had to order
the establishment of an operational committee for refugees in the north-east
town of Kukes, and the Defence Ministry reported that the army was digging
in near the Qafa e Morines pass on the Kosova–Abania border in response to
reports of Serb military deployments near the border. In a panic move, the
PASOK government in Athens sought to purge the Tirana government of
anyone suspected of Kosovar sympathies.

In the final week of April, with the war rapidly intensifying in north-west
Kosova, immense Greek embassy pressure was put on Nano to sack Culture
Minister Arta Dade and Defence Minister Sabit Brokaj, both principled
nationalists within the Socialist Party who refused to accept Greek embassy
instructions on Kosova policy issues. Athens wanted a mass arrest policy of
KLA people operating from Albanian soil. Nano complied but President
Rexhep Meidani refused to sign the orders sacking the ministers, setting
in the open a conflict between President and Prime Minister that had been

simmering ever since Meidani was appointed. President Meidani was, under the constitution, commander of the armed forces and resented Athens pressure on the Tirana government to work with the Serbs against the KLA. Greece wanted Brokaj to use the army for mass arrests of the KLA in Albania, and to close the north-east border, which he refused to do. Arta Dade was a highly intelligent, talented and uncorrupt minister who was closer to the DP on pan-Albanianism than her Socialist colleagues.

Events on the ground continued to overtake the politicians. By 25 April the first 1000 Kosovar refugees had reached Albania. A further 3000 women and children from Drenica villages were sheltering in Gjakova en route to Albania. The pattern of the war known as the 'First Offensive', pioneered around Junik and Decan, was producing large population movement.[11] On 26 April the Serbs killed 16 of a column of 200 KLA soldiers crossing the border into Kosova from Albania.

The parameters of the war in the north were being set, with the Tirana government often under huge international pressure to clamp down on the Kosovar patriots but having neither the means nor, privately, often the wish to do so.[12] On 7 May the Switzerland-based newspaper of the LPK, *Zeri I Kosoves*, carried an interview with novelist Ismail Kadare, in which Kadare said that the time had arrived for pacifism to be radicalised. Elsewhere in the paper the LPK criticised the 'dangerous antics' of Kosovar 'Prime Minister' Bujar Bukoshi towards the KLA and opened the fight for legitimacy in the leadership of the new army. Bukoshi was secretly in the process of forming a new army to compete with the KLA, as it was clear the LDK would be incapable of controlling the KLA. This was based on the old 'Defence Ministry' of the 'Kosova Government' in exile of the mid-1990s.[13] The Contact Group[14] issued a statement calling for a return to the political process, which had no influence on the ground in Kosova. The road to central Tirana involvement in the full-scale Kosova war was open, but there was no clear policy option open to the government as long as it was tied to Greek regional interests.

The same crisis of confidence and policy affected international diplomatic discourse. The Socialist government had no capacity to articulate the central Kosovar demand for independence, but instead focused on the so-called 'Third Republic' solution whereby Kosova would become a new republic within a reformed Yugoslav Federation, made up of Kosova, Serbia and Montenegro. This policy was strongly associated with Foreign Minister Paskal Milo. He has since been accused of a failure to give enough political support to the Kosovars, but the general weakness and dependence factor of the government needs to be borne in mind, along with the state of general Albanian public opinion, which was exhausted by the previous six months of violent chaos and did not relish hearing news of the outbreak of war in Kosova. Even the least politically aware understood how the country could easily get involved in the Kosova war. As a result, illusions replaced practical policy. Despite its total impracticability, the notion of the 'Third Republic' was the dominant Kosova policy in Tirana in the spring of 1998. Some ultra-collaborationist Socialist leaders even advocated a return to the 1974 autonomy within Yugoslavia.

In the official Tirana government media the war was badly reported and sometimes not reported at all. For example, in the *Albanian Daily News* bulletin for 22 April 1998, when Belgrade's First Offensive was in full flow, the main stories were Fatos Nano's plans for local government reform and changes in government structure. The shelling and barbaric devastation of Decani villages like Baballoq by artillery and helicopter gunships was only reported in a small item on an inside page. This inertia did not apply to all the political elite though, and soon prominent figures such as novelist Ismail Kadare were devoting all their spare time to building support for Kosova.

A mass demonstration was called in support of Kosova in Skanderbeg Square in Tirana on 9 March, in a rare display of inner-party unanimity. But the atmosphere remained dominated by neurotic fear among the Socialist-inclined elite that somehow the Kosova crisis might explode in their faces and lead to a return of the Democratic Party to power in government in Tirana, on the coat-tails of the Kosovars' struggle for self determination. The bruised and battered DP leadership was largely silent on the Kosova issue as it developed in the early stages, and had little to contribute to the policy debate. The Jashari massacre was a particularly difficult issue for the DP to handle, as Adem Jashari had been arrested and imprisoned by the DP government on British and French orders as long ago as 1993.[15] The DP press was more energetic; it frequently, and correctly, blamed Nano and the Crete 'diplomacy' episode as opening the door for Milosevic's terror machine in Kosova.[16]

Fatos Nano himself, with a characteristic mixture of shrewdness and egocentric calculation, seems to have seen the crisis as a way to project the importance of his own 'stabilising' role on the internationals and played both sides off against each other. This meant that Interior Minister Neritan Ceka was often unclear about what policy to follow over the key issue of control of KLA arms procurement activity and border security when the government was under intense pressure from the international community to close the border in the north-east to insurgent movements.[17] Ceka was supplied with information about alleged small arms shipments from British intelligence but was in a state of confusion as to what action he should take. Nano called for a NATO force to be placed on the Albania–Kosova border, an apparently statesmanlike gesture of support for moderation, but one that would also have helped strengthen his fragile grasp on northern Albania. NATO General Secretary Javier Solana, a past master at seeing through the apparently statesmanlike efforts of Albanian politicians to draw NATO into supporting one side or the other in Albanian politics, declined the offer. Solana said on 11 March that the time for such a force was 'premature'.[18] A week later the Albanian side boycotted talks with Serbian government negotiators in Prishtina, and Dr Rugova made a fresh call for Kosova to become independent.

The distance between the world of the Nano government and the reality of the war was growing daily. The Kosova crisis had accelerated the already nascent conflict between Prime Minister Nano and President Meidani. The two men came from the same political party, but otherwise had little in common. Meidani was not a classic Tirana or southern Tosk intellectual, although he did have a standard PLA educational background. A northerner by birth, he had taught for a time in the late 1980s at Prishtina University in the physics department, and so was unique in the government in having first-hand knowledge and experience of Kosovar society in the post-Tito period. Meidani had a clear and unambiguous view of the threat of the Greater Serbia project to all Albanians, something that was not at all clear or universal among his colleagues.[19] On the opposite wing of the Socialist Party, Nano's Foreign Minister Milo had always seen Italy as the greatest potential threat to Albania, something embodied both in his academic work as an historian and in what he saw as the errors of the Berisha period. Milo was well aware of the complete lack of military capacity in the disintegrated armed forces, and in defence of his caution over Kosova it should be borne in mind that at this stage there was no guarantee at all of the EU, WEU or NATO alighting on the side of the Albanians and Kosovars.

Only a year before the First Offensive had started in Kosova, NATO and the EU had declined to act decisively to support the survival strategy of Sali Berisha, and as recent ex-communists the Nano government was likely to be poorly viewed in international organisations and in the USA.[20] Milo felt the new Socialist government in Tirana was in an even weaker position to attract the US support needed for the Kosovars. Mishandling of the crisis, in his view, could have led to a direct attack on Albania by Belgrade, and even to a Serbian/Montenegrin occupation of part of the north of Albania.[21] Most Kosovar leaders, of all persuasions, privately sympathised with aspects of this viewpoint – for instance, leaders such as Veton Surroi in Prishtina and Arben Xhaferi in Macedonia regretted the chaos and military weakness in Albania, even if they had very critical views of Berisha and his government.[22]

As a result of these tensions, a polarity began to develop between Nano and Meidani that would continue to be a central factor in Tirana throughout 1998 until the September coup attempt and the end of Nano's time as Prime Minister. In response, diplomats in Tirana were put in the odd position of defending Nano against his critics, with smear allegations such as 'Meidani is spending too much time on Kosova' commonly put forward by EU ambassadors to visiting journalists.[23] This weakened the already flimsy authority of the government, exacerbated the tensions between pro-Nano and pro-Meidani ministers and meant that in practice little was done to restrict KLA small arms transactions. It is not yet clear what the exact effect of these policies were; memoirs of the war speak extensively of the problems of weapons shortages that affected the KLA in 1997 and early 1998, and the general foreign media image of a smooth flow of munitions from Albania to Kosova was clearly incorrect. Even when adequate supplies of small arms were available, ammunition shortages often presented insuperable difficulties in theatre. This relates to wider issues of political and military priorities, and the interplay of complex, sophisticated and largely unknown political actors and organisational forces in the KLA support apparatus.

Meanwhile in Kosova, in his account of the war, Ramush Haradinaj speaks of the difficulties of the autumn 1997 period after the death of his brother Luan, and of growing dissatisfaction with the military/political apportionment ratio laid down by the LPK leadership who controlled the funding to the nascent army. Haradinaj, Lladrovci and other key Dukagjini leaders objected to the fact that the military development of the KLA was not receiving 100 per cent of all the resources available. There were also differing political conceptions of how the struggle for self-determination should proceed. There were some who envisaged a general armed uprising of the Kosovar Albanians along the lines of the Albanian events of spring 1997, or there were those who contemplated the alternative perspective of an outright guerrilla war. In practice, the latter group won the military argument, and the KLA was relatively successful in the spring 1998 period in developing into an insurgent army, achieving its aims.

The LPK strategy was, however, something of an elitist perspective, and came under great pressure as Milosevic's First Offensive developed. In this respect small arms transfers were irrelevant, whether from Albania or elsewhere; what mattered was the inability of the KLA to hold ground under Serbian shelling. Here, the diaspora-based conceptions of the LPK and leaders like Ali Ahmeti and Xhavit Haliti may have been significantly affected by their own unavoidable personal distance from the reality of Kosova, coupled with maybe a little elitism in their own thinking. As far as Haradinaj and other Dukagjini commanders' views on finance were concerned, the LPK leaders had to evaluate many demands on party funds, and it was vital to keep activities like the newspaper *Zeri I Kosoves* going, and the League alive as a political force (and not to totally merge it with the new army).

As in the Tirana leadership, in the summer and autumn of 1997 and the early winter of 1998 within the LPK there was a case for caution as well as a case for confident advance. It was certainly not clear by autumn 1997 whether the conflict would develop satisfactorily and be able to cross the critical stage in Partisan warfare between isolated attacks on Serb security people and a general mobilisation of the population. Another dimension to this issue was the difference of policy between the LPK, who sought as a priority to build an organised, structured army, and the LKCK, which planned for an armed people to take power along classic insurgent lines. The LKCK was stronger in some Kosova towns than the LPK, particularly in Prishtina itself, and had a reputation as an organisation of young idealistic and self-sacrificing militants who had borne a heavy and brutal burden of police repression. They had an influence, particularly amongst young people, far beyond their small numbers and were often the only organisation capable of running the distribution of underground political material in Prishtina. The LKCK however did not have access to the diaspora financial resources that the LPK had, which in turn affected the development of the liberation war. The LPK had its strongest influence in the rural west and centre of Kosova, where popular support for the KLA movement was strongest.[24]

Another question central to any consideration of the development of Tirana politics during this period is that of foreign control, or attempted foreign control, of particular politicians. This is an area where accurate data is in short supply, but speculation and unfounded allegations are common. The onset of war produced acute tensions in Tirana. In general, the more intelligent politicians could see that the strengthening of the relationship with the USA was the most likely immediate effect of hostilities, but most Socialists philosophically looked towards Europe and the EU, and considered that the DP was the more 'American' of the Tirana parties. Some older Socialists still had a political psychology imbued with the Enverist ideas of the Anglo-American threat to Albania and therefore had an instinctively isolationist orientation, with suspicions of Western motives in the Balkans. Some southern Socialists also saw the Kosovars as in general being 'Islamic', an idea that Greece for its own purposes strongly encouraged.

The most salient fact to point out is the systematic Greek attempts to bring the entire political elite under its wing, and thereby weaken the influence of Italy.[25] Despite the relative success of Operation Alba, none of the traditional links between the DP government, the Vatican and the Italian Right had worked at a practical level to preserve the Berisha government, and the lack of a land border with Albania was a key issue. By comparison Greece, with its long common frontier, played a part in the southern uprising, held jobs for tens of thousands of *Gastarbeiter* and had numerous cultural and religious links that seemed to be more effective as policy levers compared to those of Italy. In the historical sense that Albania would always be a theatre of contest for interests between Italy and Greece, there could only be one winner in 1997–8. As a result, important outside powers such as Britain began to work more and more closely with Greece in Albania, something that had in any case accelerated strongly with the election of the Blair Labour government in June 1997. The dubious ties between some Tory politicians and the DP had been well publicised in the British press, and the new London government now had the opportunity to distance itself from this past.

It was not long, though, before the development of the ground war in Kosova brought these international link issues to a head. By the end of May 1998 the first significant numbers of Kosovar refugees had begun to arrive in Albania, centred on places like Shijak, near Durres, and Kavaje, both with historic Kosova links.[26] At this stage people could be accommodated with relatives, but it was obvious to the international humanitarian community that if the conflict continued much larger numbers could be expected who would put an enormous, perhaps intolerable, strain on the Albanian body politic and society in general. A refugee crisis would also undermine the Nano government's Kosova policy and bring home the reality of the war to the Albanian people generally, with unpredictable results. Optimists felt that pan-Albanian solidarity would bring people to the aid of the Kosovars; pessimists stressed the cultural differences and total separation by communist border closures, along with alleged Gheg–Tosk antagonism. The demands of patriotism and pragmatism might have conflicted. As it turned out the optimists were correct, and many impoverished communities such as Peshkopi, Kukes and Puka have outstanding records of humanitarian support for the Kosova refugees; but in Tirana in March 1998 no one could be certain what would happen, and in the international community the pessimists inevitably dominated.

By the beginning of the summer the level of violence in Kosova had accelerated and, from Milosevic's point of view, the First Offensive was bringing results. The Albanians were losing what had appeared to be securely held ground. The main players in the international community concluded that Milosevic would win and the KLA would be destroyed. Unknown to all Albanians, except Veton Surroi in Prishtina, a secret deal had been reached between the British, the French and US Balkan negotiator Richard Holbrooke to allow a Serb crackdown on the KLA in exchange for which Milosevic would agree to a Dayton-type negotiation on Kosova with Rugova.[27]

In this critical situation, President Meidiani gave a strong patriotic lead, and in a speech delivered on 9 June 1998, on the 120th anniversary of the League of Prizren, called for the unity of all Albanians to face the contemporary threat to the nation.[28] It would have been difficult to imagine any other member of the government with the vision to make the same speech and he clearly saw, which many in the government did not, that the tired initiatives of the Contact Group were likely to fail to achieve anything concrete with Belgrade to avert the historic crisis which was evolving and which would soon engulf both Albania and Kosova. In practice, the deficiencies of the Nano government's approach were irrelevant. As in many other matters in national life, popular initiatives by-passed official structures, and family, community and national solidarity for the refugees was overwhelming, albeit coupled with inevitable grumbles about theft and community disruption. Gheg–Tosk rivalry faded and the nation was able to cater for a vast refugee influx without internal conflict.[29] The nation deserved particular credit, as early in the crisis the massive dysfunctionality of the United Nations High Commission for Refugees (UNHCR) office in Tirana became apparent, and remained so until the end of the crisis in summer 1999.[30]

Elsewhere in the Albanian sphere in the Balkans, strong support for the war was developing, with the leadership of the largest ethnic Albanian party in Tetovo in western Macedonia making a clear call for Kosovar independence.[31] In the provincial centres north of the Shkumbini River, widespread military activity was already taking place, although the fragmentation of the Albanian Army meant that virtually all vehicles were useless or looted, and it was clear that the KLA was going to be a very low-technology force. KLA activity was intense in Tropoja, with the provincial centre of Bajram Curri becoming an open recruiting and training centre for the new Kosova military force, and an open-air arms market was developing in the centre of the poverty-stricken and remote town. Horses, donkeys and mules were pressed into service. The local barracks of the Albanian Army, which had been ransacked in April 1997, was taken over as a KLA administrative centre and soon neat stacks of uniforms and equipment were being built up there.

Whether it wished to or not, the Tirana government had no power to stop these activities – a far cry from the days of 1992–3 when the DP government closed down Kosovar training facilities. Sympathetic figures in the army allowed a certain number of designated military camps to become recruitment, training and logistics centres for the KLA, like the camp at Mulleti between

Tirana and Elbasan, and an informal office was set up at Durres port to cater for recruits arriving by ferry from western Europe. At this stage, the vast majority of diaspora recruits were from Europe, particularly Switzerland; the upsurge of support for the war in the USA occurred later, from July to August 1998, when the Atlantic Battalion of the KLA was formed.[32] In the diaspora 'Vendlindja Therret' (the 'Homeland Fund') was opened to collect money for the war, in place of the largely discredited 3 per cent income levy used to support the LDK.

The entrenched pro-Belgrade elements that dominated the Western police and counter-intelligence agencies viewed these developments with concern, and soon open and covert attempts were made to stop the development of the KLA. Telephones of activists were tapped and attempts made to stop arms shipments into Albania, with regular 'successes' being trumpeted in Albanian newspapers close to the Tirana diplomatic community, such as *Koha Jone*. At the same time, the European Parliament called for the deployment of a 'preventative peacekeeping force', along Operation Alba lines, for Kosova. On 11 March NATO had said that such a force was 'premature'; a decision that appears to have been largely based on British, Dutch and French intelligence assessments that saw Milosevic as always able to win on the ground over the KLA. Albanians rallied in Brussels that week to demand Western intervention, with slogans such as 'Europe – wake up!' and 'NATO – where are you?'

American concerns seem to have been more focused on stopping the conflict spreading to Macedonia, and State Department spokesman James Rubin said that the UN force in Macedonia could be reinforced 'so that if the situation does deteriorate further, the risk of it spreading is limited.'[33] It was this fear that was later to determine the change in US policy in the summer of 1998 towards more positive support for the Albanian side, leading to the recognition that the KLA was a useful, if novel and unpredictable, force against the Milosevic regime. Nevertheless, many in the US diplomatic apparatus, particularly those around Richard Holbrooke, had a strong stake in the status quo and it would take time for the Clinton administration to be prepared to face up to its difficult responsibilities.

The initial period of euphoria within the KLA was short, as the Serb army began to press in where it had taken control of small urban centres. A key turning point was the battle for Orahovac on 7 May, when the KLA lost control of the town to the Serbs. As a result, the progress of the KLA towards the Prishtina–Kacanik–Skopje main road was halted, and correspondents who had been reporting on a seemingly inexorable growth of the guerrilla movement were now writing of military reverses and setbacks. Systematic

Serb attacks began on Albanian-inhabited villages throughout western and central Kosova. Thousands of destitute and desperate Kosovars took refuge in the forests near their homes and lived under canvas or plastic sheeting.[34] This produced an upsurge in interest from the international media and for the first time the big television companies like CNN and the BBC came to Kosova. Most coverage was sympathetic to the Kosovars, whose plight rapidly rose to near the top of the international agenda. Milosevic took little heed of the pleas of the Contact Group to end the recurrent attacks on villages, and at the end of May the NATO council decided to take practical action as a warning against the development of Bosnian-style ethnic cleansing. On 8 June an air power 'flyover' was made and deployment of NATO air assets in Albania, principally Apache helicopters, was accelerated. This action was strongly welcomed in Tirana, as a sign of practical commitment by the USA, as it coincided with deployment of more NATO assets within Albania itself.

As the ground war became more entrenched NATO became more involved; the Supreme Commander, General Wesley Clark, was a man of high principle and immense energy who had no illusions about the nature of the Serbian regime. NATO gradually became more and more a central actor in the next four months, and the fears in the State Department about disturbance to the Dayton settlement were less important. The Contact Group, with its entrenched Russian veto, was no longer the only diplomatic show in town – something that transformed the atmosphere in Tirana and emboldened the more nationalist elements in the political spectrum to take on what they saw as the collaborators with the Serbs and the Milosevic regime.

Some blood would be spilt in the process, however, and by September the nation was again in danger of descending into violent chaos. The centre of the developing crisis was to move after May–June 1998 to northern Albania and the bitter and entrenched family, clan and party conflicts there. However, the power struggle would be decided on the streets of Tirana in September that year. In Kosova itself, the crisis deepened for the KLA with the news of the emergence of FARK, under the aegis of Rugova's 'Prime Minister' Bujar Bukoshi. As one US diplomat in the region commented a few weeks later, 'the KLA itself and its legitimacy are coming under question', and a very long and agonisingly difficult summer for the Albanian forces, the government in Tirana and the diaspora lay ahead.[35]

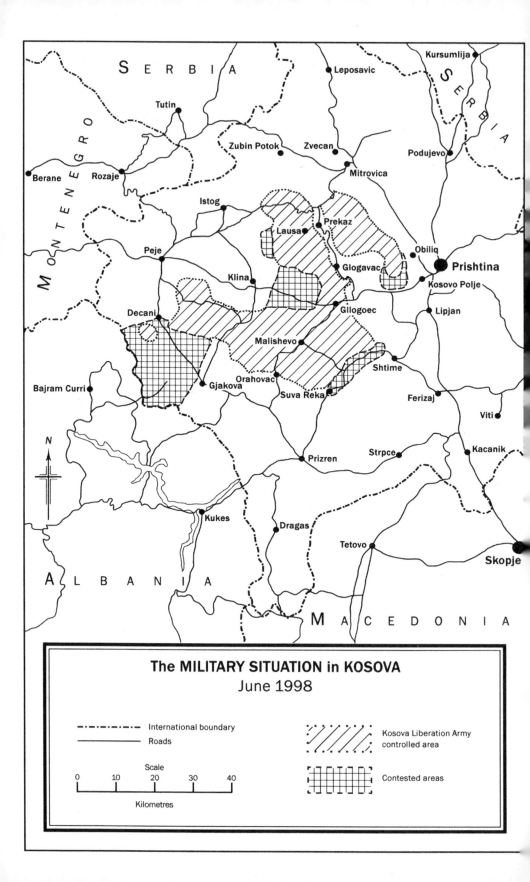

The **MILITARY SITUATION in KOSOVA**
June 1998

International boundary
Roads

Kosova Liberation Army
controlled area

Contested areas

Scale

0   10   20   30   40

Kilometres

9

Tirana and the Growing International Crisis

I
t took some time for the nature of the looming summer 1998 crisis to become apparent in Tirana. Security was slowly improving over the whole country, with the exception of Tropoja, and the economy was picking up from the chaos of the previous year more quickly than most international experts had predicted. Foreign policy began to take a back seat to domestic concerns, and this included Kosova. The government was satisfied with the degree of international engagement and had no inkling of the sellout to Milosevic that had been envisaged by some major players in Britain and the USA after the setbacks of the KLA on the battlefield during the First Offensive period. However, the ground was nonetheless moving under the Nano government, as after the First Offensive period ended the insurgency continued in the villages, particularly in Drenica in central Kosova.

As tensions in Kosova increased it had become increasingly difficult for Albania's 140-kilometre frontier with Kosova to be adequately monitored and for the Albanian government to cope with the steady influx of Kosovar refugees. The Albanian authorities were increasingly concerned at attempts by Serbia to implicate Albania as a supporter of 'terrorism', by implying in press reports that KLA fighters were being trained on Albanian territory and that arms and ammunition were being transported from Albania into Kosova. Such accusations were not new. As far back as November 1992 the then Albanian Defence Minister Safet Zhulali denied to the international press that Albania was training Kosovars for guerrilla fighting in Kosova, despite the existence of camps for this purpose. He was responding to Serbian allegations that Albania had built a system of tunnels under the border mountains to smuggle armed insurgents into Kosova. Although some Albanian army military movements in the north-east were taking place, any deployments were strictly defensive in nature and limited to the digging-in of artillery pieces along the main road.[1]

The Albanian government initially hotly denied allegations in the Yugoslav press that KLA recruits were being trained in Albania and that weapons were being freely transported across the border. However, despite strong international pressure, it was impossible for Albania to seal off its border entirely. In the spring of 1998 there were only 67 police border guards, aided by soldiers, to patrol the hundreds of miles of inhospitable, remote and mountainous terrain. Most border guards were just ordinary village policemen, who patrolled on foot because of the lack of cars and the absence of any roads. They also lacked essential equipment, such as binoculars and radio and communication equipment. Albania's depleted armed forces, which then only numbered around 11,000 troops (including 5000 regulars), were also thinly stretched in attempting to monitor the border. Having virtually disintegrated following the uprising, efforts to re-build the army had only tentatively begun in the spring of 1998.

As the border authorities denied Serbian reports of illegal KLA training camps inside Albania, the Albanian government persistently stated that Albania would not be used as a base for the KLA. There was little Tirana could do, however, to stop the activities of the KLA in northern Albania, nor could they halt the KLA's growing support network amongst the population of the Kosovar-border districts. Many northern Albanians have relatives in Kosova with whom they share the same dialect and have the same clan and kinship structure. In fiercely pro-KLA border towns such as Kukes and Bajram Curri, any Albanian border patrols trying to apprehend Kosovars smuggling weapons into Kosova would themselves be attacked immediately by armed inhabitants of these towns.

The OSCE, as well as the EU, had significantly increased their monitoring of the border. Yet in the wild and remote Albanian highlands it was virtually impossible to detect all the myriad of ancient mule tracks that snake their way through otherwise impenetrable mountains. Nevertheless, according to interviews with OSCE officials, the Serbian side had failed to provide any evidence of the involvement of the Albanian government in the smuggling of arms to Kosova. Instead the OSCE pointed to Serbia's unwillingness to cooperate with international organisations and to allow an OSCE mission to be attached to Kosova to try to make the process of monitoring the border more effective.

Throughout the spring of 1998 there had been a substantial arms build-up along the Albania–Kosova border, mostly AK-47s looted from Albanian army barracks but also a sprinkling of more sophisticated weapons from the Montenegrin drugs mafia, which was then operating almost unhindered in the region and whose business interests lay with the KLA in clearing the Kosova side of the border of Serbian police and security control. The government had therefore to begrudgingly acknowledge that although several consignments of arms destined for Kosova had been apprehended by Albanian police, a considerable number of weapons were being freely transported to the border. There they were sold openly from the boots of Mercedes cars to Kosova Albanians, and indeed to anyone wanting to purchase arms. With the demand for weapons increasing, there remained systematic attempts to loot Albanian arms depots. The price of a Kalashnikov had risen from just $10 in the summer of 1997 to around $100 by April 1998. The police had little choice but to ignore the trafficking, as they were fearful of confronting the dealers.

By the end of April the situation had become such that Fatos Nano had little choice but to declare that the border in the north-eastern part of the country was now out of control. He thus freed the government of any responsibility for any weapons trafficking going on there, and in practice provided the KLA with a border backup zone free from outside interference. In the light of Socialist government allegations that the smuggling and trafficking in that zone was conducted by DP loyalists, any eventual accusations of links between certain groups of people and the KLA would be blamed on Berisha, who was vainly trying to strengthen his weakened and discredited position. Despite the fact that Berisha was largely regarded as a spent force in Albania itself, he still had the support of prominent Kosovars – most notably Ibrahim Rugova – and of a sizeable group of loyal northern henchmen. This did not apply to Bujar Bukoshi, who had by now started to distance himself somewhat from both Rugova and Berisha.[2] Berisha was also useful to the Yugoslavs as a destabilising influence in Albania, which could also have implicated Montenegro in the developing conflict. Albanian Interior Ministry sources claimed to have proof that Yugoslav intelligence forces (the UDB-a) were encouraging smuggling operations between Albanians and Montenegrins, which contributed to the escalation of violent feuds between the participants. This in turn further enhanced the notion that the Tirana government was not in control of any of its northern regions, and gave Belgrade the excuse to build up troop reinforcements along the Montenegro–Albania border.

Despite the growing traffic in arms, Fatos Nano's administration repeatedly stated that Albania would not be used as a base for the training and equipping of KLA fighters. The government was determined to appear willing to apprehend weapons traffickers. Therefore, whilst it had no control over arms-dealing in the north, there were several highly publicised seizures of weapons consignments in the port of Durres.[3] Although the state of alert remained 'high' in northern border areas, there was no general mobilisation of the army. Soldiers remained in their barracks and not in field positions, as would have been the case on full alert. The lack of military activity was in fact deliberately aimed at trying to reduce tension along the border. The army and police forces on the Albanian side had gone to great lengths to avoid any action that could be interpreted as provocation by the Serbs. The deferential policy was also a product of the actual military incapacity of the army.

In the immediate aftermath of the killings of ethnic Albanian civilians in Drenica in Kosova in March 1998, there had been a brief show of solidarity shown by all sides of the political spectrum in Albania. This culminated in a huge demonstration in support of the Kosovars in Tirana, which was attended by both Socialist and Democratic Party leaders. Politicians from across the political spectrum had recognised that Albania's future economic prosperity was closely linked with finding a solution to the Kosova problem, without which there could not be any significant foreign investment to kick-start the stagnant economy. The acute concern in Albanian political circles over the Kosova issue was also evident amongst the general public as a whole. Although ordinary Albanians had little interest in the broader national question, being largely preoccupied with the struggle to survive, their paramount concern in the spring of 1998 was that Premier Nano did everything possible to reduce the chances of Albania's involvement in any conflict with Serbia.

As the crisis in Kosova continued to escalate, Albanian Foreign Ministry statements consistently attested to Tirana's firm belief that the international community would be able to broker a satisfactory solution to the problem. The Albanian government had no specific 'Kosova Policy' other than advocating a preference for Kosova to become a third constituent republic within the framework of Yugoslavia, having equal status with the Republics of Serbia and Montenegro. Tirana therefore put unswerving and naive faith in the ability of the international community to encourage, facilitate and maintain a constructive dialogue, which it was hoped would lead to a peaceful settlement of the conflict.

The Albanian government was severely criticised by all sectors of the Kosovar political structure for not arguing for much stronger measures to be adopted against the Belgrade authorities. However, given Albania's military weakness and economic disintegration following the uprising there was little Tirana could offer towards a solution to the crisis. Albania's policy towards Kosova had been ambiguous for some time. Nevertheless, despite these official announcements proclaiming confidence in international moves to end the crisis, there was universal scepticism amongst most Albanian politicians over the prospects of the Contact Group meeting, held in Rome at the end of April, being able to promote any form of dialogue between Belgrade and Prishtina. The deteriorating situation in Kosova and the increasing number of refugees fleeing into northern Albania prompted the Albanian parliament to unanimously approve a resolution demanding the deployment of NATO troops in Kosova to avert a spillover of the fighting into Albania. The resolution highlighted the Contact Group's deadline to Yugoslav President, Slobodan Milosevic, to withdraw Yugoslav forces from Kosova before 25 April.

In a letter to Italian Foreign Minister Lamberto Dini on the eve of the Contact Group's Rome meeting, Fatos Nano requested the deployment of NATO troops along Albania's northern borders in the hope of preventing Albania being dragged into the conflict.[4] Not all Albanians welcomed Nano's request. The Albanian opposition, as well as virtually all Kosovars, were adamantly opposed to the deployment of NATO troops in Albania, demanding instead that troops be deployed in Kosova itself. They argued that by calling for a NATO presence along Albania's northern border with Kosova, Premier Nano effectively wanted to do Milosevic's work for him – that is to cut off the escape and supply routes into Albania for both the KLA and Kosovar civilians. Western governments too remained hesitant and divided about any possible military intervention to halt the violence. The NATO alliance had been careful to condemn the violence on both sides, and to note that while it supported a return to the autonomy Kosova enjoyed before 1989, it did not back the Kosovars' call for independence.

The logistical problems relating to the deployment of any NATO troops were immense. Albania's chronic lack of infrastructure meant that electricity supplies were meagre, roads were virtually impassable, water supplies were erratic and telephone communications limited and unreliable. Most important of all, most road bridges were incapable of taking the weight of heavy military vehicles. According to a team of foreign technical experts surveying the Kukes district that spring, even if NATO had agreed immediately to the deployment of troops it would have taken a minimum of four months before the necessary technical infrastructure was in place and ready for use. Another factor to be considered was the lack of adequate security in the lawless northern border regions for both personnel and material equipment (which was routinely stolen almost as soon as it was installed).

Possibly the only positive consequence of the imminent crisis in Kosova was the announcement in mid-March of the Democratic Party's decision to formerly end a six-month boycott of parliament. The national question issue, following the Serb attack in Drenica, was the main reason behind the decision. The Democrats had persistently resisted calls from the international community to return to parliament and to cooperate with the ruling coalition to draw up a constitution. Despite its return to parliament, the DP was nevertheless totally dismissive of the government's ability to contribute to a solution to the Kosova crisis, due to its lack of nationalist credentials and legitimacy. The latter referred to the Democrat's assertion that the 1997 elections, which brought the Socialists to power, were fraudulent.

Since the start of the Kosova crisis in March, the opposition had been largely critical of what they saw as the feeble response by the Contact Group to the actions of Milosevic in Kosova, and the Socialist-led government's unwillingness to demand that stronger measures be imposed on Belgrade. Sali Berisha was able to take a more principled stand than Nano on these issues. Speaking on behalf of the right-wing political grouping Union for Democracy, he said that the Contact Group meeting in Rome had been a complete failure. It had decided to block the foreign funds of the Yugoslav government and the Serbian government, as well as all investments in Serbia, if the latter did not begin talks with the Kosovar leadership by 9 May. From the Tirana viewpoint, this was an empty gesture that would have no effect on Milosevic. Berisha was realistic in saying that the measures adopted in Rome failed to take a severe and clear-cut decision against Serbian aggression.[5] In response the international community, through its diplomatic personnel in Tirana, warned Berisha, in his capacity as leader of the main opposition party, not to play or to exploit the nationalist card. This followed numerous Albanian and foreign intelligence reports that former national intelligence (SHIK) officers still loyal to Berisha were instrumental in organising the shipment of weapons from Albania into Kosova and Macedonia for the use of the KLA.

Despite the fact that he was forced, under US pressure, to abandon calls for the unification of all Albanian-inhabited regions of the Balkans, Berisha still wished to be seen to be giving high priority to the national question. As a result he tried to forge strong links with the Kosovar leadership, in particular with the 'Prime Minister' of the Kosova government in exile, Bujar Bukoshi. The defeat of the Democratic Party and the forced resignation of President Berisha in the spring of 1997 had caused dismay amongst the Albanians still living in Yugoslavia. Hitherto, and despite his having previously backtracked on the notion of Kosovar independence, Berisha had presented the world with the possibility of a united pan-Albanian front. The anarchy and violence in Albania, and the election of a government dominated by southern socialists, destroyed that notion. Following Berisha's resignation the Kosovar leadership immediately distanced itself from Fatos Nano's government. The Kosovars were instinctively sceptical about the strength of the commitment of Nano's administration to the national cause. Nano, as well as his political adviser Gramoz Pashko, Foreign Minister Paskal Milo and other prominent officials in the Socialist-led administration, had Orthodox, southern backgrounds and were close to Greek diplomatic circles.

During the 86 years that the Albanians of Kosova and those of Albania had been divided, contact between the two groups had been minimal, except during the Second World War and in the 'thaw' in the late 1970s and early 1980s when Albanians were in control of the communist party in Kosova. Even then, contacts had in the main been confined to approved exchanges by intellectuals and a few specialist workers who worked in Kukes on the hydroelectric schemes. This considerably weakened and hindered the Albanian government's capacity to help broker a solution to the crisis. Albania's attitude towards Kosova during the communist period from 1945 to 1992 had varied according to circumstances and had not always been supportive. Preoccupations with the survival of Albania's ruling elite and Balkan geopolitics often took precedence over concerns about Yugoslavia's Albanian minority. On a few occasions, Kosovar political activists taking refuge in Albania were even said to have been sent back to Kosova into the hands of the Yugoslav secret police. Economic relationships had been grossly exploitative, with the Yugoslavs stripping bare swathes of Albanian beech forest for the Yugoslav furniture industry in the 1950s and 1960s, and securing rock-bottom prices for Albanian mineral ores in the next decade. Albania–Kosova relations had improved significantly with the victory of the Democratic Party and the election of Sali Berisha as President of Albania in 1992.

The Kosova Albanian's deep mistrust of the motives of Fatos Nano's government in relation to the all-important national question had been enhanced by the controversial meeting in Crete between Nano and Yugoslav President Slobodan Milosevic in November 1997. The Kosovars saw as virtual treason the fact that Nano had actually agreed to meet with Milosevic during the Balkans heads of state summit in Crete. Unlike his predecessor, Nano was not concerned about consulting with the Kosovar leadership on matters relating to pan-Albanian political strategy. Although Nano claims he urged Milosevic to reopen dialogue with the Kosova Albanians over educational issues, he must have known that such advice would never have been even remotely heeded by Milosevic. At the Crete summit, Nano had concentrated on issues relating to wider cooperation between the Balkan states as a means for diffusing national tension. He was anxious to improve economic and trade relations with Albania's neighbours, and was therefore unwilling to promote Kosova, other than to state that Kosova was an issue to be addressed by Belgrade and Prishtina. Various statements emanating from the Albanian Foreign Ministry during the First Offensive period, which had labelled the KLA 'terrorists' rather than 'freedom fighters', also angered the Kosovars. Consequently, there was little personal contact between the Albanian government and the official Kosovar leadership. Indeed, instead of the red carpet treatment awarded to such personnel under the Berisha administration, prominent Kosovars visiting Albania now had to make their appointments with government officials through their 'embassy' of the so-called 'Republic of Kosova' in Tirana.

With their limited knowledge of internal events in Albania, the Kosovar Albanians failed to understand that Tirana had other priorities aside from the national question. Albania's economy and infrastructure were shattered, poverty was endemic and the rule of law was still confined to just the capital and a few central districts. The vast majority of Kosovars had little understanding of the events that had led to the overthrow of the Berisha government, or had any knowledge of the complexities of the political situation in Albania at that time. In general, Kosova's Albanians remained convinced that Albanian foreign policy was being dictated by Greece, a regional Orthodox ally of Serbia. Nano's government was seen as being strongly influenced by Athens, and not at all committed to the pan-Albanian national idea that Berisha had attempted to espouse during the very early days of his government. Relations between the Kosovar leadership and the Albanian government thus remained very tense and reserved.

To a large extent, therefore, the Tirana government remained isolated and ignorant of events amongst the divergent elements within Kosova, and par- ticularly of the wealthy and powerful Kosovar diaspora based in Switzerland, the USA, Germany and Belgium, which was greatly influencing the pace of events on the ground in Kosova. Given that the organisational command of the Kosovars and the KLA was in exile amongst the large Kosovar diaspora groups, the Albanian government wielded little influence nor had any ability to attempt to curb funding to the Kosovar militias. In defence of accusations of Tirana's lack of interest in the national question, in his meetings with Kos- ovar leaders Nano repeatedly stressed the very difficult economic and pol- itical situation of the Albanian nation. Those who were actively connected with political debate in Albania were largely preoccupied with problems of internal national reconciliation following the previous year's uprising.

In the meantime, the number of refugees arriving in Albania from Kosova continued to grow. By mid-May the Interior Ministry announced that although 15,000 Kosovars were then estimated to be in Albania, only 9000 had actually registered as refugees in the Albanian border towns of Tropoja, Bajram Curri and Kukes; the majority had filtered southwards to stay with relatives in Shkoder, Tirana, Shijak and Durres. Albania was totally ill-equipped to deal with the refugees. A team of experts from the UNHCR visited the Kukes and Tropoja regions to help prepare contingency plans for a larger influx of refugees. Discussions on various forms of humanitarian relief programmes were hurriedly taking place between government officials and representatives of the relevant non-governmental organisations (NGOs) operating in Albania. Doctors and emergency medical supplies were dispatched to the northern towns of Bajram Curri and Kukes to help prepare for potential casualties, and all but urgent medical operations were suspended in order to conserve blood supplies.

There was a reluctance by some Albanians to accept unrelated Kosovars into their homes due to the widespread, and not unrealistic, belief that amongst the refugees were a certain number of Kosovar-Albanian agents working clandestinely for the Yugoslav Secret Intelligence Service (the UDB-a). On walls in the northern towns one could see graffiti proclaiming 'Death to the agents of UDB-a'. Many southern Albanians were concerned that the Democratic Party was encouraging the settlement of Kosovar refugees in the lowland region in order to alter the political balance in their favour. But when asked, the majority of Kosovars, wherever they had settled in Albania, appeared to want to return home as soon as they were free to do so in safety. The government issued repeated statements of its support for those Kosovars who were genuine refugees, whilst ordering border police to apprehend bogus arrivals, whom the government termed 'Kalashnikov merchants' (i.e. Kosovars who crossed into Albania to purchase arms for the KLA).

Looking at Albania's regional policy at this time we see a paradoxical situation, and one that confirmed many Kosovars' suspicions regarding the true patriotic nature of Fatos Nano's government. At this critical time Albania's relations with her immediate neighbours, Greece and Macedonia, were on a far better footing than those with the Albanians of the former Yugoslavia. The Greek embassy held a stranglehold over Albanian foreign policy in the spring and summer of 1998 (which was dramatically broken by the coup attempt in September and the replacement of Nano by Majko). Relations between Tirana and its Balkan neighbours had significantly improved since Nano's government came to power. The Italian government aid programme was expanded in 1998,[6] and at the end of March 1998

Albania and Macedonia had signed a military cooperation agreement ahead of a scheduled visit by President Meidani to Skopje. A month later Albania and Greece signed a similar agreement on military education within the framework of the Partnership for Peace programme between Albania and NATO. During the discussions then, Nano had reassured the Greek Defence Minister, Tsohatzopoulos, that he had no regard for the KLA, with its ambiguous structure and suspicious financing – a reference to the profits of serious crime that Greek and Serbian propaganda claimed provided the bulk of the KLA's funding. There had been particular cooperation between the defence and interior ministries of Italy, Greece and Serbia in a bid to escalate inter-regional cooperation in matters relating to border security and the fight against the rapid increase in the smuggling of cigarettes, drugs, weapons and illegal migrants.

One of the hottest political issues in the spring of 1998 was smuggling, which had become the Albanian government's Achilles heel in terms of its image with the EU. Smuggling and the resultant corruption were poised to become weapons to threaten political rivals within the government itself. This had eroded the public's confidence in the government. In the June 1997 elections the Socialist Party had won considerable support on its anti-corruption ticket and the public's general reaction against corruption in the Democratic Party's administration. Much of the inflammatory material released to sympathetic journalists by the CIA in the autumn of 1996 about the ills of the Berisha government had been about the 'mafiaisation' of the economy and corruption. In less than a year, however, public confidence in the Socialists' ability to stem corruption had all but evaporated. So much money was to be made from smuggling that it was impossible to curtail the practice. In fact, to a large extent the smuggling was not considered a crime, as cigarettes are a normal, legal commodity. In Balkan eyes, the EU's policy was based on empty moralism, when EU governments were collecting huge sums of money in taxation themselves from rising tobacco duties. If, for example, contraband cigarettes were confiscated by the police, they were simply locked away for a week before being sold in clandestine auctions to 'friends and acquaintances'. The same would apply to confiscated drugs and weapons. Underlying the smuggling crisis was the 'prohibition effect' engendered by the EU's policy of ever-increasing tobacco prices, which provided massive and ever-increasing profits for the smugglers.

From mid-May the state began the partial drafting of the civilian population along its northern border districts of Kukes, Has and Tropoja. Military alarm drills had also been organised amongst the civilian population. In general people responded positively to the draft, but problems had arisen with inaccurate lists of potential recruits. This was due to the migration, since the collapse of communism in 1992, of hundreds of families to the southern lowland areas, and of the estimated 400,000 young men then working abroad. Thus the military lists were inaccurate and local authorities were ordered immediately to draw up new lists – a procedure that was both difficult and time-consuming.

During the period following the killings in Drenica in March until the renewed attacks on Kosovars at the beginning of June, the Albanian press gave equal coverage to events in Kosova, on a par with that of internal affairs. Albanians themselves were still deeply preoccupied with trying to boost their meagre incomes – the average wage was $320 per month – or to find ways of leaving the country to work abroad. This resulted in a largely apathetic attitude not only towards the Kosova crisis but also in regard to internal political developments. Nevertheless, those newspapers supporting the Socialist Party attempted to explain the government's stance on Kosova, i.e. accepting the decisions of the international Contact Group as the best solution to the problem, whilst those supporting the right-wing opposition were predictably scornful of government policy, claiming it to be a betrayal of the national question.

The Socialist daily *Zeri-i-Popullit,* had been careful to explain the government's stance against a change of borders through the use of violence and for the settlement of the Kosova question through peaceful dialogue. In a bid to appease opponents the paper had, however, also tried to equate government policy with support for the national interest. In an editorial it argued that: 'True, mature and determined Albanian patriotism should stand out at these moments. We should work without nationalist charges but with devotion, to accomplish our tasks in defence of our national interests.'[7] Opposition papers concentrated on criticising the government for its feeble stance on Kosova, taking the view that the international community had failed in its hurried and ill-thought-out Kosova policy. The pro-Berisha daily *Albania* stated that the continual deadlines set by the Contact Group were merely offering Milosevic more time to seal Kosova's borders in preparation for further atrocities to be committed against Albanian civilians.[8]

On the whole, however, there was a marked show of restraint by the press, with little jingoism. Even the right-wing nationalist media refrained from inflaming the issue by calling for every true patriot to reach for his gun. In fact, the most strident call to arms came from the independent daily *Koha Jone,* which urged the government to arm the population in the north of the country. 'The Serbs have felt our arms on their backs more than once this century',[9] the paper warned. It went on to criticise the government's manoeuvres of military forces in Kukes and the equipping of hospitals with more beds and medical supplies as an insufficient and cosmetic approach. The daily argued instead for the partial mobilisation, arming and training of the population along the northern border as priority emergency measures that should be adopted.[10] Overall, Fatos Nano was praised by many Albanians for his skilful conducting of negotiations with the Contact Group and NATO over Kosova, and of having helped keep Albania from direct involvement in the conflict. Indeed, *Koha Jone* hailed Nano's request for the deployment of NATO troops on the border with Yugoslavia as part of a well-thought-out policy. The daily reported that using such terms as to prevent 'illegal arms trafficking' or 'the unlawful crossing of the border', to justify the request, implied that NATO troops would be deployed more to get these phenomena under control than to defend the Albanian border against Serbian attack.[11]

By the end of spring 1998, Albania's internal politics and other developments were becoming increasingly overshadowed by events in Kosova and the associated international involvement. The conflict in Kosova was steadily spreading and would soon inevitably involve the entire territory. The Albanian government therefore warned that its policy on Kosova could not remain static. Its previous stance of exercising restraint in the face of escalating violence in Kosova may have gained international approval but it had seriously damaged the Tirana administration's nationalist credentials amongst the Albanians of the former Yugoslavia and their large and influential diaspora. Yet Albania's political elite still remained deeply divided over how to respond diplomatically and materially to the escalating crisis, and support for Fatos Nano was beginning to show signs of weakening – largely because of his low-key approach to the escalating violence in Kosova. The Albanian government's reaction was quickly shifting from initial concerns regarding human rights abuses in Kosova to urgent requests for an increased international military presence in Albania itself.

The deepening crisis in Kosova had highlighted, amongst other things, the acute lack of knowledge about Kosova in Albania, other than historical. In order to address what was acknowledged as totally inadequate specialist information on all aspects relating to the Kosova question, Fatos Nano set up a special advisory group on Kosova, made up of diplomats and specialists on the region. According to its brief, 'the group, which was to be in constant contact with the Foreign Ministry, was to intensively study the situation and to make proposals for Albanian and foreign diplomatic initiatives.' Before long, Foreign Ministry spokesmen claimed the advisory group was effectively providing the relevant ministers with information relating to

Kosova as soon as it was received, and thus enabling a quicker and more informed response by Tirana to events in Kosova. This was just as well because the Albanian government was going to need all the information it could muster, as reports were now coming in of a build-up of Serbian troop reinforcements and heavy armament along the north-eastern border with Tropoja and Kukes, as well as at Lake Shkoder on the border with Montenegro.

PART

IV

THE POLITICAL CRISIS IN ALBANIA

10

Northern Developments – Preparing for a Coup d'État

Kosova in June 1998 had become the scene of a full-scale guerrilla war, which was beginning to have a seriously destabilising effect on the north-eastern border areas of Albania. In these bleak and tough little towns, villages and isolated windy upland farmsteads, all normal life other than agriculture and family care had been overtaken by the demands and sudden opportunities of the Kosova conflict. For most of the twentieth century the region had been one of the most obscure backwaters in mainland Europe, used as a place of exile and punishment by both King Zog and the communists. A year before, all talk in Tropoja's smoky cafés had been of events in Tirana and the armed uprising in the south. Now attention was focused on Kosova.

Rows of tents housing refugees started to sprout up along the bare land near the old Kukes airstrip, which dated from Zogist times. Young men from the Kosovar diaspora turned up at random, travelling east on the Fierza ferry and through the fiords on the Drin River with AKs in their plastic holdalls, ready to risk their lives to fight Serbia in their home villages. The accents of Hamburg and Munich mingled with those of the Bronx. Groups of refugees fled west towards the Adriatic and Europe in the opposite direction on the ferry's return trips towards Shkoder. In particular the Tropoja region, adjacent to western Kosova, was vibrating ominously from the sudden influx of refugees, KLA recruits, gunrunners, journalists, aid workers and criminal opportunists – each group having appeared either as a cause or consequence of the conflict in Kosova. Tropoja, birthplace of former president Sali Berisha and the key staging post for Kosova Albanians travelling to and from Kosova to fight, had been dominated by the KLA for several months. The Kosovar Albanian leadership themselves were becoming acutely aware of the dangers to their cause of the continuing political disunity in Tirana, and on 20 June the journal of the Kosovar Ministry of Defence carried a long article warning of the 'dangers of political egotism' in Tirana, a clear reference to the looming crisis that would dominate the summer in the Albanian capital.[1]

Although Yugoslav troops had refrained from actually advancing onto Albanian territory, the Albanian authorities were nervously anticipating an incursion as the Milosevic regime in Belgrade became increasingly frustrated with the KLA 's ability to flee rapidly over the border and to use Tropoja as a recruitment and training area. In fact many Kosovars could enter Albania with ease quite legally, largely due to former President Sali Berisha, who in a generous pan-Albanian gesture handed out thousands of Albanian passports to his Kosovar supporters between 1992 and 1997. Particularly favoured contacts were given diplomatic passports, most of which were cancelled as a result of British pressure on Fatos Nano's government after coming to power in 1997, but many ordinary KLA guerrillas, armed with their Albanian passports, still had a legal right of abode in Albania.

During the summer and autumn of 1998 there were between 5000 and 10,000 KLA soldiers and supporters in Albania at any one time. The Albanian side of the KLA war machine was run by Ali Ahmeti, the Macedonian-Albanian LPK activist who was to lead the NLA in the 2001 Macedonian conflict. On 16 June Yugoslav army helicopters opened fire on refugee camps on a mountain near the Kosova border with Albania, by the Padesh border crossing post. Inside Kosova the same helicopter gunships attacked four villages in western Kenova, near the border. In response the Albanian Air Force held an exercise, the first since the 1997 uprising shattered the armed forces, and UN Secretary General Kofi Annan commented on 15 June that 'all of you who have been following the last few months in Kosova must begin to wonder if another Bosnia looms on the horizon', and added that 'already the shellings, the ethnic cleansings, the indiscriminate attacks on civilians in the name of "security" are taking place'.[2]

In an ironic response to the Democratic Party attacks on him, Fatos Nano took a car down to the south of the country and toured the high security prison at Bence, near Tepelena, where Berisha had held him, while the television bulletins in Tirana were dominated by speculation that prosecutors were about to rule on DP leader Sali Berisha's future, particularly on his use of the intelligence agencies to shore up his regime the previous year.

The role of the SHIK[3] intelligence service was also a difficult issue for the Nano government. The head of SHIK, Fatos Klosi, was a staunch Nano henchman who came from a southern family with strong Hoxhaist roots. Klosi had, like ex-President Berisha, studied as a post-graduate student in France, and was inevitably accused in the Tirana bars of having unhealthy connections with foreign agencies. This was also an ultra-sensitive subject for Berisha (having been in France on a medical scholarship), who was privately accused by some Socialist leaders of having first ingratiated himself with the West as a result of his exposure of Albanian agents in France.[4] The relationship between the KLA and the Albanian authorities in the developing war context was informal and unquantified. The intelligence service evidently tried to monitor KLA activity as far as possible but, like everything else in Albania at that time the organisation barely functioned and was heavily factionalised along party lines. Some groups of SHIK officers who had been sacked in 1997 had effectively set themselves up as hit squads in the north of the country, and could be hired by foreign government agents to murder KLA activists.

In the aftermath of the controversy about the death of DP leader Azem Hajdari later that summer, SHIK leader Fatos Klosi has been blamed for orchestrating a campaign against the Kosovars, at the behest of foreign interests, and there have been many allegations and conspiracy theories put forward to account for particular events. It is unlikely, given the lack of hard evidence for many allegations, that much will ever be firmly proved but it is nevertheless a fact that some of the most prominent assassinations and murders of key KLA figures that took place that summer bore the mark of professional killings (where the location of the murder victim was probably provided by a trace on his mobile telephone and the information relayed to the assassins). This could not have taken place without the active participation of a NATO country, where NATO technological capacity could be used for the former purpose and the information leaked, probably via Greece, to Serbian agents active in the region.

There is also the known fact of rivalries between different government agencies dealing with Albania and Kosova. In the USA and Britain the 'law and order' agencies such as the FBI and MI5, dependent for intelligence on French-situated and French-oriented Interpol, were believed to have a much more pro-Serb inclination than the British MI6, the CIA, the US State Department or the Pentagon. The new arrivals in the region focused on 'law and order' issues and caused internal tensions.[5] The FBI and MI5 generally saw the KLA as a 'terrorist' organisation and they adopted traditional Serbian perspectives, often as a response to what they saw as pro-KLA attitudes in the other agencies. Whatever the desires of the authorities in Tirana to stay out of any conflict, Albania would inevitable be drawn in as both a supply route for arms and a haven for KLA fighters. There was intense and growing pressure from the diaspora for the Tirana government to do more to help the insurgents. In the USA local Albanian community centres were being taken over for KLA support and fundraising activities, and not only in traditionally militant centres like Kosovar-dominated north Bronx in New York City. In a little town like Waterbury, Connecticut, over $30,000 had been raised in two weeks in June for the 'Homeland Calling' Fund, and speaker after speaker at a meeting held at the local Hasan Prishtina centre criticised the LDK and Rugova in Prishtina, and Nano in Tirana, for blocking military aid to the KLA.[6] On the ground this meant a rapid increase in war-funding capacity.

Local Albanians were regularly crossing into Kosova to sell weapons and ammunition, and KLA fighters were incurring the wrath of the Yugoslav Army by seeking sanctuary over the border in Albania. The cross-border clashes, often including Albanian farmers and shepherds, sparked official protests from Tirana. Yugoslavia, meanwhile, complained that Albania was ignoring the growing weapons markets and KLA training camps, which were springing up in the border districts. This accusation was basically true as Tirana was virtually powerless to intervene in the war-based activities in the northern districts of Tropoja, Puka and Shkoder, which still remained under only nominal state control. The sheer demand for weapons and other supplies in Kosova led to the proliferation of criminal gangs, which presented a severe setback for the government's attempts to promote political and economic development. Within NATO these developments were causing alarm. German Defence Minister Volker Ruehe called on 10 June for new military actions to contain the crisis and attacked the ideas of UN official Carl Bildt, including his call for NATO troops to be stationed on the Albania–Kosova border, as 'pseudo solutions'.[7]

As summer began the presence of heavily armed men in and around the Tropoja region increased. The KLA issued a general call to arms of all able-bodied men through the pages of Veton Surroi's Prishtina newspaper *Koha Ditore*, and called in particular for those who had fled to Albania with their families to return to fight, stating that 'we must all be the KLA. Only that way can we save our people and liberate Kosova with the least sacrifice.' This was reproduced the next day in nearly all Tirana newspapers. The atmosphere in this notoriously violent district had grown brooding and menacing. Groups of men, with Kalashnikovs casually slung over their shoulders, met in front of the main administrative building in Tropoja town, which was next to the warehouse from where humanitarian aid was regularly distributed. They would eye up the aid packages, looking in particular for precious medical supplies that could be sold to the KLA for a hefty profit. Although international NGOs attempted to physically separate the armed groups from the distribution point of humanitarian aid, large quantities still went 'missing', as local distributors sold on as much as they could get their hands on.

For local Albanians the Kosova conflict had come as a welcome economic lifeline, as entrepreneurs made a good living selling weapons, equipment and supplies to the Kosovars. In lawless Bajram Curri the local mafia was in control and would not tolerate anyone – Albanian or foreigner – interfering with their 'business's' profit margins. A foreign doctor working for an international aid agency was forced to leave the town after receiving death threats simply because his pharmacy was cutting into someone's cousin's profits. Although a massive amount of humanitarian aid had been arriving in Bajram Curri, up to 50 per cent was immediately disappearing from warehouses and the backs of lorries, only to reappear for sale in Tirana and other towns further south. In reality, weapons and the Kosova conflict were proving to be the only job providers for local Albanians, and the northern towns were rapidly becoming the rear-front bases of the undeclared war beyond the border. The war acquired an economic momentum of its own, as all wars do – something that was not clearly understood by much of the foreign community in Tirana, let alone outside the country. Although the summer of 1998 was an appallingly difficult time for the KLA from a military point of view, it was also a time when the mechanisms of war support became deeply entrenched in Albania, particularly in northern Albanian society, and this enabled the embattled guerrilla movement to have the flexibility and support structures to survive setbacks and losses.

At the same time it was not only the conflict brewing over the border that was threatening to destabilise the north, as the Democratic Party had had its own motives for intensifying local conflict since the beginning of the year. As the lawlessness and criminality in the north escalated, the government's futile attempts to bring the region under control were being hampered by the lack of cooperation from the opposition. As early as 21 January an armed group, which included several sacked policemen, had rampaged through the town of Shkoder firing automatic weapons and briefly occupied some local government offices. Apparently, they had the support of the local DP branch. Special armed forces were hurried up from Tirana to quell the unrest as the government accused the Shkoder branch of the Democratic Party of supporting efforts by criminal elements to disrupt law and order in the town. The following month trouble-making attendance at a football match in Shkoder in mid-February by the maverick DP deputy and close aide of Berisha, Azem Hajdari, had led to a stand-off between his entourage and the local police. DP activists had continued anti-government protests in the town throughout the spring and early summer.

By the beginning of July the Serb offensive had driven hundreds of rebels across the border into Albania, which resulted in an increase in border clashes. The Albanian government was now actually considering war with Serbia in response to the threat of Yugoslav aggression. Defence Minister Luan Hajdaraga told an Italian newspaper that Albania was considering the possibility of military confrontation with Serbia if the Serbs continued with their 'ethnic cleansing' in Kosova. He said that Albania's military reconstruction was making progress thanks to the support of two regiments from Italy, the training of Albanian commandos by Turkey and several hundred troops from Greece.[8] The minister's confidence regarding a possible confrontation with Serbia was bolstered by the knowledge that NATO was now threatening retaliation against Serbia and that the USA had officially recognised the KLA as guerrilla fighters rather than 'terrorists'.

Since the end of May official statements from both Prime Minister Fatos Nano and the Foreign Ministry had also abandoned the collaborationist term 'terrorist', and were referring instead to the people of Kosova taking up arms in order to defend their lives and property. Tirana now referred to the KLA as a people's movement created as a result of the right of people to defend themselves from aggressors. This turnabout occurred primarily because the Albanian government had had to recognise that the KLA was more than just a motley collection of disaffected Kosovar émigrés, with little support for their 'unrealistic' goal of an independent Kosova. In a televised statement at the beginning of June, Fatos Nano declared his government's acknowledgement of the growing strength and popularity of the KLA, saying 'The people of Kosova have taken up arms in self-defence and their organisational structure is a reality that should not be ignored.'

With the Belgrade government showing no sign of abandoning the use of force, the position of the Albanian government regarding Kosova had to be reviewed and adapted to the new situation unfolding on the ground. There were now reports of Serbian military incursions into Albanian territory. Villages near the border were being shelled. Under such circumstances Albania's already fragile party-political truce was being further undermined. In mid-August Albania complained of a number of border violations whereby Serb troops had fired artillery and small arms fire onto its territory. Around 600 refugees had also crossed the border into Albania on 13 August – the largest number in a single day since the Serb offensive had begun; prior to this an average of 30–50 refugees had been crossing into Albania daily.

In the meantime the Serbs' image of Albania as a rogue state, harbouring not only criminal mafia but also Islamic terrorist elements, had been further enhanced following the bombing of American targets in East Africa in August 1998. Several press reports had linked the explosions with the extradition of four Islamic extremists from Albania a month prior to the attacks. The four, who were wanted in connection with the killing of 58 tourists in Luxor in November 1997, had been working in Egyptian-controlled Islamic NGO charity organisations. Some anti-terrorist agencies had alleged, strongly supported by Belgrade, that some of the many Islamic charitable foundations in Albania were used by terrorists to provide a cover for their activities and their links with other Islamic organisations outside Albania. The militants in question were apprehended by the SHIK with the cooperation of the US CIA, and were escorted aboard a plane at Tirana's Rinas Airport on 2 July. In response, Egypt's banned Jihad group warned that it would retaliate against the USA for its assistance in the extradition. As a result the USA closed its already heavily fortified embassy in Tirana as a precaution against a potential terrorist threat.

The government was quick to deny media accusations that Albania had become a 'hotbed of Islamic intrigue'. Given the then barrage of disinformation emanating from Serbia and Greece about Albania's alleged export of Islamic extremists, Tirana was keen to present the accusations as groundless. This was a legitimate concern in view of the generally very moderate Islamic religious traditions in Albania and the lack of concrete evidence to back up the foreign claims that the Egyptians had had any connection with explosions in Nairobi attributed to Al Qaeda. Most Albanians in the pre-9/11 atmosphere sincerely appreciated the genuinely valuable charitable and aid work of many of the Islamic foundations and NGOs.[9] The head of SHIK, Fatos Klosi, refuted any links between the terrorist acts in Kenya and Tanzania with Islamic Jihad activities in Albania. He admitted, however, that 'there were fundamentalist terrorist elements in Albania but not actual structures as such'.[10] In reality this meant Albania was a convenient bolthole for a few Egyptian militants on the run. According to Klosi, the number of Islamic groups present in Albania had risen substantially after 1997, and some of their members had 'assisted people coming from the Middle East, who went on to commit terrorist acts elsewhere'.[11] In evaluating the substance of Klosi's remarks, it is important to bear in mind the overwhelming degree of Greek (and thus surrogate Serbian) influence within SHIK and other key Tirana government structures in these summer months prior to the coup. In July, Greek Foreign Minister Papoulias spent two days in Tirana and was photographed so frequently in the newspapers that an unitiated visitor from a foreign country or from Mars might have believed that he was the actual leader of Albania rather than Fatos Nano.

Israel was also interested in what was happening in relation to Islam in Albania. At the end of May Klosi had given an interview in Tirana's *Klan* magazine, in which he had attacked Berisha's intelligence chief Bashkim Gazidede who had fled the country after the 1997 uprising, allegedly to Syria. He had been named commander of the armed forces by Berisha for a period during the uprising. Klosi said he had turned SHIK into an 'instrument of violence' against individuals like the old communist Sigurimi.[12] In the Tirana press stories ran the following week blaming Gazidede for taking Albania into the Islamic conference, and stating that he was on the 'watchlist' of the Israeli intelligence agency Mossad because of his links with Islamic organisations.[13]

During these months Greece, and to a degree Israel, were playing the 'Islamic card' in Tirana on behalf of Serbia in a last-ditch effort to keep the Tirana government away from active support of the KLA. Hardline Zionists in Israel and USA were content to back Milosevic against the emergence of what they saw (wrongly) as possibly becoming an 'Islamic' state in an independent Kosova. The 'respectable' argument advanced by Athens was that being drawn into the war would threaten the future of Albania against the overwhelmingly superior Serbian army; the real purpose of the argument was designed to keep the USA and NATO out of its growing involvement with Kosova, and to allow the Yugoslav army to create a 'military' solution there and smash the KLA if it could. In the first week in June NATO had made its first real threat to Kosova with the overflight exercise 'Operation Determined Falcon', and the Greeks and pro-Serb circles in often anti-USA countries like France in NATO saw the danger that NATO involvement represented to Serbian hegemony in Kosova.[14] In reality the NATO operation was a minor PR-inspired stunt, with most aircraft going nowhere near Kosova airspace, but it did have a symbolic importance.[15]

By the end of July Serbian military commanders felt sufficiently emboldened by international community and particularly Contact Group inaction, that the first bombing of Albanian territory took place on 20 July. In response, diaspora activity in support of the KLA was stepped up, and an editorial in the US diaspora community newspaper *Illyria* on 22 July contrasted the behaviour of 'Christian Greece, that stood firmly by Christian Serbia in the Bosnian war', with the Contact Group's 'vicious clamour to cut down on the flow of funds for the Kosova Liberation Army'. In the US Senate a motion was passed calling for Milosevic to be indicted as a war criminal. The scene was being set for a showdown in policy between the USA and Britain, and the Europeans, led by Greece and France. Albanian Foreign Minister Milo responded to the Senate decision with a speech in which he said 'that if efforts to end the bloodshed peacefully failed, Albania would have no choice but to encourage its ethnic kin in Kosova to resist'.[16]

Albania then began an immediate crackdown on the very few Arab and Islamic groups operating in the country, which had been picked as a haven by Islamic extremists for a number of specific reasons. For one, Albania's geographical proximity to the former Yugoslavia meant easier access to the oppressed Muslim minorities fighting Serb oppression in Bosnia and Kosova. Also, because of its impoverished economy and the social chaos resulting from the uprising in 1997, Albania's immigration and law-enforcement controls and its judicial system had been left in tatters, thus providing a safe refuge from foreign law-enforcement agencies.

Although the crackdown was no doubt legitimate in strict anti-terrorist terms, it was also a political godsend to the pro-Greek and anti-Kosovar forces in Tirana, mostly but not exclusively southern Socialists, who were able to try to identify the KLA as an 'Islamic' force, in alliance with 'Islamic' militants in the Democratic Party. It also served to identify Albania in some quarters (particularly in media coverage) in the USA as an 'Islamic' country, and to boost support for Serbia amongst a few people. This crude attempt to drag religion into the Kosovar conflict helped to produce a polarisation in the political atmosphere, and inadvertently assisted the dark forces in the north that were preparing for an attempt to overthrow the coalition government and seize power in the following month.

Meanwhile, the relative progress achieved in domestic politics had gone into reverse mode at the beginning of July when the Democrats resumed their boycott of parliament.[17] The stresses and strains that the deep crisis in Kosova were producing in the nation were causing new political fragmentation and conflict. Although Berisha claimed the decision was in response to a 'wave of terror exerted against the Party',[18] the real reason was to protest at the endorsement by parliament of a report blaming the former Berisha government for instigating the anarchy that had engulfed Albania in the previous spring. The spectre of the conflict of the previous summer had not been laid to rest in Albanian politics. The report published by the Attorney General's Office, entitled 'Berisha and the Events of 1997' accused the former president and other senior Democratic Party officials of having 'violated the constitution, exceeding their authority and using the police and army unlawfully against protesters'.

As the summer progressed, demands in the Albanian press and in Parliament grew for the lifting of Berisha's parliamentary immunity. If his immunity was revoked, Berisha faced the death sentence if convicted on a charge of organising an armed insurrection. Fearing further political instability should the former President be arrested, representatives of the international community warned the government and its coalition allies to be careful in their persecution of Berisha in relation to his role in the previous year's turmoil. The role of Dutch ex-Foreign Minister and OSCE head Daan Everts was crucial in these initiatives. The priority of the OSCE and the international community was to keep Albanian institutions functioning despite the intense stresses the political crisis was putting upon them. Despite intense pressure from the international community to end their parliamentary boycott, the DP demanded a guarantee that Berisha was not going to be arrested in order to return to parliament. If Berisha were imprisoned, Albania would once more have a jailed opposition leader, and would thus have returned to the cycle of politically motivated revenge. For the government it was a difficult decision. If the former President was arrested, there was a risk of a possible uprising in northern Albania. If however Berisha and others went untried, this would send the message that any politicians could do anything whilst in power because when they found themselves in opposition they would not face any charges for fear of causing civil unrest. In the view of some observers, perhaps the only solution would have been to try Berisha in an international court.

Although Berisha himself may have escaped trial, others were not so lucky. The arrest on 22 August of several senior ministers and officials from the previous Democratic Party government for 'crimes against humanity' before and during the 1997 uprising greatly enflamed the situation. Those arrested included the former Defence Minister Safet Zhulali, Interior Minister Halit Shamata, Deputy Chairman of the Intelligence Service Bujar Rama, the Vlora Police Chief, Sokol Mulosmani, and the Chief of the State Audit, Blerim Cela. The Democratic Party's National Council issued a statement saying the arrests of the former officials were 'an act of personal revenge by Fatos Nano, in an effort to scare, attack and liquidate the political opposition in Albania'. Cela, who faced charges of supplying weapons to DP supporters in the southern town of Tepelena in March 1997 had initiated the investigation into corruption charges against Fatos Nano in 1992 for which the Socialist leader was sentenced to 11 years imprisonment (of which he served four).

The court ruling that the former officials should stay in prison indefinitely dashed any hopes of the Democrats returning to parliament or the talks on a new constitution. In fact, any meaningful dialogue between Albania's two main political factions had now totally evaporated. This seriously jeopardised the crucial constitutional reform process, although a new constitution was an essential precondition for the rebuilding of political stability in Albania. The country had remained without a constitution since 1991, when the first multi-party parliament abrogated the old communist constitution and approved a package of provisional constitutional laws to govern the country. A draft constitution proposed by the Democratic Party had failed in a popular referendum in 1994 following a successful campaign by the then opposition parties against the draft, which was presumed to give too much power to the then president, Sali Berisha.

The arrests plunged the country into the worst political crisis since the wounding of the Democratic Party MP Azem Hajdari by a Socialist MP inside the parliament building the previous September. Democratic Party supporters saw the measures as an attack on the legitimacy of the remaining DP influence within the security apparatus and the military. Although Zhulali had become a fierce critic of Berisha, whom he accused of trying to have him killed before he fled the country at the height of the 1997 uprising, the Democratic Party reacted to his arrest by threatening to topple Nano's government by force.[19] The DP dailies reiterated their appeals for the ousting of Nano, highlighting threats of the return of a neo-communist dictatorship in Albania and issuing calls to prevent it.

When news of the arrests spread, thousands of DP supporters staged a demonstration in the capital's main Skanderbeg Square. There Berisha made an aggressive speech, saying the arrests were 'a political act aimed at eliminating the opposition', and describing Fatos Nano as a 'criminal' and a 'drug addict' – a reference to the SP leader's then chronic smoking and drinking habits. He and other DP leaders then called for the overthrow of the Socialist-led government, which was the 'source of all the misfortunes in the country during the past year'.

The arrest of such prominent opposition figures was a bold move by such a weak and inefficient government. The team in power in Tirana would never have had the confidence to take such action without having had the endorsement of Western allies. Ever since the violence in Shkoder in January, it had become widely believed that the Democratic Party was trying its utmost to destabilise the country. For the West, the possibility of Albania once again imploding into anarchy was to be avoided at all costs. The situation in Kosova was now dangerously near to developing into open conflict, and this threatened the stability of the entire southern Balkans. Therefore, the stability of Albania was vital if NATO and the West were going to confront Belgrade.

Three days after the arrests, a worried-looking Fatos Nano made an address to the nation on Albanian state television to refute allegations that he had masterminded the arrest of the group of officials. Citing his own bitter experience of being arrested solely for political motives, Nano claimed that:

As a former prisoner convicted as a result of a farcical trial just because I represented the opposite political opinion to [the then president] Sali Berisha, I know better that anyone what it means to be a victim of the judiciary's dependence upon political basis. That bitter experience is for me irrefutable evidence of the blindness of political revenge.

The following day in an interview with *Voice of America*, Berisha claimed that the 'Democratic Party was facing the challenge either to accept the re-establishment of a dictatorship by a mafia clique, or to accept sublime sacrifices and save Albanian democracy.' On 27 August the Democrats defied a police ban and held another rally in Skanderbeg Square. To the baying crowd Azem Hajdari bitterly denounced Fatos Nano. 'Albanians, you are being governed by a master criminal', Hajdari told the crowd, which joined him in chanting: 'Let's get rid of him.' The demonstration climaxed with skirmishes between DP supporters and police in front of Nano's home. By now the Premier was clearly far from fully being in control of developments. His cabinet, fraught with disagreements, appeared barely to function. Nano was reduced to performing something of a balancing act between the international community, including NATO, and the north of the country, which was out of his control.

In the weeks following the arrest of the six former DP officials, various acts of sabotage occurred throughout the country. On 2 September a bomb attack demolished walls at the office of the Socialist Party in Lezha, 70km north of Tirana. There were several attacks on electricity sub-stations, which produced widespread disruption in the capital and the south of the country, and, together with a campaign of small terrorist bombings against politicians of Greek ethnic origin, were clearly designed to destabilise the country. The now daily opposition demonstrations were putting an even bigger strain on the police, who were already stretched by the fallout from the Kosova crisis and efforts to track down Islamic militants. Many Berisha supporters had memories of how Greek inputs, although unofficial, had been instrumental in destabilising 'their' government only a year or so earlier in the key weeks of March 1997, and saw the power struggle in Tirana as an opportunity to settle scores with local ethnic Greeks. They perhaps forgot, conveniently, how much of a privileged position Berisha had created for the Greek speakers in the land privatisation process in the first place.

The ongoing escalation of political tension in Albania witnessed the demands of the independent media that the Democratic Party be outlawed. The daily *Shekulli* argued that the DP, which Berisha had 'converted into a terrorist gang', had gone way beyond the limits of the law. The paper warned that Albania should not be left hostage to the DP, and that the judicial institutions had to act hastily to stay the DP Chairman's hand to stabilise the country, otherwise there would be a repeat of March 1997.[20] Another daily, *Koha Jone*, called openly for the DP to be outlawed,[21] whilst the Socialist Party paper *Zeri-i-Popullit* said that Berisha and Hajdari were inciting people to take up arms in a call for civil war.[22]

The security situation appeared to be deteriorating rapidly as violence in the north spread. Interior Minister Neritan Ceka was fighting against the odds to establish rudimentary security in the north – partly because of entrenched corruption at ministerial level and throughout the administration. There was thus a real possibility that an armed insurrection could spread from the north. Intelligence service sources had information that some form of coup to topple the government by force was actually being prepared. There were reports of the existence of a so-called 'Liberation Anti-Communist Army' in Shkoder, which was recruiting and training a pro-democrat force of around 500 men in preparation for an assault against Tirana. According to intelligence sources the armed operation was expected to begin in mid-September. The anticipated scenario was as follows: several hundred armed men would leave Shkoder en route for Tirana. They would be joined by other forces, mainly from the districts of Tropoja, Kurbin, Kruja and the newly settled Democratic Party strongholds in the suburbs of Tirana.

In order to prevent any reaction from the south, other forces would be activated in the southern DP stronghold of Kavaja, whilst the main road south into Greece would be blocked by the maverick and fiercely pro-Berisha village of Llazarati on the outskirts of Gjirokaster.[23] Llazarati had not been under any form of government control since March 1997, and had effectively established an armed and well-organised DP mini-state to the south of Gjirokaster. The main goal of these groups would be their occupation of the major state institutions in Tirana and the overthrow of the Nano government. The armed operations would culminate in a huge rally in Tirana's main Skanderbeg Square.

Presumably the organisers of the coup hoped to create the impression, for the benefit of international observers, of a popular uprising against the threat of a new neo-communist dictatorship. Interior Minister Neritan Ceka's claim that the Yugoslav security service was behind the plan has not been substantiated, although it was not a wholly unrealistic scenario; the military and police crackdown in Kosova during the spring and early summer could have been connected. In the context of the overall advancement of the Albanian national question, there was no doubt that the Democratic Party should have submerged its grievances against the coalition, legitimate and illegitimate, until the future of Kosova was secure. Instead, its leadership allowed internal and external forces to manipulate it in an irresponsible and anti-national activity.

In Kosova, the KLA were fighting with their backs to the wall in many difficult theatres of the war, and were increasingly able to recruit soldiers from many different backgrounds and political orientations. However, in northern Albania sectarian and personal feuds still overrode the wider national interest. The growing anti-government disturbances were not confined to the north. On 1 September gangs from the village of Llazarati blocked the country's main north–south road to Greece for an entire day, injuring six policemen in violent skirmishes. The same gangs had already blocked the road between Saranda and Gjirokaster twice that year. Hundreds of special police were sent to the heavily fortified village to search for the gunmen. But although the police had regained control of the road, they had been driven back by blistering fire from the gangs during two attempts to enter the village. All police units were subsequently withdrawn to the nearby town of Gjirokaster, whose Police Chief, Islam Qibini, resigned as a consequence.

As the political situation deteriorated, Berisha was becoming increasingly hard-line, and contemptuous of public or international opinion. On 9 September Berisha spoke at a rally of around 3000 supporters in Tirana, where he threatened to use force against the government. Renewing his call for the six DP officials to be freed, he warned that the SP leader could meet the same fate as the Romanian dictator Nicolae Ceauşescu.[24] Berisha told his cheering supporters 'We shall crush Nano into powder, force will know no bounds.' Within days an attempt at this prophecy would be put into action. In essence the crisis days of June and July had been much more dangerous for the Albanian nation than many outside observers realised at the time, and without the growing presence of NATO there had been, in hindsight, the real possibility of a major Serbian attack in the north. There was no linkage between the remaining patriotic forces in the army and the security apparatus, and in society in general, to slow or stop the fragmentation process.

This was also reflected on the Kosova side of the conflict, with the emergence in early June of the new military force in Tropoja controlled by LDK 'Prime Minister' of Kosova, Bujar Bukoshi – the so-called 'FARK' army (the National Army of Kosova) of his shadow Defence Ministry of Kosova. Although never numbering more than a few hundred men, and in military terms never a match for the commitment or organisational capacity of the KLA, it represented a new destabilising paramilitary force of the Right in the northern borderlands. It provided a new story for the media, which in turn emphasised the growing confusion and danger in the general regional situation.[25] By the end of August 1998 the international community was faced with the real possibility of a repeat scenario of the chaos of 1997, only spreading over the entire region, which in turn would threaten the stability of former Yugoslav Macedonia and threaten a wider regional war.

11

The Assassination of Azem Hajdari and the Attempted Coup

In the stifling heat of the first week in September, the political climate in Tirana was becoming increasingly tense. The city seemed to be at the centre of the whirlpool of a vast and all-encompassing geopolitical crisis as the Kosova conflict developed. The recent rumours of a possible attempt by forces loyal to Sali Berisha to topple the government had created an electric atmosphere in the capital. The security forces were put on high alert as hooded police patrolled the curfew-imposed streets whilst everyone anxiously waited for something to happen. They did not have to wait long.

On the evening of Saturday 12 September 1998, opposition leader Azem Hajdari, 35, one of Albania's most popular politicians, was shot and killed as he left the Democratic Party HQ in Tirana.[1] He was fired upon by gunmen in a car parked in front of the DP building and a bodyguard was also killed. Hajdari, the darling of the Albanian Right, had led the Tirana students in the uprising against the country's communist rulers in 1990. Like Berisha, he was from the northern district of Tropoja and had been a candidate for leader of the Democrats in 1991, but a US-engineered coup in the party brought Berisha to power instead. Hajdari, who was described by one observer as 'a young, portly, uncouth loudmouth',[2] knew he was living on borrowed time after surviving several attacks, including an assassination attempt in parliament the previous September.

No proper investigation of the crime scene was possible because, just minutes after the killings the corpses of Hajdari and his bodyguard were transported to hospital without being examined. No official autopsy or examination was made on Hajdari's body, and investigators were unable to

6. The site of the assassination of Azem Hajdari, Tirana, September 1998

acquire any of his personal belongings at the time of the killing. His bloody clothes and personal documents, as well as his mobile phone, were removed before the police arrived at the scene. Hajdari had reportedly received his final phone call just minutes before his murder, which made him come out of his office into the street. His mobile phone has never been found. In a compelling piece of evidence of foreknowledge of the assassination, the Democratic Party HQ had a press release, in very good English, issued about the murder within 20 minutes of its occurrence.[3] According to one observer, an official DP announcement of Hajdari's death arrived at the OSCE office in Tirana, via fax, within an hour of his death. Not only was the fax well written, but also it was very detailed, accusing specific people of a role in the killing. The fax appeared unusually crafted for such an incident on a Saturday night. DP faxes during business hours rarely matched this one for clarity and precision, and a number of people speculated that this fax could have been prepared in advance – for what end, nobody was sure.[4]

As word spread of the assassination, the nation's shock turned to anxiety. Foremost on everyone's mind was what political capital Berisha would make from the murder of a man whom most people believed he personally loathed, but was now more than useful as a martyr, 'sacrificed for democracy'. Crowds gathered throughout the night at the DP headquarters where early the following morning a hastily arranged press conference was held. There in front of the growing crowds, an ashen-faced Sali Berisha blamed Prime Minister Fatos Nano for Hajdari's murder, and warned him to resign within 24 hours or face 'catastrophic consequences'. The opposition media was also quick to apportion blame for the killing of the popular opposition leader squarely on the shoulders of the Prime Minister. The inflammatory headlines of the pro-DP daily *Albania* screamed 'Nano killed Azem Hajdari'.[5] Government supporters, however, were convinced that Berisha himself had engineered Hajdari's death, in order to create a martyr and thereby get popular support for his attempt at a return to power through a popular uprising. In a television interview earlier the same day, a clearly anxious Nano appealed to Albanians not to let his opponents seize power by force.

Berisha was certainly implicated in the events of 12 September by one of the three men later suspected of killing Hajdari – a police chief, Jaho Salihi (Mulosmani), also from Tropoja (Hajdari's district of origin). In May 2001 Salihi confessed to the court to having murdered Hajdari. However, just two months later he told the court that although he had assisted in the murder, Hajdari was actually shot by Fatmir Haklaj, who was not only Tropoja's Police Chief but also the head of the town's criminal world. Hajdari had been heavily involved in the shady business of selling weapons to the KLA, which had based itself in Tropoja. This was such a lucrative business that numerous blood feuds had been activated as a result of the fierce competition amongst the weapons dealers.

Whether Berisha directly or indirectly had a hand in Hajdari's death is but one as yet unproven allegation. The same is true of the DP's reverse allegations against Fatos Nano. There is also a possibility Hajdari was shot by a faction within the KLA, which had a bitter dispute with him over gunrunning to Kosova. As the MP for his own Tropoja district, Hajdari had been well placed to get involved in the arms business. Alternatively, he may have been killed by any one of his many sworn enemies. In fact, it is surprising that Hajdari lived as long as he did. This was at least the third attempt on his life. The first attempt to kill him was in 1996, on the Fierze Ferry when a fellow passenger – reputed to be senior DP official Vili Minaroli – borrowed Hajdari's distinctive white coat and was subsequently shot at from the banks of the river. The second attempt occurred inside the parliament building on 18 September 1997 when, during a heated argument, Hajdari had put the head of a Socialist deputy, Gafur Mazreku, between his legs. This was such an insult witnessed by so many people that Mazreku was forced to take revenge to restore his honour. He therefore shot and seriously wounded Hajdari inside parliament. Shortly after this incident more than 150 bullets hit a motorcade in which Hajdari was travelling.

Meanwhile, following Berisha's ultimatum for Nano to resign, around 2000 of his followers marched on the parliament buildling, chanting 'kill

Fatos Nano', firing pistols in the air and pelting the building with stones. The crowd forced its way inside where Nano and his cabinet were holding an emergency meeting, and traded pistol shots with the guards before setting fire to the ground floor. Ministers fled in panic through a side exit amidst explosions of the petrol tanks of cars the protester's had set on fire. Armed men then looted the Prime Minister's office and residence, as carloads of heavily armed opposition supporters, waving national flags, raced through the streets. OSCE Ambassador Everts, US Ambassador Lino and Italian Ambassador Spataforo were then meeting with Fatos Nano and other senior officials to discuss the crisis.

The next day witnessed even more violence, following the funeral of Azem Hajdari, his bodyguard and a protester who had been killed in Sunday's rioting. During the funeral, Berisha repeated allegations that Nano was responsible for Hajdari's death and called for a 'day of peace' to honour the charismatic former student leader. This contradictory rhetoric only served to inflame the situation. After the funeral ceremony, hundreds of anti-government demonstrators carried the coffins along the capital's main street to the Prime Minister's office (which had been attacked and set on fire during Sunday's rioting). Fierce fighting began as the crowd tried to bring the three coffins inside the Premier's office. The mob literally pounded the coffins against the doors, which gave way as looting began and all hell broke loose. Later DP officials claimed that this was in response to shots fired from the PM's office, but OSCE's Deputy Chief of Mission Tim Isles was an eye witness standing across the main boulevard with an unobstructed view, and he reported that there was no evidence of such shooting.[6] Grenades were also thrown into the building. After an intense exchange of fire, the crowd moved off in the direction of Nano's nearby residence. Tanks and armoured personnel carriers appeared on the streets, and a couple were quickly seized by the gun-toting mob. One group of protesters stormed the state-run television studios, sending the staff fleeing. Viewers then saw an unidentified man on their screens announcing, 'We have taken over.' He then urged people to wait patiently until the government resigned.

The situation deteriorated rapidly as the government appeared to be losing control of the capital. By mid-afternoon, thousands of people were milling about in Skanderbeg Square, randomly firing weapons in the air and looting shops (which had closed for Hajdari's funeral). Looters brazenly pulled up cars to the Ministry of Justice and began loading furniture, carpets and computer equipment. At this point, according to one observer, OSCE Ambassador Everts decided to reach out to all the major leaders to get a temperature reading. He called Kastriot Islami, President Meidani and Sali Berisha – Premier Nano was nowhere to be found. Islami was totally panicked and asked the Ambassador what he should do; President Meidani was concerned but much calmer, and he expressed reservations about negotiating with Berisha. Everts then reached Gramoz Pashko, who was barricaded in the Interior Ministry. According to Pashko, he and the Interior Minister Perikli Teta had around 100 armed men, and they intended to kill every protestor who tried to enter the building. Pashko said he wanted Ambassador Everts to get a message to the protestors, that they had better pull back immediately from the building or his men would open fire. Everts then placed two calls. First he got Islami on the line, and then, with Islami listening in, he called Genc Pollo.[7] Everts then asked Pollo to get the protestors to pull back from the building. Pollo said he would try, but 'popular uprisings' were hard to control. Ambassador Everts responded with anger that 'This is an armed confrontation that must stop. Negotiations cannot take place under these circumstances.' Shortly thereafter, the protestors miraculously pulled back from in front of the Ministry.[8]

Amid the chaos, several of Berisha's supporters were killed and 14 were wounded in the counter-attack. Berisha himself remained holed up at the DP headquarters in Tirana until late on Monday night. To the consternation of the government and Tirana's international community, Fatos Nano's whereabouts were unknown. To the disbelief of all, the Premier had switched off his mobile phone and simply disappeared. Nano had been taken totally by surprise when the DP mob stormed his office, and had fled the building and was driven to Macedonia where he went to ground for several days, leaving President Rexhep Meidani to hold the fort. Meidani, in his capacity as Commander-in-Chief of the armed forces, and in the absence of Nano, had called in the special forces to put Berisha's motley army to rout and to seal arterial roads into the capital. By late evening government forces had regained control of the key installations seized by Berisha's supporters during a chaotic day of violence. President Meidani issued a televised statement to the nation calling for calm and for the police to find Hajdari's assassins as quickly as possible, whilst the Interior Ministry announced a $200,000 reward for information leading to the arrest of the killers.

By 16 September the situation had calmed considerably. The government had regained control of the city centre, having faced down armed supporters of Berisha who had been guarding the DP headquarters with Kalashnikovs and two tanks taken from army troops on Monday. Both tanks had been surrendered without a fight late on Tuesday, as Berisha's gunmen melted away from the DP building before a dawn deadline to leave it. Special forces were then poised to storm the DP headquarters to arrest Berisha, fearing he would try to leave the country. But the DP leader told CNN-International that he 'would never leave Albania'. The final death toll in three days of violence was eight dead and nearly one hundred injured.

The unrest, which had plunged Albania into its second major crisis in just 18 months, caused serious alarm in international circles. Envoys from the USA and the EU issued a joint statement deploring the violence and hinted that they might cut off economic aid if the government fell. NATO Secretary General Javier Solana commented that all sides should return, throughout the country, to peace and stability. Besides concern over the stability of Albania itself, NATO was worried that a further breakdown of law and order in the politically weak republic could aggravate the worsening conflict in Kosova. Neighbouring Greece was fearful of a possible spread of violence to the south of Albania, and consequently Greek border posts were put on high alert. During the violence Berisha's supporters had burnt down three Greek banks, including the National Bank of Greece.

The next few days saw security tightened in Tirana as police special forces wearing black balaclavas set up armed roadblocks to search any vehicle heading towards the capital. On 17 September Parliament rushed through a law transferring the military police and commando units from the control of the army directly to the Interior Ministry. The decision gave the government the ability to maintain order without calling in the army. Despite such moves, the government remained insecure and nervous. In an attempt to ensure support amongst the police, a beleaguered Premier Nano hastily doubled their salaries. Nano, having returned from his panic trip to Macedonia, put the blame for the violence squarely on Sali Berisha, calling him the 'chief organiser of the attempted coup d'état'.[9] Berisha, however, remained defiant, describing the accusations as 'ridiculous', saying the unrest had been 'provoked' by the intelligence service, the SHIK. He called Nano a 'Leninist terrorist' and demanded that he resign in favour of a 'technical government' to arrange new elections.[10] In the days that followed, a hard core of around 1000 supporters joined Berisha in regular street protests. To the jeering and whistling of onlookers, Berisha led his rent-a-mob provocatively through central Tirana, chanting 'Death to Nano – death to Communism'.

Hajdari's murder was the culmination of a year of political polarisation and a long-running campaign by the Democratic Party (DP) to undermine the government and to block moves to introduce and agree upon a new constitution. Indeed, ever since the Socialist-led government had come to power the previous year, the DP had, in essence, been holding the government hostage. Despite calls from Nano and the international community for the Democratic Party to assist in the general reconstruction of the country, there had

been virtually no functioning parliamentary opposition. Apart from organising street protests, the DP had boycotted almost all parliamentary institutions, claiming that the government was illegal because it was born out of 'illegitimate elections' supported by 'communist-led mafia gangs'. Berisha liked
to describe Nano and the government as 'the Red Pashas and Blockmen', in
many speeches, aiming a jibe at Nano's elevation to the top of the old Party of
Labour before 1990 under the patronage of very hard-line communists.

As a result of the unrest, and despite its successful suppression, the already
weak Socialist-led coalition was thrown into a state of turmoil. With daily
attacks on government personnel and the killings and arrests of opposition
supporters, a climate of fear and uncertainty gripped the country. Albania
was once again locked in a state of limbo, with complete paralysis of
parliamentary institutions and the scaling down of international aid projects
as foreign personnel refused to return to Albania until the situation had
stabilised. The Democratic Party rallies continued to be held every day in
Skanderbeg Square, with Berisha bellowing into a microphone, intoning
the late Hajdari's name over and over again in a desperate attempt to whip
up enthusiasm amongst the hired rabble that constituted a substantial
proportion of his crowd of supporters. His exploitation of the assassination
of Hajdari was disingenuous in the extreme.

Hajdari's murder had created the opportunity for Berisha to set in motion
what he hoped would have been a popular armed insurrection that would
catapult him back into the presidency and the government. Berisha had been
dismayed at the speed with which his opponents in the south of Albania had
mobilised in March 1997. In essence, he was thus trying to recreate a similar
popular uprising based in the north. Yet the predicted revolt against the
government did not happen. The Albanian people were exhausted and weary
of the endless chaos and violence of street politics. Berisha's call for a nationwide revolt failed to strike a chord with a weary and frightened population.
The ex-President, whose support base was relatively small and ideologically
fickle, had made a grave miscalculation by imagining that enough people
around the country would back him to have him catapulted back into
power. Even in the 1997 elections the majority of voters in his home district
of Tropoja had voted for the Socialist Party, albeit in the hope of getting back
the money they lost in the pyramid collapse rather than through admiration
for Nano or his Socialist Party. The fact that the mayhem in Tirana was not
copied in other towns around the country – not even in traditional hotbeds
of anti-Socialist dissent such as Kavaje or Llazarati – proved Berisha's overall
lack of majority support in the country, as the polls had shown in the June
elections.

Immediately following Hajdari's death, Berisha's support had temporarily grown as people demonstrated their anger at the attack on such a popular figure. Nevertheless, apart from a few hundred people in Tirana, including his gun-toting, die-hard supporters and unofficial bodyguards, there was almost no sign of support. In the frequent anti-government demonstrations before the crisis of September 1998 Berisha had never been able to muster more than 3000 people. This rent-a-mob had largely represented a loose alliance of thugs and former SHIK personnel, who were implicated in various criminal activities, and faced an uncertain future should they disassociate themselves from the 'protection' of their former president. The Albanian people generally had no stomach for a repeat of the previous year's violence; their overriding attention was focused on finding means for survival amidst the country's continued economic ruin. The coup attempt had been a predictable farce, which left much of the population traumatised and further alienated from politics and the democratic process. Although this translated into chronic apathy towards the political process (an unhealthy development in such an immature democracy as Albania), it also meant that there was very little appetite for yet another popular uprising. In all probability, the only event that could have provoked further instability would have been the arrest of Berisha. Nano was intelligent enough to avoid this course of action.

The government was now nonetheless tightening the noose on Berisha by threatening him with legal action for attempting to overthrow the government. A parliamentary committee had voted to strip the former president of his political immunity, thus paving the way for the government to charge him with organising an armed uprising. Given the volatility of the situation, however, it was hard to see how arresting Berisha would do anything other than fuel a further escalation of the crisis. There was strong pressure from the international community not to arrest Berisha for fear of provoking his followers into causing more unrest, which in turn could further destabilise an already volatile region.

Eventually foreign pressure, most notably exerted by the EU troika (of Austria, Italy and Greece), which visited Tirana shortly after the coup attempt, saw to it that Berisha was not arrested. If he had been arrested, however, the chances of him turning into a martyr figure would not have been that high judging by the lack of support he had nationally. As it was, Berisha was allowed to get away with the attempted coup but in the process had managed successfully to discredit himself and his party, which had degenerated into a rabble. In an attempt to rescue the credibility of the opposition, 12 right-wing parties and several nationalist and anti-communist associations formed a 'Dictatorship Refusal Front' against the government.

At the same time, the government was also coming under pressure from the Left. The newly reformed Communist Party was also ready to join the anti-government fray.[11]

Unfortunately, the crisis in Tirana had deflected attention away from the deteriorating situation in Kosova and in particular from the recent wave of refugees from Kosova that were arriving in the northern town of Shkoder following their expulsion from Montenegro. On 12 September Montenegro had closed its borders to ethnic Albanians fleeing the fighting in Kosova, and sent some 3000 refugees across the border into Albania. By then Montenegro had around 45,000 refugees from Kosova, but officials said that no more could be admitted because reception facilities were severely overstretched. However, facilities (apart from family accommodation) for the refugees in Albania were virtually non-existent, and as winter was fast approaching the humanitarian situation was becoming critical.

The latest bout of unrest in Tirana had compounded the government's lack of control in the north of Albania, which had now become the main staging area for the Kosova conflict. Amongst those benefiting from the Albanian government's further loss of border control were increasing numbers of Albanians profiting from the growing illicit border trade in the sale of weapons, ammunition, equipment and medical supplies to the KLA. Many were senior officials from the north of the country, utilising the all-important extended family structures straddling the border between northern Albania and Kosova. The turmoil in Tirana had concentrated internal police and military attention on protecting the capital and its surroundings, leaving local weapons dealers and the KLA greater room to freely manoeuvre in the north.

In the meantime, investigations were continuing into finding those responsible for the coup attempt. There were growing allegations of Kosovar Albanian involvement in Albania's internal political crisis. In early June another ethnic Albanian guerrilla force, which like the KLA advocated independence for Kosova, at least theoretically, had emerged in northern Albania. The new paramilitary group, known as the Armed Forces of the Republic of Kosova, or FARK, was controlled by Bujar Bukoshi, the LDK's 'Prime Minister'-in-exile of the Kosovar Albanians' parallel government. FARK had an antagonistic relationship with the much larger KLA, and friction between the two groups was substantial. Although never numbering more than a few hundred soldiers, and in military terms never a match for the commitment or organisational capacity of the KLA, FARK represented a new destabilising paramilitary force of the Right operating in the northern borderlands. It provided a new story for the world's media, which in turn emphasised the growing confusion and danger in the general regional situation.[12]

Bujar Bukoshi, who was based in Germany and had been a strong supporter of Sali Berisha, was responsible for raising funds to finance the parallel government and to fund its 'armed forces'. FARK was led by former ethnic Albanian Yugoslav officers who had fought against the Serbs as volunteers in Bosnia. These men were far more knowledgeable about contemporary Yugoslav military tactics than the older Yugoslav Army officers from the Kosovar diaspora, who were prominent in the KLA but were more idealistic than realistic in the eyes of FARK. In contrast, as far as the KLA were concerned, FARK had a dubious commitment to fighting the Serbs and was content to settle for greater autonomy rather than full independence for Kosova.

The existence of two ethnic Albanian armies presented several difficulties on the ground. If FARK were to have grown, it would have become impossible to determine who was responsible for military actions. The emergence of a second ethnic Albanian army based in northern Albania also seriously endangered the territorial integrity of Albania. Since both groups were by necessity forced to launch most of their offensives from the country's northern border there was an increased risk of direct military intervention in Albania by Belgrade's forces. Also, the allegations that FARK members had played a role (if small) in the armed uprising was a worrying indication of an inter-ethnic Albanian conflict that could be conducted on Albanian soil. Berisha seems, unwisely, to have relied on support from FARK for manpower in his attempt to overthrow the government. Certain FARK commanders had promised Berisha 400 armed supporters to help him seize power in Tirana. In the event, only 180 or so turned up and they vanished as soon as it became clear that the coup attempt had failed. Two of Bukoshi's men, both Kosovar Albanians, had been among those arrested when security forces recaptured Tirana's state-run television station from anti-government protesters. Other supporters of Bukoshi quickly went into hiding in Tirana, Durres and Shijak.

The following week a leading Socialist MP publicly claimed that Kosovar leaders were involved in the failed coup attempt by supplying Democratic Party supporters with weapons. According to Spartak Braho, then chairman of the mandates and immunities committee, 'some Kosovo leaders such as Bujar Bukoshi were involved in the coup.' Braho accused Bukoshi's government-in-exile in Germany of supplying Berisha's DP with 'armed men who were given specific tasks to undertake during the coup attempt'.[13] On 21 September police arrested 11 Kosovars, who claimed to be KLA but were in fact members of FARK, for illegal possession of weapons. They were arrested whilst travelling from Tropoja to Tirana. In a further dramatic development on the same day, the chief commander of FARK, Ahmet Krasniqi, was shot and killed by two masked gunmen in Tirana. Two high-profile assassinations in the capital within nine days suggested to many that the country was now in danger of a 'wave of political assassinations'.[14]

Although no person has so far been arrested for the killing of Krasniqi, the incident served to focus attention on the activities of Kosovars involved in the war in Kosova who were coordinating their activities increasingly from Tirana. As with the death of Hajdari, there were numerous theories as to who killed Krasniqi. Democrats were insistent that the FARK commander, who was residing temporarily in Tirana, was assassinated by the Albanian intelligence service, the SHIK, possibly in collaboration with the UDB-a. Suspicions had been aroused a few hours after Krasniqi's death, when it was discovered that a branch of SHIK had ransacked his house the night before his assassination. The arrival of four police vehicles immediately after the killing also raised suspicions. Socialists, on the other hand, tended to dismiss allegations of the involvement of SHIK, but admitted that it was most probably some foreign intelligence service. At this time ordinary Albanians were unaware of the extent of the bitter rivalries between the various Kosovar Albanian factions and were convinced that the 'Great Powers' were behind all major events connected with Kosova.

The murder of Ahmed Krasniqi had given an added impetus to the hunt for the main organisers of the armed rebellion. On 24 September police arrested the leader of the small monarchist Legality Movement Party, Ekrem Spahia, and two other former military officials: Sali Shehu, a former senior police official, and Fatos Hoxha, the ex-commander of the army commando unit. The three were charged with organising and participating in the armed uprising. Spahia was one of three people who had appeared live on Albanian television to announce the alleged fall of the government following the takeover of the Prime Minister's office, parliament and the radio and television stations on 14 September. The retired senior officers had also been supported by some elements in the Albanian National Guard and the Ministries of Public Order and Defence.

In the meantime there had been great pressure on Fatos Nano either to reshuffle his cabinet, as one way of strengthening the government's efforts to get to grips with the consequences of the unrest, or to step down. Western diplomats were also urging Nano to act swiftly to restore security in the north of the country. On 24 September Nano told a meeting of the Socialist Party Steering Committee that he did not intend to resign before the year 2001. However, the immense efforts of Nano to hold onto political and institutional power were put to the test the following day when parliament discussed an anti-crisis package that included the issue of fundamental changes in government, governmental structures and style of governance. Unexpectedly, Nano easily obtained a full mandate from the Steering Committee to form a new government. Paradoxically, he appeared to have reinforced his position at a time when he had lost much credibility in the international arena because of his sluggishness in combating the country's rampant corruption. The economy was beginning to revive, and substantial patronage money was available within Nano's and his friends' party networks. Nano's purely political reputation had waned even within the ranks of the Socialist Party and their coalition partners because of his disappearance for several days during the attempted coup.

The sudden resignation of Prime Minister Fatos Nano, which was announced on television late in the evening of 28 September, therefore came as a complete surprise to all observers. Nano's departure broke the political impasse that had paralysed Albania over the previous two weeks. Although the opposition had been calling for his resignation since the inauguration of his Socialist-led coalition government in August 1997, Nano had ruled out any possibility of resigning as late as the evening of 27 September. In his final days as premier, Nano had managed to restore a vestige of credibility to his short-lived premiership, but could no longer conceal the inter-party squabbles that exposed the fundamental weakness of his position. Attacked from all sides, Nano wisely came to the conclusion that he had little support within his own party.

The demise of Nano had been a virtual certainty since his disappearance in the wake of Berisha's coup attempt. The haste with which he submitted his resignation and stepped out of office appears to have been organised by President Rexhep Meidani, who was then the most respected politician amongst an otherwise discredited political establishment. For some time Meidani had been dissatisfied with Nano's performance as Premier, particularly his drinking problem, and had been considering how best to engineer his replacement. During the height of the mid-September disorder, and Nano's subsequent disappearance, the President had summoned Socialist Party Secretary General Pandeli Majko for crisis talks at which Majko's appointment as Nano's successor had been secured.

Since Nano personally appeared to be the focus of Berisha's wrath, his departure was deemed necessary in order to diffuse the tense political atmosphere. There was an enormous sense of relief following the move, which, it was hoped, would end the political impasse that had paralysed the country since the arrests of the six former DP officials back in August. His young successor Pandeli Majko (31) was generally regarded as untainted by a communist past and thus more acceptable to a population weary of older politicians burdened by a 'communist' mentality. Majko, who, like Hajdari, had played a significant role in the student demonstrations that eventually brought down the communist government, represented a new generation of Albanian politicians that, it was hoped, could breathe some fresh air into the stale political atmosphere. The West, however, was concerned at this change of leadership at a time when the crisis in Kosova was entering a dangerous stage. Majko's position on Kosova was unknown, whereas, rhetorically at least, Nano had been a reliable partner for the international community on the issue of Kosova, ignoring calls for the independence of the province and urging a peaceful resolution of the crisis.

One of Majko's first tasks in the autumn of 1998 was to call for the dismissal of the chief of the state intelligence service, Fatos Klosi, because of his alleged implication in the killing of Azem Hajdari. President Meidani, however, refused to endorse Majko's request for Klosi's dismissal, apparently at the behest of a certain foreign intelligence service that was concerned not to change the head of SHIK at a time of increasing tension in Kosova. According to Meidani, his decision not to dismiss Klosi was prompted by a member of 'an important intelligence service that was concerned with the evolution of the situation in Kosova'. Meidani explained that he had been handed a sealed piece of paper, 'which attested that the accusation against Klosi, was an issue they (the foreign intelligence service) were also involved in so they could manage to control the nature of events in Kosova. This note asked forcefully not to make structural changes to the leadership of SHIK at that time.'[15] Although definite proof is not available, there seems little doubt that the request concerning Klosi was made by the Greek intelligence service to Meidani.

The involvement of Berisha, SHIK, the KLA, FARK and certain 'foreign intelligence services' in the murky events of September 1998 have served to conceal to this day the real perpetrators of the various destabilisation processes then at work in Tirana and northern Albania. The crisis in Kosova was about to turn into actual warfare and there was too much at stake for something as messy as 'the truth' to win out.

PART
V

ALBANIA AND THE DEEPENING

KOSOVA CONFLICT

12

The Spread of War

The final week of September 1998 saw Tirana still in a state of extreme but subsiding tension, as the resignation of Fatos Nano from his post as Prime Minister brought a marked improvement in the atmosphere and meant that a key objective of the opposition had been achieved, although without Nano's replacement by Berisha or a DP figure. The police gradually reasserted themselves during the day, although AK-47 fire echoed through the night. Outlying districts such as the new northerners' suburb of Kamza remained firmly under the control of armed pro-Berisha gangs, and any policeman venturing there would have been shot dead on sight. Inner-city police stations were guarded by armoured vehicles, some left over from Operation Alba, but the buildings were not attacked. The coup attempt and the subsequent unrest in Tirana had seemed to be at first sight an unqualified disaster for Albania and perhaps also for Kosova. The world media had yet again been filled with pictures of Kalashnikov-wielding young Albanian men shooting thousands of rounds of ammunition at each other for no apparent reason. To the world at large the country seemed to be deranged and beyond reason.[1]

Yet the very seriousness of the situation, and the possibility that a general descent into chaos might encourage Milosevic to begin the final ethnic cleansing of Kosova and destabilise Macedonia, emboldened US diplomacy to move behind Tirana and to try to broker an agreement over Kosova that would protect basic Albanian interests. This decision was not a matter of sentiment, or the power and efficiency of the Albanian lobby on Capitol Hill, as some have alleged. It was taken as a result of a clear view of the risks of a general regional conflagration that the continual internal strife in Albania represented. Some US experts thought that a mass refugee exodus from Kosova could cause the total collapse of Macedonia and risk a conflict between Greece and Turkey, both NATO members, over the territory. A refugee influx into Greece would cause major social tensions with the overwhelmingly anti-Kosovar Greek population. The same would apply, to a lesser extent, if the refugees went to Bulgaria.

These fears, even if exaggerated, removed regional objections to US policy in many quarters. Although the Albanian ex-communists in the Socialist Party leadership were widely disliked in the international community, they were perceived as more of a factor for regional stability than any alternative government. Within NATO the arrival of the Blair government in Britain had brought a rebalancing of influence, with the pro-Serb, anti-interventionist inclinations of the Tory government replaced by the activist perspectives of Foreign Secretary Robin Cook and Prime Minister Blair himself. After a period of early uncertainty, Cook had realised the full extent of rampant Serbophilia among many of his officials and had moved to counter it by appointing his own expert advisers on the region who were loyal to humanitarian ideals. This meant a united Anglo-American front could move NATO in directions that were new, and overcome the inertia and Serbo-centric world views of the 'Old Europe' component of the organisation.

The September coup attempt and its diplomatic aftermath also provided another, and as it turned out, final, opportunity for negotiations between the Clinton administration's US Balkan envoy Richard Holbrooke and his old adversary from the 1994–5 Bosnian war period, Slobodan Milosevic. From the point of view of NATO and the international community, the key issue was to get refugees to return from the camps back to the villages before the tough Kosova winter really started, and provide a breathing space in which some wider settlement might evolve. The more intelligent people in NATO were well aware of the feeble nature of the 8 June 'flyover' and what little effect it had had upon the Serbs. They were now determined to make a more substantial threat of specific air strikes and a major bombing campaign if the Serbs did not comply with NATO directives to remove heavy armour from Kosova and stop the ethnic cleansing process.

On 9 October, in dense fog, journalists watched as columns of Yugoslav Army vehicles left Kosova, or so it appeared. In reality, however, much vital equipment had already been hidden by the Serbs in factories and under camouflage cover in the forests weeks before. The limited withdrawal was officially seen as a success for NATO, and it took Serbian military pressure off the KLA at a key time and enabled the guerrilla army to regroup. In late summer 1998 the command structure had been reorganised with help from US military contractors. Lieutenant-General Agim Ceku became head of the KLA, an experienced ex-JNA (Yugoslav People's Army) officer who had worked with the Americans in 'Operation Storm' in the war in Croatia in 1994–5. There is no evidence that these positive developments (from the Kosovar Albanian viewpoint) were at all understood in government circles in Tirana, where the idea persisted, derived from Serb propaganda, that the KLA had a more 'extreme' political leadership than other parties. From the narrow military point of view, both sides could be said to benefit from the effective truce. In the time-honoured tradition of local Balkan warfare going back to Ottoman times and earlier, the wet and foggy autumn followed by heavy winter snow caused a pause in operations, which assisted the KLA. The Serbs' heavy armour and tracked vehicles often had serious operational difficulties in the bad weather and ground conditions. To some extent, the Holbrooke agreement sanctioned something that would have happened anyway.

In Tirana, the agreement was regarded as manna from heaven, as it appeared to confirm that the USA would protect if not defend Albanian basic interests in the region, if only in the interests of stability. This would reduce the degree to which the Kosova issue could be used by Berisha and the opposition as a counter in Albanian politics. The Socialist leaders were essentially correct in this strategic analysis, and this has remained a given of Tirana politics ever since: a great asset to Fatos Nano that was strengthened, after 11 September 2001, by his undoubted 'non-Islamic' credentials. The USA had always disliked the fact that Berisha had taken Albania into the Islamic Conference organisation in 1994. Nevertheless, basic contradictions in US policy remained. As soon as the dust had settled on the 7 October agreement, US Balkan specialist and ambassador to Macedonia Chris Hill revived the summer peace plan, which aimed at restoring Kosovar autonomy along the lines of the 1974 constitution.

Although this plan had already been rejected by all the Kosovar Albanian parties in acrimonious exchanges in Prishtina in late summer 1998, and was actually first leaked out in *Koha Ditore*, the newspaper of star 'moderate' figure Veton Surroi, in the autumn it was enthustically backed by Foreign Minister Paskal Milo. He said on a visit to Denmark that 'All the main parties and actors are working now with the KLA to convince them that it is not the time to ask for independence for Kosova.'[2] In reality private talks had been held between the Tirana government and KLA political spokesman Adem Demaci, and the subject of a peacekeeping force including Albanian Army soldiers had been discussed, but Milo and Nano persisted in seeing the KLA as an extremist force in calling for independence.

In reality future independence for Kosova had been the long-held position of all Kosovar Albanian political forces, including the so-called 'moderates' in the LDK of Ibrahim Rugova. Fatos Nano and the Tirana Socialist leadership in this period never really came to terms with the fact that the KLA was no longer a small guerrilla group led by 'extremists' or 'leftists' but was becoming a broadly based popular military force, with substantial recruitment of LDK supporters and others from all currents of political opinion in Kosova. Underlying their concerns was an almost obsessive desire to do what the international community wanted, which the Socialist leadership saw as tied up with the manoevres of their opponents in Albanian politics, and linked to their own doubtful political legitimacy after the spring 1997 events.

During the summer of 1998, the size of the KLA had risen from a few hundred soldiers in March to about 10,000 by November, before rising to its final total of about 18,000 men and women by March 1999.[3] As many as 2000 soldiers were in training or in camps in Albania by the end of October, and in real terms the war effort was becoming increasingly integrated between these military assets in Albania and the KLA on the ground in Kosova. The key towns in western Macedonia, Tetovo and Gostivar, were playing an ever more important part in the war support effort. It was not long before the KLA leadership took advantage of the rising pan-Albanian popular sympathy for the war and began to emerge openly in Tirana. By the end of September key members of the inner circle such as Bardyl Mahmuti, Swiss-based fundraiser Visa Reka, and top strategist Xhavit Haliti were regular members of a KLA Tirana 'kitchen cabinet' based in the prestigious Rogner Hotel. This was an astonishing development for the traditional Tirana elite. These men had the whiff of gun smoke and conspiracy about them, and were soon enjoying celebrity status. In the Albanian popular mind, fed on nationalist history under communism, they were natural successors to the Kacaks of the 1920s.[4]

Tirana kiosks were soon selling KLA T-shirts, and a rapidly produced propaganda book about the Jashari family and their martyrdom became an autumn bestseller. A military magazine of the united KLA and FARK 'Defence Ministry of Kosova' was on sale. It was a very long way from the world of anonymity in the political underground, or the long years in Serb jails endured by Mahmuti and others in the 1980s. Xhavit Haliti had been given the role of opening close liason for the KLA with Nano and the Socialist top brass, which as a member of the older generation with a similar cultural formation and a vast array of international contacts he was well qualified to do.[5] The LDK as a serious factor had virtually ceased to exist in Tirana, and the unofficial 'Kosova Embassy' in its prestiguous building on the capital's Embassy Row saw little activity.

After Tirana's dismal response in spring 1997 to the horrors of Serb ethnic cleansing in the First Offensive period, and the fratricidal strife of the summer leading up to the attempted coup, the KLA had finally 'arrived' in Tirana and was quickly able to alter the quality of media and diplomatic debate in the Albanian capital about the situation in Kosova. With the arrival of the Majko government there was an increasing convergence in both the content and presentation of policy in the media between the new government, the KLA political spokesmen and the Albanian media. Advice from US State Department and CIA operatives was important in this process. They had taken over the role played by the Greeks in the time before the coup crisis.

The KLA leaders understood the international media much better than the Tirana Socialist or DP leaders. Many of them, such as Mahmuti, were young, sassy, wore good clothes, and knew how to use television. Their personal histories appealed to the public, with their periods in jail or exile universal. Most Albanians in Tirana had always felt (with reason in the Titoist period) that Kosovars were materially much better off, and lowland Albanians were bored or resentful about their complaints after 1990. But the KLA leaders were quite different. They had been prepared to take real risks and suffer personal hardship for their beliefs, and did not expect outsiders to solve all their political problems – an image the LDK often engendered, if unintentionally.

Foreign reporters were under intense pressure from editors to find out about the KLA leadership and get good stories, which the media-savvy Tirana group easily provided. They were a new phenomenon in the Albanian capital city: usually tall, thin and with cool Italian designer suits and fast BMW cars, and speaking excellent English or German (or French in Mahmuti's case). It was clear that there was little or no difference between their political outlook and that of any other Kosovar political party on the independence issue, something that caused an even greater sense of unreality to surround pre-October 1998 Albanian foreign policy positions. The homely and self-effacing Tiranite bureaucracy with its inherent deference to foreigners was green with envy. The Foreign Ministry had little idea how to cope with these KLA spokespeople who changed and reset the political agenda. Above all, the KLA spokesmen were confident and did not suffer from the inferiority complex of many Albanian leaders towards the outside world. An almost immediate result after September 1998 was the final end of any attempts by the government to restrict arms supplies to the KLA in the north.

There were soon two currents of policy running simultaneously within the Albanian government: the 'American', centred on President Meidani and new Prime Minister Majko, and the 'European', led by Foreign Minister

Milo (in turn heavily dependent on the Nano southern party machine). This has remained a given of political and diplomatic life in one form or other in Tirana ever since, with the former closer to the military (Majko's father was one of Enver Hoxha's generals), the USA and NATO. The 'Europeans' were seeking pacific solutions in line with the EU without making Kosova an integrated or central part of Albanian foreign policy. With his mastery of tactical movement within the Socialist Party, Nano initially belonged firmly in the 'Greek/European' camp, and lost his position in September 1998 as a result. The 'Europeans' had the serious problem in the government in that national security for both Albania and Kosova after 1991 always depended on NATO and the US, a fact exemplified as long ago as 1992 when the then US President Bush (senior) issued his famous 'line in the sand' warning to Belgrade over Kosova.[6] The US kept its promises, eventually (something no superpower had ever done with Albania before), and in the end, after 1999, the road to Kosovar freedom and independence was opened. This has made Albania and Kosova, at popular level, two of the most pro-American nations in the world.

In essence, in the autumn of 1998 there were two parallel discourses in US policy. First was the orthodox open diplomacy led by Chris Hill, concentrating on impressing on Belgrade that change in Kosova was inevitable, but with Holbrooke gradually becoming supplanted by Secretary of State Madeleine Albright. Second was the military/National Security Council/CIA side, where it was assumed increasingly that a final NATO confrontation with Slobodan Milosevic and the Serbs was inevitable, and where policy was increasingly determined by purely military criteria, some of which had little to do with Albania. For example, many intellectuals concerned with US naval policy in Washington were strongly in favour of a very pro-Albanian, anti-Serb policy because of the priceless strategic asset of the Albanian Adriatic coast in an era where more and more of the projection of power by the world's only superpower was made through sea power and sea-launched ordnance.

This was later borne out in the 78-day NATO campaign, where cruise missiles launched from the US Navy in the Adriatic were pinpointed onto Prishtina targets such as the Serbian Interior Ministry Police headquarters. General Wesley Clark firmly supported a strong line within NATO, and on the ground on the Kosova border CIA activity was evident that could only be explained in the context of a future NATO intervention in Kosova using ground forces.[7] At this level of geostrategic long-term planning for Albania's defence and security it did not matter very much what Foreign Minister Milo or any other Tirana politician or official said about events; the real decisions were being made elsewhere. Many of the Kosovar leaders did not have this impairment in their understanding, as virtually all of them except the Thaci–Haradinaj group – who were in any case immersed in running the war – had very extensive US experience and contacts.

Whatever criticisms might be made of Dr Ibrahim Rugova's general policy over the years, he had visited the USA frequently and had many friends and contacts there, togther with an active and powerful wing of the LDK party machine. Although the majority were loyal LDK supporters at the political level, the US Albanian diaspora has an atmosphere of fierce nationalist commitment and many Rugova loyalists were now strongly supporting the military campaign, with both money and recruitment into the KLA Atlantic Battalion.[8] In Prishtina leaders like Blerim Shala or Veton Surroi and Arben Xhaferi, who were seen as 'moderates', had extensive practical knowledge of the USA, which led them to believe that the USA would be prepared to support a degree of Kosovar nationalism on geostrategic grounds. Many people at lower levels in the US machine had had experience of British Conservative government collaboration with Russian geopolitical interests in Bosnia in the Bosnian war period in the mid-1990s that had led to near-genocide, and felt that the Blair government would back the USA in a more radical position and firmly back US policy initiatives. This duly turned out to be the case, and the British change of position was a major factor in the success of the 1999 NATO campaign.

On the ground in Kosova in October 1998, international involvement had increased with the arrival of the international verification teams who were tasked to oversee the implementation of the Holbrooke–Milosevic agreement. A headquarters under US control was set up at Kosova Polje and some local offices opened, although progress in some places was slow. There were widely differing political agendas among the international verifiers, who were nearly all active or retired diplomats or intelligence officers.[9] Predictably the Americans were mostly concerned about Serb violations of the Holbrooke–Milosevic agreement, whilst the British and European military officers still saw the KLA as their main target. Despite having little long-term effect on events, during October and November the verifiers' mission was generally respected and they had a restraining influence on military activity.

From the point of view of Tirana, and most mainstream Albanian opinion elsewhere, these were the most optimistic months of the entire Kosova crisis. The Tirana government had secured major diplomatic gains, and with international community activity in Kosova it seemed as though a 'solution' could be found without regional political change or military confrontation, in a way that might avoid a greater refugee crisis in Albania. NATO was increasing its profile in Tirana day by day and was providing a near certain deterrent to a Serb attack on Albania itself, whatever happened in the wider war in Kosova. It seemed as though the days of the old simplicities in Albanian world relationships might return, with the additional input of US security.

The over-optimism of the government in Tirana rested on essential ignorance of the military realities on the ground, as in earlier stages of the crisis. Milosevic had not actually withdrawn his forces from Kosova as the Tirana government believed, and after just two months the influence of the verifiers in the Kosova localities had begun to decline. There was also no serious political force in Kosova, inside or outside the KLA, which was prepared to abandon the goal of total independence from Belgrade. The old patterns of Tirana-based Albanian diplomacy as represented by Milo seemed to depend more and more on wishful thinking and a denial of the fundamental changes that were taking place in the Albanian world as a whole. Thus, insofar as the Kosova crisis opened up a new pan-Albanian agenda, it did so on the basis of a polycentric nationalist development where the Tirana elite and ex-communist political class was often not really fully in touch with events. They were even less able to control them, as the Tirana diplomatic community would have wished in an ideal world.

The Albanian nation was evolving from the artificial division of the Albanian people that originated in 1878 at the Congress of Berlin and was later entombed in the Ambassadors Conference of 1913. The nightmare existence for the Albanians of Yugoslavia was coming to an end; an event so momentous that it was beyond the imagination of much of the Tirana elite, but not that of the ethnic Albanian leaders in Tetovo or Prishtina, Zurich or New York. The underlying logic of the situation was not, however, new. Virtually all Tirana governments have had problems of democratic legitimacy since the foundation of the state in 1913, whether during King Zog's inter-war pro-Italian period under the communist one-party state, or in the successor transition governments after 1991. As a result the political class has often lacked the ability to put forward a united vision of the national interest. Individual politicians have traditionally been easily bought off by foreign powers or become de facto representatives of foreign interests. This occurred even under communism, so that key Hoxhist insiders, like sometime Prime Minister Adil Carcani and Foreign Minister Hysni Kapo, were universally seen as 'Russia's men' in the central leadership group.

In contemporary Tirana foreign influence is projected through open corruption and/or the influence of foreign embassies over the media. Despite the atmosphere of an overwhelming regional crisis, the process of reconstruction in Tirana nevertheless continued slowly forward, with the continuation of the work towards a new constitution. A constitutional committee, led by Sabri Godo and Arben Imami, proposed that the new constitution should be debated in Parliament in February 1998 and a referendum should be held to verify it the following month. The work of clearing up the pyramid crisis also continued, with Fatos Nano telling the annual meeting of the World Bank in Washington on 3 October that he was going to 'uproot VEFA Holdings'. VEFA boss Vehbi Alimucaj remained in hiding, but new border controls were instituted to prevent his escape abroad. British auditors Deloitte and Touche were brought in to begin auditing the pyramid schemes. Tirana was awash with rumours about what had happened to the embezzled money. In Rome the Pope met Albanian President Rexhep Meidani later in February, and the Pope blessed the reconstruction process and began talks on opening a Roman Catholic university in Albania. The extraordinary events of the spring and summer of 1997 had focused the minds of central figures and institutions in international life on the Albanian national future in a way that had not occurred since the time of the Tito-Stalin split and the Corfu Channel incident nearly 60 years earlier.[10]

A crude political evaluation of this period might suggest that Albania had followed the Maoist invocation that power comes from the barrel of a gun, but a more accurate view might be that power comes from many different centres of national feeling and activity. In the Tirana courts the conviction of Ramiz Alia was quashed, and the exile of the former communist leader in France seemed likely to end. News on the economy was good, with the Bank of Albania and the World Bank noting an 8 per cent increase in GDP for the year, although inflation still ran at a high 10 per cent. In the north, British aid worker and activist Sally Becker, the 'Angel of Mostar', abandoned her aid operation in Bajram Curri and condemned British Foreign Office apathy over the Kosova crisis, saying 'my government doesn't want witnesses to the tragedy of Kosova in Britain.'[11] In July she had been held by the Serbs for trying to smuggle an Albanian man out of Kosova, and in November had been hit in the leg by a bullet in a shooting incident in Tropoja.

In Kosova itself, in Llausha village, the KLA held a commemoration ceremony to remember the first anniversary of the first public appearance of the rebel army in Kosova, a sign of the returning confidence in the guerrilla force after the setbacks of the late-summer period. A speaker reaffirmed the central demand that the overwhelming ethnic Albanian vote for independence in the 1991 referendum should be recognised by Belgrade and the international community. This was a traditional Rugovist policy position, a sign of the growing convergence of the KLA and most of the LDK in the Kosovar political scene around a few key demands for the international community, the OSCE and the UN Security Council. On the border between Albania and Kosova, the Kosova Media Centre reported a pitched battle between Albanian arms smugglers and Yugoslav border guards – a sign of the accelerating tempo of the war as the Kosova Verification Mission had less and less effect on military developments on the ground. Tension also rose on the Greek border with a Greek farmer, George Makris, shooting dead two Albanian brothers, Afrim and Gezim Kazma, near the village of Radat.

In a statement issued to the London *Sunday Times* newspaper, Tirana Secret Service Chief Fatos Klosi, a close Nano henchman, claimed that networks controlled by terrorist chief Osama Bin Laden had been discovered in Albania.[12] This was the first mention of activity, or at least alleged activity, by Bin Laden in the region. The Saudi had visited Albania as part of a business delegation in 1994. Klosi's comments were eagerly seized on by the Serbian and Russian press but were received with derision in Tirana itself, where no concrete evidence of 'Islamic' terrorism linked to the Kosova freedom fighters had ever been produced.[13]

Of greater military and political significance was the decision announced by the newly elected Macedonian Parliament in Skopje to allow NATO troop deployment in the country, in the first place so that a force could, if necessary, extract the unarmed Verification Mission. In the DP Berisha faced a leadership challenge from veteran Shkoder Catholic politician Pjeter Arbnori, which he easily defeated thanks to the continuing cohesion of his bedrock of Tropoja and northern support. Events in the military and security sphere were dominated in the early autumn by the reconstruction of Rinas airport, which insiders attributed to NATO plans for Kosova if and when the conflict accelerated. Meanwhile in the world of the poor, migrants were still trying to leave the country, and over 60 people drowned in the last week of September when their ship sank near Brindisi.

A precarious equilibrium seemed to have been reached in Tirana, with Nano and Berisha still at daggers drawn in terms of their personal animosity. However, given that the Democratic Party was absent from parliament and Nano was out of the limelight, the DP street demonstrations gradually declined in size as the tide of international support for the new government increased. The role and position of President Meidani continued to improve now that Nano was no longer Prime Minister, and he became a figure of increasing respect within the international community with his cheerful and unpretentious personality, modest lifestyle and sensible patriotic outlook. He was also able, as the Kosova crisis deepened, to project his role as President of all Albanians, his technical constitutional role, and to articulate national question concerns as Berisha had rarely succeeded in doing clearly. He was thus able to make an important contribution to the stabilisation of the Kosova crisis, and the prevention of any exploitation of it for party ends. In the spring of that year Meidani had been an obscure figure and many people could not understand why he should be considered a suitable candidate for President. Yet in emergency conditions he rose to the occasion with considerable political skill and surprised many, particularly Rightists, who had been critical of his appointment. Most importantly, in the critical days of the late summer crisis, he was a barrier (with Defence Minister Sabit Brokaj) to Greek efforts to steer Nano's policy away from support for the KLA and towards opening direct negotiations with the Milosevic regime.

Foreign governments though still regarded Fatos Nano, correctly, as the main power behind the government, and he was rewarded with a visit to London in December to discuss the future of the region with Foreign Minister Robin Cook. Nano did not, however, have a meeting or photo opportunity with Prime Minister Tony Blair, which was perhaps a sign of lingering unease about whether the Socialist Party had really moved sufficiently far away from its Party of Labour origins to be considered a modern political party. The Foreign Office and MI6 bureaucracy also contained many individuals who had been active collaborators with the Berisha government (MI6 particularly), usually with a strong covert Royalist agenda and often with private links to ceaselessly plotting monarchist circles in London, Serbia and Greece.[14] For these people the events of 1997 had been a disaster, and they were not inclined to recommend rolling out the red carpet of VIP welcome to Nano.

It was nonetheless an important milestone for the Albanian leader. In the communiqué Nano was unrepentant about the Crete meeting, but in an interesting change of emphasis also stated that 'the recognition of Kosova's legitimate rights' was needed, which 'cannot be solved within the framework of the status quo in Kosova'.[15] This represented a major policy shift from the Milo policy of the summer months of 1998, where Tirana saw the crisis as something to be defined and solved within the existing setup and borders of Yugoslavia. In turn this illustrated the increasingly radical atmosphere in Tirana after the September events and the arrival of the KLA representatives. In the pro-Serb areas of the international community, this was matched by an increasing determination to keep Kosova and Albania apart at all costs.

On the ground in Kosova by mid-November a major crisis in the peace process following the Milosevic–Holbrooke deal was becoming apparent. Refugees from the 30,000 or so people who had left their villages in the summer arrived home in October to find scenes of medieval devastation, and very often most or all of their farm animals and livestock dead. A return to the old life was simply impossible in many places, and the State Department brief that had been given to Holbrooke on refugee return contained many superficial assumptions and faulty intelligence about what had actually been happening in Kosova in the previous months.[16] In central Drenica whole villages had been laid waste by Serbian troops and police and, contrary to the image in the minds of international community policy-makers, there was no stable society to regenerate. People began to move into Prishtina and other towns to survive the winter, or back to camps in Albania like Kukes where they had been in the summer.

It was clear to almost everybody that the war would be renewed in the spring, if not before, and Milosevic began quietly to move heavy armour and truck-mounted artillery pieces back into Kosova. As there were virtually no verifiers at all on the northern Kosova border roads this was easy from a logistical point of view, and illustrated how far the verification mission had adopted the Serb agenda that the KLA was the main danger to regional 'peace'. The Serb build-up was witnessed with alarm in the ethnic Albanian communities and the young men from the wrecked villages became a rich supply of recruits to the KLA.

This had immediate effects in Albania itself. In the north, the American adviser's attempts to integrate the old FARK fighters with the KLA had only had partial success and some FARK commanders, like Tahir Zemaj, who had refused to join the unified KLA, were still in the field with their own soldiers, threatening what little law and order there was in Tropoja. They were on very bad terms with the KLA within Kosova, who saw them as a splitting and diversionary force.[17] The KLA, now reorganised and with much better weapons and a more functional command structure, reoccupied the semi-abandoned Drenica villages, and local skirmishes accelerated with the Serb forces. In Dukagjini the KLA forces under the command of Ramush Haradinaj had been able to clear all Serb forces from the Decani area, and a second 'liberated zone' was appearing. Reuters reported from the Morina border area on 23 December that 'few borders in the world appear more ominous than the one between Albania and Yugoslavia as it passes through the crossing point at Morina', and noted the views of an OSCE observer, who commented that 'the writ of the Albanian government doesn't extend to the highlands. Psychologically, the people in the northern Albanian border area are as much part of Kosova as Albania. That and its geographical isolation make it a perfect KLA base.'[18]

A combination of bad weather and the resumption of hostilities prevented many of the verifiers from leaving their bases very much, and the mission became increasingly irrelevant as Christmas approached. OSCE Ambassador Daan Everts noted that 'the north of Albania is still a staging ground for the war and the KLA are very busy. They don't see much prospect of a negotiated settlement for Kosova that they would be willing to accept, so they are getting ready for the alternative.'[19] The Serbs launched a major operation to mine all possible border crossing routes where they still controlled the territory, to try to restrict KLA movement in the spring. They laid thousands of mines, which were illegal under the Ottowa Convention, something that the OSCE verifiers knew about but failed to publicise or condemn.[20]

Meanwhile, in Macedonia the Democratic Party of Albanians (DPA), led by Arben Xhaferi and Menduh Thaci, entered the Skopje government in coalition with the Internal Macedonian Revolutionary Organisation (IMRO). The emergence of the most radical party then existing in the Albanian minority community into government in November produced a major change in the political situation. Although Kiro Gligorov remained President, his party, the ex-Communist Social Democrats, were in opposition in Parliament for the first time since 1992. This had the general effect of reducing Belgrade's influence in Macedonia considerably, and opened political space for Albanian activity in support of the Kosovars. Gligorov's plan for refugee corridors through Macedonia into Albania had been abandoned, and some refugees were beginning to gather in Tetovo, Gostivar and the western Albanian-dominated towns during the late summer months. The KLA began to use Tetovo hospital to treat wounded combatants. By the end of the summer, a small number of refugees were also evident in the Albanian-minority area of southern Montenegro in towns like Tuzi (ironically the family-origin town of the Milosevic clan), and a few were to be found as far away as Blageovgrad in Bulgaria. The Kosova crisis was spreading inexorably over the whole region, and the social order (if it can be called that) dependent upon the isolation of Albania from Yugoslavia since the Tito–Stalin split in 1948 was breaking down irrevocably. Albania itself, as much as Kosova, was now at the centre of the international crisis.

The Albanian national question had arrived at the centre of the international stage, for the first time since the Ambassadors Conference in 1913. The calls of the international community for the maintenance of existing borders were increasingly irrelevant. As British commentator Jonathan Eyal once put it: the people can move, even if the borders do not (in reference to the situation when the Warsaw Pact collapsed). A good deal of the vapid misapprehensions of the international diplomats depended on ignorance of geography. All Albanian borders, except a short section of the border with Greece and a very short section with Monetnegro, run through remote and often mountainous land and thick forests, and only communist-period shoot-to-kill policies were a deterrent to population movement.

7. Kosova: the Americans arrive. Shaun Byrnes speaks to the press, October 1998

In response to these realities, NATO launched in autumn 1998 preparatory moves for what was to become, in April 1999, 'Operation Allied Harbour' with enhanced deployment of NATO assets in Albania. The headquarters at Durres under British soldier John Reith was in essence designed to help stabilise Albania in the refugee crisis, and designation of sites of tented camps was a priority. There were some remaining elements from Operation Alba still in place such as modernised barracks, the presence of units of the Italian Carabinieri and a modest number of Greek, Turkish and other Alba-force component troops. US troop strength had been built up slowly throughout the autumn, and by Christmas there were almost 700 in theatre along with 450 French and nearly 1100 Italians. NATO drew heavily on Italian expertise and experience, and although the main purposes of the operation were to show Milosevic that any action leading to the destabilisation of Albania was off-limits and to provide a factor in the internal stabilisation process, there was also a new element in background NATO thinking that the operation might also help to reduce the growing influence of the KLA in northern Albania. Several different internal national NATO country agendas thus existed more or less simultaneously: the structural stabilisation programme; the internal pacification role; the humanitarian relief role; and even a covert counter-insurgency role. It was perhaps unsurprising that as the crisis deepened during the winter months, some internal tensions within the mission began to show. To the Albanians NATO meant, above all, air capacity along the lines that had been used against the Republika Serbska army in the Bosnian war, while within 'Old Europe' NATO countries there was often quite a different priority, that of social stabilisation, law and order, and control of the movement of the population, refugees and internally displaced persons.

13

Tirana and the January Political Crisis

The accelerating conflict in Kosova in early January 1999 was much better understood in Tirana than similar events a year or even six months earlier. The presence of KLA representatives in the capital for some time, the continual arrival of refugees, and an enlarged US and NATO presence meant that the traditional prejudice and often ignorance about Kosovar matters had all but disappeared among the political elite, although traditional differences remained in the population as a whole.

In the first week of January 1999 armed clashes between the Serbs and the KLA intensified, as Milosevic moved more and more heavy armour back into Kosova. On 16 January, at the little village of Racak, an event of enormous significance took place that embodied all that the war had become and provided a major atrocity story that led to calls for international intervention. Racak, just outside the town of Shtime on the edge of the Drenica highlands, had become a focus in the battle for central Kosova for several months, as control of the Shtime/Racak area would give the KLA an open run east to try to cut the main Prishtina–Skopje road and effectively divide Kosova in two. After weeks of minor clashes the Serbs decided to make Racak an example and groups of defenceless villagers, including whole families, were slaughtered at the edge of a wood and their bodies thrown into a ditch. The head of the OSCE mission in Kosova, William Walker, was soon on the scene accompanied by representatives of the world's media, and the record of the Racak killings soon appeared on front pages all around the world.

In Brussels NATO moved forward plans for intervention, and it was made clear to Milosevic that a Bosnian-style emergency would not be tolerated and that prompt action against the 'Butchers of Belgrade' would be initiated. At the same time diplomatic activity accelerated, with Madeleine Albright putting forward plans for an international peace conference on Kosova, which would be held at the chateau of Rambouillet, outside Paris, the following month. In Macedonia inter-ethnic tension intensified under the pressure of the Kosova crisis, with explosions at police stations in Kumanova and Prilep and a sense that the long-feared 'spillover effect' from Kosova might be beginning to develop. The ethnic Albanians' unofficial 'capital in Macedonia', Tetovo, was crowded with refugees and deeply involved in munitions supply to the KLA.[1] The leader of the Tetovo Albanians, Arben Xhaferi, was developing into a key intermediary political leader between the different Kosova groups, and the roots of the permanent change in the importance of Tetovo within the Albanian world lie in this period.

In Albania itself all these events produced general satisfaction, although there were still doubts in some quarters, mostly the more old-fashioned parts of the Socialist Party leadership, as to whether NATO really would be prepared to go to war to protect Kosova. The developing Monika Lewinski sex scandal with President Bill Clinton provided an amusing diversion for the public, in Tirana as elsewhere in the world. Political leaders mulled over its significance. In Belgrade the film *Wag the Dog* was showing, and politicians openly ridiculed what they saw as US government incapacity. Doubts spread about US commitment to the support of Albania and Kosova. In Prishtina the liberal daily *Koha Ditore* ridiculed the crisis in the Democratic League leadership caused by the onset of impending war, with Kosovar Albanian leader Ibrahim Rugova lampooned as Christ at a last supper for the old LDK, his party, surrounded by quarrelling old associates. The KLA stood waiting outside the room.[2] A monopoly on Kosovar political leadership was about to be broken after nearly a decade, but it also raised the question as to the depth of commitment of the USA and NATO in the situation. For many foreigners the LDK 'was' Kosova, and it was not clear how the international community would see a pluralist leadership, which by necessity would also have to include the radical political forces that were developing.

In Tirana politicians of the generation of Nano and Milo had grown to political maturity in a climate where almost their whole political lives, from the early 1960s onwards, had been dedicated to understanding and coping with difficult superpower relationships. Countries such as Russia and China and minor associate powers such as North Korea had let Albania down or betrayed trust. It was still difficult for politicians of their type and background to trust the capitalist superpowers such as the USA and Britain, historic enemies of an old communist Albania that had only quite recently disappeared. The same doubts and worries arose in every apartment and café in Tirana. Would the Americans really let loose air strikes against Yugoslavia when, until the Milosevic period, Yugoslavia had been the main ally of the USA in the region? It was difficult for the Tirana leaders to consider these questions dispassionately and rationally when an often paranoid atmosphere existed in the city's hotels and key political watering holes such as the Hotel Rogner bar. Here, the talk was still whether the government was going to prepare a criminal case against Berisha, something his own followers often promoted as an imminent threat in order to mobilise and keep up an atmosphere of martyrdom for their 'lost' Presidential leader.

Three months earlier, in November 1997, the rightist *Albania* newspaper had run an editorial claiming that Berisha's arrest was imminent and that the state was preparing the trial process against the leader of the Albanian opposition. It commented:

> In order to hide the hands of the state, of the government, and of the party which governs the country, the communists have chosen the Bolshevik ways of people's consciousness, used more than half a century ago ... the truth of the events of the spring this year can not be considered as something belonging to the past and to be forgotten for the sake of reconciliation.[3]

Yet it was reconciliation that Albania, and particularly Kosova, needed in early 1999, when it would be clear whether the forthcoming Rambouillet negotiations were to result in a peace deal, or more likely a step towards NATO's first war, which would put Kosova and the region in a veritable maelstrom of conflict. The agitation of the DP extremists seemed not only irrelevant and backward looking to the Socialist coalition leadership, but also deeply irresponsible given the crisis in the national question – a crisis where every Albanian would have to face their responsibilities, from the KLA soldier in the forests to the fundraiser in the diaspora or the Albanian family hundreds of miles from Kosova offering hospitality to refugees.

All schoolchildren in Albania and Kosova are educated in a long historical tradition of understanding national oppression, principally by Serbia, which illustrates how disunity in the Albanian leadership has played into the hands of the country's enemies, usually the Greeks and Serbs. The main problem with developments, from the Tirana and international community viewpoint, was the disunity among the Kosovars, and the major split between those who supported the KLA and the followers of Rugova's LDK. Rugova had not visited Tirana since June 1996 and did not recognise the legitimacy of the Socialist-led government. The LDK representatives in the

Kosova 'embassy' in Tirana were patriotic figures who were involved in war support activities and were very detached from the official LDK leadership. They had little or no active contact with Rugova for prolonged periods.[4]

Official Tirana had to formulate a policy to deal with the crisis. The minds of Foreign Minister Paskal Milo and other leaders were overwhelmingly dominated by the need for Albanian unity, fearing that the forthcoming Paris conference could turn into a debacle with Albanians quarrelling publicly and the Serbs laughing their way home to Belgrade, and with NATO unable to proceed with military action. Therefore although the attention of the world in general was understandably focused on Racak, with the French and other European officials in collusion with Belgrade in trying to discredit OSCE chief William Walker's version of events, Tirana leaders found themselves with an important role to play, almost by accident.[5] It was also an important factor that it was in their interests to boost the KLA side of the Kosova spectrum; given that Rugova was seen as very close to Berisha, it suited the Socialists to have 'their' Kosovars as an alternative, and this meant practical support for the KLA leadership.

Talks began on 5 January between Foreign Minister Milo and KLA political spokesman Adem Demaci on what needed to be done to try to secure a united Albanian delegation. Demaci made a public statement when he arrived in the Albanian capital, saying that he would be prepared to meet Rugova. Even the moribund Contact Group was moved to action by this dramatic statement, with Russian Foreign Minister Ivan Ivanov telling Belgrade that it was time to negotiate with the Albanians. The following day, 6 January, Democratic Party leader Sali Berisha met Demaci and pledged the Democrats' support for a united Albanian front at the conference, an illustration of the great difference the KLA factor had made in Tirana politics. Two years before, after the chaos of 1997 and Berisha's breach with the Kosovars, it would have been difficult to imagine Demaci and Berisha together in the same room, let alone acting harmoniously in the diplomatic sphere. President Meidani also added his weight to the unity campaign, with a speech calling for the West to play a more active part in the Kosova conflict. Leading Kosovar intellectual Rexhep Qosja, of the United Democratic Movement (who had been based partly in Tirana since mid-1998), met Meidani and sought to synchronise policy with him.

In a key but little noticed decision Prime Minister Majko appointed an intelligence service watchdog, Arben Isaraj, with a brief to purge the service of Greek/Serb traitors.[6] The US Special Mediator Chris Hill was still in the field, although with a gradually reducing role as a close associate of Richard Holbrooke, who was becoming increasingly marginalised by the domination of US diplomacy by Madeleine Albright.[7] At first sight Adem Demaci and Paskal Milo were an unlikely diplomatic pair, with the urbane and southern Milo working with the steel-hard legendary Kosova veteran of 27 years' imprisonment in the Titoite prison gulag. The advocate of armed force in the political underground and the ever polite, profoundly Tiranite Milo had to form a common front over KLA participation. At a slightly later stage, British and US diplomats like Foreign and Commonwealth Office Albania-expert David Slinn became more closely involved in trying to integrate the KLA into the talks. The central problems were whether the KLA would attend, and related to that, the composition and leadership of the delegation. The KLA would not accept Rugova as leader, and if there was any serious prospect of this happening not only would they not attend, but also the conference would probably never take place at all. Authority in the KLA was diffuse, and the views of ground commanders were important on this issue. Many of them, particularly in the key Drenica and Dukagjini sectors, loathed Rugova.

This tendency was being accentuated by the development of the KLA itself. December 1998 and January 1999 had seen a flood of new recruits and a marked improvement in operational efficiency, as the reorganisation pushed through by General Agim Ceku and top regional commanders like Rrustem Mustafa (nicknamed Captain Remi) and Ramush Haradinaj began to bear fruit. This successful development led to political complexities, as quite a number of the new soldiers came from an LDK background and had little or no contact with the original KLA leadership with its LPK, LKCK or LPRK background. Demaci was himself sceptical about the Rambouillet prospect, something that led to his resignation from the post of KLA political spokesman at an earlier stage, only to be reinstated before the talks began. The military realities in Kosova, as ever, were often unclear, and it was difficult for the Albanian leadership to be sure about the military capacity of the KLA and how real its revival might be. It was even more difficult for the Tirana government to be sure about the murky relationship between the KLA and Western governments. Unlike earlier stages of the crisis, though, there was at least now plenty of accurate information about the real military situation.

The KLA was increasing in size and retaking large areas of central Kosova, some of which had not been controlled by the KLA since the 'First Offensive' period in early 1998.[8] The Racak massacre had clearly shifted international opinion away from the Serbs. The Europeans were marooned on the sidelines. The nefarious influence of the Greek Embassy in Tirana was subsiding, and even the most pro-European members of the government leadership group were looking towards NATO and the USA as the key international players. This was not clear in the traditionalist part of the international community, and Premier Pandeli Majko was summoned to Italy for talks with the Rome government, which pushed for Tirana to take a 'moderate' line over Kosova. There was still a profound link between the Italians, the Milosevic regime, the Vatican and the LDK and Rugova leadership (as Rugova's Italian 'exile' in the latter stages of the war showed), and the Dini Foreign Ministry clearly found the possibility of the emergence of the KLA as a major political factor very unsettling and a sign of a major reduction in their influence on events. The visit was overshadowed by the deepening military crisis, with Yugoslav jets overflying Albanian airspace as Majko sat in talks in Rome. The Tirana Foreign Ministry issued a statement accusing Belgrade of warmongering. In turn Belgrade attacked the Tirana government for sponsoring 'terrorism', and other abusive exchanges followed. In a hardening of policy towards the international community Belgrade also threatened to expel William Walker's OSCE verifiers, while the Albanian Defence Minister Luan Hajdaraga issued a statement saying that the 'armed forces will be ready to realise their noble mission to defend the country'.[9]

The conflict was also spreading into neighbouring northern Montenegro, used for some time by the KLA as a relatively safe operating area for running the war around the strategically important town of Peje (Peć). In the last days of January bitter and fierce fighting spread along the Peje–Montenegro road, with hundreds of houses set on fire, resulting in a Kosovar refugee influx into Montenegro itself. The southern Montenegrin Albanian-majority regions of Plav and Gruda adjoining northern Albania had always been militant strongholds of nationalist feelings, and the conflict here was opening a new front of great concern to the international community.

The Montenegrins had a strong pro-independence lobby in the government of leader Milo Dukanovic, and there was a real prospect of regional destabilisation spreading further along the Adriatic coast. Montenegro was important to the KLA as a conduit for recruits and for organising fighters, weapons and munitions supplies to the Peje front. While the mountain villages could be controlled by the insurgents, the roads could not. They were dominated by the shelling and heavy armour of the Serbs, who fired rockets and shells indiscriminately into villages to try to clear fighters away from the road. Montenegro also provided passage for Western journalists to reach the Kosova front with a fair degree of safety, and the deep cleft of the Rugova Pass was an important artery of the war for many actors on the ground.[10]

During the third week of January the parameters for the war over the next six months were really set, and NATO was irrevocably drawn into a position where it would have to act over Kosova or risk irrelevance. A significant risk of open armed conflict between Albania and the Yugoslavs had also appeared, as it was clear that Milosevic could, if he wished, attack Albanian targets from the air and so draw Tirana into open military conflict. In Germany, a member of the Bundestag commented on 11 January that 'we cannot allow Belgrade to reach as far as Tirana'.[11] Equally the Albanian army, poor as it was, could make incursions into Kosova in support of the KLA or to defend border villages. This realisation was not widely reported in the international media at the time, but it had a profound effect on the political atmosphere in Tirana and helped engender a rare unity among the politicians. After so long when Albanian incompetence, faction fighting and confusion had been an unchanging part of the diplomatic scene, a tenuous unity was now formed around the recognition that the political vacuum caused by Rugova's refusal to engage with the new government in Tirana had been filled. This had to be done for the future of the nation, and in filling it as an interlocutor, the Tirana government had an opportunity to engage with the Kosova issue that was unprecedented since the 1920s and the betrayals then of Kosovar patriots by King Zog.[12] The arguments that some Greek-influenced Socialists had used against this in the summer of 1998, to the effect that association with the KLA would lay Tirana open to charges of supporting terrorism, collapsed with the open engagement of US and other diplomats with the KLA leadership as a negotiating partner and member of the Kosovar team at Rambouillet.

The Rambouillet talks marked a new phase in the national question, and one that has brought revolutionary changes to the diplomatic position of Tirana governments. In terms of the national question, the break in political discourse in the post-war period caused by the 1948 Stalin–Tito split and the consequent international isolation of Albania had ended. It is likely that future historians will see January 1999 as a major turning point in Albania's history. As so often happens with major historical turning points, the importance of the events and their full significance was not apparent to participants, who worked 20-hour days with little sleep and, like the journalists in the field in Kosova, only had a sense of an all-embracing international crisis unfolding before them whose consequences would be far-reaching and impossible to predict.

The change of fortunes of some leading political players was extraordinary. The transformation in Fatos Nano's life and status over the previous two years must be one of the most extraordinary in twentieth-century Europe: from a despised jailbird in January 1997 who could only expect a long sentence, to Prime Minister and being a central figure in negotiations with figures such as

Javier Solana of NATO as the alliance prepared its first war. The atmosphere of imminent crisis and confusion over NATO's real intentions increased with the expulsion of William Walker from Kosova by the Yugoslav government, and by a statement on 19 January by key Rugova aide Fehmi Agani to the effect that he doubted whether NATO would intervene in Kosova. This had a jarring impact in Tirana, where political leaders in the Socialist party felt they were going out on a limb with some of their own followers to help Kosova, only to find Rugovaist LDK leaders like Agani sowing doubt and confusion.

Meanwhile the internal instability in parts of Albania continued. Government security forces fought a pitched battle on 18 January with citizens in the southern village of Llazarati, near Gjirokaster. A notoriously militant and rebellious DP village, it had been out of government control since the 1997 uprising, and the episode demonstrated how fragile the effective control of the Majko government was over even some southern areas of its territory. In Kosova itself the Serbs launched a major offensive in the north, where villages were heavily shelled, starting new inflows of refugees into Albania and Montenegro.

In response, intense behind-the-scenes work intensified, involving senior CIA and US State Department figures to unify the Albanians ready for the international conference. Rugova was prompted to issue a statement saying that the LDK envisaged a KLA presence in the Rambouillet delegation. This statement was a valuable aid to the KLA and dealt a final blow to the fiction, popular in official Italy and France, that Rugova and the LDK might be maintained as the sole Kosova representatives leading to a collaborationist deal with the Serbs.

Elsewhere in Europe, on 29 January the Contact Group in Paris called for talks to start as early as 6 February. The different cross-currents in the Kosovars' political world put Demaci under intense pressure and on 2 February he stated that he felt the KLA should stay away from the Paris talks. By taking this position he was reflecting his own distrust of the international community but also the views of several important KLA field commanders, who felt they were seizing the military initiative in their own localities and making major advances. They feared an international conference would be a sell-out, a modern-day echo of the Ambassadors' Conference of 1913. In turn this put the Tirana government under great stress. They feared that if the talks did not take place, Milosevic would simply carry the war into Albania.

The LKCK and some other groups in Prishtina were still pressing for a general popular uprising to drive the Serbs from Kosova, and there was an ominous sense in the last days of January that unless the talks in Paris began soon, the whole crisis might spin out of control, with a violent confrontation on the streets of Prishtina. In turn Milosevic would then have nothing to lose by spreading the war. It became clear that KLA political spokesperson Hashim Thaci was becoming a more and more central figure to the negotiations, as someone with sufficient military credibility and political militancy to be able to 'deliver' the more extreme Kosovars.

Tirana was centrally involved in this process, and Thaci made a secret visit to Albania to consult with colleagues and to exchange views with the KLA senior political figure in Albania, Xhavit Haliti. Haliti had direct access to Nano and was able to impress on a reluctant Tirana Socialist leader that the war option was the only remaining course open for the Kosovars if Rambouillet failed to produce a deal. Prime Minister Majko made a rushed visit to the USA on 2 February to convey the government's views to the Pentagon, who shared his worries. Pressure from the USA on the different factions intensified, and on the following day, 3 February, talks started on forming the final Kosova delegation, including KLA representatives, Rugova for the LDK, Qosja for the United Democratic Movement, and journalists Veton Surroi and Blerim Shala to represent the intellectuals and the wider Kosovar Albanian community.

There was considerable concern in Tirana that some sections of Kosovar opinion might only be represented by second-line figures, and Foreign Minister Paskal Milo and British Ambassador Stephen Nash made a joint appeal on 4 February, with Nash saying on behalf of the Contact Group countries that:

> We are keen to ensure there is a high-level representation at such a level that firm commitments can be made. We see this [Rambouillet] as a unique opportunity for the parties in the conflict in Kosovo to reach a fair negotiated solution which will be in the interests of both parties.[13]

In terms of the personal relationships aspect in the Albanian delegation, some of the discourse had more in common with born-again Christianity than normal diplomacy, with that evening Rexhep Quosa telling a newspaper that he had had a 'reconciliation' meeting with Rugova earlier in the day. Surroi had for some time been acting as an unofficial Kosovar foreign minister and spending a good deal of time in the USA. He acted as an important behind-the-scenes interlocutor and Kosova advocate, and with his polished manner and perfect English was a vital figure in this period with major international community actors such as British Foreign Minister Robin Cook and US Secretary of State Madeleine Albright. Although never as popular with the electorate inside Kosova as outside it with foreign diplomats, he played a vital role in this period.

A new political dimension came with the emergence of Hashim Thaci as the political spokesman for the KLA. Hashim Thaci was one of the key leadership group of the KLA, and had been on Serbian wanted lists since 1993. A tall, thin young man with film star good looks, he came from the small village of Broje in western Drenica, from a family with long patriotic antecedents. His grandfather had fought against the Bulgarians in eastern Kosova in the Second World War with the famous Partisan leader Sadik Rama. He had early political ambitions and had become a student leader and a top-secret member of the LPRK at Prishtina University in the early 1990s. He was also a close associate with the fabled Jashari family from Prekaz, who were wiped out in spring 1998. Thaci had taken part in various armed actions between 1993 and 1994, after which he had been chosen by the LPRK core group as a future national leader and had been sponsored to study at Zurich University.[14] Thaci had a notoriously bad personal relationship with Ibrahim Rugova, whom he had known since student days, and although he had lived in the political underground on occasion in Tirana since 1992, he had few top-level contacts there. He had been put under arrest by the Berisha government for a short time in 1996, when he had a reputation as a talented, dangerous young man.[15] His emergence from almost total obscurity had begun in mid-January, when his photograph began to appear in some Kosova newspapers.

Back in Tirana, on 13 January the Majko government had concluded its turbulent, extraordinary first 100 days in office, a period dominated by the failure of most international community attempts at reconciliation between Berisha and the Socialist government. The former President marked the day by addressing one of the many demonstrations of his motley rabble of 'supporters' that were regularly held in Skanderbeg Square. He called for new elections, which non-DP commentators noted as the height of irresponsibility given the need for national unity in the looming and overwhelming Kosova crisis. DP supporters were still clashing with opponents in many parts of the country in often-unpublicised incidents. In Shkoder on 21 January armed groups entered the town from the nearby countryside and terrorised the inhabitants by shooting into the air and attacking a local police station. They then occupied the town hall for two days and forced the district prefect Gezim Podgoritsa to resign at gunpoint. The local office of the centrist Democratic Alliance Party condemned the attack, coming only two days after a visit of Berisha and his deputy Pjeter Abnori to the city. They claimed that the former government leaders were looking for an armed revolt, and requested that criminal proceedings should be started against them, a call that fell on deaf ears in Tirana.

The distance between the official world of ministers like Paskal Milo, who that week was meeting ex-Yugoslav bigwig Milan Panic (after immense pressure from the US State department to start Albanian–Serbian dialogue), and the reality on the ground was very great. If by some extraordinary miracle an agreement over Kosova had resulted from the talks, it is doubtful whether Milo would have been safe to hold a public meeting to even talk about it in many parts of central and northern Albania. Milo's visit to Moscow for talks with the Russian government on Kosova the previous month had been attacked strongly in the Kosovar media, and his diplomatic initiatives were unlikely to affect the tide of events. In response to the DP's endless agitation about government legitimacy, the coalition parties issued a joint statement calling for national stability in the face of the threat of war, and demanding that the DP leaders cooperate with the government. The same week a bomb went off near the DP HQ in the southern industrial town of Fier.

Although the usual domestic preoccupations of crime, violence and public order had dominated the agenda, the Majko government had a noticeably different tone from the Nano government that had preceded it, with much closer liaison with the USA and NATO, and a cooling of relationships with Athens and other European powers. An important marker to the future was a speech by Milo back in November 1997 when the Foreign Minister, to the astonishment and irritation of Athens after what the pro-Serb collaborators in the Foreign Ministry saw as the triumph of the Nano–Milosevic meeting on Crete, reopened the long-dormant Cham issue by calling for the restitution of lost properties in north-west Greece belonging to Muslim Albanians resident in Greece who had lost them in the Greek ethnic cleansing and genocide of the Cham regions in 1943–4. This was an issue new to the national discourse and illustrates that some Kosovar criticisms of Milo's allegedly collaborationist and 'anti-national' policies may have been slightly misplaced.[16] When President Sali Berisha had erected a monument to the Chams tragedy in 1994 the issue was largely unknown outside Albania.[17]

The following week saw another symbol of the ever closer relationship between Tirana and the USA, with US president Bill Clinton announcing, to the surprise and pleasure of the Tirana government, that Albania was being accorded 'most favoured nation' trade status with the USA. It was widely assumed in Serbia and elsewhere that the Albanian lobby in the USA was only a real factor in the Republican party but in fact there were many wealthy and influential Democrats of Albanian origin, such as Bardhyl Tirana (ex-President Jimmy Carter's lawyer) and the National Albanian-American Council (the NAAC, then essentially a Democratic Party organisation) that had been energised over the Kosova crisis.

Many new factors were being put into play as a result of the Kosova crisis and the reopening of the national question and consequent reorientation of priorities within the Albanian world. The announcement that $200 million had been recovered by the state from a bankrupt pyramid company produced only minor interest, and few newspaper headlines.[18] The centre of Tirana was a familiar place to see foreign military vehicles but within what seemed like the blink of an eye at the time, the trucks of Operation Alba soldiers coming to restore order had metamorphosed into US humvees with NATO markings who were clearly coming to the aid of Albanians in neighbouring Kosova.

It was an astonishing and complex situation, hard for the average citizen to understand or credit. Some did not, and took refuge in cafés away from politics, while hard-line middle class DP supporters in the better districts of Tirana called the KLA 'hajdutis' (bandits) who had brought yet another crisis to Tirana. However, most citizens were profoundly grateful to see the NATO vehicles and forces on the streets.

In a further sign of the spread of the crisis throughout the region NATO began to put into practice the decisions that had been taken at the end of 1997, and 'Operation Allied Harbour', a major refugee relief operation, was planned and the US Air Force began stockpiling rations and humanitarian aid packages in bases in Europe. The modernisation work at Rinas airport continued (by the German Siemens company), so that the runway was improved for larger planes, and a naval build-up started at Durres port. A visit by Foreign Minister Milo to Brussels produced little, with much talk of a revival of the EU 'troika', discredited years before, and awkward exchanges between Milo and Italian leader Dini, who took up much of the meeting with concerns about the civil rights of the Italian-allied ex-DP leadership and the possibility of a return of the DP to the Albanian parliament. Even 18 months after Berisha had fallen from power in chaos for the country, he could still rely on Italian backing.

Yet throughout the turmoil and confusion, a new reality was coming into being, and it was clear by the end of this terrible and dramatic month for the Albanians that a crisis of world proportions was at hand, in which they would play a central part. The NATO preparations on the ground for conflict continued without interruption, and in the background a series of informal understandings were developing between the Kosova Albanian leadership that would result in a functional delegation, mainly by the expedient of leaving the leadership issue open until they arrived in France. In Belgrade, Milosevic viewed the process with disdain and the government announced that if Rambouillet was held, he would not be attending and Yugoslavia would be represented by a modest-level delegation.

Whatever the difficulties in the White House, the Pentagon continued with the support agreed at Majko's visit on 2 February, and by the end of the month five US warships had reached the coast, while the Prime Minister himself visited troops on the Albania–Kosova border. The US Air Force at Ramstein base in Germany and at several bases in Italy began to mobilise for a future conflict in which, based on the Bosnian model, air strikes against Milosevic were envisaged. The Royal Air Force in Britain planned a short, five-day air campaign against Yugoslavia, based on increasingly clear intelligence warnings about Milosevic's ethnic cleansing plans.[19] Only a few senior commanders knew the scale of General Clark's planning at NATO HQ or the determination of other leaders like British General Rupert Smith to avoid the confusion and indecision of the Bosnian war precedent that Milosevic had exploited.

The preparations for war on the ground were in full swing and it remained to be seen what the talks in Paris would bring as the members of the delegations – numerous diplomats, journalists and advisers – left for Paris in the first day or two of February in bright, cold weather. The fate of the Albanian nation would be decided far away from the Albanian lands, as had so often happened in the past.

14

Rambouillet and NATO Commitment

The Rambouillet conference marked the arrival of the Albanian Question onto the international stage, in the formal sense that a major diplomatic conference was held to try to decide on an agreed future for Kosova between Serbs and Albanians, under international mediation. The stasis in which the Kosova issue had been held since the Second World War and the false 'solution' of Yugoslav communism was now decisively broken. The events at the chateau at Rambouillet are of great interest for students of the nature of modern diplomacy. Rambouillet, was, of course, billed in the international media as part of the 'Kosova Dayton', but from the first day, 6 February, the circumstances were very different.

The conference at Dayton, Ohio that formalised the end of the Bosnian conflict in 1995 came as the war in Bosnia was drawing to a natural close, with exhausted participants and a general acceptance, if not welcome, for a deal to be signed under US supervision. [1] Rambouillet had a very different background, with a ground war very much in progress and neither side with an inclination to cease hostilities. The difference was perhaps most symbolised by the choice of location. Dayton was a very American affair, whilst the Paris conference was an opportunity for traditional European diplomacy, in a traditional setting, and it is hard not to surmise that at least some Americans who wanted a military showdown with Milosevic were willing to see it fail. They knew that NATO had to evolve into an international peace intervention force and that the Kosova conflict was a perfect pretext, with most key liberal opinion firmly 'on message' against the Serbian dictator and happy to support NATO. In Britain and elsewhere it was mainly the traditional

Right who were anti-intervention, but by the structure of national politics they were firmly pro-NATO in the way many liberals and leftists were not. A Kosova war by NATO was a perfect opportunity to solidify the legitimacy of the 'new military humanism' for NATO commanders and the Pentagon across the Centre and Left of the European political spectrum.

At Dayton there was a highly controlled and militarised environment, in geographical isolation and with ample means to keep the press away from the participants. There were various methods of psychological coercion available to make negotiators pliable: principally the laid-down time frame for negotiations and for an agreement. Delegates were largely isolated from opinion and the state constituencies they represented. At Rambouillet, negotiators could go where they wished in Paris and were free to make contact with friends and journalists on their mobile phones. Outsiders, whether a KLA commander in the field in Has, or a political figure in Tirana, or the editor of a Belgrade newspaper, could all take part. Dayton depended on physical isolation, where the diplomats could effectively totally control the environment and the agenda. It took place before mobile phones with international 'roaming' agreements were widely available. In Rambouillet the situation was quite different, and this meant that Albanian preoccupations generally had a much more important role than might have been the case. The new developments in communications and technological progress also played a really central and important role. In 1995 at Dayton mobile phone, Internet and digital communications technology had not reached the ubiquitous state that it had by 1999.

At Rambouillet it enabled exiles and the Albanian diaspora to become a significant factor in the external factors affecting the negotiations. Before roaming and satellite phones it would not have been possible for Thaci and Haliti to speak to the KLA commanders in the field and make them a factor in the negotiations, and it is possible that Thaci could have been marginalised. At Dayton there was a strongly prearranged plan in the negotiations; at Rambouillet such a plan may have existed but it disintegrated under pressure of events within a day or two of the start of negotiations.[2] There were in fact two Rambouillet conferences, the first lasting from 6 to 23 February and the second from 15 to 18 March. The first was a genuine attempt to secure an agreement through negotiation; the second[3] was often little more than a process of legitimising the failure of the first stage in February in a form that would give NATO a mandate for war.

Difficulties multiplied from the moment the delegations tried to assemble, although the overwhelming general wisdom was that there would be a deal because, as Tim Judah put it, 'the alternatives were too awful to contemplate.'[4]

Experienced diplomats present, particularly those who had been actually involved in Dayton, were more cautious. This instinct deepened rapidly when the Serbs announced that they would arrest the Albanian delegation – or some members of it – on terrorism charges, and they were only able to travel when a French military plane came to Prishtina airport to collect them.

The French government tried to get the Albanian delegation changed to leave Thaci and Haliti behind, something that enraged the KLA in general and turned several KLA commanders with only lukewarm support for the talks into opponents. The key problem for the KLA commanders was that, like all guerrilla movements, there is a long and painful learning curve before military efficiency is achieved and in the last part of 1998 and early 1999 there had been a great step forward for the KLA in its capacity and organisation. In the eyes of the KLA commanders, it was being asked to stop fighting and disarm just when it was becoming a more coherent and successful force. It was only a short step from this perception to the view that the Rambouillet Conference was basically an international community attempt to pull the Serbs' chestnuts out of the Kosova fire, and a plot against the KLA.

A precise military assessment of the situation on the ground is difficult, but there was no doubt that the KLA was gaining ground over the whole of central and western Kosova in late January and February 1999, and that from the Serbs' point of view the threat to Prishtina was real. On the other hand, Milosevic had substantial reserves of heavy armour, which could be, and after 20 March were, pushed into Kosova to remove all the civilian population. At the time, some pro-Serb figures in the British intelligence world took the view that the refugee movement was partly organised by the KLA to force NATO to intervene.[5] There is no evidence to support this, characteristic of the recurrent failure of swathes of the British political elite to appreciate the realities of Kosova. The immediate priority for the international community was to find a way to bring the two sides together around the negotiating table and to resolve the problem of the composition of the Albanian delegation. It took intervention by the Britain and the USA, plus a threat from Geneva from Jashar Salihu, head of the Homeland Fund, that the Albanians would withdraw from the talks altogether without Thaci's presence. The row illustrated the difference between the British and French perspectives, and the seemingly eternal attachment of the Europeans to Rugova and the LDK.[6]

In reality, the negotiations had immediately hit the problem of the legitimacy of the KLA, which was to dog Rambouillet throughout. At Dayton, however much many participants might have loathed each other, there was no doubt that they were representatives of 'governments', or 'entities'. This was not the case in Paris, from the Belgrade viewpoint. In Serbian eyes, to have recognised the KLA would have entailed recognition of loss of effective sovereignty over Kosova. Judah also points out, correctly, that there was another fundamental problem in the form of the disparity between the two delegations, with the 16 in the Albanian delegation including almost all of the central figures, from Thaci and Haliti for the KLA to Rugova and his LDK colleagues, and independents such as Surroi and Blerim Shala of *Zeri* magazine. In marked contrast, the Serbs fielded a hard-line team of Milosevic acolytes, including a deputy Prime Minister, Nikola Sainovic, and various lawyers, but nobody of any real power – let alone Slobodan Milosevic himself. Rambouillet was thus in many ways doomed before anyone entered a negotiating room.

At first sight it might appear as if Tirana and Albania was to be irrelevant to this process, but this was not the case. The Albanian delegation lacked legal expertise, and the lawyers who were available were recruited and paid by Bujar Bukoshi, the Kosovars' erstwhile 'Prime Minister', who was by now a marginalised and often unpopular figure, especially with the KLA delegation. In this situation, the Tirana government provided an Albanian of Kosovar descent, Shinasi Rama, from Columbia University in New York. Britain-based lawyer Marc Weller from Cambridge also played an important role, along with international lawyer Paul Williams from Washington. It has been claimed that by the end of Rambouillet, Tirana controlled the KLA. This is an overstatement, but it is certainly true to say that without the quiet backing of Tirana, the KLA would have had more difficulty in making itself the central voice of Albanian opinion in the negotiations.

At a deeper level there are also important geopolitical issues to consider. Whatever the details, which are now long passed into history, Rambouillet was very much a French and European event and the talks had little effect on NATO war preparations, particularly at important NATO air bases in Italy, at sea and in Albania itself. The French were perhaps conscious of this, and after the fanfare and massive press attention of the opening, they downgraded the event in their statements, saying, as Judah observes, that it was ' a meeting' only, and not an overall test of European diplomacy.[7]

An important factor in US planning seems to have been, according to Madeleine Albright, the fact that the CIA had received intelligence reports indicating that the Serbs planned a massive offensive in mid-March against the KLA, regardless of what happened in Paris.[8] Whatever the military outcome, this would result in a massive international refugee crisis with the potential to destabilise Macedonia, always a central preoccupation of Washington. Albright had fought a hard internal battle in the administration against Pentagon doubters over military action in the 19–25 January crisis week, and, having won it, the vast technological and engineering capacity of the US military machine was moving. Once that had happened there were limits to what could be done to stop it, unless the Serbian government suddenly capitulated to the demands of the international community. In a certain technical sense that was impossible without Milosevic in Paris.

Critics of Rambouillet in the British and EU diplomatic world have claimed that Milosevic was presented with a non-negotiable package involving the surrender of Serbian sovereignty over Kosova. This is said to have led to the NATO intervention. In reality it is probable that the momentum towards war was virtually unstoppable from the time the Pentagon agreed on US troop involvement on 19 January, and this in turn depended on the effects of international opinion on the outcome of the Racak massacre a few days before. It is not surprising that such efforts were made to discredit the Racak events by pro-Serb elements in the international community.[9] Time was of the essence in these days. It was not on the side of the Serbs. Thaci and Surroi knew that time was on their side once Rambouillet had been convened, something Milosevic does not seem to have understood as clearly.

The external factors of the wider Albanian world were in many Kosovar and Albanian minds throughout the negotiations, and Xhavit Haliti acted as the main conduit of news and comment from the delegation to Nano and the government in Tirana. Prime Minister Majko was in touch with the US embassy almost daily. The Tirana news magazine *Klan* caricatured Haliti as 'that mysterious Kosovar' who had suddenly become a big wheel in the capital city.[10] Nano's personal role in this period is obscure, and he does not seem to have had any central role in the dealings with the international community. Public opinion in Albania was expectant of a deal from the conference at the outset, largely because of the massive media promotion of the 'Dayton model' and the obvious degree of involvement of the USA.

Ordinary Albanians found it difficult to see how the military and political realities would interact, as US generals visiting Albania had already ruled out the possible deployment of ground troops. It was, though, in practical terms, hard to see how Milosevic could be stopped without them. They were not aware of the change in Pentagon and NATO policy in January, and the determination of key figures in the international community, starting with US President Bill Clinton and British Prime Minister Tony Blair, to stop a repetition of the Bosnian genocide. On the other hand, experienced heads that knew the history of the region and the nature of the Kosova problem had few illusions about the nature of the Serbs' plans to remove as many Albanians from Kosova as possible by force. In the background to Rambouillet, there was a sense that events might be on the Albanians' side, and that the entrenched powers of the international community might finally be losing patience with Belgrade.

When talks started the election of Hashim Thaci to be head of the Albanian delegation was a sensation, and, if Madeleine Albright is an accurate guide, was also unexpected in the US State Department. In her record of the conference she described him as 'a lanky 29-year-old with whom we had had little contact. Thaci's designation appeared to reflect the continuing decline in the standing of Rugova, who responded to the affront by saying almost nothing.'[11] Although this ignorance of the standing of Thaci was not the case with all Americans, it does indicate the fact that the international community had never appreciated the deep and abiding unpopularity of Rugova across a wide spectrum of Albanian political opinion, from leaders like Arben Xhaferi in Tetovo to Fatos Nano in Tirana and Veton Surroi in Prishtina.[12] The internationals did not understand either the fact that even during the height of its power and popularity between 1991 and 1995, the LDK had never represented everybody or all strains of political opinion in Kosova (although Rugova often claimed it did, and the diplomatic visitors he received usually took his claims at face value). Internationals could not meet the members of banned organisations such as the LKCK and the LPK openly in occupied Kosova, but they could and did meet a monopoly of the LDK leadership, and this was but a short step to seeing the LDK as the only significant political force.

The influence of the more radical parties, particularly the LPK, had expanded rapidly in the 1998–9 period in central and western Kosova. Later Albright commented on Thaci's 'brilliant potential', but in the first week of talks little that was concrete was achieved, with Italian leader Lamberto Dini putting pressure on his friend Rugova for the Kosovars to abandon their demand for an independence referendum, and the Americans doing the same on Thaci to accept the framework agreement that had been prepared, which envisaged the total disarmament of the KLA. Unsurprisingly, Thaci was unable to give this assurance, and other delegation leaders backed him. The talks were supposed to end on Saturday 13 February but in reality almost nothing had been agreed by then, and a further extension was planned. By the middle of the following week more Albanian leaders were on board but Thaci still refused to sign, and he felt that his position, perhaps even his life, was threatened if he did. The mobile phone once again played a key role in events, with different KLA field commanders telling him from the war zones that the only reason the KLA had been formed was to achieve independence and until it was gained, or at least a referendum on it granted, they would not disarm.

The Americans tried to contact Adem Demaci to persuade him to pressurise Thaci to sign, but Demaci refused to intervene, saying he supported Thaci and the KLA's position.[13] As a result the international community leaders effectively adopted Veton Surroi as leader of the delegation, a redrafting of the agreement began, and Surroi signed the final text for the Kosovars while Thaci promised to spend the next two weeks 'selling' it to the KLA leadership in Kosova. In effect the international community was trying to make the Kosovars give up the long-held dream of independence, which no leader could be expected to do. Thaci's critics have called his position intransigent and dogmatic but in retrospect there is no doubt he was reflecting the opinion of many, perhaps most, Kosovars, for whom, as even Serbian President Kostunica has said, 'the word independence is written on every Kosovar's heart when they are born'.[14]

The elevation of Surroi to effective delegation leader, from being its secretary, was a sign of growing British influence over the situation. Surroi had been a British payroll leader in Kosova since the early 1990s when British government finance had backed his first journalistic and media ventures. The 'head-bashing' and highly coercive approach of the US diplomats and EU figures such as Austrian leader Wolfgang Petritch had not succeeded in changing Thaci's mind, and in a few quarters he has since been blamed for the failure of Rambouillet to produce a peace deal between the Serbs and Albanians. Given the realities of the situation and the conflict on the ground, this is a harsh judgement, and indicative of wishful thinking rather than rational analysis among those who hold this view.

Thaci's decision marked the interaction of the military and political factors in the conflict in the clearest possible way. The key issue, as always, was the control of the ground by the military and police. If the deal were signed in its original form, the Belgrade security and repressive apparatus would remain intact in Kosova. The NATO 'peace implementation force' sounded, to Kosovar ears, something much too close to the UN force in Bosnia that had been so easily controlled by the Serbs in the 1993–5 period, and they feared that without the KLA they would be unable to resist the pressure to reincorporate the state within Yugoslavia.[15] In this sense, both the KLA and Milosevic were at least realists; the conflict was not about human rights reforms or educational autonomy or a return to the 1974 arrangements. This was a Western diplomatic pipedream; it was about control of the territory and independence.

The Albanians were alarmed by the Rambouillet concession to Milosevic that the NATO troops would be designated as an 'anti-terrorist force'; it seemed as though they would be picking up the Serbs' mission. There were also worries about this policy in the Pentagon, the CIA and in parts of the British military. US and British special forces advisers and private military contractors had been working with the KLA in northern Albania for some time, and were aware of the real situation on the ground and the explosive potential of the conflict. Behind these concerns was the anxiety in the Pentagon and EU defence ministries about the increasing flow of recruits to the KLA, the KLA force strength having reached about 18,000 soldiers plus many armed sympathisers. Intelligence reports were appearing on the planning of a Prishtina uprising by the LKCK and other militants in the city. Having witnessed the terrible difficulty of controlling an Albanian insurgency as President Sali Berisha floundered in 1997, US infantry commanders had no wish to be involved as a 'piggy in the middle' between the Serbs and Albanians, and told the administration that they were only prepared to put up troops for a force if there was a 'permissive' military environment. In practical military terms, this really meant that the Serbian forces would have to be reduced to wreckage by an air campaign before ground troops could be put in theatre.

The Director of the CIA, George Tenet, was of Albanian-American origin, from post-Second World War emigrants from Himara near the Adriatic coast north of Saranda, and unlike any other senior figure involved in the West had a deep knowledge of the politics and culture of the Albanian side. The CIA knew that politics in Albania and the Albanian lands had been changed irrevocably by the 1997–9 period, and that there was no longer a 'moderate majority' of leaders who could be easily manipulated by the international community. This logic also led to more and more commitment to NATO air power as a way to deal with Milosevic. The CIA considered that the forces being assembled in and near Kosova under the Niš military command area were about 50 per cent larger than those used in the First Offensive in 1998.[16] On the other side, Yugoslav generals still believed they could win their counter-insurgency campaign, and Milosevic told the Americans that the deployment of an outside military force in Kosova was unacceptable.[17]

During the next two weeks, from the end of February until the negotiations resumed on 15 March, there was ferment throughout the Albanian political world. In Tirana the newspapers and the government toed the official line, which supported the Rambouillet deal, but under the surface the situation was more complex. It was an axiom of the situation that NATO could not afford to lose any war that it fought, and there was a good deal to be said from the Tirana point of view for a conflict that could only have one winner in terms of changing the place of Albania in the world. NATO was effectively taking the side of the Albanians and a successful war could, once and for all, change the balance of forces in the region. Although the government called for a peaceful outcome and the adoption of the Rambouillet formula, few government ministers had any illusions about the underlying situation. In these circumstances, many people felt that common sense would force the Serbs to come to a deal. This applied to KLA leaders as much as Tirana politicians.

As far from Tirana as it is possible to be in the Albanian world, in the Llap hills of north-east Kosova, a leading KLA commander such as Rrustem Mustafa (Remi) felt the same doubts about the onset of war as the Tirana media. In a war memoir Remi noted that during the week before 23 March:

> Personally I was sceptical until four–five days before the beginning of bombardments. I did not believe such a thing. I believed Serbia would sign the agreement. I believed Serbia would pull back before the bombing started. However, she did not back off.[18]

Thus by the time NATO began hostilities on 23 March, the process of Rambouillet itself had brought Tirana and the Socialist-led coalition into an increasingly central role in the Albanian-inhabited lands and in the Balkan region as a whole. The projection of US military power in the world was itself increasingly dependent upon the projection of air power, which in turn depended on sea power. Aircraft were launched from ships in the Mediterranean. The same applied to many of the cruise missiles that were fired during the conflict. Albania's key position on the Adriatic coast was an asset of great value to the USA and other NATO navies, and the 78-day bombing campaign that was to follow had many wider geopolitical implications.

US policymakers had in many ways to pick up the threads of the old Eastern Question where, as Julian Amery wrote when describing the wider strategic realities:

> The highroad to the East is the Mediterranean; but those who would reach it from Eastern or Central Europe must first travel in one of three ways: the Black Sea; the Danube, Morava and Vardar valley; or the Adriatic sea. These ways are joined to the Mediterranean highroad at the Dardanelles, the port of Salonika, and the Straits of Otranto; and the strategic importance of these three positions has made them the storm centre of the Eastern Question. The Straits of Otranto … divide the Apulian heel of Italy from the land of Albania.[19]

Tirana was only 30 miles from the Adriatic coast, and one of the few things the Albanian dictator Enver Hoxha and his British ex-MI6 opponent Julian

Amery were able to agree on was the centrality of that coast and its control in world politics.[20]

Surprise has sometimes been expressed about the success of the KLA in attracting at least tolerance and later active support among some parts of the international community, in a way that previous radical popular movements in the Balkans, like the IMRO, had not been able to achieve – but geopolitics can provide an explanation. The IMRO was a pro-Bulgarian organisation that, had it succeeded in 'liberating' large sections of Macedonia and northern Greece from Athens control, would have led to the weakening of a key naval ally of the British Empire in the eastern Mediterranean, and would have changed control of Salonika to a pro-Bulgarian and pro-Russian direction. US tolerance of the KLA rested in the last analysis on geopolitical factors, where US power projection is greatly assisted by a network, or in more modern terminology 'clustering', of influence focused on chains of pro-US states, such as Israel. The intervention on the Albanian side in Kosova was to produce a profoundly loyal and enthusiastic pro-US population and a future state which will depend on US and NATO security structures for its security and survival. In the words of President George Bush in 1991, a 'line in the sand' was drawn on 23 March 1999, the full implications of which have still not been grasped in all sections of the international community. Meanwhile, on the ground the Kosova population had to meet the full force of the Serbian assault, and a period of going through fire and brimstone to achieve freedom was ahead. The greatest burden would fall upon over a million refugees. [21]

In Paris, after the failure of the first phase of the talks, it became obvious that war was not far away. Veton Surroi was dispatched to London to meet British Foreign Secretary Robin Cook, and to attend a Kosova crisis conference at Wilton Park in Sussex. There he swept up the gravel drive and into the Foreign Office's rural retreat in a long black coat, and appeared to be a future candidate for national leadership. These weeks were the height of Surroi's influence. The Foreign Office had been a long-time supporter of his newspaper *Koha Ditore*, and the media aspect of the war was a very British affair.[22] In the conference he concentrated on the presentation of the new leader, Hashim Thaci, and for the first time revealed his own closeness to Thaci over the last period. Most of the assembled diplomats, politicians and experts had no idea who Thaci was, and Surroi played an invaluable role in his legitimisation during this key time. Surroi acted in the same way as NATO General Secretary George Robertson's interlocutor with NLA leader Ali Ahmeti in the Macedonian conflict in 2001.

In the US State Department plans were made to wheel out Richard Holbrooke for one last time to try to persuade Milosevic away from a course that would lead Yugoslavia into a suicidal war. There was still a section of opinion that felt that while air strikes might be necessary a full-scale war could be avoided, and this opinion constituency still continued to be influential for several weeks after the air strikes had started. It was made up, in the US, mainly of the more mildly pro-Serb Foreign Service officers, and those in and around the US Air Force who tended to see the Kosova conflict through Bosnia spectacles.[23] The main practical effect of their activity was, though, to produce confusion and delay the major strategic strikes that finally brought the Serbs to the negotiating table.

The threat of force could mean many different things to many different political and military actors, a major difficulty for NATO throughout the time of its Balkan involvements. The Belgrade leadership took the opportunity during the political confusion in the last two weeks of February and the beginning of March to accelerate the process of the ethnic cleansing of Kosova. By the second week of April over a hundred thousand people had moved from their homes. US Secretary of State Madeleine Albright noted that 'we had underestimated the speed, scale and ferocity of the Serbs' terror campaign.'[24] The talks in Belgrade between Holbrooke and Milosevic only produced a series of delaying tactics by Milosevic and it was clear that the ethnic cleansing of Kosova would have been completed by mid-summer 1999 if NATO had not acted.

In Tirana and throughout Albania the entire attention of the government was directed to refugee and humanitarian aid operations, although more soldiers were moved to the Yugoslav border and kept on high alert. On 11 March the Shkoder division and the tanks available at Lac were mobilised to be ready to defend the border with Montenegro. On the political front in Kosova Thaci had succeeded in getting the agreement of most KLA commanders to a signature on the Rambouillet deal, and on 16 March he issued a statement saying that the Kosovar Albanian delegation would sign. On the same day Albania moved soldiers to Tropoja, the first real demonstration of Tirana state power there since March 1997. They were received well by the local population. The previous day Yugoslav forces had crossed the border near the Prushi Pass above Gjakova and fired on Albanian villages. Thus the prospect of outright war between the two countries moved closer.

The Kosovar Albanian delegation in Paris finally signed the agreement two days later on 18 March, but an event that might have been so important a month before had now become largely irrelevant. The signature gave the Albanians the moral high ground but little more than that. It was, though, received with relief in Tirana, where officials who had been in regular contact with Thaci and Haliti had been quite unable to exert effective pressure in favour of any compromise on the independence issue. The decisive voice was that of the armed men on the ground in the KLA, and Thaci's timing in 'delivering' them at this stage was immaculate, with the event making a good image for the Kosovars. However, it was now much too late to slow the momentum towards war. In a sign that the diplomatic process had run its course, Tirana Foreign Minister Paskal Milo called for an emergency meeting of NATO on the Kosova crisis, while Prime Minister Majko flew to Paris for talks with the Kosovar delegation. A de facto pan-Albanian front had been formed.

In Tirana President Meidani went on television to call for national unity and for immediate foreign intervention in Kosova. It is a sign of the failure of the Democratic Party to reintegrate itself into Albanian political life that during these crisis hours for the wider Albanian nation, Sali Berisha was not put forward as a prominent figure in the largely state-influenced media. New relationships were forming in the Albanian political world but a deep fissure still existed in Albania itself within the political elite, although, as the welcome the army received in Tropoja showed, the attitudes of many rank-and-file Albanians were more sensible than some of their leaders. In a general sense the war now fully involved Albania itself, as well as Kosova, and in terms of logistics and supply issues it also affected Montenegro and most importantly, north-west Macedonia. Only Chameria and the border areas of north-west Greece were exempt from patriotic activity, with the Greek army reinforcing the Ioannina barracks in case of any spillover effect of refugees into Greece.

NATO Secretary General Javier Solana gave the go-ahead for the air campaign to begin on 23 March, and the Alliance joined the contest for Kosova. By the following morning airfields in Montenegro and northern Serbia had been hit by NATO bombs and rockets. The Yugoslav government declared a state of war throughout Yugoslavia and all borders were closed. Tirana newspapers reflected upon the momentous events with a sense that a new era for the Albanian people might be emerging. The tide of events appeared to be running the Albanians' way, although most of the Tirana leadership had only a limited influence over the course of events. As Michael Ignatieff has pointed out, this early stage of the war was almost virtual, with a high technology contest (unseen by the wider world) between NATO's forces and the technicians of the Yugoslav air defences. Only a few thousand people took part.[25]

In the view of the politicians and the world at large, little was being achieved, with Madeleine Albright stating bluntly that 'During the first days of fighting, just about everything went wrong.'[26] Many targets were missed, the weather prevented some operations, and a Lockheed stealth fighter-bomber was shot down over Serbia. The Serb armour was able to pour into Kosova almost unheeded and the savage ethnic cleansing of historic Kosova towns such as Peje and Gjakova occurred during this period. In Prizren the Serb quarter was surrounded with heavily armed supporters of Vojislav Seselj's Radical Party, and the historic headquarters building of the first League of Prizren was set ablaze and burnt down. Perhaps the most important secular national monument for the entire Albanian nation, the event sounded an alarm bell about Belgrade's seriousness in the Kosova campaign that resounded around the Albanian diaspora communities throughout the world.

Refugee flows into Albania, Montenegro and Macedonia accelerated markedly, so that some days as many as 4000 people an hour were leaving Kosova. Hashim Thaci, still in Kosova and living a nerve-racking life in hiding in daytime, described Prishtina as a 'dead city', while the old railway station was crowded with thousands of displaced persons, like a scene from a film about occupied Europe in the Second World War.[27] Special units of the Serbian paramilitary police and army tried to target the Albanian political leadership. Key Rugova aide Fehmi Agani was murdered by Interior Ministry soldiers as he attempted to board a train. Agani was one of the few people in the LDK leadership with any credibility among the KLA and his death was a severe loss to the Rugova leadership group. The vast flood of humanity arriving in Albania meant that in Albania almost all politics quickly became refugee and aid politics, and the fixed contest between the Socialist-led coalition government and the Democratic Party opposition lost relevance – although the Democrats were not slow to accuse Nano, Majko and their associates of defrauding the aid funds. There were now, in a sense, two governments of Albania: the Socialist-led coalition and NATO's Operation's Allied Harbour HQ at Durres and in the old military academy building in central Tirana by the little Lana River.

While these political developments unfolded, the crisis on the ground began to explode. The roads from Kosova to Albania began to fill with tens of thousands of hapless and destitute people, the flotsam and jetsam of the war. They moved steadily by day and night towards Tirana, Durres and the lowlands, a human tide that was to change Albanian history.

15

The Kosova Refugee Crisis in the Region

Three weeks after the beginning of the NATO bombing campaign the influx of over 400,000 Kosovar refugees into Albania, combined with increasing border clashes with Yugoslav forces, placed a huge burden on the Albanian authorities. By the third week in April the government decided to try to move refugees away from vulnerable camps close to the Yugoslav border. Yet in trying to do so, they were acting very much as the Belgrade government wanted. Once the refugees were far from Kosova, it was probable that they might never return. Security was the essence of the appeal of the camps but disaster was never far away, and camp life could only be a temporary solution for most families. A refugee, only 13 years old, wrote later: 'We were in the camp for two months and felt safe there. We had the basics to live by, but we were worried about granny's health. She was growing weaker.'[1]

The USA acted more quickly than the Europeans in facing this threat, with President Bill Clinton informing Congress on 3 April that he planned to send at least 1000 US military support personnel to Albania and Macedonia for refugee relief work. By 6 April thousands of tons of food and materials were being airlifted out of Ramstein Air Base in Germany by the USAF 86th Airlift Wing, with half a million daily humanitarian rations in transit and 700 large tents, but there were major distribution problems once the cargos reached Albania. By then the UN refugee authority, the UNHCR, had assessed the refugee flow as 226,000 people in Albania, 120,000 in the Republic of Macedonia, 36,000 in Montenegro, 8000 in Bosnia and 6000 in Turkey.[2] These figures were probably underestimates. The human tide was becoming a flood, with people moving on foot or with their vehicles or animals through the mountains in an exodus of a truly Biblical scale. Little tractors struggled along mountain tracks, with children and elderly family members riding in them, along with the few possessions they were able to pack with them for the journey.

8. Chaos at the Kosova–Macedonia border, Blace, April 1999

On the Macedonian border the situation was particularly bad. A refugee observed:

> Eventually we reached the Macedonian border at a place called Blace. I felt miserable and cold. The weather was wretched. Flurries of snow came down from the mountains. We were forced to stay out, fully exposed. We were encircled. The Serbian paramilitaries were guarding us on one side, the Macedonian police made sure that we remained where we were.[3]

The situation in the north-eastern town of Kukes, which hosted the majority of new arrivals from Kosova, worsened each day as a never-ending flow of people entered the town. International community officials were able to do little more than try to assess the numbers of people in their locality. The 100,000 refugees in Kukes itself were very exposed as the town, which by then was being described as a 'war zone', is just 15km from the Yugoslav border – well within reach of Serb artillery and mortar fire. The Tirana authorities were therefore determined to quickly reduce the number of refugees in the Kukes district by transporting them to camps further south in the country. The evacuation of the Kosovars, however, was being done in a very chaotic and haphazard manner, as lack of adequate planning meant there were not enough vehicles to transport the refugees to the south. Kukes had an airstrip, which originally had been built as one of the nation's first airstrips in the Zog period in the 1930s, but it had fallen into disrepair. A priority for NATO would be its reconstruction and extension to take large, modern military supply aircraft.

As always in wartime, improvisation solved many problems at local level that central planning had created. The UNHCR in Tirana was a deeply dysfunctional organisation in this period, with problems of organisation, leadership and often a poor relationship with the Albanian authorities.[4] The UNHCR directorate in Geneva under Ron Redmond had a depressing Yugophile atmosphere and poor intelligence about the scale and magnitude of the disaster overwhelming Kosova. The brunt of the relief effort fell directly onto big NGOs like CARE International, World Vision and Oxfam. Unlike the UNHCR, they were efficient and capable, and saved the face of the Western aid community in this crisis. The World Food Programme was much better organised than UNHCR and was the only really effective part of the UN effort. Within quite a short time a 'bush telegraph' within the refugee community carried news about which were the most functional and best organised camps, and people headed towards them.

A notable centre was at Elbasan, where there was plenty of good land made available by the Democratic Party Mayor of one of the most progressive and best-run local authorities in the country, and within a short time two large camps holding as many as 12,000 people were built by the Turkish, French and British armies. Relatively civilised conditions were established, with good relations with the people of the town.[5] In general the provincial towns such as Kukes, Elbasan and Durres carried the heaviest burden, and Tirana did not host very many refugees (with no tented camps at all in the vicinity, and only a small minority of families offering to host refugees). In other provincial centres where there were no tented camps, like Bulqiza, Librazhd or Peshkopi, local hotels and empty buildings were pressed into service to provide basic accommodation. Some of these towns, Peshkopi in particular, had quite extraordinary achievements in refugee relief, given the limits of local resources and the difficulties of accessing international relief supplies in the early weeks of the crisis. A few camps, like Korca, received very few refugees at all at any stage of the crisis.

The refugees did not long remain passive. More enterprising members of families soon entered the street commerce world, and made small cash incomes from cigarette trading and the resale of aid surplus. This contributed further to the demolition of the last vestiges of communism in Tirana, as even if young traders were living in a camp in Elbasan or Durres, they often travelled to the capital to trade goods in the big Tirana street markets. Older inhabitants of Tirana, the Albanian social group with much the strongest anti-Kosovar prejudices, found the whole situation quite extraordinary and very unsettling. The Kosova crisis coming so quickly on the heels of the 1997–8 political turmoil was still a traumatic and difficult experience for older members of the more socially privileged groups, whilst in contrast young Albanian people with shared interests in pastimes like popular music were much more easily able to interact with the refugees. Some minority groups in Tirana who had been refugees themselves, such as the Chams, carried out a disproportionate amount of relief activity.

Although NATO's Operation Allied Harbour HQ outside Durres was meant to coordinate camp-building and management activities, under British General John Reith, it found difficulty in doing so. A cheerful, mild anarchy prevailed, with individual national governments running their own shows once camp-building land had been allocated. It was very fortunate for NATO, and for the Albanians and the Tirana government, that the crisis was occurring in late spring and early summer, where the warm weather after a wet spring meant that physical shelter requirements were much less pressing than they would have been during autumn or winter. The tough Kosovar rural people were often critical of some international aid personnel but fundamentally unconcerned by lacunae in camp organisation. There had been major delays in NATO planning for the refugee crisis, another key indicator of how the progress of the Kosova war had not been envisaged clearly. The preparation for the deployment of NATO troops to aid the refugees did not begin at all until two weeks after the bombing campaign had started, when on 7 April a NATO team led by an Italian general was deployed from NATO South East Europe HQ. In NATO, pro-Serb elements still clung to the illusion that a short period of bombing could force Milosevic to the negotiating table.

Difficulties on agreeing targeting within NATO high command were encouraging the Serbs to drive out as many refugees as they could as quickly as possible, and the bombing campaign was making little impression on Serbian strategic capacity.[6] The first plan for the bombing campaign was for attacks of only five days' duration, and only on tactical targets.[7] General Reith's full team from Allied Command Europe Mobile Force finally arrived on the 10 April to make final preparations for the opening of the NATO Immediate Reaction Force HQ, in an empty building at Plepa on the outskirts of Durres.

About 3000 soldiers from NATO national contingents were already in place, mostly from Italy, France, Greece and the USA. On 13 April NATO approved plans for a 10,000-troop deployment, authorised to construct camps, repair selected roads, provide refugee transportation and distribute food water and supplies. The US operation, called Shining Hope, was based on the pre-positioning of 36,000 tons of food in Albania that was planned to be enough to feed up to half a million people for three months. A second US operation had been planned, called Task Force Open Arms, aimed to airlift refugees from Albania to the USA, although as events turned out, few of the 20,000 refugees the American Red Cross expected ever crossed the Atlantic.

Large numbers of Kosovar Albanians near the border were an alleged 'provocation' to the Serbs, who claimed the camps were providing a support base for the recruiting and training of KLA guerrillas. There was also a specific Tirana government decision to clear the Kukes camps to make room for the possible arrival of thousands more refugees if and when they arrived. This did not take place, with the massive Kukes camp support organisation being coordinated by big NGOs like CARE, the Swiss-based International Committee of the Red Cross and Oxfam, who in reality were the real political authority in Kukes and had by far the most authority over practical decision-making. Their staffs was experienced in emergencies and disaster relief in many parts of the world, had excellent top-level contacts with donor governments, and soon accessed basic organisational, logistics and communications capacity on a scale that Tirana government officials could never have achieved. The more able local government officials in the north, where municipalities were not dysfunctional, soon saw the personal advantage in working directly with the big INGOs, coming to view them as a godsend and unique opportunity to make their own names on the Albanian national scene without having to go through the centre in Tirana. Before the 1999 refugee crisis Tirana, in general, had taken no interest in these remote north-east communities in the post-communist period.

With the imminent arrival of an estimated 60–70,000 refugees from over-crowded camps in Macedonia, new camps were being built deep inside Albania, away from the vulnerable northern border. In less than two months the population of Albania had increased by nearly 17 per cent. As a result there was concern about what socio-economic impact the long-term presence of so many Kosovars would have on Albanian society if they were not able to return to Kosova relatively soon. The number of refugees leaving Kukes for other districts had fallen greatly since the last week of April, due to a severe lack of adequate transport to disperse people to different regions. Most NATO vehicles were still based in parks near southern towns like Durres. The always poor road to Kukes from Tirana was beginning to collapse in some mountainous regions, as heavy military vehicle use compounded the usual problems of erosion, snow and water damage in the high mountains. The main road was not capable of taking very heavy vehicles beyond Burrel, only about halfway to Kosova from Tirana, something that constrained NATO's food distribution capacity. There was also acute psychological reluctance on the part of the refugees to move away from the Kukes camps. They wanted to remain as close to Kosova as possible, and persuading them to leave Kukes proved extremely difficult for both the UNHCR and the Albanian authorities.

This insistence on remaining in Kukes stemmed from several factors. Firstly, many were families who still had relatives missing in the aftermath of their flight from Kosova and were remaining in Kukes in the hope of being reunited. Secondly, there was an initial lack of information about where the refugees would be taken and what living conditions were like in other camps. Few refugees had ever been in Albania in their lives, and thus people had only a vague idea of local geography in many places. Many Kosovars were shocked and appalled at the general poverty and lack of modern infrastructure they found in the poorest parts of northern Albania. Thirdly, there was a degree of scepticism about the type of reception the Kosovars would receive from local Albanians should they move to southern districts. Kukes region had been part of the villayet of Kosova in Ottoman times, and some prominent Kosovar politicians from Prizren, like Veton Surroi and Edita Tahiri,[8] had family roots and connections in the Kukes hinterland. In the diaspora leading figures such as Prizren League General Secretary in the USA Gani Perolli came from a family that owned land on both sides of the Albania–Kosova border just north of the town, above the Quaf e Morines Pass. The big hydroelectric dams on the White and Black Drin rivers meeting there had been a Hoxhaist showpiece that had involved the drowning of the old Kukes village, Ottoman *Kukush*. Some Kosovar specialists had been allowed to be employed on this project in the 1980s. Although so remote from Tirana, many key elements in Kosovar Albanian life were present in Tropoja, and in a certain sense if not 'home' it was unlike total exile.

The concern of some Kosovars about settling in southern areas of Albania also stemmed from what the Kosovars had heard about the violent uprising of 1997, which emanated from the south of Albania. The events of 1997 were mistakenly believed by many Kosovars to have been directed against the government of Sali Berisha, in part because his administration was identified as northern Gheg 'nationalist' as opposed to southern Tosk 'Socialist'.[9] Thus, due to the fact that the Kosovars are Ghegs, at the onset of the crisis many believed they would not be welcome in southern Tosk areas of Albania. In understanding these fears, the basic lack of information in Kosova consequent upon Milosevic's closure of the Albanian media in 1990 should be remembered. For over ten years Kosova had been pitifully short of information about Albania. It was not the refugees' fault that they initially believed these myths; the Rugova leadership in Prishtina had never done anything to enlighten them. They had no independent media and except for a tiny number of specialist workers, artists and intellectuals they were unable to experience Albania in the past as normal visitors.

In Kukes it was the men who appeared the most reluctant to move south, not only because they were uncertain of their reception elsewhere, but also because they wanted to return to Kosova as soon as possible and believed that their dispersement would delay that return. Some wished to join the KLA and fight to regain their land if they could buy a weapon and find a way to do so. As the international community began to have more of a permanent presence in Kukes, some KLA operations had been moved north to Kruma in the Has region, and contacting the insurgent recruiters was more difficult. Women, on the other hand, showed a greater willingness to relocate away from the overcrowded and wholly unsanitary Kukes camps, mainly because they were concerned about the health of their children. Women also did virtually all the domestic chores such as clothes-washing, standing in long provision queues, cleaning, cooking and child care. Even for those used to the tough life of the Kosovar farms, camp life was primitive and they were consequently curious to know what conditions were like elsewhere in the hope that they would hear of somewhere better than Kukes.

One aid official described his impatience with some of the Kosovar men in Kukes, saying that they spent their days 'cussing and discussing', whilst their womenfolk tried desperately to maintain a semblance of domestic routine amidst such appalling conditions. An Albanian journalist from Tirana was so angry at the Kosovar men for refusing to discuss what conditions were like in camps in southern Albania, that he demanded the men go back and fight in Kosova, and let the women and children move away from the filth, damp and squalor of the Kukes camp.[10] To compound the problem of Kosovar refugees, there had recently been an increase in cross-border military clashes, which had caused the displacement of many local Albanian families living near the Yugoslav border. Serb artillery had widened the conflict by shelling several Albanian villages near Bajram Curri, killing several people and forcing hundreds to flee their homes. Those who remained gathered for safety at night in abandoned hillside tunnels and mine shafts.[11]

By the end of April, around 6000 inhabitants of border villages in the Kukes and Tropoja districts had been evacuated from their homes, with only the men staying behind to protect livestock and property. For the first time, on 22 April, Serb forces used depleted uranium radioactive shells in fighting with KLA troops close to the border with Albania. For almost a year similar incidents had taken place. Now, however, it appeared that the firing of artillery shells made of radioactive material into Albanian territory was targeting civilians. Further use of such weapons increased in May because Serb forces found it difficult to return to their previous positions along the Kosova–Albania border after severe fighting with the KLA. The Serb attacks were aimed at destroying KLA training camps in the area, as well as causing general instability in the border districts.

Another reason why it was thought advisable to move the refugees from the northern border districts was to protect them and the aid agencies from the violent local gangs that preyed upon any strangers, Albanian or foreign, who were thought not to have adequate armed protection.[12] The arrival of the Kosovars had provided rich pickings for local Albanian criminal elements. In the northern border area local gangsters robbed some of the refugees with impunity, whilst illegal immigrant traffickers in the coastal town of Vlora were doubling their number of trips across the Adriatic with boats crammed full of Kosovars hoping to join relatives in Western Europe. Some refugees complained of being victimised by local Albanian gangsters, who had stolen their cars and tractors and sold them back at exorbitant prices. This was especially so in the Tropoja district where international border monitors, foreign journalists and Kosovar refugees had been robbed at gunpoint of their money, equipment and vehicles. At the end of April a BBC crew was attacked by two masked men, who fired over their car and then stole their cameras and money. Even NATO officers dispatched to reconnoitre the area for possible troop deployment had to be escorted by lorry loads of Albanian soldiers.

Local criminals were quick to exploit the arrival not only of refugees and foreign media crews, but also of the dozens of international relief agencies that descended on Kukes and the notoriously bleak and lawless town of Bajram Curri. Dozens of truckloads of international aid was disappearing daily en route between the port of Durres and Tirana, into the hands of the local mafia and then onto the black market. In mid-April $300,000 worth of antibiotics disappeared from the port of Durres. The constant movement of refugees into the central and southern districts of Albania, together with the lack of proper registration of refugees scattered throughout the country, made it relatively easy to divert aid supplies. Aid representatives estimated that only four out of every ten relief consignments were actually being distributed to the refugees without prior resale.

Although the Albanian authorities set up an emergency committee to coordinate the arrival and distribution of aid, the weakness and sometimes complete absence of any effective Albanian administration in many areas, combined with problems of division of responsibility between various international relief agencies, severely limited the committee's effectiveness. In some northern districts regional authorities were involved with the local mafia. With the scale of the thefts some relief organisations were pulling out of the most dangerous areas. A special refugee police force of 1600 officers was quickly established, in part to maintain public order in the camps but also to protect the refugees and to accompany the relief lorries. Due to the enormity of the crisis, however, this force was wholly inadequate to protect all but a few districts in and around Kukes.

Vehicles and construction supplies at reception centres for future refugees were urgently needed, as were food supplies to local Albanians who were sheltering refugees. Local families, who had taken in hundreds of refugees, were finding it almost impossible to continue feeding their Kosovar 'guests' as well as their own families. This was a difficult time of year. Unlike September or October, there was little food to harvest when the peasants were just planting crops. Having spontaneously invited the Kosovars into their homes, local Albanians did not expect to have to feed so many people for such a long time. Most families had exhausted their winter food supplies. Thus there was an urgent need to supply local families sheltering refugees with extra food in order to prevent a destabilising of the situation.

There appeared little willingness amongst international aid agencies to coordinate with the Tirana government, some members of which believed that many NGOs had a real fear of a transparency that might expose their organisation's inefficiencies.[13] Kukes District Council Chairman, Shefqet Bruka, praised the work of the UNHCR but criticised other international organisations for not coordinating their activities between either themselves or the Tirana authorities, thereby hampering relief work.[14] In reality, the UNHCR had been one of the organisations worst prepared for the crisis, with an inefficient bureaucratic structure. Another factor that needed to be urgently addressed was the allocation of suitable sites for the construction of sizeable refugee camps. The Albanian government kept offering sites for refugee camps, which were state-owned and invariably turned out to be flooded or otherwise physically unsuitable. Any land that was half-decent was privately owned.

The people of Albania were largely sympathetic to the plight of the refugees, but many were concerned that their settlements might take on signs of permanency. There was resentment from some elements of the ethnic Greek community about the numbers of Kosovars (although modest) arriving in the eastern town of Korca near the Greek border, where NATO was building

9. Kosova refugee at Kukes camp, June 1999

several camps. Absentee landlords from the Greek-speaking community then owned much of the land around the vast plain of Korca. The owners were living and working in Greece. At the height of the crisis, local people agreed that there would not be a problem if the refugees stayed for a relatively short time. However, if they remained for any length of time, there was concern that they may start growing vegetables around their dwellings, looking for work in a region with chronic unemployment and receiving better material benefits than local people, such as fresh running water and reliable electricity. In practice, none of these fears came to much, with the fairly limited number of refugees being well organised by the German army, and many mothers with small children being accommodated in old school buildings near the centre of Korca itself, a sign of community acceptance.

The greatest dimension to the refugee crisis in terms of the coming together of the Albanian people was in Macedonia. After the initial movement of people southwards had begun after 28 March, a huge mass of thousands of refugees had begun to build up in the 'no man's land' between the border of Kosova and Macedonia at Blace village, on the border crossing point at the south end of the dramatic and imposing wooded Kacanik Gorge. In increasingly insanitary and desperate conditions, the international press witnessed the brutality of the Macedonian army and police against them, which seemed exactly similar to that meted out by Milosevic's police.[15] British Development Minister Clare Short called for international intervention, and a new focus for the crisis emerged that took some of the refugee and internally displaced person movement pressure off Albania. The Skopje government viewed the whole process as a disaster for Macedonia, and attempts were made to revive the old idea of ex-President Gligorov for 'corridors' in Macedonia to drive the refugees through the country and into Albania.

The Macedonian security forces did not in fact have the capacity to do this, with a small and badly organised army, and once the border was broken at Blace, after intense international pressure, there was no prospect of controlling refugee movements. A reception camp was set up and run by CARE International at Stokenovac, between Blace and Skopje, and soon it was bursting to capacity with 6000 refugees. Conditions were dismal, with the British army attempting to enforce reasonable humanitarian standards, whilst the Macedonians controlled the perimeter with savage dogs. A second reception camp, 'Stokenovac II' was soon in operation, and by the middle of April the whole 20-mile zone between the border and Skopje was a seething refugee city, barely under any kind of control. A massive camp under CARE management was quickly constructed in the second week of the month at Cegrane, north of Gostivar, and this became the largest single camp in the entire crisis, housing over 43,000 people by the end of May in a camp that had been designed for 12,000, under the aptly named Snake Hill.[16]

The internationalisation of the crisis had profound internal effects in Macedonia, as President Kiro Gligorov envisaged that it would.[17] The old neo-communist system of government in Skopje, with its nationalist and chauvinist 1991 constitution embodying Slav power, was one of the most unreformed and backward governments of the ex-Yugoslav republics. Under a façade of ethnic harmony, the 25-plus per cent Albanian minority suffered a variety of serious human rights problems, which had exploded into violence in July 1997 in Gostivar.[18] Other minorities, such as the 5 per cent of Turks, were leaving the country, and the large Roma community centred on Skopje were some of the poorest and most disadvantaged people in the whole of Eastern Europe. Macedonian Slav dominance had been traditionally maintained by a close alliance with Serbia, a product of the states' Titoist origins.

The refugee crisis and the effective takeover of Macedonian security by NATO, and the free run that NATO and other international community personnel had in the country, considerably eroded the old government system. It was therefore soon possible for a sense of liberation to sweep through the Albanian communities in the west, centred on the towns of Tetovo and Gostivar. Although in a formal sense Skopje government jurisdiction still existed throughout Macedonia, the demands of the crisis broke through many of the old communist survivals in terms of local government, and subsequently opened the way for popular local political and social initiatives for the Albanians. They managed to recover a degree of control over their communities that led to the conflict of 2001 and the democratisation of the country through the Ohrid Accords.[19] But all this was far in the future.

The Albanian-dominated town of Tetovo had been deeply involved in the Kosova war since the spring of 1998, and a few of the top KLA officials came from Tetovo, such as Bardhyl Mahmuti. Many educated Albanians in Tetovo under 50 years of age had attended Prishtina University before it was purged of Albanian teachers by the Milosevic regime in 1989–90, and there were also many family links.[20] Before 1990 there had, of course, been no border of any kind for 50 years between Kosova and what became the Republic of Macedonia. Tetovo Albanian political leader Arben Xhaferi was one of the most acute and intelligent politicians in the region, and had close contacts with the non-LDK Kosova leadership.

A new political centre appeared in Tetovo, and with its own refugee camp four kilometres away at Neprostino, the town was soon at the centre of the crisis. It was close enough to the old Sar mountain passes for KLA people to cross into Macedonia on a horse, or even travelling on foot. It was within particularly easy reach of the key town of Prizren, the traditional fountainhead of Albanian nationalism. The Prishtina Albanian-language newspaper *Koha Ditore*, owned by Veton Surroi, moved its production to Tetovo after the Prishtina operation was closed on 25 March, and soon much of the elite of Prishtina were based in Tetovo. In contrast, many LDK and Bukoshi people had fled to Skopje in Macedonia. The first elements of the pan-Albanian world had appeared as a result of the refugee crisis, in a way that was to have very fundamental long-term consequences.

The Macedonian-Albanian leaders had even fewer productive contacts with the Tirana leadership than the Kosovars had, and were viewed from the Albanian capital as complete provincials, with perhaps a little too close a relationship with Islam. This was quite untrue in terms of the ethos of Xhaferi or his party, but it was a convenient stereotype. The mutual ignorance and indifference meant that the Tirana leadership had little means of moderating Macedonian-Albanian nationalism or of preventing the growth of local support for the Kosova war. The political world of the new Albanian space was being formed by the breakdown of communist-era borders and the development of free markets as opposed to Slavo-communist command economies and state socialist social restraints, but at this stage it was a process that was largely invisible to the international community. Few Skopje-based diplomats ever visited or spent much time outside Skopje, a natural result of the excessive centralisation of all Macedonian government functions there, and the political vitality and high leadership quality of the Tetovo leaders was often unknown. In Montenegro, Bosnia and elsewhere, the small refugee inflow was contained without long-term social and political effects, but this was not the case in Macedonia. It acted as a decisive lever to open the new national question in that country.

In another regional dimension to the refugee crisis that was to have long-term seminal effects in opening the national question but was generally unnoticed at the time, the Greek government refused to take any refugees whatsoever, in a cruel decision that was in breach of international humanitarian law. As Serbia's main regional ally, Greece had stood against the main direction of Western policies in the region for most of the crisis, but NATO required the use of the port of Thessaloniki for the Kosovar and Macedonian logistics and supply operation. The Greek government of Costas Simitis had a strong hand, and used the excuse of the developing war and anti-Albanian public opinion to exclude the refugees. In return NATO got what it wanted in Thessaloniki. It was, in retrospect, a foolish and short-sighted decision, as it produced a feeling of bitterness against Greece in the Albanian world that has yet to subside.

None of the Western countries or NATO members involved in the crisis had any clear notion of the effect of refugee flows on this scale on the politics of the regional world. This was not surprising at one level: such movements of people in Europe had not been seen since the Second World War. The central political motive for NATO's intervention was to enable the people to return to their homes, but the process of war would also irrevocably change Kosova itself. Wars, notoriously, bring social revolutions, and the region would never be the same again. It is as yet unclear what NATO leaders really thought they would finally achieve. Recent publications by American scholars such as David Halberstam indicate that in some quarters in Washington there was a hard core of opposition to the Clinton administration's Kosova policy throughout the war, centred on figures in the US army, and that this led to the sacking of NATO SACEUR (Supreme Allied Commander Europe) General Wesley Clark soon after the war.[21]

The hard fact was that after the Rambouillet conference NATO was forced to take action in support of the Kosovars or look ineffective and ridiculous. Events had moved the Kosovar Albanians' way in a direction that only a very few people could have imagined a year or two previously. In turn, they opened the new national question wherever they went. At a human level, during the refugee emergency, life went on and the spirit of the people overcame the humiliations of refugee existence. Remzije Ujkupi observed in Renfrew, Scotland, later in that summer: 'When we left home during the war, I was glad to have my baby in a safe place. My son was born in Scotland, so we called him "Shpetim Scot Ujkupi", which means "Safe Scot Ujkupi".'[22]

PART

VI

THE NEW ALBANIAN SPACE AND THE FUTURE

16

Tirana and the New Kosova

When NATO forces entered Kosova on 11 June 1999, they found departing Serb forces and also departing Serb refugees. Over 50,000 Serbs left Kosova within the first few days of the NATO operation. Some were employees of the repressive Milosevic state who knew they were likely to be killed if they remained; others were ordinary peasants and working families. Some had committed crimes against their Albanian neighbours during the war, others had not. Some families fled with their belongings in cars and lorries so that there were no Serbs at all left in many Kosova towns, apart from isolated elderly people, and many Serb villages were almost completely depopulated. Intimidation began against remaining Roma and Serbs, for a variety of reasons. There was widespread 'score-settling' within local communities over the next six months, and naturally the vast majority of Milosevic-era state officials fled, given their complicity in war crimes and long years of repression.

Within a month, by mid-July 1999, the old Yugoslav state had collapsed, and the new United Nations mission in Kosova (UNMIK) administration was faced with the task of building a new multi-ethnic, democratic Kosova from the ruins of the old Yugoslav system.[1] The international community had not anticipated the speed and rapidity of the transition of power. The Provisional Government of Hashim Thaci and the KLA that had been declared on 5 April was the only effective authority on the ground in Prishtina, although after a few weeks Ibrahim Rugova returned to Kosova from Italian exile and stated that he felt he was the legitimate leader, based on elections held in the Milosevic period.[2] It is worth bearing in mind that the NATO Kosova force deployment plan had originally been designed to police a 'settlement' agreed with Milosevic, along Bosnian lines, and this accounts for some of the force deployment decisions, particularly the fateful decision to give the French Army control of the northern Serb-dominated sector at Mitrovica and in Leposavic *opstina* district. Major Serb population movement does not seem to have been anticipated in the planning parameters. The international community seems to have envisaged that whole sections of the old Kosova state machine and its personnel would remain more or less intact, and that this 'planning' was in turn based on the assumption of a short air campaign and then a successful peace negotiation.[3]

As the air campaign was long and difficult, the land war between the KLA and Serb forces had carried on regardless, and violence in Kosova in that period was very severe. By the first week of June the KLA was present everywhere in Kosova, even in areas of the south-west around Gjilan where until early 1999 it had had little influence. It controlled a swathe of territory, perhaps 30 per cent of Kosova in the centre and west, stretching from Istog and the Montenegrin border in the north to Mount Pashtrik above Prizren in the south-west. This success underlaid the apparently dogmatic and rejectionist view taken of Rambouillet and peace negotiations and initiatives during the 78-day war by Adem Demaci and some KLA field commanders. They knew that if the NATO air campaign continued for long enough they could cut the Serb supply lines north along the roads leading to Serbia, causing the campaign of the Prishtina Corps to become unsustainable. By late May this had begun to happen, and the LKCK scenario of a general Albanian uprising in Prishtina would become feasible.

NATO bombing had its successes and failures but there was no doubt that the big Yugoslav Army barracks on the edge of Kosova Polje to the west of Prishtina was a smoking ruin, and that key cruise missile hits on strategic targets like the Prishtina Post Office tower with its central electronic communications were at long last taking place. After the 23 May missile on the Post Office tower, military communications for the Serb forces suffered very badly. If the bombing had continued for another three or four weeks, there is every probability that the KLA would have been in sole control of all of Kosova. This is perhaps the central unresolved and unanswerable question of the war.

With the beginning of the appearance of an anti-war movement in Serbia itself, continuation of the war was a real option for the Albanians. The fact that Hashim Thaci was able to moderate the more extreme demands of many KLA commanders gave the international community a breathing space to persuade the Serbs to accept the Russian peace plan. From the mainstream Albanian point of view, after about the end of June 1999 the critical

10. NATO's war: cruise missile strike on a Prishtina building, May 1999

issue was that Kosova was now almost entirely an ethnic Albanian space, where only a few tens of thousands of Serbs and other minorities remained, living alongside over a million Albanians. Irrespective of the difficulty that has naturally followed in deciding the future of Kosova, this represented a massive strategic advance for the Albanian people in the region. The liberation of Kosova from Milosevic's forces and the puppet 'government' the Serbs had created in the 'Greater Serbia' period of 1989–99 in turn created a new Albanian political space, irrespective of border change and sovereignty issues. The history of the years after June 1999 is in essence the attempt of the international community to come to terms with this new reality.

In June and July in Albania the central issue was the return of the refugees. There had been a total failure of the UNHCR strategy for refugee returns, which had anticipated a slow and orderly return, under international community supervision, and reintegration into a multi-ethnic Kosova society. The refugees in Albania did not wait for government or international orders, though, and began streaming back to their homes in very large numbers in the three or four weeks after 11 June. Roads in northern Albania were jammed with tractors, cars, carts and buses, led by the hundreds of thousands of people who were still in the Kukes camps. Although in theory NATO had set up a border control post at Quaf e Morines, in practice there was no obstacle placed in the path of the refugees. It was the largest movement of people that had been seen in Europe since the end of the Second World War, and it provided wonderful television pictures for the international media. The big NGOs and the World Food Programme set up way stations along the roads to provide rations, but to all intents and purposes this was the limit of their relief activity. For those humanitarian workers, journalists, diplomats and soldiers who had been connected with the long epic of the Kosova struggle after 1989, this was perhaps the happiest time, before immersion in the manifold and complex problems of Kosova reconstruction and government.

When the refugees arrived at their homes, they often found scenes of medieval devastation. In the camps there had been few newspapers, and even fewer people had transistor radios or access to television. Hence the refugees did not know what was happening to their home communities in any detail. In general they had often only been poorly informed about the extent of the physical damage caused by the Serbs' ethnic cleansing. This particularly applied to town-dwellers who had had no experience of the war in the rural areas prior to their exile. Many were unaware that the entire old town centres and market areas of Peje and Gjakova were burnt out ruins. Entire villages in Drenica and Dukagjini were uninhabitable. In these confused circumstances, relief operations run from Albania and Macedonia concentrated on the provision of tents to provide basic shelter.

In Albania, this news slowed the flow of people somewhat. Families were anxious to leave tented camps and wished to return to proper houses as soon as possible, and when news of the devastation did arrive, they were shocked and disoriented. Some families left old people, women and children behind so that they could live in the support network provided by the NGOs in the Albanian refugee camps. Their menfolk and younger unmarried women returned home and put their homes into some sort of habitable order. If this was impossible, they erected tents next to the houses. This discovery of wartime devastation set the scene for the widespread revenge attacks against remaining Serb communities in rural Kosova, which the NATO force was unable to protect satisfactorily. Throughout Kosova in the next six months Serb churches were burnt down or dynamited, and attacks on individual Serbs proliferated, along with aggression against Roma communities who were seen as having worked with the Serbs under Milosevic.[4]

The new situation in Kosova provided many opportunities and dilemmas for the Tirana government. In terms of practical government, by the end of the bombing campaign NATO and its activity was a dominant element on the streets of the capital city. On some issues, for those connected with security in the north for instance, NATO was the real government of Albania and local ministries were only rubber-stamping decisions taken elsewhere. Many Tirana residents felt they had lost control of their destiny as a result of the Kosova war. The scale of the psychological change was dramatic, after so many years when the Titoist entity had seemed to dominate the Balkans. A Kosova dominated by ethnic Albanians was more than many people could easily imagine after the Milosevic years. Others were curious, and anxious to visit what had been a forbidden land for so long. A few intrepid people began to make the long journey up to Prizren, and Tirana journalists were able to work unhindered in Prishtina for the first time for over 50 years. Tirana publishers filled their cars to the gunwales with books on all subjects that were snapped up by Prizren kiosk owners, hungry for Albanian language vernacular literature after so many years of unavailability.

The more intelligent ministers in the Albanian government tried to find political formulations to match the new reality. As early as 12 April, Foreign Minister Milo had made a speech in which he said that the Rambouillet document was now obsolete and that Kosovar Albanians could no longer live with Serbs, and on 17 April President Rexhep Meidani called for an international protectorate to be set up. During May relations between Hashim Thaci and the KLA on one hand and Ibrahim Rugova had deteriorated sharply, with Thaci declaring on 11 May that the Provisional Government was the sole legitimate authority in Kosova. The following day the Albanian parliament passed a resolution recognising Thaci's government, and also recognising and supporting the KLA, calling for NATO to establish an international protectorate and for the return of displaced people.

Tirana had thrown its weight decisively behind Thaci, whereas the international community had not. Although Rugova was enjoying a life of ease in Italy as a 'guest' of Lamberto Dini, he was still the leader preferred by all European states. Tirana nevertheless pressed ahead with support for Thaci, with Prime Minister Majko suggesting a week later, on 21 May, after talks with Thaci, that the Kosovars should set up a 'Council of National Salvation' to reunite the Rambouillet delegation and bring together a coherent leadership for a post-war Kosova. At a crowded news conference in Tirana, Thaci said that 'there is a vacancy within the government for political forces absent from it', referring to the possibility of Rugova and the LDK joining it.

As in the pre-war period, the imperative for Tirana was to bring unity to the Kosovar leadership, a task no less difficult in the period of the bombing campaign than it had been before it. In practice familiar divisions were reappearing, with the USA and the Great Britain recognising the reality of KLA power and being willing to work with Thaci, while the Europeans led by Italy were keen to revive Rugova's old supremacy. In the Albanian capital Prime Minister Majko wrote to LDK leader Rugova on 21 May inviting him to come to Tirana for talks with the Albanian government. This initiative was however undermined by a wild and intemperate attack from Sali Berisha on the KLA the same day in a Hungarian newspaper, in which he said that parts of the KLA were being led by communists mixed up with the Yugoslav secret police, and alleging that members of the Socialist coalition in Tirana had been profiting from the cross-border arms trade with Kosova.[5] In a demonstration of the political contortions the war had brought upon the DP, in the same interview Berisha also said that his party supported the KLA but it needed 'reorganisation', emphasising that the 'Kosovars are fighting for their own independence, and not for joining Albania'. This was certainly true, but the interview caused uproar in Tirana and the next day Thaci, Majko and Kosovar academic nationalist Rexhep Qosja made a well-publicised visit to a refugee camp together, at Mullet village near Tirana. They sent a message to Berisha that only the Socialist coalition knew the realities of the war and stood unreservedly shoulder to shoulder with the Kosova Albanians.

The new regional situation now meant that, in practice, the Kosovar struggle could not succeed without Albania, whether in the pre-war phase (where the KLA needed safe recruiting and training areas) or in the current wartime phase (when humanitarian aid and refugee support operations along with NATO's operations were run from Tirana). In the minds of some Kosovars and the Democratic Party leadership in Tirana, there was the unspoken question that Majko and the American advisers he followed might be planning a rapid de facto unification of the two territories, which, if it was successful, might exclude the Right from power in both countries for a very long time.

In the region, Greece viewed developments with increasing concern. After the apogee of Greek influence in 1997–8, Greece had suffered massive diplomatic setbacks during the late 1998 and 1999 wartime period, as a result of Nano's departure from power in September 1998. Within NATO, Greece, along with France, had played the major role in delaying the decision to bomb strategic targets in Yugoslavia, and in early May Prime Minister Costas Simitis had ruled out any ground war contribution from Greece when the Clinton administration was actively considering the possibility.[6] Greece was the only neighbouring country to refuse to take Kosovar refugees during the humanitarian crisis. A priority for Greek diplomacy was to destabilise the government of Prime Minister Pandeli Majko and try to engineer the return of Nano, whom they felt more comfortable with, and who was easier to pressurise into closer relations with Serbia. By late May 1999 there was a widespread sense that the war might soon be ending, symbolised by the visit of UN envoy Sergio Vieira de Mello to Kosova on a three-day fact-finding trip. Although not allowed by the Serbs to visit many combat zones, he was shocked by the devastation and spoke of 'the clear evidence of ethnic cleansing by the Serbian forces'.[7]

Another important imperative for the Tirana government during this period was to argue for the maintenance of the unity of Kosova. The Italian government was in favour of setting up 'zones' in Kosova territory, along Bosnian lines, that would effectively partition the land into Serb and Albanian 'entities'. This in effect was promoting an old Serb 'plan' from years before. Albanian Foreign Minister Paskal Milo was sent to Rome at the end of May for talks with the Italian Foreign Minister to try to squash the idea of any partition of Kosova. The Chernomyrdin–Ahtisarri peace plan was making progress with the Serbian government in Belgrade, and on 3 June the Serbian parliament voted for the proposals.[8] Slobodan Milosevic had been forced to recognise that the Russians were not going to risk their ongoing relationship with the West over Kosova. The end of one stage of the war was drawing near.

Provisional Government leader Hashim Thaci continued to attend a whirlwind of meetings in Albania and elsewhere, the most important of which was an appeal issued in Paris on 28 May to Ibrahim Rugova for 'reconciliation', and for Rugova to recognise the realities of the military, diplomatic and political situation and to join the new Kosova 'National Security Council' that Thaci wished to set up. Heavy fighting was continuing in Kosova, particularly in the west near the Albanian border in Dukagjini, with the KLA threatening Serb control of the Prishtina–Podujevo road after cutting the supply lines to the Serb military bases around Prishtina, which were running short of food as a result. Although the internal organisation of the KLA had improved a good deal in 1999, there were still major communications difficulties between different commanders in the localities, and the international community diplomats had little idea what they felt about the new Russian-brokered peace plan[9].

The indictment of Milosevic as a wanted war criminal by the International War Crimes Tribunal at The Hague on 27 May seems to have been timed to impress the Kosovar Albanians and convince them that the international community really would take decisive action against Belgrade. The same day Yugoslav Prime Minister Momir Bulatovic called for a halt to NATO bombing and a political settlement by 'diplomatic means under United Nations aegis and in strict observance of its Charter' – the latter presumably meaning an open recognition of Serbian sovereignty over Kosova. Simultaneously, rumours of an attempt by dissidents in the LDK leadership to remove Rugova from the party presidency swept Prishtina, and his office was forced to put out a press statement confirming that he remained leader of the LDK.

The end of the war came on 11 June with a suddenness that few had expected. Slobodan Milosevic had been forced to recognise that Russia was not going to come to his aid, and that the deteriorating military situation in Kosova posed risks to his forces.[10] In Prishtina, the Serb army stripped the museum of its exhibits and loaded them onto trucks to take to Serbia, and an orgy of firebombing and other attacks on mosques took place. Almost every Islamic library was destroyed, a prelude to the destruction of Serb religious buildings that followed in the ensuing months. As the trucks loaded with soldiers left, the first forces from NATO replaced them. A savage and oppressive occupier was replaced by a benevolent occupier, or so it seemed. Happy Albanians threw flowers at the NATO soldiers as they arrived and took up their places in the barracks that the Serbs had so recently left.

British soldiers suddenly dominated the centre of Prishtina. The NATO KFOR (Kosovo Force) HQ was established in the old Kosova film studios, on a hill overlooking the city. The Grand Hotel, for so long owned and run by Serbian war criminal Arkan and his men, was now full of young British paratroopers. A new Kosova was emerging from the ruins of the old. In Prizren there was a huge street party, with musicians playing in the summer sun as the soldiers of the KLA swept into the historic city from their bases on Mount Pashtrik and the Has hills. Long chains of people hundreds strong danced and sang into the night under the benevolent eyes of German KFOR soldiers, enjoying the limelight of the first serious foreign deployment of German infantry since 1945. The first returning refugees came back to their homes to discover houses stripped of all furniture by the departing Serbs, who had billeted soldiers and policemen in them.

It did not take long for the people to understand that the new life would contain elements of the old, with Russian forces seizing Prishtina airport and British general Mike Jackson refusing the order of NATO Supreme Commander General Wesley Clark to eject them. In Mitrovica, a de facto Serbian enclave in the area north of the Ibar River was already being established by hard-line Milosevic loyalists, and the French KFOR troops there were unable, or unwilling, to confront them. The new Albanian space might be without the Serb security apparatus, but it was not wholly free.

Almost immediately, marked differences in atmosphere began to emerge quickly between the different KFOR regions, with the German and US KFOR most sympathetic to the Albanians, the British and the Italians somewhere in the middle, and the French in the north seeing their role as primarily to protect the Serb, Roma and Bosnian minority sheltering in Mitrovica and Leposavic from further reprisals by ethnic Albanians. Although the British government of Tony Blair was probably the most pro-Albanian major

11. NATO as liberators: the Turkish army enter Prizren, July 1999

government in the world, the British military had an entrenched and historic pro-Serb lobby within it, which had been strengthened, to some extent, by the Bosnian peacekeeping experience. Rank-and-file soldiers tended to see the KLA as the same sort of force as the IRA they had spent so long fighting in Ireland, and rightly saw the remaining Serbs as an oppressed and often elderly minority needing protection. They did not know, and were not told in briefing material, the full story of the horrors of the last ten years under Milosevic, and as a result tensions between their mandate and the political leadership soon began to grow.

In the wider Albanian world the removal of the Serbian security apparatus from Kosova and NATO's first victory in a war (if formally undeclared) had seismic, if often unseen and hidden effects. Those who had argued for a strong national position over Kosova had been vindicated and those who had said that the USA and NATO would never come to the aid of Albanians were proved wrong. The most obvious losers were the Greeks. The USA had a unique position of influence, and the future history of Albania would now be inextricably involved with the new superpower partner. Others who had been vindicated were the leaders of the little underground groups in the diaspora, who had argued that the future of Kosova could not be entrusted to Rugova and the LDK, and that other forms of organisation and a different political perspective was necessary.

These groups had other agendas, though, as inheritors of the nationalist traditions of the Second World War Balli Kombetar (National Front) and monarchist organisations. This applied even if they had a formally 'Marxist' ideology. They stood for what is now generally called an 'ethnic Albania', disparagingly referred to by Serbs and others as merely another name for a 'Greater Albania' that would unite the Albanians of Albania itself with those of Kosova, Macedonia, Montenegro and the Chameria region of north-west Greece. In most Albanian eyes, however, an 'ethnic Albania' is defined as a region where Albanian language and culture are dominant, within the political parameters of a uniting moderate Europe. This definition appeals to moderate Albanians as it avoids the issue of border changes and difficulties with the Helsinki Final Act and its provisions. As the then President Rexhep Meidani said on one occasion, 'the task of Albanians in the Balkans is not to change borders, but to open them.'[11] This did not, though, rule out bringing forward issues of concern within states where Albanians were living in a minority, as the evolution of events in Macedonia would soon demonstrate. The liberation of Kosova gave confidence to Albanians everywhere.

An immediate result, in terms of the evolving national question, of the displacement of the Greeks from their special position of influence in Tirana during the Kosova crisis was the emergence of the Chameria issue. The Cham problem, essentially a leftover from the Second World War, is an interesting illustration of the re-emergence of legitimate Albanian human rights concerns in neighbouring states after the end of the Cold War and Albanian communism.[12] The region of north-west Greece concerned, stretching from Arta[13] in the south to the Greek–Albanian border north of Ioannina, had a very mixed population in Ottoman times, with a large number of Albanians, both Christian and Muslim. The region only became part of the modern Greek state in 1913, and many Albanians and other minorities continued to live there. There was an internal division in the Cham world between coast-dwellers, who tended to be rich Muslim beys who prospered on the food and olive export trade to Corfu, and the mountain people who were more often Christian and always poorer. An abandoned village such as Lisi, near Sagiada, is a typical Cham upland settlement. Many place names on the coast are Hellenised fakes, so that a place which was called Murtos for hundreds of years is now called 'Sivota'. In a town such as Igoumenitsa (Albanian *Goumenitsa*), the Albanian language is still spoken by a minority of inhabitants.[14]

The modern Cham problem is essentially the creation of the British and the Greek extreme Right in the Second World War, when in 1943 the Royalist paramilitary leader Napoleon Zervas was encouraged by Christopher Woodhouse, the British military adviser to the Greek anti-Axis Resistance, to liquidate the Cham communities, who were seen as a possible obstacle to Allied plans for an invasion of the Balkans on that coast. Recently released classified British Foreign Office papers reveal a world of racialist and chauvinist prejudice in British official circles against the 'Muslim Albanians' (despite the fact that many, such as the Suliot families were and remain actually Orthodox Christian), and traditional British imperialist backing of Greek expansionism also played a part in what took place. After their expulsion, some Chams moved to Turkey and a life of what often became quite prosperous exile, while others settled in Albania, in Tirana, Fier, Vlora and southern districts around Saranda.[15] In Tirana the main Cham area is to the east of the central park and parliament building. Under communism Enver Hoxha abandoned their cause in the interests of a collaborationist relationship with Greece.[16]

In the post-communist period, political progress for the Cham cause was at first slow. Although a 'Chameria' association was formed in Tirana after the end of communism in 1990, and a monument to the Chams was erected by the Berisha government at Konispol in1994, it is only since the Kosova war that the Cham issue has become internationalised, with hearings in the US Senate on the issue and a speech on the subject by Hilary Clinton in the US Congress. Those families that remained in Greece did what they could to preserve their culture in the face of clerical and government hostility.[17] The Chams now have a new HQ in Tirana, a newspaper and a growing national organisation. Cham literature, particularly poetry, is being republished, and Cham associations in Germany and the USA are being revitalised. Under international law, Greece should pay reparations to those who lost their property in the Second World War; some commentators believe that this is the only reason Greece keeps the state of war issue unresolved. Nevertheless, the Athens government has been forced into serious consideration of the issue for the first time for two generations. There were reports in European media in 2003 of a new paramilitary organisation, the 'Chameria Liberation Army', in the region, and the international community has a strong interest in putting pressure on Greece to open negotiations to resolve what should be a routine matter of property compensation left over from the Second World War.

The position of the Albanians in Montenegro, consisting of about 8 per cent of the population, is in many ways analogous to that of the Chams, as a small minority at a serious cultural and educational disadvantage within a neighbouring state. During the Milosevic years there was a considerable rapport between Tirana and the Podgoritsa government of Milo Djukanovic, as the pro-independence orientation of Podgoritsa was seen as a counterweight to Milosevic in Belgrade, and there were economic links through the Albanian community at tourist centres such as Ulcinje, Venetian *Dulcingo*.[18] In the Kosova wartime period, Montenegro was a very valuable conduit for people and supplies to Kosova, and was used as a supply route by the KLA. Albanians in Montenegro have their own newspapers, radio stations and cultural organisations. They also have an influential position in the US diaspora and a strong political and religious (mostly Catholic) presence. However, during the period since 1999, there has been some deterioration in their position. Traditionally Montenegrin Albanians had intermarried more with Slavs than other Albanians, their family and clan structures were similar, and their percentage of the population is in decline compared to the rising proportions of Albanians in neighbouring states. Montenegrin independence, as it has developed in 2006, may open opportunities for Albanian human rights grievances to be addressed.

As elsewhere in the Albanian world, pan-Albanian development is concentrated along the Montenegrin coast, and is focused on changes in road and transport infrastructure that free markets encourage following the end of the one-party state. The new dual carriageway road linking Tirana and Shkoder has cut journey times considerably for those wishing to travel from the capital to the north and Montenegro. A new bridge across the estuary of the Buna River is to be built linking the Albanian resort of Velipoja with the Albanian-dominated Montengrin centre of Ulcinje. A new economic zone of activity is also coming into being with the opening of the Muriqan border crossing point south of Lake Shkoder, closed since the Stalin–Tito split in 1948. Similar beneficial effects are anticipated from the opening of the Vermosh border crossing between Tropoja in northern Albania and the ethnic Albanian regions of Plav and Gruda in southern Montenegro. As elsewhere, pan-Albanian development is polycentric and it is unlikely that the influence of Tirana will be very strong in these localities.

An important question for these communities will be the future of the Serbian–Montenegrin federation. With the federation break-up in 2006 and Montenegrin independence, this would be a course strongly supported by the Albanian political parties in Montenegro.

There was clearly a limit to what bilateral initiatives to help the Montenegrin Albanians from Tirana could achieve if all meaningful decisions were actually taken in Belgrade. The general fear of destabilisation in the international community is likely to be linked to the growth of paramilitarism and community disintegration and inter-ethnic relations in Montenegro. As in Chameria, there have been a few reports of the beginning of Montengrin–Albanian paramilitary organisation, but these tendencies may grow if legitimate human rights issues are lost by default. It is, however, unlikely that this will be the case. All citizens of the coastal regions can expect a major improvement in the local economies and infrastructure as a result of the end of communist-period borders, and there is every possibility that a 'moderate majority' of ethnic Albanians will resist the temptations of political extremism and separatism. Whether in Croatia, Montenegro, Chameria or Albania, the new dynamism in the Albanian world is intimately linked to the Adriatic coast. A sign of this in the security world was the signature, under American aegis, of the Croatia–Montenegro–Albania coastal charter in 2003, and geostrategic factors favour a form of pan-Albanian development linked to the gradual opening of all borders and the end of Belgrade-centric political and economic dominance of the region.

It is of course possible that there will be differing political priorities within the Montenegrin Albanian world itself, with the predominantly Catholic coastal Albanian communities looking more towards Shkoder, with its large Catholic population, and Italy, with the Muslim Albanians of Plav and Gruda having closer links with Kosova and particularly the strongly reviving Kosovar town of Peje, always the regional economic centre. Plav and Gruda are much poorer than the coastal centres and it remains to be seen what the effects of differing levels of economic and social progress on the two communities will be. Many of these contradictions and dilemmas for the Albanians have already begun to work themselves out in Macedonia, as the 2001 conflict indicated.

17

Preshevo, Macedonia and the National Question

Conflict in Macedonia had been long forecast, with a history of preventative diplomacy and peacekeeping there dating back to the Ahrens plan for political reform in 1993.[1] The Albanian factor, however, was not widely understood. Before the Kosova war period, the existence of the 25-plus per cent minority of Albanians in Macedonia was largely unknown in the West outside specialist Balkan circles within the international community. Unlike their kinfolk in Kosova, the Macedonian Albanians had no newspapers, political offices or advocacy capacity in Tirana, and few people outside the Skopje diplomatic circle had ever met their leaders.

The Preshevo Albanians were even more obscure. Preshevo was known, if at all, as a remote small town near the Niš–Skopje motorway in south-east Serbia. Equally few, or perhaps even fewer people, in Tirana and elsewhere in Albania knew that the Preshevo Valley, which dominates the road route in ex-Yugoslavia between Serbia and Montenegro, was predominantly Albanian inhabited and until Titoist communism had always been part of Kosova. The Kosova war and ensuing refugee crisis brought the issue of the ethnic Albanian population of other regions of what remained of Yugoslavia to prominence. Preshevo became, after 2000, the most sensitive new point of development of the Albanian national question. Without the Kosovar refugee crisis and its effects in Preshevo, the structural crisis in Macedonia would not have developed to the point of social breakdown and paramilitary activity. The fate of the Preshevo Valley, *Kosova Lindore* (Eastern Kosova) in Albanian, was essentially unfinished business from the Kosova war.

There was no KLA presence in the Preshevo Valley during the late 1998 and early 1999 period when it was growing strongly elsewhere. During the NATO bombing campaign between March and June 1999 there had been widespread destruction of Preshevo Valley mosques and other Albanian buildings by the Serbian army, associated security apparatus units and independent paramilitary groups.[2]

In the summer and autumn of 1999 violence began there almost as soon as NATO entered Kosova, with small local groups of ex-KLA fighters trying to enter the Preshevo Valley from the Gjilane region of eastern Kosova. By March 2000 Preshevo had became a major focus for international concern in the region, with Miranda Vickers writing in a leading US newspaper on 24 March 2000 that the Preshevo crisis was closely linked to the failure of the international community in Mitrovica, and that the emergence of the Liberation Army of Preshevo, Medjeve and Bujanoc (the UCPMB) was in fact symptomatic of the wider problems affecting this part of the Balkans. Vickers argued that:

> The fighting in the Preshevo Valley has coincided with the rising level of violence in the divided Kosova town of Mitrovica. French KFOR had allowed the Serbs to effectively partition the town, a slow process of appeasement that begun in summer 1999 and culminated in February 2000, NATO fed Albanian suspicions that Slobodan Milosevic was preparing to annexe northern Kosova to Serbia.[3]

On the ground NATO appeared to be preparing for the partition of Kosova. This strategic trigger was to dominate the next three years and led to a renewed crisis in Preshevo in autumn 2000, as Albanian leaders feared enforced negotiations with Belgrade following the fall of Milosevic that would rule out full independence for Kosova.[4] The Preshevo conflict spread into Macedonia in the February of the following year.[5]

In 2001 Macedonia was convulsed by violence between the Albanians and the Slav Macedonian majority, and a small war developed that was ended by negotiations during July and August 2001 and the signature of the Ohrid Accords that set out a programme of institutional reform.[6] In essence this was designed to ease the human-rights and cultural grievances of the Albanian minority, but it was also a sign of the emergence of the Albanian national question as the predominant political issue in the southern Balkans. Contrary to the views of many diplomats at the time, this process was substantially unaffected by the fall of Milosevic in Belgrade in October 2000, although this event did disadvantage the Albanian cause in Preshevo in the short term and lead to the negative aspects of the first imposed settlement of the fighting in Preshevo in spring 2000.

The Albanian minority in Macedonia had long-standing grievances against Belgrade that went back to before the Second World War.[7] During the interwar period, the Albanian-inhabited lands in western Macedonia had been subject to extensive and planned colonisation by Serbs and Montenegrins as part of the construction of a 'South Serbia' *banovina* (administrative region), within Royalist Yugoslavia, and Tetovo was to all intents and purposes made into a Serbian town. The colonisation was linked economically to the development of the rich mines in the Sar Mountains nearby. There was even a small White Russian community in the town. Slav numbers were further augmented after 1949 with the arrival of Slavophone refugees from the defeat of the Democratic Army in the Greek Civil War. With the collapse of Royalist Yugoslavia and the advent of communism and the Socialist Republic of Macedonia, many of these people left, and Albanian numbers have risen progressively over the years, as elsewhere in western Macedonia.

The Albanian democratic struggle has always been to secure cultural and human rights in these areas, commensurate with their numbers.[8] Following the end of the Second World War, in the Preshevo Valley there had been major fighting between Titoists and Albanians until 1949, and refugee movement of Preshevo Albanians into Kosova. An entire district of Prishtina became mainly populated by Preshevo refugees. These people and their human rights grievances effectively disappeared from general view during the Cold War period. Macedonia after communism became a state where the national identity was defined in terms of the majority ethnic group, the Slav-Macedonians, and their view of recent history. This identity had never been accepted by Greece or Bulgaria, and ever since 1991 the state has existed in periods of tension, often acute, with its neighbours. Until 1999, ethnic Albanian history and interests in the region were often hidden and unknown, as was the major assault of the Yugoslav military against the Preshevo mosques in May 1999 that led to widespread damage and the loss of several important historic buildings.

Under communism various minority rights provisions existed, which to some extent were put into practice, but many of them were lost to all minorities under the post-communist 1991 Constitution, which embodied the assumptions of the new Macedonian nationalism. A series of small crises, such as the Bitpazar violence in 1992, the arms plot of 1993 and the bloody riots at Gostivar in July 1997, punctuated the succeeding years and the general alienation of the Albanians from the state produced a very favourable atmosphere for nationalist political activity in the post-2000 period. The dangers of the situation had been foreseen for some years by more far-sighted members of the diplomatic community, and numerous attempts had been made to reform the Skopje-based state, such as the proposals but forward by German OSCE Ambassador Geert Ahrens in 1993, but it was difficult to convince the government of Kiro Gligorov of the need for change. The Skopje government was receiving strong support from France, Israel, Bulgaria and the British Conservative government throughout the mid-1990s, which saw little need for social or political reform and were only concerned with preserving the Belgrade–Skopje––Athens axis as the mainspring of power in the southern Balkans. This had been reflected in the botched MI6 covert operation known as the 'arms plot' in November 1993, when weapons had been planted on the ethnic Albanians in the government in an attempt to discredit them.[9]

The USA and NATO were acutely aware of the need to keep Macedonia stable, seeing the danger of conflict between two NATO members, Greece and Turkey, if it should disintegrate. American diplomats in particular, unlike their non-Swiss European counterparts, were aware of the strength of nationalist feeling amongst the large Macedonian-Albanian diaspora, centred mostly in the mid-West of the USA. The extent of Macedonian-Albanian support for the Kosova war was well known in the USA, whereas this was often not the case in Europe. Some US cities, such as Chicago, had a substantial number of Albanian migrants from Macedonia, and they formed an important constituency of opinion and activity within the US diaspora as a whole. The Macedonian-Albanians also contributed a number of key leaders from an LPK background to the national movement, such as Ali Ahmeti and Fazli Veliu.

When the Kosova war ended, a small but significant number of demobilised KLA figures who came from Macedonia were faced with a serious dilemma; the KLA was in process of demobilisation and they had little future role in Kosova. The exact early history of the NLA in Macedonia is unclear, something compounded by the reluctance of some of the main actors, such as Ahmeti, to make public their view of events. Although it is clear that the decision to mobilise an insurgent army was taken by the LPK, the leadership was not limited to LPK figures. As Skopje journalist Iso Rusi has written in his monograph *From Army to Party – The Politics of the NLA*, the leadership group composed quite a number of people and some, such as Xhezair Shaqiri ('Commander Hoxha'), who led the first NLA group into Tanusche village in mid-February 2001, have challenged the views of Ahmeti and others about some events.[10] He claimed, for instance, that in 1999 Ahmeti believed that armed actions in Macedonia could not be considered before

2003 or 2004 at the earliest. The Preshevo crisis that unfolded in the autumn of 1999 only involved local insurgents, with their own local commanders, and the question inevitably arose in their minds as to their future. Some of the most prominent figures in the LPK leadership were from Macedonia, like Veliu, and were known to be close to the Kosovar political leadership, with senior Kosovar politicians like Xhavit Haliti having belonged to the same underground group in the north-east of Kosova in the 1980s as the young Ahmeti. The crisis began to unfold in the spring of 2000, when the KFOR 'crackdown' on the Albanian movement began and the international community sought to placate the Kostunica leadership in Serbia with a key role in settling a long-standing dispute over the Kosova–Macedonia border.

In response to the departure of Serbs from Kosova during the summer/autumn of 1999 and winter of 2000, the climate in some parts of the US government began to change. This was linked to the election of the George W. Bush administration in the USA. The Clinton administration was seen as pro-Albanian and so the Bush group sought to back the opposite Balkan client group (i.e. Serbia), which in any case closely corresponded to their traditional Titoist period loyalty. Influential figures from the early 1990s like Brent Scowcroft began to reappear in policy-making circles, and they were ideologically and practically inclined to favour the Serbs. The influential figure of Henry Kissinger in Republican circles was important, as his consulting firm, Kissinger Associates, had worked for the Yugoslav government in the past and also for Yugoslav commercial companies. Attention was also redirected to Belgrade with the possibility of the end of the Milosevic regime in a peaceful way in the forthcoming autumn 2000 Serbian elections. Another key figure was British diplomat and fanatical Yugophile Charles Crawford, who had been a member of the Tony Blair orbit of law students at university and became British ambassador to Belgrade.[11] Another British member in touch with the new policy thinking was David Landsman, later to become British Ambassador to Tirana in 2000.

A secret USA–Great Britain planning group was set up in 1999, based in Budapest, with the object of 'regime change' in Belgrade and the reconstruction of a new Serbian-dominated Yugoslav Federation, of which Kosova would be forced to remain part. Few of the Albanian leaders in Kosova knew what was happening, and assumed the Blair government was as committed to freedom and independence for Kosova as hitherto. This certainly was the case with most British government ministers and the members of the parliamentary Labour party, but the bureaucracy still contained many people who had been involved in the Bosnian policy debacle and had never broken with the British

Yugoslavist psychology and tacit or active collaboration with Serb war crimes in the name of 'opposing' Islam in the Balkans.[12]

In fact in a 'Tony's cronies' issue, and with the change of US administration, there had been a change of emphasis, linked to the unswerving determination of many in the Foreign Office and secret intelligence service (MI6) officials to make a last-ditch attempt to protect Serbian hegemony in the region. The laudable aim of the removal of the genocidal Milosevic regime was also linked to this second and largely hidden agenda, something that many observers of the largely bogus ' revolution' of October 2000 in Belgrade did not notice at the time. A complex and sophisticated strategy to keep Kosova within Serbia in a post-Milosevic 'democratic' regime was developed, and the main emphasis was put on media operations. Journalists likely to be critical of the strategy were as far as possible removed from reporting positions in the region, and pliable figures put in their place who would accept the 'revolution' at face value.

As well as this open agenda, a counter-insurgency campaign against the Albanian paramilitaries was authorised and the anti-Albanian propaganda machine was cranked up in London in police and security circles, with stories fed to sympathetic journalists stressing the alleged and exclusive threat of the 'Albanian mafia'. Although the Kosovars had won the media war in the 1998–2000 period, their leaders were quite unprepared for what was to come in the period that followed. A key factor in forming opinion was the employment of ex-Milosevic policemen as 'expert advisers' to international agencies such as Interpol, who quickly succeeded in politicising the agenda of these bodies in their preferred direction. This was hidden from the world at large in the 2000–01 period.

It was, however, quickly noted by the Kosovar Albanian leadership after May 2000, when the period of repression that had begun with the crushing of the enormous mass march from Prishtina to Mitrovica for the reuniting of the latter city on 12 February culminated in the assassination of Ekrem Rexha ('Commander Drini') outside his house in Prizren. Drini was a popular and effective KLA commander who had been tipped to become Mayor of Prizren in the local elections to be held in Kosova that November. He was an ex-Yugoslav army officer who had been the KLA representative in Bosnia, and was seen by the Serbs and their sympathisers in the international community as tainted with Islamic sympathies.

Prizren was of great strategic importance in the development of Kosovar life, with its proximity to Albania and the strong radical undercurrent in its political culture. There were some family links between Prizren Albanian families and the Preshevo insurgents, and one or two Prizren-origin soldiers were in the UCPMB, and several fatalities resulted for Prizren families in the Preshevo conflict. Prizren had more links to the Preshevo Valley than geography might immediately suggest. After the Titoist genocide in the 1945–9 period, some Preshevo imams had fled to Prizren.[13] The circumstances of the assassination suggested a professional killing, and allegations have been made that Drini was murdered as part of an anti-Albanian counter-insurgency operation involving a British military contractor. Others have alleged that foreign police special units were involved, or that Serb hitmen were used by the British secret service for the murder. It has since become clear that the Foreign Office ministers were not aware of what was happening.

In a crisis in Whitehall after the murder, the head of the government Joint Intelligence Committee, Thomas Packenham, a career diplomat, was replaced, allegedly on CIA and Pentagon insistence amid allegations that the Foreign Office was never informed about what was happening on the ground in Kosova, or about the Drini murder plot.[14] Two months earlier the international community in Kosova had been shaken to the core by a superbly organised and planned mass march of miners and their supporters from Prishtina to Mitrovica to demand the unification of the city, which had never been brought under proper UNMIK control since July 1999 and where northern Mitrovica and the adjoining Leposavic *Opstina* was dominated by gun-toting pro-Milosevic gangs. In this climate of desperation, counter-insurgency death squads seemed a legitimate tactic, but quite apart from issues of morality or legality, those planning them could not have been aware of the difficulty of keeping operations of this kind secret in Kosova or the sophistication and political skill the ethnic Albanian leadership would employ in dealing with the issue. The running sore the murder created in Kosovar relations with the international community in Prishtina soon negated the short-term gain of the counter-insurgency operation.

Against this background of what has to be called a largely secret and undeclared war against independence aspirations for Kosova, within key sections of the British and US government apparatus, the reaction of much of the Albanian political leadership to the situation became increasingly focused in the autumn of 2000 on the possibilities for struggle against the repression of the ethnic Albanian people in Preshevo and Macedonia. The Preshevo campaign was reigniting in the absence of political progress in the region, and the 2000 agreement to end the first Preshevo violence had been drafted in Belgrade with British and NATO help. The strategic situation from a military point of view for the Albanians in the Preshevo Valley was always poor, with the Yugoslav army always able to contain the insurgency within a fairly small area with only a limited number of UCPMB fighters.[15]

After the departure of Milosevic in October 2000 Kosova was swept with rumours that a new 'Dayton' was planned, where a settlement that fell far short of independence would be imposed on the Albanians. There were fears that the government in Tirana might be bribed and/or threatened to support such a conference.

In this climate of intense suspicion of the intentions of the international community and deteriorating relationships between the Albanians in Kosova and NATO forces, particularly in the British and French sectors of KFOR, the arguments of the hitherto largely isolated and tiny minority of mostly LPK-background activists who had advocated opening a military campaign in Macedonia (to secure a strong negotiating position to advance Albanian human rights and take international pressure off Kosova) suddenly fell upon fertile ground. In Germany, Macedonian-Albanian LPK leader Fazli Veliu had been jailed for a time on trumped-up charges during the 'crackdown' period of the spring of 2000, and he was released after several weeks in prison as a bitter and angry man who felt that the time had come to open a Macedonian military front.[16] This view was shared by other LPK leaders such as Emrush Xhemali. If a war was in progress, it would be difficult or impossible for the international community to open negotiations on the future of Kosova, and within Macedonia itself there was a strong constituency of opinion that favoured more militant action, given the total lack of progress made on human rights issues by moderate leaders over the previous ten years.

 In Tetovo a substantial economic underground support system for a paramilitary campaign was still in place only a year after the end of the Kosova war, which had diverted its energies to activities such as cigarette-smuggling, but there was no reason why it could not quickly become mobilised to support a paramilitary campaign. Much of this had been the case for some time, in structural terms, and the Skopje government had always been on weak ground against growing Albanian nationalism, exemplified by President Kiro Gligorov's concerns expressed to the international community in the summer of 1998 when he called for refugee corridors to channel people from Kosova away from the main Albanian areas of Macedonia. In doing so, he was aware of the dramatic effect refugee movement would have on energising the national issue in the Macedonian-Albanian communities.

The Macedonian insurgency developed in the early spring of 2001, as a calculated response to the setbacks in Kosova in 2000 and to the threat posed by the attempts of pro-Serb extremists in the British and other diplomatic and security apparatus to reverse the results of the NATO campaign in 1999. The main link, in formal military leadership terms, between the new insurgency and the KLA was the figure of General Gezim Ostreni, a portly and conventional ex-Yugoslav army officer from Dibra in western Macedonia who was a senior commander in the Kosova Protection Corps (KPC) after a period in the KLA in the wartime. He was also a military historian, and had made a careful study of the Second World War Partisan war in Macedonia, that 'coincidentally' was published on the eve of the Macedonian campaign.[17]

If 1999 had been an *annus mirabilis* in the context of NATO intervention on the side of the Albanians, 2000 saw pro-Serb forces within the international community working to reverse what had been achieved, and to secure the increasingly fragile but traditional predominance of Belgrade as the nexus of regional politics. This was always a chimera but that did not stop it being pursued by the traditionally Serbophile elite in some European chanceries. The heart of the conspiracy against Kosova was in London, in the orbit of senior Serbophile officials in the Ministry of Defence and the Foreign and Commonwealth Office, who seemed to have learned nothing from the debacles in Bosnia. London was the key link to the USA.

The Republican administration's preoccupation with building strong and stable states, coupled with the advanced age, ignorance of current realities and Yugonostalgia of many advisers, and with their desire to do something diametrically opposite to the Clinton administration, meant that pro-Serb traditionalists in Britain could attempt to highjack the Kosova issue in US policy terms and turn it against its progenitors. They did not understand the increasingly complex, flexible and polycentric nature of modern Albanian nationalism, the quality and experience of the diverse political and military leadership, and in particular the sophisticated understanding of the significance of counter-insurgency as a sign of political manipulation of the Albanian polity by foreign states, something that had developed in the aftermath of the arms plot in 1993 against the Tetovo-Albanian political leadership.[18]

The murder of Commander Drini was an alarm signal to virtually all Albanian leaders in the region, and friends of Albania and Kosova elsewhere, and led to revulsion from the international community administration in Kosova in their private discourse. At rank-and-file level, it meant that the key informal networks for arms and supplies procurement would be eager to return to the fray. In turn, a strong military response was seen to be required in Macedonia, the only promising military option open to the Albanians. Throughout this key period, the government in Tirana had little or no knowledge of the direction of events. Socialist government leader Fatos Nano had a close and generally harmonious relationship with the similarly ex-communist leadership around Macedonian President Kiro

Gligorov, and more or less non-existent relations with the key Macedonian Albanian leaders.

The international community had attempted to resolve the first Preshevo insurgency in the aftermath of the fall of Milosevic in autumn 2000 with an amnesty for fighters, an agreed programme of social and political reforms, such as the introduction of a multi-ethnic police force, and a strong intervention by NATO negotiators.[19] The UCPMB insurgents disbanded and entered politics, at least in theory. In fact, apart from some improvement in policing, few of the elements of the agreement were ever put into practice, with the Yugoslav army building massive new military facilities in the Preshevo Valley and a continual undercurrent of paramilitary activity remaining in the Albanian villages, leading to a steady stream of minor but violent incidents.

In late January 2001, a few mostly ex-UCPMB fighters were deployed to spread the Preshevo campaign into Macedonia, something that was very easy from a military point of view. Very militant ethnic Albanian villages such as Haracine (Arachanovo) were halfway between Preshevo and the Skopje capital and had themselves been subject to recent conflicts with the authorities, as with the violence in Haracine in January 2000, and provided a strongly supportive environment for the new force.[20] At the same time, the Macedonian police began a crackdown against militant villages, with searches for arms and ammunition that raised tension considerably. It is generally agreed that the first NLA direct offensive action against a Macedonian state target was an attack on the police station at Tearce village on the Tetovo–Kosova road on 23 January 2001, in response to Macedonian police violence in that community.[21] The NLA communiqué issued afterwards stated as a first principle that 'the NLA is committed to the preservation of the territorial integrity and sovereignty of Macedonia', a key principle in obtaining international community support. Meanwhile, the focus of conflict moved from Tearce to the northern mountains.

High on the Macedonia–Kosova border, the little village of Tanushe straddled the border and was subject to Macedonian police violence and coercion. The village land lay in both Kosova and Macedonia, and the new state border after 1990 (where previously there had been no border at all) had caused serious economic problems for the village. It was the home of many nationalist villagers, and a small land conflict quickly spilled over into violence. Within a few days about two hundred members of the new insurgent force, the NLA,[22] were in the field.

Some had fought in the KLA in the Kosova war, but it would be a mistake to see the new NLA as merely the old KLA in different uniforms. There was little overlap in active membership. The LPK leadership had carefully

considered the military lessons of the Kosova war, and they had no wish
to fight with an over-large, poorly organised force. The NLA was planned
as a mobile elite force, capable of quick military initiatives for specifically
defined political objectives, using classic guerrilla tactics that could be used
with precision against the Macedonian army. The KLA had begun to falter
when it fought like a conventional army, as in Rahovec in May 1998. The
Macedonian-Albanian insurgents had no intention of making the same
mistake. To the onlooker, even the well informed, the NLA were, as one
European military observer put it at the onset of the war, '127 guys in a
forest that no one has ever heard of'[23] but in reality they were all that was
required to prise open the rotten and tottering structure of the unreformed
Macedonian state.

In the last week of February and the first week of March 2001 the conflict
had quickly spread from Tanushe along the Crna Gora mountains in both
directions, with the insurgents confining their presence to the high ground
and sympathetic villages with a predominantly ethnic Albanian population.
The Macedonian army mobilised against the insurgents, with a crude attempt
to shell NLA positions in villages above Tetovo. The German NATO soldiers
based in Tetovo were unable to affect events, with no mandate to intervene
even if the Macedonian government had agreed it should try to do so. The
Special Units of the Macedonian army under the direct control of Defence
Minister Boskosvki, nicknamed the 'Lions' and 'Tigers', soon gained a
reputation for brutal random attacks against ethnic Albanian villages, and
duly drove more support towards the insurgents. A key place was little
Shipkovica, above the old Ottoman fort at Selce, where NLA leader Ali
Ahmeti set up his headquarters. The choice of response by the Macedonian
army was not surprising, but all observers and the Albanian insurgents were
surprised by the crass level of military incapacity, with ill-directed random
fire having no effect on the insurgents but setting light to numerous houses
and agricultural buildings, and driving the local population to support the
insurgents.

A German military observer watching the fighting commented that he
thought the Macedonian army was the only army in history where it was
more dangerous to stand behind it than in front, referring to the arbitrary
pattern of their artillery fire. By 10 March, two weeks after fighting started,
it was clear on the ground that the Macedonian army would be incapable of
delivering a military 'solution' by breaking the insurgency, and there would
have to be negotiations. US diplomatic envoy Bob Frowick met the Albanian
leaders in Prizren, in Kosova, to hammer out a common platform for reform,
much of which closely resembled the 'Ahrens plan' of 1993 in trying to bring

Macedonia away from nationalist dogma and into line with US and EU standards on minorities. This attempt by US diplomacy to impose rationality on the situation was regarded with horror by the Skopje government, who immediately declared Frowick *persona non grata* in Macedonia.

Throughout this period, Tirana was an onlooker to events and its leaders such as Foreign Minister Ilir Meta and Europe Minister Paskal Milo were unable to exert any influence on developments. Small arms transfers continued without serious hindrance across the northern Albania–Kosova–Macedonia border triangle, although this supply route was of less importance than in the Kosova war. Macedonia had for several years been a centre of arms trading, and manufacturing nations like Serbia and Bulgaria could easily trade there. The international community here was a victim of its own policies, in that the energy that had gone into inserting pliable politicians of a pro-European and non-national viewpoint into the Socialist Party leadership meant that while Tirana could be forced into their approved political model, it meant that they had little knowledge of, or connection with, events in the wider Albanian world. It was an irony that having adopted the threat ideology of the Serbs, in terms of the prospect of a so-called 'Greater Albania', in reality the political practice used to dissuade Tirana leaders from forging organic relationships with their fellow Albanians removed a key policy lever from the international community during this crisis period.

The only political relationships that mattered for the NLA leaders were with the Kosova leadership, the USA and the diaspora, particularly in Switzerland and Germany. The only Tetovo political leader with significant Tirana connections was Arben Xhaferi, but as his party was part of the Macedonian government coalition he was effectively marginalised once fighting had started and all diplomatic and military attention was focused on Ali Ahmeti, General Ostreni and the NLA leadership. The Democratic Party leadership had few connections with Albanian leaders in Skopje or Tetovo and played little part in the crisis. In Tetovo, Sali Berisha had never been regarded as popular and effective a political leader as he was in Kosova, and he had no significant personal relationship with the Tetovo leadership.

The Kosova leaders played a much greater role. Although the main ex-KLA political leaders such as Hashim Thaci of the Democratic Party of Kosova (PDK) and Ramush Haradinaj of the Alliance for Kosova were closely following events, it was essential for them to keep out of any active involvement, let alone support the insurgents, as any activity would only have fuelled allegations from Belgrade and Skopje that the NLA was in essence a Kosovar 'export'. Haradinaj was actually removed from his position as deputy commander of the Kosova Protection Corps, the legal successor organisation to the KLA, in April 2001. KPC commander General Agim Ceku was put under intense pressure to use his influence to bring the insurgency under control, but he was quite unable to do so and had not even been informed that his subordinate Ostreni was in Macedonia when the conflict started, apart from knowledge that he was planning a holiday there.[24]

The Kosovar leaders were still a vital channel of communication however, and newspaper editor and long-time Kosova spokesman Veton Surroi was used by NATO Secretary General George Robertson as an intermediary to contact NLA leader Ali Ahmeti, despite the fact that Surroi had never actually met Ahmeti, who had been based in Switzerland for some years. Surroi informed NATO that Ahmeti was a 'responsible guerrilla leader' and would be open to negotiations about ending the conflict.[25] It would have been impossible for any Tirana leader to have played Surroi's key role in bringing about the negotiations that led to the Ohrid Accords and the demobilisation of the NLA in the August–November 2001 period. Arben Xhaferi's involvement in the process actually went through an informal caucus of leaders in Prishtina, not in Tirana, and in the latter stages of the war he worked closely with Surroi.

Thus, as regards the pan-Albanian development, the Macedonian war marked a major landmark, where the Prishtina leadership was a key determinant factor in the development of events. It is also undeniable, in analysing the causes of the 2001 conflict, to observe that the highly risky and politically difficult insurgency only resulted in a partial victory for the Albanians because of the massive popular support for the war in Kosova at every political level, from the ex-KLA political leadership who suddenly went from near pariahs in international community eyes to essential intermediaries, down to the rank-and-file and general population who turned a blind eye to arms procurement and logistics activity in Kosova, to the young men and women who volunteered to go to fight in Macedonia. In fact, the NLA was a difficult organisation to join, and few of the willing Kosova recruits were accepted unless they had a Macedonian family connection and competent military skills. Nevertheless the conflict changed the atmosphere in Kosova in a fundamental way and decisively reversed the pro-Serb climate of autumn 2000 and winter 2001 when sections of the international community were trying to reverse the developments of the 1998–9 period based on the new leadership in Belgrade. Success for the Albanians in the Macedonian conflict was a real defeat for the Crawford-Landsman group in London and their allies in the Whitehall bureaucracy.

The Ohrid Accords that ended the conflict were signed in August 2001, with promised reforms to open Tetovo University and correct cultural and educational discrimination. This was to the regret of some militants who felt that in the war the NLA could have taken Skopje if NATO had not intervened in May 2001 and effectively rescued the Macedonian army from the mess it was in. They also felt that once demobilised, it would be difficult to build up the NLA again. These were legitimate military concerns but in the judgement of the highly experienced and astute key LPK leaders, like Ahmeti and Veliu, the war had achieved about as much as could be expected. The Albanian leadership were not in favour of the cantonisation of the country, or a split, something that was essential to keep at least a degree of support for their human rights demands within the international community. The continuation of the fighting could easily have led to the federalisation of Macedonia, on possibly highly disadvantageous terms for the Albanians. Confidential Greek proposals made in July 2001 envisaged a division of FYROM where the Albanians would only get a small north-west corner and the majority of the country would be left with the Slav Macedonians, in circumstances that were only a short step away from the latter section of the land becoming a Greek protectorate.

The situation recalled the old 1990 jibe that the real reason for Slovenians wanting independence was to become a suburb of Vienna. It was nevertheless a difficult decision, and significant leaders like Ostreni were not at the time happy with the Ohrid decisions, exemplified by the General's well-known comment about 'two million wasted bullets' in the war.[26] The intervention of NATO in late spring had certainly saved Skopje from the NLA, along with a possible mass exodus of the Slavophone population. Arben Xhaferi, the main ethnic Albanian negotiator, felt that there was considerable value in the Ohrid deal but also decided that 'never again would foreigners decide the future of Macedonia.'[27]

In reality, though, the leadership were not prepared to risk igniting a full-scale civil war that would have meant the end of the 'Macedonian' state and in all probability a NATO occupation force. The real and tangible military defeat of the plans of the Macedonian army was compensation for most Albanians, coupled with the radical human rights and institutional reforms promised by the Ohrid agreement.[28] In practice the Macedonian army and security apparatus has never returned in any real sense to the Albanian communities in the west of the country as a highly coercive force, and multi-ethnic policing has developed to some extent. This has produced a degree of Albanian community autonomy in these regions. The sense of an Albanianisation of western Macedonia has also been assisted by the opening of new border crossings between Albania and Kosova in the Dragas Mountains, and between Macedonia and Albania in different locations.

In general, however, the Ohrid Accords have not been an unqualified success. In northern Macedonia, the situation has been more difficult, with serious social and political tension remaining in some villages, and occasional violent incidents. Some aspects of the Ohrid Accords have been put into practice, such as the foundation of Tetovo's Albanian language university in 2003, while others have not, but deeper problems remain. The Accords did not affect in any way the basically chauvinist and racist 1991 Constitution, with its exclusive definition of the 'Macedonian' identity, and it remains to be seen if the Slav majority really wish to implement Ohrid in the key areas of the army and the security apparatus. In order to get the Accords through the Skopje Parliament, Arben Xhaferi and Ali Ahmeti had to accept this constitutional reality, and there is as yet no sign of much enthusiasm in implementing the Accords among the non-Albanian majority. Another key issue that remains unresolved is that of citizenship, with thousands of people of Albanian ethnicity living in Macedonia unable to vote or take part in normal political life.[29]

These contemporary reservations pale into insignificance, though, when compared to the enormous strategic political advance that the 2001 insurgency and the Ohrid Accords represent for the Albanians. For the first time in their history in the region, the Albanians have the prospect of social equality with the Slav majority in the state, with their own culture and history having a secure and respected position in education. The new economic space (NAPS) opening up between western Macedonia, Kosova and Albania is a product of the end of communism and the planned economies, and the democratisation of the southern Balkans. Although the military situation is not currently in the Albanians' favour in Preshevo, it is also taking part in the new space, with greatly improved cross-border transport and cultural links, and some advances in policing and the removal of the most coercive aspects of Yugoslav structures from their communities, although there is much to be done before they achieve full freedom. Although the Kosova question is at the heart of the future of the Albanians in the southern Balkans, the onset of the Preshevo and Macedonian conflicts has changed the arithmetic of the international relations calculations concerning the Albanian national question in an irreversible way.

18

Pan-Albanianism: Tirana and the Wider Albanian World

Albania has undergone a remarkable and unprecedented political, social and economic transformation since it emerged from the ruins of the harshest form of communism in 1991. Then an utterly poverty-stricken population was wholly dependent upon international food aid, and the state was in a condition of advanced disintegration. Within a year, however, Albania's international isolation had ended as the world's major powers hurried to establish their diplomatic missions in this impoverished but strategically important Balkan state. Despite chronic internal political unrest during the latter half of the 1990s, Albania gradually became a respected partner of the West in the region. During the Kosova crisis the country proved itself a worthy NATO ally, and following the 9/11 attacks on the USA, Albania has resolutely joined the 'War on Terror', by firmly monitoring the activities of radical Islamic individuals and groups in the country. Albania has also contributed soldiers to US-led coalitions in the wars in Afghanistan and Iraq. Albania's gradual integration into the socio-economic framework of the EU has been boosted by the opening of negotiations on the Association and Stabilisation Agreement with Brussels, which began on 31 January 2003. The Agreement came into full force in January 2006.

From a national standpoint, perhaps the most important development over the past decade has been the ability of ethnic Albanians living in neighbouring lands to engage fully for the first time in their history with the Albanian capital Tirana that was established after the Second Balkan War in 1913. This radical new development, which has substantially weakened

Shqiponor madhe [handwritten margin note]

the hold of Slav power in the southern Balkans, has reopened many difficult and historic questions with Albania's neighbours. Most worryingly it has led to allegations that a formal reunification of the Albanian lands is a hidden agenda for most Albanian politicians, which could lead to a so-called 'Greater Albania' that could become a threat to the region. The nature of this 'threat', however, has rarely been specified, although all border changes are seen as destabilising in this school of thought. In Serbia, nationalist extremists see the process of border openings often advocated in Tirana as part of an Islamic plan to set up a new pan-Islamic state comprising Albania, Kosova, western Macedonia, Bosnia, the Sandjak and parts of Montenegro.

Critics of the policies of the Tirana government to the national question in the recent period have often seized upon the keynote speech of former President Rexhep Meidani, referred to earlier in this book, in which he described the correct ambition for Albanians as the opening of all borders to their neighbours.[1] In this statement he indicated that he was aware that the dynamic effects of free markets after 1990 were sweeping aside communist-period borders and internal movement restrictions in a way which could not have been foreseen a decade earlier. This less than provocative statement is actually a reference to the increasing Europeanisation of Albania, and the country's popular support for European integration and the opening of all European borders, in both Old and New Europe.

The economics of free markets have begun several irreversible changes in this direction. During the nineteenth century, throughout the Balkans Albanians thrived in the open economy of the late-Ottoman world, as part of a very large multinational and multi-confessional empire, where central authority was gradually disintegrating to the point where most internal restrictions upon trade, apart from onerous local taxation, had collapsed. The post-1913 borders politically, culturally and geographically divided the Albanian people, but the communist regimes in Tirana and Belgrade also placed many bans and restrictions upon economic life that were accentuated by the effects of the 1948 Tito–Stalin split on Albania and Kosova. As a result, Albania remained chronically weakened and impoverished and its inherent backwardness was compounded by international isolation and lack of development. Although the ethnic Albanians of the former Yugoslavia managed to retain their cultural identities, they had little or no opportunity to benefit from the extensive mineral wealth of the regions they inhabited. Royalist Yugoslavia mortgaged key economic installations in Kosova and western Macedonia, such as the Trepce and Tetovo mines, to foreign interests and local client Serb control, a situation that remained until the break-up of Yugoslavia.

There were of course some important economic and infrastructural developments that took place under communism, in areas such as road construction and hydroelectricity generation. However, in Kosova and western Macedonia, within the framework of a planned economy, most of the benefits went to northern Yugoslavia and the revisionist bureaucratic elites in Belgrade or Zagreb. During the Milosevic period, a sustained policy of asset-stripping and exploitation was followed, so that most of the Trepce mine production was sold at knockdown prices to Russia and the proceeds plundered by the Milosevic circle and their friends.[2] The effects of the removal of these restraints upon the economic capacity of the Albanian people have yet to be widely appreciated by the international community.

The post-1999 period has led not only to a major political reorientation for the Albanian population of the southern Balkans, but also to many changes in local trade and cultural patterns. Nowadays the people of Tropoja in northern Albania can communicate easily by public transport with their traditional trading towns of Peje and Gjakova just over the border in Kosova. Villages in north-east Albania can now more easily obtain goods and services in Prizren than they can in Tirana, although this may change when the new Prizren to Durres road is constructed. For the first time since 1948 Montenegrin Albanians can easily travel to northern Albania, and more importantly Albanians from the Shkoder district can find desperately needed work in Montenegro. These developments have been eased by the opening of a number of new border posts, or more often the reopening of posts and roads that were closed after the 1948 crisis with Yugoslavia, such as the important crossing between Albania and Montenegro at Vermosh, or the Kosova–Albania crossings in Dragas, and the southern Lake Shkoder crossing at Muriqan to Albanian-dominated Ulcinje in Montenegro.

A significant, but often little acknowledged, effect of the violent conflicts and political instability that engulfed the Balkans during the 1990s has been a marked reduction in the power of central authority in many of the region's capital cities. These capitals, of which Belgrade is the most obvious example, had been built up as centres of all meaningful decision-making under undemocratic governments during the communist and pre-communist periods. In Belgrade particularly, the political elite functioned as a surrogate for British and French geopolitical interests in the interwar period, and more general Western interests vis à vis the Soviet Union in the post-1948 period. Bloated capitals were developed with expensive and exploitative revisionist-communist bureaucracies. Tirana had the same role in Albania, in the foreign-patronised nation-building process under King Zog and Enver Hoxha, and one way of explaining the violence of the 1997 uprising and its aftermath is as a rejection of this authority, at that time embodied in the highly centralist Berisha regime. Although Tirana has grown in size very quickly since the end of communism and has become the economic motor for the whole country, far fewer decisions are taken in many fields in Tirana now than in 1990, and significantly fewer than in January 1997 (the last functional month of the first Berisha government).

The 1997 uprising was a significant defeat for the power of the ex-communist SP bureaucratic and elite strata, as well as for the Berisha government itself. The uprising opened the way for the democratisation of Albania and rejuvenated a process of rejection of traditional central authority that has affected many aspects of life outside the political arena. In the cultural sphere, for example, publishing has been thriving in Albania's regional centres, particularly Shkoder, and also in Kosova and Tetovo, whereas ten years ago virtually every Albanian-language book or literary journal was published in Tirana. There are now a number of new and expanding publishing houses producing material in the Gheg dialect.[3] New churches and mosques are centres of a modern civil society where religion plays a positive role for many different people. Local NGOs and issue campaign groups are developing, with many different civil society objectives.

Another key issue has been population mobility, which under communism was controlled rigidly in Albania. The mobility of Albanians is a controversial issue for the international community, with the traditional fears of mass population movement after the crises and ship seizures of the early 1990–02 post-communist period, and the epic refugee crises during the Kosova conflict.[4] These fears are heavily focused in Greece and Italy, the main receptor countries for Albanian economic migrants. Many knee-jerk diplomatic and official responses to the 'new Albanian problem' are far more a product of fear about demography and about 'disorder' linked to population movement than any particular objection to a reorientation of South East Europe and the Adriatic to being more in favour of Albanian interests. In this mindset, Serbian domination of Kosova is linked to the notion of a 'control factor' in a 'Yugoslavia' as a force for 'order' in the region. There is also a widely perceived link between the spread of serious crime and social dislocation, where Albanians are blamed for many developments in trans-national crime, such as people- and drug-trafficking that are intimately linked to the processes of poverty and globalisation and are not a product of the moral nature or social activity of any individual nation.

A second important determinant to the future development of the Albanian people is likely to be whether the international community finally comes to terms with the reduced significance of Serbia in the region. During the Kosova conflict most central decision-makers within the international community appeared to accept Serbia's regional decline in influence. However, there have been significant setbacks following the October 2000 removal of Milosevic's dictatorial regime, where Serbophile elements within the international community were able to reassert themselves following its overthrow. This has enabled many Serbs to remain in denial about their national responsibility for the tragedy of Yugoslavia and the wider region.

Backing for the 'new' Serbia against the claims of Albanians in the region has come from a variety of disparate sources, such as some Christian Right conservatives in the USA and places like Bavaria (fearing 'Muslim' advance in the region), Europhile economic theorists who mistakenly see Serbia as the key to economic progress in the Balkans and those who always privately sympathised with Serbian hegemonic ambitions in the first place (a significant if often hidden group in Europe, although now more or less non-existent in the USA). In the view of these groups the independence of Kosova will be a destabilising factor for the region that could lead to a possible break-up of Macedonia and a 'Greater Albania', which in turn will produce a nationalist reaction in Serbia and further wars. Opponents of this view see Kosova's independence as a way to calm and satisfy the central problem of the region.

Ideological factors and academic interpretations of history are more important influences on government Balkan policy than is often realised. The traditional, often British, argument for support for a 'strong Belgrade' has rested on a fixed and unchanging view of Russian ambitions in the region, and the theory that the British and French 'special relationship' with Yugoslavia led to the breakaway from communism of the Tito government and 'progress' in the region.[5] This was supposed to have restricted Russian influence in the Balkans. In fact, events showed that European collaboration with the Serbs helped to keep Milosevic in power and communism, or his version of it, actually lasted much longer in Serbia than anywhere else in Europe.[6] Some memoirs of British participants in the Balkan crisis, such as *Fighting for Peace* by General Sir Michael Rose, illustrate the degree to which leading British figures collaborated with Russians, and Adam Le Bor has noted how the Serbtelecom privatisation deal struck with Milosevic by Lord Douglas Hurd and Dame Pauline Neville Jones helped Milosevic to stay in power and to keep his regime going long enough to pay for the next conflict in Kosova.[7]

The European view of the benevolent influence of Yugoslavia as a concept or a Titoist reality had never been generally accepted in the USA. Although there were always strong 'Titoists' in ruling circles, like Brent Scowcroft

12. Kosova elections, 2001: Flora Brovina and Hashim Thaci

and Warren Zimmerman, there were always serious and informed critics of the whole Titoist project in ways that were not common in Europe outside of Germany. Leading figures in the USA during the Kosova crisis such as Madeleine Albright were brought up on a view of history derived from her father's book exposing Titoist communism, and her own exile.[8] The most prominent historian of contemporary Yugoslavia in the USA, Ivo Banac at Yale, is from a Croatian background and his major academic works are dedicated to the exploration of the national question in Yugoslavia, something most London 'Titoists' saw as solved and an irrelevant and destabilising diversion. American analysts, on the other hand, have always appeared more realistic about the economic realities of Titoism, seeing the achievements as more dependent upon massive Western funding rather than anything inherent in the Titoist system itself.

What then is the nature of the pan-Albanian process likely to be?[9] It is clear that the economic and cultural integration processes are now effectively outside the Albanian government's or the international community's control, as they depend upon free markets, democratic cultural freedoms, technological independence for ordinary people brought about by Internet and mobile phone technology, and the end of government-imposed personal movement restrictions. The orientation of the EU for the removal of national borders is also helpful. The political process will thus inevitably be complex and multi-dimensional. The reality is that the various Albanian entities in the southern Balkans have several different interlocking agendas, ranging from the war reparations and property restitution concerns of the Chams to the wider human rights issues in Montenegro, the political status of Kosova, democratisation and possible cantonisation in the Republic of Macedonia, or the reintegration of the Preshevo Valley with Kosova. Political authority in the new Albanian world is highly decentralised, and even if there was a single planning and conspiring centre for the expansion of the Albanian nation, as is alleged sometimes in Greek and Serb propaganda, it is difficult to see how these agendas could be centrally coordinated. For the Albanian people in general, the term pan-Albanianism is an umbrella reference to a package of progressive measures that include democratisation, free markets and polycentric and accountable populist political authority.

It is easily demonstrable that the agenda of the new national question is not being coordinated through Tirana, where evidence based on the events of the last five years shows the Tirana political elite as inherently cautious and careful not to do or say anything that stirs up nationalist feeling. This has sometimes led to Tirana's official acceptance of the international community's misgivings regarding some Albanian national claims, such as the dismal response of the Socialist-led government to the massacres in Kosova during Belgrade's 'First Offensive' in the spring of 1998. Also, during the ethnic Albanian insurgency in Macedonia in 2001, the Albanian government allowed the deployment of NATO countries' military intelligence officers on the border with Macedonia to try to prevent supplies reaching the NLA, just as 30 years earlier Enver Hoxha's regime handed back fleeing ethnic Albanian students from the violent 1981 riots in Kosova to long jail sentences in Yugoslavia. During the interwar period, in his fight to establish his central authority in Tirana, King Zog waged a relentless campaign to destroy the then liberation struggle of the Kosovar Albanians. Zog's secret agents hunted down the main Kosovar Albanian leaders, who were all killed before Zog then instigated moves to curtail the activities of the Kosova Committee, which he believed constituted a danger to the maintenance of his good relations with Belgrade.[10] Such is the tradition of narrow, localised power struggles amongst Albania's elite, which have precluded any political vision or sense of mission that would lead to alignment even with Albanians from another region of Albania, let alone ethnic Albanians from the former Yugoslavia.

Alongside concerns about a possible Greater Albania, an abiding fear within the international community is that the Albanian model of para-military organisation, originating with the KLA and developed in Preshevo into the UCPMB in 2000 and refined in the more sophisticated NLA of the 2001 conflict in Macedonia, could become a model for other insurgent military organisations. This seems unlikely, however, as the KLA and its successor organisations depended upon particular local cultural and political circumstances that are unlikely to be reproduced elsewhere. The principal feature of this is a largely youthful and oppressed population that has been deprived of normal domestically held Balkan small arms capacity for a long time, and which is suddenly presented with the possibility to rapidly arm itself. Although the movement of munitions into Kosova from the 1997 Albanian uprising has been exaggerated, it was nevertheless a seismic event in a very unique and particular historical context that, by the nature of things, is unlikely to repeat itself.

Another salient factor is the absence of a normal and effective army in Albania, which has given full opportunity to those in the political and military twilight to claim that their clandestine arms-trading and paramilitary activities are legitimate in patriotic and national defence terms, even if illegal. As long as Albania is without the normal means to defend itself, and the KPC is less than a Kosovar army, paramilitary capacity and small arms possession will be seen as an essential necessity in the Albanian communities of the southern Balkans. Many Albanians who see NATO as having been a great friend of Albania during the last ten years are also concerned about the lack of sovereignty involved in over-dependence upon NATO and the lack of a national Kosovar defence capacity. A central challenge for Tirana governments over the next few years will be to remedy this situation.[11]

The key dynamic for the next stage of the national agenda is likely to be the triangle of interaction between the main Albanian centres in Tirana, Prishtina and Tetovo, and the increasing number of projects that will dramatically improve communications between the various Albanian populations of the southern Balkans. The process of economic development is being accelerated by the construction of the new Durres–Prizren road, which began in late 2005. The importance of this road cannot be overestimated for it will link Kosova with the Adriatic Sea, and is seen by Albanian leaders as a key factor in the stabilisation of Kosova as a Western-oriented and stable state after its political status has been decided. Without the road, communications with the Adriatic coast would be limited due to severely deficient existing roads, which would hinder Kosova's development. An electricity exchange between Albania and Kosova is planned, to ease power outages, and the full modernisation of Prishtina airport will follow, thus opening the area to trans-Atlantic-sized aircraft.

In marked contrast to the snail's pace of progress in institutional reform, Albania's economic development is generally encouraging. Recent reviews published by the IMF report favourably on a high growth rate and stable macro-economy, but continue to criticise shortcomings in structural reform.

In view of Albania's relatively improved political stability, the number of tourists visiting Albania has been gradually increasing over the past three years, with more than 500,000 visiting the country in 2004. Income from tourism is now one of the main sources of foreign currency for Albania's economy. Tourism was rated as one of the most dynamic sectors of the economy during the first quarter of 2005, generating around $200 million during this period, when the number of foreign visitors to the country increased by 15 per cent compared to the same period in 2004.

A new regional airport at Kukes and projected new airports near the southern towns of Vlora and Gjirokaster, will considerably improve internal communications. The rail link with Macedonia is being restored, and more border openings are planned between Albania and its neighbours, particularly with Macedonia, and a fibre-optic cable network is being built to link the country with Montenegro and Croatia. The US mega-corporation General Electric has signed a contract for various modernisations of the Tirana–Durres railway. The main Albanian bank, the Bank of National Savings, has been purchased by an Austrian bank with massive development plans. There will be more investment in the next ten years in the Albanian and Kosovar economic and transport infrastructure than in the entire twentieth century.

At the time of writing the vast part of the new wealth that has been created in the new Albanian political and economic space in the southern Balkans is held at most by the top 10 per cent of the population, and much of that by a very much smaller number of people. This concentration of wealth and related power bases centred around a very small number of very wealthy businessmen is unlikely to bring stability in the long term. The opening of the new Albanian space needs to be accompanied by a real effort to reduce poverty and lack of opportunity, especially for those in rural districts, in order to remove the fertile soil in which organised crime and corruption grow. Without development and poverty reduction, it is very unlikely that there will be fundamental change in this direction.

Underlying all developments, political, economic and cultural, is the central issue of the independence of Kosova. There is widespread misunderstanding of Albanian national aspirations. Albanians have got used to the idea of separate Albanian entities in the Balkans. They are well aware of the cultural and ideological divisions between them, and are therefore content to preserve their separate political entities as long as business, cultural and travel restrictions are removed. At the present time, most Albanians do not wish to join a single political unit. However, if the final status of Kosova is not resolved within the foreseeable future, the southern Balkans will inevitably see a resumption of conflict.[12]

The independence of Kosova remains at the core of the national question. The international community and the UN has adopted the 'Standards before Status' policy, which imposes several stringent requirements upon the Kosovar Albanians in terms of protection of minority rights and other issues. Following the death of Ibrahim Rugova in January 2006, talks on the political status of Kosova opened in Vienna in February 2006 under UN auspices. The current concentration on the Kosova independence issue is the main focus of current pan-Albanian thinking. Albanians look at the gains made by Slovenia, Croatia and the initial Western support for the independence movement in Montenegro, and ask themselves why they cannot have what has been granted to others.[13] In the next period it will be possible to see how far the international community is prepared to recognise this, the central reality in the Balkans today.

Appendix

Summer 1997 Parliamentary Election – the Coalition Government

Title	Name	Party affiliation
President	Rexhep Meidani	SP
Prime Minister	Fatos Nano	SP
Deputy Prime Minister	Bashkim Fino	SP
Ministers		
Agriculture and Food	Lufter Xhuveli	AP
Culture, Youth and Sports	Arta Dade	SP
Defence	Sabit Brokaj	SP
Education and Science	Et'hem Ruka	SP
Finance	Arben Malaj	SP
Foreign	Paskal Milo	SDP
Health and Environment	Leonard Solis	HRUP
Interior	Neritan Ceka	DAP
Labour, Social Affairs and Women	Elmaz Sherifi	SP
Public Economy and Privatisation	Ylli Bufi	SP
Public Affairs and Transport	Gaqo Apostoli	SDP
Trade and Tourism	Shaqir Vukaj	SP
State Ministers		
Minister	Kastriot Islami	SP
Legislative Reforms and Parliament Relations	Arben Imami	DAP
Economic Cooperation and Development	Ermelinda Meksi	SP
Secretaries of State		
Euro-Atlantic Integration	Maqo Lakrori	SP
Defence Policy	Perikli Teta	DAP
Interior	Ndre Legisi	SP
Local Power	Lush Perpali	SP
Central Bank Governor	Shkelqim Cani	SP

Note: *Socialist Party (SP); Social Democratic Party (SDP); Democratic Alliance Party (DAP); Human Rights Union Party (HRUP – ethnic Greeks); Agrarian Party (AP).*

Parliament Elected on 29 June and 6 July

Party	% of vote	Seats
Socialist Party	52.8	99
Democratic Party	25.7	29
Democracit Alliance Party	2.8	2
Human Rights Union Party	2.8	4
Social Democratic Party	2.5	1
Republican Party	2.3	1
National Front	2.3	3
Movement of Legality Party (monarchist)	n/a	2
Party of National Unity	n/a	1
Agrarian Party	n/a	1
Non-partisans	n/a	3
Run-offs	n/a	2
Total		*148*

Note: Some 9 per cent of the votes were either spoilt, corrupt or otherwise disallowed by the Electoral Commission.

Notes

PREFACE

1. Vickers, Miranda and James Pettifer, *Albania – From Anarchy to a Balkan Identity* (C. Hurst & Co., London, second edition, 2000).

2. For convenience, after the recognition of what is known by the UN as 'Former Yugoslav Macedonia' (FYROM) and/or the 'Republic of Macedonia' by the USA, we generally use the term 'Macedonia' for the current state entity.

3. For a representative view of the Albanian national question prior to the 1997 uprising, see 'The Albanian National Question – the post-Dayton pay-off', War Report No. 41 (London, May 1996).

4. For an Albanian view on the attitude of the Democratic Party government to the national question up to 1999, see Bucpapaj, Muje, *Partia Demokratike dhe Ceshtja Kombetare* (Koha, Tirana, 2000).

5. For the refugee crisis and associated events, see Selm, Joanne van (ed.), *Kosovo's Refugees in the European Union* (Continuum, London and New York, 2000); Friend, Melanie, *No Place Like Home* (Midnight Editions, San Francisco, 2001); also Booth, K. (ed.), *The Kosovo Tragedy – The Human Rights Dimension* (Cass, London, 2001).

6. See Pettifer, James (ed.), *The New Macedonian Question* (Palgrave, London and New York, 2001).

7. For a discussion on the historical background to the Cham question, see Vickers, Miranda, *The Cham Issue – Albanian National and Property Claims in Greece,* G-109, April 2002 (Conflict Studies Research Centre (CSRC)) at www.csrc.mod.uk. The Cham issue arose after the Greek genocide committed by the forces of EDES in 1943–4 in the Second World War, led by Napoleon Zervas. Most of the Albanian Cham population were driven from Epirus to exile in Turkey, the USA or Albania.

8. After the foundation of the Albanian state just before the First World War, its stability was threatened by an invasion of Greek irregulars in the south and much of the energy of King Zog in the 1920s was taken up with creating physical security within the country and along its borders. This process was overtaken by the annexation of Albania by the Italian fascists. In the Second World War, Greek forces once again entered Albania, this time to oppose the Italian invasion of Greece in 1940.

9   In general, Gheg Albanians were those that lived north of the Shkumbini River and in
        Montenegro, Kosova and north-west Macedonia, while Tosks lived south of that river
        and in south-west Macedonia and Chameria. Ghegs speak a slightly different dialect
        of the language, and are often taller and thinner than Tosks, but these traditional
        differences (often exaggerated in vulgar anthropology) have been much diminished by
        population movement in the post-communist period.

10   Pettifer, James, *Kosova Express* (C. Hurst & Co., London, Wisconsin University Press,
        Madison and Liria Books, Prishtina, 2004; Libri, New York, 2006).

11   We would like to take the opportunity to correct the error we made in *Albania – From
        Anarchy to a Balkan Identity* where we wrongly stated that Ambassador Ryerson had a
        long background of work in Latin America.

12   Carlson, Scott N., *Some Reflections on Experiencing an Attempted Coup in Albania*,
        (Washington, DC, 2002).

PART I, Chapter 1

1   Dr Ibrahim Rugova (1943–2006) was a prominent Kosovar Albanian literary critic
        and author. He was involved in founding the Kosova Democratic League (LDK) in
        1989–90 and led the party until his death.

2   The so-called 'small package' agreement was negotiated by US envoy Richard Holbrooke
        and signed by Greek and Slav Macedonian leaders in October 1995. It resolved the
        FYROM/Macedonian flag design dispute and opened the Macedonian economy to
        Greek asset-stripping and exploitation.

3   World Bank, 'Albania – Country Assistance Review' (Washington DC, 18 June 1998).
        This report is the best general guide to the financial crisis of 1997. For a general economic
        analysis, see Vaughan-Whitehead, Daniel, *Albania in Crisis* (Edward Elgar, Cheltenham
        and Northampton, MA, 1999) and Clunies Ross, Antony and Peter Sudar (eds), *Albania's
        Economy in Transition and Turmoil* (Ashgate, Aldershot and Burlington, VT, 1998).

4   The Albanian pyramid banking schemes were in essence following the modus operandi
        pioneered by the corrupt US financier Charles Ponzi, where the very high returns paid
        to existing investors were maintained by exploiting the contributions of new investors
        to the pyramid banks. These schemes are at high risk of collapse when the supply
        of new investors dries up. See Zuckoff, Mitchell, *Ponzi's Scheme: The True Story of a
        Financial Legend* (Random House, New York, 2005).

5   Kokodihma is now a multi-millionaire in Tirana and owner of *Shekulli* newspaper and
        other businesses. He was originally a prominent figure in the Party of Labour youth
        organisation in Fier.

6   For a technical economic analysis, see Korovilas, J., 'The Albanian Economy in
        Transition: The Role of Remittances and Pyramid Investment Schemes', *Working
        Papers in Economics* No. 28 (University of the West of England, November 1998).

7   See Vickers, Miranda and James Pettifer, *Albania – From Anarchy to a Balkan Identity*
        (C. Hurst & Co., London, second edition, 2000), pp.286 ff. See also 'Albanians refuse
        to awake from prosperity balloon dream', *Albanian Daily News*, 11 October 1996.

8   *Albania,* Tirana, 10 October 1996

9   Vickers, Miranda, 'Pyramid banks crisis looms in Albania', *Independent*, London, 3
        January, 1997.

10   Gramoz Pashko died in a helicopter crash in July 2006.

11   There have been allegations in Tirana that the French government, through a Swiss legal intermediary in Geneva, extensively funded the DP in this period. In London prominent members of the pro-Berisha Anglo-Albanian Association, such as Julian Amery, also had contacts with the Serbian monarchists and Greek Royalists.

12   See Wheen, Francis, 'Conservative pillars of the Albanian state', *Guardian*, London, 12 February 1997.

13   See Vickers and Pettifer: *Albania – From Anarchy*.

14   See Pettifer, James, *Kosova Express* (C. Hurst & Co., London, Wisconsin University Press, Madison and Liria Books, Prishtina, 2004; Libri, New York, 2006).

15   Vickers, Miranda, 'Huge losses in Albanian savings fraud', *Independent*, London, 3 January 1997.

16   Ibid.

17   *Albanian Daily News*, 2 January 1997. See also Smith, M.A., 'Albania: pyramid crisis', *CSRC Occasional Brief* No. 52, www.csrc.mod.uk.

18   Commentator Mero Baze stated this on the *Voice of America* on 9 January 1997. It was widely repeated in the Albanian media the next day, but denied by Vlora police.

19   *Voice of America* broadcast, 12 December 1996.

20   *Albanian Daily News*, 16 January 1997.

21   See Pettifer: *Kosova Express*, pp.104 ff.

22   Done, Kevin, 'Albanian company keeps up the show', *Financial Times*, London, 31 March 1997. See also pamphlet published by VEFA Holdings, 'Our aim is to create as many jobs as possible' (Arberia, Tirana, 1996).

23   *Albanian Daily News*, 22 January 1997

24   Named after the Chameria region of north-west Greece where they had lived for hundreds of years.

25   VEFA Holdings: 'Our aim is to create'.

26   See Associated Press report 'Circular logic that dazzles the unwary' and interview with Xhaferi, 21 January 1997; see also report on the blockade of Lushnja by Joanna Robinson, *Guardian*, London, 25 January 1997.

27   *Guardian*, London, 28 January 1997.

28   Editorial, *The Times*, London, 27 January 1997.

29   SHIK was the successor organisation to the communist-period Sigurimi secret police.

30   Done, Kevin, 'Albanian company keeps up the show', *Financial Times*, London, 31 March 1997.

31   *Guardian*, London, 11 February 1997.

32   Author's interview with Neritan Ceka, former Interior Minister, November 2002.

33   Almond, Mark, 'Albania's riots aren't what they seem', *Wall Street Journal Europe*, 5 March 1997.

34   *The Times*, London, 15 February 1997.

35   Done, Kevin and Kerin Hope, 'Country Survey – Albania', *Financial Times*, 19 February 1997.

36   See Metropolitan Sevastanios of Dryinoupolis, *Northern Epirus Crucified* (Athens, 1986) and similar publications. In essence, the Northern Epirot agenda has remained unchanged since the end of the First World War and has always sought to 'recover' this region for Greece.

37   World Bank: 'Albania – Country Assistance Review', p.61

38   See Owen, Richard, 'Is Albania on Europe's conscience?', *The Times*, 4 March 1997; also Pettifer, James, 'Berisha's fall vital to end the anarchy', *The Times*, 15 March 1997.

PART I, Chapter 2

1   For Meksi's views on what was happening see the interview series in *Zeri* newspaper, Prishtina, 18–26 February 2001. Also, Meksi interview with James Pettifer, Tirana, February 2004.

2   The Sigurimi (from the Albanian word for 'security') was the communist-period political police.

3   For insights into the basic crisis in the political class, see Danaj, Koco, *Populli I Tradhtuar* (Java, Tirana, 1998).

4   See, for instance, Owen, Richard, 'Enver Hoxha haunts Berisha's Tirana', *The Times*, 4 March 1997.

5   Owen, Richard, 'Berisha declares emergency to quell Albanian revolt', *The Times*, 3 March 1997. It is not clear exactly which agencies Berisha had in mind, but Greece is the most obvious candidate.

6   For Meksi's views on some of these issues, and the 1990–7 period in Albania generally, see Meksi, Alexander, *Permes Fjales se Tij* (Luarasi, Tirana, 1997).

7   See Pettifer, James, 'Scapegoat sacrificed to rising militancy', *The Times*, 3 March 1997.

8   See Lane, Col C. Dennison, 'Once upon an army – the crisis in the Albanian army 1995–6', CRSC Document G-114, 2002 (www.csrc.mod.uk). For an Albanian historian's view, see Katana, Halil, *Ringritja e Ushtrise Shqiptare 1997–2000* (Rinia, Tirana, 2004). Katana gives a very useful account of the army position in the north, in particular.

9   Associated Press report, 6 March 1997, quoted in *Hellenic Times*, Athens, 6 March 1997.

10   Robertson, Joanna, 'Berisha sacks army chiefs', *Guardian*, London, 5 March 1997.

11   Interview by James Pettifer with Greek Army officers, Ioannina, 12 March 1997.

12   Front page article, *International Herald Tribune*, New York/Paris, 5 March 1997, compiled by staff from *Dispatches*.

13   See, for instance, article by BBC Foreign Affairs editor John Simpson, *Sunday Telegraph*, London, 'Sali Berisha objects to my last column', 9 March 1997.

14   Pettifer, James, 'General's decision to dragoon troops', *The Times*, London, 5 March 1997. Many of Berisha's Ministers were less optimistic about the situation than the President himself. Foreign Minister Arian Starova believed 'the reality was that there was no army' (document written in response to questions from the authors on the crisis, July 2006).

15   Front page article, *International Herald Tribune*, New York/Paris, 5 March 1997, compiled by staff from *Dispatches*.

16   Tepelena was probably the town with the strongest Partisan and communist support in the region, dating back many decades.

17   Daly, Emma, 'Protestors fear Berisha's army is out for blood', *Independent*, London, 6 March 1997. This air force activity was also reported in *The Times*, London, 6 March 1997.

18   Special Operations Executive, a clandestine British Second World War agency.

19   Walker, Tom, 'Rebel barricades go up in south as army advances', *The Times*, London, 6 March 1997.

20   For further background, see Cupi, Frrok, *Vlora '97* (Fan Noli, Tirana, 1998) and Pettifer, James, *Blue Guide to Albania and Kosova* (A&C Black, London and Norton, New York, 2001), pp.470 ff.

21   Forum for Democracy document, 6 March 1997. It stated 'The meeting throws into serious doubt the determination of President Berisha to achieve a peaceful solution to this crisis.'

22   See Judah, Tim, 'Albania prepares for war as rebels dig in', *Daily Telegraph*, London, 9 March 1997.

23   Permet was predominantly Orthodox and pro-Socialist. In communist times it had been an Enverist 'Hero City', a sign of favour under the communist regime.

24   Robertson, Joanna and Helena Smith, 'Concession failed to quell Albania revolt', *Guardian*, London, 10 March 1997.

25   It was claimed at the time, in some sections of the Tirana media, that Hajdari was acting as a conduit for funds from an Islamic nation in the Middle East. These claims were never proven, but may account in part for the extreme reluctance of some sections of the international community to discuss his later murder.

26   See Part II, Chapter 5 on 'Operation Alba' for more on Italian and international community attitudes during this critical week.

27   Similar failures were, of course, a common feature of the Bosnian war period and were to persist in the Kosova conflict.

28   In some cases, much longer (i.e. the purging of the army was not completed by Berisha until late 1995).

29   The most important aspect of this was that the BBC and *Voice of America* broke Berisha's attempted media blackout after 3 March.

30   Interview of the authors with Qeparo citizens, March 2003.

31   Goudapple was working closely with the British-financed Butrint Foundation at the time, and had previously had difficulties with unfair competition and unethical business practices from Greeks on Corfu, and had suffered harassment from the Greek internal security police (cf. interview with James Pettifer, September 2005).

32   See Vickers, Miranda and James Pettifer, *Albania – From Anarchy to a Balkan Identity* (C. Hurst & Co., London, second edition, 2000).

33   For the aftermath of this, and the military reform issues, see Binaj, Agim and Beatrice Pollo, *Buxheti dhe Shpenzimet per Mbrojtjen* (Geer, Tirana, 2002).

34   See, for instance, the attack on the authors of this book by Anthony Daniels in 'The media backs the Communists – as usual', *Sunday Telegraph*, London, 9 March 1997, and the activities of the Oxford Helsinki Human Rights Group throughout the crisis. Some US neo-conservatives took up similar positions, although others did not.

35   In the communist period, a 'biographi' was the term used by the secret police to describe a person's political record.

PART I, Chapter 3

1   The impetus for this was also probably connected with fear of mass emigration. See Phillips, John, 'Italy mobilises anti-immigrant force to repel Albanian exodus', *The Times*, 4 March 1997.

2   For example, Alliance party leader Perikli Teta, a former Minister, said 'The place for negotiations is in Tirana, not out at sea with the Italians' ('Berisha loyalists raise spectre of north–south war', *The Times*, London, 12 March, 1997).

3   A decree to set aside Nano's sentence was signed by Berisha on 14 March.

4   Fatos Nano was born in 1952 into the family of a Communist Party official, and received a degree in political economy and a PhD in economics from Tirana University. In the last years of communism he worked in the Institute of Marxist-Leninism in Tirana. He was nominated to the post of Prime Minister by communist leader Ramiz Alia in 1991 but was forced to resign after popular protests and strikes. He was imprisoned by Berisha in 1993 for corruption. After returning to power in mid-1997, he was leader of the Socialist Party and held various top government posts until the election defeat of 2005.

5   See Katana, Halil, *Ringritja e Ushtrise Shqiptare 1997–2000* (Rinia, Tirana, 2004). Also Lane, Col C. Dennison, 'Once upon an army – the crisis in the Albanian army 1995–6', CRSC Document G-114, 2002 (www.csrc.mod.uk).

6   Smith, Helena, *Guardian*, London, 10 March 1997.

7   See Pettifer, James, *Kosova Express* (C. Hurst & Co., London, Wisconsin University Press, Madison and Liria Books, Prishtina, 2004; Libri, New York, 2006), pp.115 ff.

8   The nucleus of FARK was this paramilitary force in Tropoja. It later merged with soldiers loyal to ex-Kosova 'Prime Minister' Bujar Bukoshi in the 1998–9 period in the Kosova war. Bukoshi had begun to build a military force for the Kosova Democratic League of Ibrahim Rugova in response to the failure of the Democratic League to control the KLA.

9   Commentators have consistently overestimated the amount of weaponry that actually arrived safely in Kosova. See Haradinaj, Ramush, *A Narrative about War and Freedom* (Zeri, Prishtina, 2001) and other memoirs by war veterans.

10   See News Flash, Greek Foreign Ministry, from the Greek Embassy in Washington DC, 11 March 1997 (Albanian News Agency).

11   For a DP view of the Greek plot alleged to be behind the uprising, see Berisha and Harxhi (eds), 'Komploti Greko Komunist kunder Demokracise Shqiptare 1997-2000' at www.users.erols.com.

12   Under King Zog (1926–39) a trading and administrative middle class grew in the capital, a process carried on in the Italian annexation in the 1930s.

13   See Smith, Helena, 'Albania sinks deeper into anarchy', *Guardian*, London, 13 March 1997.

14   Ibid.

15   Although collectivisation had been the official policy, as elsewhere in communist countries, it never found much support among the people, and after 1990 and land redistribution, many traditional holdings were restored. For a view of this period, see Lemel, H. (ed.), *Rural Property and Economy in Post-Communist Albania* (Berghahn, New York, 2000).

16   Author's correspondence with Ms P. Peacock, UK, 1997.

17   Col Dennison Lane was technically US military adviser to the Albanian Ministry of Defence, not the President. See his published reports of this period on the President of Albania at www.csrc.mod.ac.uk.

18   Gumbel, Andrew, 'God save us, God save Albania', *Independent*, London, 14 March 1997.

19   Author's interview with Bob Churcher, ex-head of the OSCE, Peshkopi, October 2001.

20   At the time, in the Albanian media, the Vranitsky mission was often referred to as the 'European Mission'. This was incorrect: it also contained non-Europeans, such as Congressman Eliot Engel from the USA.

21   Sweeney, John, 'Gun Law', *Observer*, London, 16 March 1997 (front page story).

22   I.e. a leader in the *New York Times* on 16 March had commented on the need for the EU to develop mechanisms to support the Balkans, and said part of the Albanian problem was the Bosniacentric preoccupations of the Europeans.

23   Quoted on the BBC Albanian Service, 10 March 1997.

24   See Part II, Chapter 5 on Operation Alba for an analysis of this process.

25   Briggs attained unwanted prominence later in the crisis after being shot at a party in Tirana, allegedly by a Tirana prostitute after a fight involving members of the British SAS. See Owen, Richard, 'British diplomat stabbed', *The Times*, 10 June1997; also interviews by the authors.

26   Many leading French Albanologists had been, or still were, communists in 1997.

27   Interview by James Pettifer with US State department official, Paris, May 2001.

28   See, for instance, Elez Biberaj's book *Albania in Transition* (Westview, CT, 1998). Biberaj is a distinguished and universally respected *Voice of America* Albanian Service commentator of rightist leanings from northern Albania who had become increasingly critical of the Berisha government after the controversial 1996 election.

29   See Pettifer, James, 'Berisha's fall vital to end anarchy', *The Times*, 15 March 1997.

30   For a typical statement of this viewpoint, see Almond, Mark, 'Albania's riots aren't what they seem', *Wall Street Journal Europe*, 5 March 1997.

31   The so-called 'Tetovo Factor' in the development of the national question should not be underestimated. See Rexhepi, Zeqirja, *Partia Demokratike Shqiptare-Lindja Zhvillimi dhe Verprimtaria* (Tringa, Tetovo, 2004) for an account of the 1990s power struggles in Tetovo and the north-west Macedonian Albanian communities that later led to the intense support for the Kosova campaign.

32   An exception was the anti-globalisation theorist Koco Danaj. See his analysis in Danaj, Koco, *The Clinton Doctrine and the Twenty-First Century* (Erik, Tirana, 2000).

PART II, Chapter 4

1   Author's interview with Col Dennison Lane, 8 April 2001.

2   *Koha Jone*, Tirana, 2 May 1997.

3   Lloyd, Anthony, 'War gives Coke a taste of the real thing', *The Times*, 17 March 1997.

4   Klosi, Ardian, *Anarchy by Design*, War Report, IWPR, London, April 1997.

5   In the 1980s he had been a candidate member for the higher organs of party authority and leader of the Party of Labour medical group.

6   In the internecine feuds that paralysed Vlora between late 1997 and the end of 1999, Zani's power waned, and his brothers were all killed or arrested. Zani's joint operations with the Italian Mafia were closed down by Interpol.

7   For an excellent account of the history of the political struggle for leadership of the Macedonian Albanians in this period, see Rexhepi, Zeqirja, *Partia Demokratike Shqiptare-Lindja Zhvillimi dhe Veprimataria* (Tringa, Tetovo, 2004).

8   See Part II, Chapter 5 on Operation Alba for a detailed analysis.

9   *Koha Jone*, 18 April 1997, unattributed leading article.

10   *Koha Jone*, 16 April 1997, unattributed article.

11   Leka Zog's father, Ahmet Zog, was born in the Mat district of central Albania in 1895. He proclaimed himself King Zog I in 1928, and in order to gain financial assistance Zog began overt political ties with Italy. Within a decade, the Italians controlled every

essential sector of the Albanian state. Following the Italian invasion of Albania in April 1939, Zog fled into permanent exile with his wife Geraldine and two-day-old son Leka. The monarchy was abolished by the Communists in 1946. Leka was crowned king in 1961 after the death of his father.

12   It is likely that British monarchist activists linked to MI6 also played a role in the decision Leka Zog took to return to Albania at this point.

13   Albanian Television, Tirana, 1800 GMT, 19 April 1997.

14   Albanian Television, Tirana, 1800 GMT, 17 April 1997.

15   There has always been considerable debate about the extent to which the Yugoslav Secret Intelligence Service (UDB-a) had infiltrated the royal orbit, particularly in Britain and the USA. See Misha, P. (ed.) *Dosja Sekrete e UDB-se-Emigrationi Shqiptare 1944–1953* (Koha, Tirana and Prishtina, 2005). Some leading supporters of Zog, such as Lord Julian Amery in the Britain, were also on good terms with the exiled Serbian monarchists. See *Illyria* newspaper, New York City, 12 July 2005 and also interviews by the authors with various US Albanian émigrés.

16   Klosi: *Anarchy by Design.*

17   Sir Reginald Hibbert, *The Times*, 10 March 1997.

PART II, Chapter 5

1   See Favretto, Marcella, 'Anarchy in Albania: the collapse of European collective security', *Basic Papers on International Security*, No. 21, June 1997.

2   There are numerous books about the Bosnian intervention and settlement. For the peace negotiations and the role of the UN, see Holbrooke, Richard, *To End a War* (Random House, New York, 1998). For a critical view of the UN and the Dayton Accords, see Chandler, David, *Bosnia – Faking Democracy after Dayton* (Pluto Press, London, 1999).

3   See 'Lifting the lid on Operation Alba', *Jane's International Police Issues*, London, December 1998.

4   See Williams, Abiodun *Preventing War – the United Nations and Macedonia* (Rowman and Littlefield, Lanham, MA, 2000).

5   See, for instance, paper by Fatmir Mema, former Albanian Deputy Defence Minister, 'Did Albania really need Operation Alba?', *Security Dialogue*, Vol. 29, No. 2, June 1998 (see also article by Ettore Greco in the same issue, 'New trends in peacekeeping – the experience of Operation Alba').

6   The standard history of the deployment is Orofino, Giuseppe, *L'Operazione Alba* (Rivista Militare, Rome, 2001). We are grateful to the office of the Italian military attaché in London for various help in obtaining information about Operation Alba, and also to the Italian KFOR officers in Peje. For comparison with the role of the UN in Macedonia, see Phillips, John, *Macedonia – Warlords and Rebels in the Balkans* (I.B.Tauris, London, 2004).

7   For background on previous Italian aid programmes, see Ministry of Foreign Affairs, 'Italy supports Albania/Italia aiuta L'Albania', Rome, 1998. About $130 million was spent in 1997.

8   Quoted in Mema, Fatmir, 'Did Albania really need Operation Alba?', *Security Dialogue*, Vol. 29, No. 2, June 1998.

9   For example, Col Lane, Dennison, 'Once upon an army – the crisis in the Albanian army 1995–6', CRSC Document G-114, 2002 (www.csrc.mod.uk), author's correspondence with former US Ambassador William Ryerson, and publications by the US Helsinki Committee in New York City.

10   Ambassador Ryerson contends that in our earlier book *From Anarchy to a Balkan Identity* we overestimated his direct influence over Berisha in even the earlier period of DP government.

11   Mema: 'Did Albania really need Operation Alba?'

12   See, for instance, material published on the Internet by the 'Albania in Rivotla' group, a faction in the Italian Communist party (www.ecn.org/est/albania).

13   See OSCE papers in archive of Bob Churcher on the election period in Peshkopi and the region, for instance.

14   Interview with Franz Vranitsky in *Koha Ditore*, Prishtina, March 2003.

15   James Pettifer's conversation with General K. Karolli, Tirana, 2001; also Orofino: *L'Operazione Alba.*

16   See, for instance, the websites of the Albanian-American Civil League (www.aacl..com) and the Albanian-American National Council (www.naac.org).

17   See Vickers, Miranda and James Pettifer, *Albania – From Anarchy to a Balkan Identity* (C. Hurst & Co., London, second edition, 2000).

18   See various articles in *The Times* by James Pettifer in March 1997.

19   Proceedings of the UN Security Council, 1997 (www.un.org).

20   James Pettifer's conversation with US diplomat Shaun Byrnes, Washington, 2004.

21   In the experience of the authors with official contacts in the 1992–6 period, the same strong supporters of the DP government in the Tory party and those close to it were the most entrenched pro-Serbian force outside of Russia in the international community. See Hodge, Carole, *The Serb Lobby in Great Britain* (Glasgow, 1997) and Simms, Brendan, *Britain and the Tragedy of Bosnia* (Penguin, London, 2002).

PART II, Chapter 6

1   There was no doubt that Berisha was correct from the point of view of constitutional law. Few of the internationals involved in the Vranitsky-led negotiations realised that the electoral law dated in essence from the 1991 and 1992 elections. Berisha, as victor in the latter contest, was happy to assume the near-dictatorial rights over election matters vested in the Presidency under his predecessor Ramiz Alia. The international community in the 1990–1 period had been willing to see Alia assume these powers as a means of reducing the influence of Hoxhaist hardliners in the Politburo over the transition from communism. See Commission on Security and Cooperation in Europe, *The Elections in Albania March–April 1991*, Washington DC, April 1991.

2   For a detailed account of the May 1996 elections, see Vickers, Miranda and James Pettifer, *Albania – From Anarchy to a Balkan Identity* (C. Hurst & Co., London, second edition, 2000).

3   Unattributed article, *Gazeta Shqiptare*, 3 May 1997.

4   For a pro-Royalist account of Leka's return and bid for power, see Germenji, Flujurak, *Mbreti ne Atdhe 12 Prill–12 Korrik 1997* (Koha, Tirana, 1998).

5   It was later claimed in the Albanian media that she had also been working as a prostitute there. Four months after the affair, she fled to London. In an interview with the authors (February 1998) she claimed that the violence started at the party after Briggs was attacked by a British special forces soldier who accused him of failing to organise the Embassy evacuation properly.

6   OSCE, 'Albania – parliamentary elections 1997' (www.osce.org).

7   Noel Malcolm, televised statement quoted in the *Sunday Telegraph*, London, 13 July 1997.

8   Albanian TV, Tirana, 16.35 GMT, 30 June 1997.

9   ATA News Agency, Tirana, 9 July 1997.

10   For Monarchist views on all these events, see unattributed article 'Mbreti ne Atdhe 12 Prill–12 Korrik 1997', *Koha*, Tirana, 1998.

11   Reported by the ATA, 4 July 1997.

12   *Albania*, 3 July 1997.

13   Presented 23 July 1997. From a strictly legal point of view, Berisha was correct.

14   Agence France Presse, 23 July 1997.

15   Remzi Lani, War Report, IWPR, London, April 1997.

16   *East European Newsletter*, Vol. II, No. 14, 24 July 1997.

17   Unattributed article, *Zeri-I-Popullit*, 14 July 1997.

18   Ibid.

19   When speaking to the General Leading Committee of the Socialist Party in Tirana on 4 July, Fatos Nano said that on 29 June, the 'Socialist Party had achieved a victory of historic proportions', but would seek to work with all non-DP political forces (see www.Albania_in_Rivolta.com).

20   Many localities had tried to solve the spring 1997 security crisis through community-based initiatives. For a fine account of this period in the north-east town of Peshkopi, see Ademi, Astrit, *Ne Dditet e Shtetit pa Pushtet* (Dardania, Tirana, 1998).

21   *Rilindja Demokratike*, 13 July 1997.

22   Unattributed article, *Koha Jone*, 10 July 1997.

23   Unattributed article, *Gazeta Sqiptare*, 18 July 1997.

24   ATA News Agency, Tirana, 16 July 1997.

25   *East European Newsletter*, Vol. II, No. 13, 3 July 1997.

26   For useful economic background, see Council of Ministers, *Republic of Albania, Public Investment Programme 1996–1998* (Tirana, 1996).

27   Author's discussion with N. Ceka, March 2001.

28   *Albania*, 12 July 1997.

29   For Milo's views on the wider national question issues, see Milo, Paskal, *'Greater Albania'– Between Fiction and Reality* (Tirana, 2001).

PART III, Chapter 7

1   For useful background see Mertus, Julie A., *Kosovo – How Myths and Truths Started a War* (Los Angeles, 1999).

2   The KLA had several small precursor paramilitary organisations. The most important of these were associated with Adem Demaci and Ahmet Haxhiu. See Pettifer, James, *Kosova Express* (C. Hurst & Co., London, Wisconsin University Press, Madison and Liria Books, Prishtina, 2004; Libri, New York, 2006). See also Neziri, Ibish, *Ahmet*

Haxhiu nje Jete te Tere ne Levizjen Ilgale (Ibrezi, Prishtina, 2001); Bajrami, Hakif, *Dosia Demaci* (Shoqata e te Burgoserne Politike, Prishtina, 2004); Veliu, Fazli, *LPK dhe UCK: Nje Embleme, Nje Qellim* (Dritero, Tirana, 2001).

3   Bulletin of the Ministry of Information of the Republic of Kosova, No. 289, Prishtina, 24 January 1997.

4   Unattributed open editorial, *Rilindja*, Tirana, 23 January 1997.

5   See Mustafa, Rrustem (Commander Remi), *War for Kosova* (Zeri, Prishtina, 2001).

6   Pajaziti was a great loss to the war leadership in north-east Kosova and had been targeted by the Serbs for some time.

7   For background on the KLA see Judah, Tim, *Kosovo War and Revenge* (Oxford University Press, London and Yale University Press, New Haven, CT, 2000). .

8   See Dobra, Islam, *Lufta e Drenicas 1941–1945 dhe NDSH deri 1947* (Prishtina, 1997).

9   See Sell, Louis, *Slobodan Milosevic and the Destruction of Yugoslavia* (Duke, NC, 2002) and Pettifer: *Kosova Express*.

10   See Pettifer: *Kosova Express*.

11   Interview with Bujar Bukoshi, Prishtina, October 2005.

12   Kosovars were in training in the Albanian Military Academy from 1989 onwards. This was stopped by the Democratic Party government in 1992, probably on foreign instructions. Adem Jashari was an early trainee under this scheme.

13   Visit by James Pettifer to Labinot camp, Elbasan, December 1992.

14   For basic background information on the LPRK, see Judah: *Kosova War and Revenge*, pp.104 ff.

15   Author's interviews with Mr Z. Qira in Kosova and New York City, 1999–2002; also see Qira, Zhelajdin, *Cell 31* (New York, 1979) for a fine account of this period.

16   There has been widespread speculation that Thaci was the real target of the hit squad and the killing was a case of mistaken identity.

17   For background on the military crisis see Leci, Elmas, *Eliminimi I Lidershipit Ushtarak* (Instituti i Sigurimit dhe Mbrojtjes, Tirana, 2002) and Col Lane, Dennison, 'Once upon an army – the crisis in the Albanian army 1995–6', CRSC Document G-114, 2002 (www.csrc.mod.uk). For more general background and analysis of the key July 1997 to January 1998 period for the KLA and its relationship with Tirana, see International Crisis Group, 'The view from Tirana – the Albanian dimension of the Kosova crisis', Balkans Report No. 36, 10 July 1998. For a view of the military issues from a senior Tirana officer, see Lama, Kudusi, *Kosova dhe Ushtria Climitare* (Borim, Tirana, 2005).

18   Veton Surroi, currently leader of the Ore party in post-1999 Kosova, was then the main independent media voice for the Kosova Albanians, through his newspaper *Koha Ditore*.

19   Authors' interview with serving MI6 officer, 2000.

20   At that time, in the Second World War, Alia was a young political commissar, and in Kosova was involved in demobilising the Albanian Partisans in the interests of Titoism – an irony in view of his later career.

21   See Kekezi, Harillaq and Rexhep Hida, *What the Kosovars Say and Demand* (8 Nentori, Tirana, 1985) and other similar material from the 1980s.

22   See Part IV, Chapters 1 and 2.

23   Klosi came from the southern farming area of Mallakastra, from a family of complex political loyalties. One of his relations, Bilbil Klosi, had been Minister of Justice for a period under the Hoxha regime.

24   Rondos was later to play an important role in organising the Greek Royalist end of the anti-Milosevic opposition in Serbia.

25   His family are actually of mixed background, partly from the Greek-speaking community and partly Albanian, from the Qeparo-Himara area.

26   *Rilindja*, Tirana, 13 April 1997.

27   The British Ambassador in the 1998–2000 period, Peter January, was a technical expert in this field with previous experience of work with the British Government Communication HQ at Cheltenham.

28   See Hamzaj, Bardh, *A Narrative about War and Freedom: Dialogue with Commander Ramush Haradinaj* (Zeri, Prishtina, 2000).

29   ENTER News Agency, Tirana, 9 November 1997.

30   See Hamzaj: *Narrative About War and Freedom*; see also Cetta, Muhammet, *Me UCK – ne Ne Koshare* (Prishtina, 2000) and other war memoirs of the period.

31   See Pettifer: *Kosova Express*.

32   See Lambert, Ben, *NATO's Air War in Kosova* (RAND Corporation, Santa Monica, 2002) for a masterly history of the eventual 1999 air war; see also Ignatieff, Michael, *Virtual War* (HarperCollins, London, 2000).

33   The Federal Yugoslav Ministry of Foreign Affairs *White Book on Terrorism in Kosovo and Metohija and Albania* (Belgrade, 1998) records 25 minor battles in the Koshare/Morina corridor, between 1 January and 31 August 1998, more than in the rest of the Albania/Kosova border areas put together.

34   See, for instance, Zejnullahu, Safet, *War for Kosova (Commander Remi Speaks)* (Zeri, Prishtina, 2001) for the views of a KLA commander from a 'rightist' background, and Neziri: *Ahmet Haxhiu* for material on the earlier stage of paramilitary activity in the pre-KLA period. The issue of command structure function has assumed considerable importance in the International War Crimes Tribunal trials of ex-KLA commanders such as Fatmir Limaj.

35   In 1995–6 in Belgrade the authors witnessed consistent contacts between British and Yugoslav intelligence officials exchanging information about Kosova.

36   See Pettifer: *Kosova Express* for a detailed study of the media and the war in summer 1998.

37   See *Ushtria Clirimtare e Kosoves- Dokumente dhe Artikuj* (Zeri I Kosoves, Aarau, 2000). For earlier documents from the LKCK, see *Misioni I Climirit* (Rilindja, Tirana, 1998).

PART III, Chapter 8

1   See story by James Pettifer, 'Tensions are mounting in Kosova' in *The Times*, London, 8 January 1998. For biographical material on the events and the Geci family, see *Fenikset e Lirise – Deshmoret e Ushtrise Climtare te Kosoves* (Shvluc, Prishtina, 2002). For a participant view of the war around Klina, see Geci, Gani, 'Lufta pa Maska', *Bota Sot* (Prishtina, 2001); also interview with Gani Geci by James Pettifer, Germany, 2005.

2   See stories by Miranda Vickers in the London *Guardian* and James Pettifer in the *Wall Street Journal* during May 1996.

3   Cf. Pirraku, M., *Tivat 1945* (Prishtina, 2004).

4   See Pettifer, James, 'The Kosova Liberation Army – the myth of origin', in K. Drezov, B. Gokay and D. Kostovicova (eds) *Kosovo Myths, Conflict and War* (Keele,1999).

For general historical background on the post-Second World War anti-communist resistance in Drenica, see Dobra, Islam, *Lufta e Drenicas 1941–1945 dhe NDSH Deri 1947* (Prishtina, 1997). The best book illustrating the key transition period in pre-KLA history before 1991 is Neziri, Ibish, *Ahmet Haxhiu nje Jete te Tere ne Levizjen Ilgale* (Ibrezi, Prishtina, 2001). Also Bajrami, Hakif, *Dosia Demaci* (Shoqata e te Burgoserne Politike, Prishtina, 2004).

5   See LeBor, Adem, *Milosevic* (Bloomsbury, London, 2002) for illuminating insights into the British view of Serbia. He notes that the British-organised privatisation of Serb Telecom in 1996 effectively paid for the Kosova war and ethnic cleansing campaign.

6   For a good account from a Kosovar Albanian viewpoint, see Baftiu, Fehmi, *Kosova Krize Nderkombetare* (Clirimi, Prishtina, 2004).

7   James Pettifer's interview with BBC correspondent Paul Woods, July 1999.

8   See Judah, Tim, *Kosova War and Revenge* (Oxford University Press, London and Yale University Press, New Haven, CT, 2000) and Pettifer, James, *Kosova Express* (C. Hurst & Co., London, Wisconsin University Press, Madison and Liria Books, Prishtina, 2004; Libri, New York, 2006).

9   For a good account of the war here, see Fejza, E., Z. Gocaj and I. Miftari, *Vushtria– Viciana me Rrethine* (Vushtrri, 2003).

10   See, for instance, unattributed article, 'Kosovo violence spreads as Serbs send in troops', *Albanian Daily News*, No. 750, 14 March 1998, where the views of an official of the neo-fascist Serbian Radical party are given equal space with those of Dr Ibrahim Rugova.

11   The term 'First Offensive' was pioneered by Professor Stefan Troebst of Leipzig Univeristy in his periodisation of the different phases of the 1997–9 war. We use it for the period from early March 1998 to June 1998.

12   See Vickers, Miranda, 'The view from Tirana', International Crisis Group briefing paper, May 1998 (www.crisisgroup.org).

13   Bukoshi is believed to have approached the British government around February 1998 for support in forming a competitor force to the KLA. The pro-Serb cabal in the Foreign Office that controlled Balkan policy supported the plan but Foreign Minister Robin Cook refused to support the recommended policy option. Bukoshi then took on British military consultants Sandlines as expert advisers. A consultant's report was produced, advising Bukoshi on how to proceed with his plans, but the British government prohibited Sandlines from further involvement.

14   The Contact Group was first established in the Bosnian war as a group of Western nations to involve Russia in largely collaborationist diplomacy with the Milosevic regime. In the Kosova war it played a more independent role under US and UK pressure. See Pettifer: *Kosova Express* and material by John Norris and other authors who have studied its diplomacy.

15   The sequence of events appears to have been that after the discovery of the Labinot training camp in autumn 1992, an Albanian military intelligence officer, Astrit Mulita, was sacked for revealing the whereabouts of the camp to James Pettifer, who wrote about it in December 1992 in the London *East European Reporter* newssheet. The DP government then sought to placate its British and French backers in the intelligence world, who had been shocked by the discovery of the camp. There was a crackdown on the nascent KLA, including the arrest of Jashari and other militants training in Albania. In retrospect many features of the affair prefigure elements of

the later crisis between the unpatriotic DP government and the Socialist-dominated officer corps of the army. The latter embodied the patriotic element in the Partisan military tradition.

16   *Relindja Democratika*, Tirana, 14 March 1998.

17   Interview of Neritan Ceka with the authors, Tirana, May 2000. Ceka stated that sometimes Nano instructed him to arrest arms traffickers and other times to ignore them.

18   *Albania Daily News*, Tirana, 12 March 1998. See Part I, Chapter 2 of this book for similar NATO dilemmas in March 1997.

19   For Meidani's views, see Nazarko, Mentor (ed.), *Presidenti Meidani dhe Kosova* (Toena, Tirana, 2000).

20   Great Britain was probably the closest friend of the Nano government in Europe after Greece, but in his autumn 1997 visit to London Nano was not allowed to meet Tony Blair and spent most of his time with middle-level officials. See 'Friends of Albania', *BESA* journal, Vol.1, No. 3, Truro, autumn 1997 for details.

21   Conversation with James Pettifer, Tirana, 11 September 1998.

22   There was even some discussion at the time in the Belgrade military press of setting up a 'security zone' in northern Albania, with anti-KLA forays across the border along the lines of the Israeli security zone in southern Lebanon. Israel, through its large Mossad station in Belgrade, played an influential role in Serbian military thinking.

23   Conversation between Miranda Vickers and British Embassy official in Tirana, March 1998.

24   It is worth bearing in mind that the LPK had existed for much longer than the LKCK. The former was founded in 1982, whereas the LKCK emerged over a period after 1990, becoming influential in Kosova after 1993–4.

25   The Turkish Foreign Ministry was heavily pro-Yugoslavist in this period, seeking to preserve as much of the old system as possible in order to protect the interests of Turkish minorities in the Balkans and avoid the vulnerability of Turkish-oriented Muslims and subsequent carnage that had occurred in the Bosnian conflict.

26   See the *The Times*, story from Shijak by James Pettifer, 8 June 1998 and Hamzaj, Bardh, *A Narrative about War and Freedom: Dialogue with Commander Ramush Haradinaj* (Zeri, Prishtina, 2000) for more detail on this period.

27   See Pettifer: *Kosova Express*.

28   Ibid., p.252.

29   See Albanian NGO Consortium document, 'Albania – the great shelter' (Tirana, 2000).

30   There are numerous accounts of the problems with the UNHCR. See relevant publications of Care International (www.careinternational.org) and Mercy Corps (www.mercycorps.org), who were among the big INGOs that had to cope with the practical results of UNHCR failures. For a UNHCR view, see UN documents 'UNHCR in Albania' (Tirana, 1999) and also 'The Southeastern Europe humanitarian operations' (Geneva, November 1999).

31   *Fakti*, Tetovo, 12 March 1998.

32   See Lushi, Uk, *New York–Prishtina–New York Batalioni Atlantiku* (Zeri, Prishtina, 2001). Also, for a generally excellent account of the KLA in New York City, Sullivan, Stacy, *Be Not Afraid, For You Have Sons in America* (Random House, New York, 2004).

33   *Albania Daily News*, 20 March 1998.

34 See Pettifer: *Kosova Express* for more detail on this period.
35 See 'New Guerrillas Rival Old Rebels to Free Kosovo', *Christian Science Monitor*, 3 September 1998.

PART III, Chapter 9

1 The tunnels referred to were almost certainly part of the old Hoxhaist defence system, and largely irrelevant to the activity of the KLA.
2 James Pettifer's interview with Bujar Bukoshi, Prishtina, October 2005.
3 British military intelligence is believed to have been the main source of intelligence data to the Nano government that made these seizures possible, and publicity for them in the Tirana press (usually in *Koha Jone*) was carefully synchronised with intelligence officers in the British embassy. Serbian influence in the British army and British secret intelligence was strong in the aftermath of the Bosnian war.
4 ATA News Agency, Tirana, 29 April 1998.
5 ATA News Agency, Tirana, 30 April 1998.
6 See Italian Ministry of Foreign Affairs, 'Italy Supports Albania', Rome, October 1998.
7 *Zeri-i-Popullit*, 26 April 1998.
8 *Albania*, 30 April 1998.
9 *Koha Jone*, 28 April 1998.
10 *Koha Jone*, 28 April 1998.
11 *Koha Jone*, 1 May 1998.

PART IV, Chapter 10

1 G. Bolincaj, 'Egoizmat Politike Rrezikonje Qenien Kombetare', *Reviste Ushtarake*, Kosova Ministry of Defence, Geneva, 20 June 1998.
2 Speech in Rome at Javier Solana press conference, 15 June 1998.
3 SHIK was the successor organisation to the notorious Sigurimi of communist times, and contained many of the same personnel.
4 In the crisis involving Klosi's departure from his job in 2001–2 there were well-substantiated allegations in the Tirana press that Klosi's main external loyalties were to the FBI and CIA, and that these links played a key role in the timing of the exposure of the Egyptian Islamic radicals in Albania in June 1998. Klosi handled the event skilfully, and the Americans may well have been unaware of how much the exposure and expulsions from Albania were really designed to strengthen Fatos Nano and his government. See *Klan*, Tirana, 16 July 2001 and other publications of around that time.
5 Controversy about the pro-Serb role of Interpol in Kosova has continued up to the present, as for instance in the arrests of ex-KLA leaders under Milosevic-period arrest warrants in 2003 in Hungary and Slovenia. The FBI in 2002–03 tried to remove British Director Ronald Noble from his post, but failed to do so.
6 *Illyria*, New York, 8 June 1998.
7 See Pettifer, James, *Kosova Express* (C. Hurst & Co., London, Wisconsin University Press, Madison and Liria Books, Prishtina, 2004; Libri, New York, 2006). Bildt's policy could only have been put forward by someone with little knowledge of the geographical terrain.

8   *Corriere della Sera*, Italy, 6 July 1998.

9   An Egyptian Islamic charity had, for instance, reconstructed Kukes mosque.

10   *Koha Jone*, 14 July 1998.

11   *International Herald Tribune*, 31 August 1998

12   *Klan*, issue week of 30 May 1998.

13   The Israeli intelligence agency Mossad was widely believed to have opened a station in Albania in the late 1990s. In fact, this did not occur until 2004–5. Mossad activity had always been focused on Skopje and Belgrade.

14   Interviews with ex-Greek Ambassador to Albania, Alexandros Mallias, by the authors, 1999. See also Pettifer: *Kosova Express* for further details on the situation in Prishtina in June 1998.

15   See Pettifer: *Kosova Express*.

16   *Zeri I Poppullit*, 24 July 1998.

17   Having begun their boycott of parliament after the Socialist victory in the 1997 elections, the Democrats had finally agreed to return to Parliament in March 1998, citing the need for national unity as violence began to erupt in Kosova.

18   *Albania Daily News*, 8 July 1998.

19   See Lane, Col C. Dennison, 'Once upon an army – the crisis in the Albanian army 1995–6', CRSC Document G-114, 2002 (www.csrc.mod.uk) for background on Zhulali as Defence Minister.

20   *Shekulli*, 28 August 1998.

21   *Koha Jone*, 28 August 1998.

22   *Zeri-i-Popullit*, 28 August 1998.

23   Since 1997 the strongly pro-DP village of Llazarati had become a focus of local opposition to the Socialist-led administration in Tirana.

24   Nicolae Ceauşescu was executed after the collapse of his communist government in December 1989.

25   There was a strong British background component in FARK. Bukoshi had approached the British military contractor Sandline for advice earlier in 1998. Foreign Minister Robin Cook had refused permission in early spring 1998 for Sandline to get involved with the Kosova war. Later in 1998, ex-Liberal Democratic party leader Paddy Ashdown is believed to have advised Prime Minister Tony Blair that British support for FARK should be continued, to avoid giving the KLA a monopoly of power in post-conflict Kosova. See also numerous works on the wartime period published in post-July 1999 Prishtina. Bukoshi now considers that his attempt to intervene in the war with FARK was a mistake (interview with James Pettifer, Prishtina, October 2005).

PART IV, Chapter 11

1   For biographical background on Hajdari, and views (often polemical) of the events, see Polovina, Ylli, *Kur u Vra Azem Hajdari* (Tirana, 2003) and Lushaj, Ramiz, *Po vjen Azem Hajdari* (Tirana, 1998). (The latter work concentrates on Hajdari's achievements as a student leader in the 1991–2 period, rather than his later career in the DP or his death.)

2   Scott Carlson, Legal Adviser to the OSCE Presence in Albania (1997–8), *Some Reflections on Experiencing an Attempted Coup in Albania* (Washington, DC, 2002) (memoir document).

3   Document 'Vritet deputi I Partise demokratike, Azem Hajdari s bashku me shqeruesit e tij' (translation from document received from international community official), 12 September 1998.

4   Carlson: *Some Reflections*.

5   *Albania*, 13 September 1998.

6   Carlson: *Some Reflections*.

7   Genc Pollo was a co-founder of the DP, in December 1990, and had continued in recent years as a leader of the Centre Right.

8   Carlson: *Some Reflections*.

9   *Albania Daily News*, 17 September 1998.

10   Associated Press report, 16 September 1998.

11   In April 1998 the Albanian parliament had lifted the 1992 ban on the establishment of communist parties, thus legalising the new Communist Party led by Hysni Milloshi and independent MP Maksim Hasani (both followers of Enver Hoxha). By autumn 1998 the new Communist Party had an estimated 25,000 members.

12   See Part IV, Chapter 10, Note 25. See also Pettifer, James, *Kosova Express* (C. Hurst & Co., London, Wisconsin University Press, Madison and Liria Books, Prishtina, 2004; Libri, New York, 2006) and numerous works on the wartime period in Kosova published in post-1999 Prishtina.

13   *Albania Daily News*, 24 September 1998.

14   *Shekulli*, 23 September 1998.

15   Interview with Rexhep Meidani on Top Channel TV, Tirana, 10 September 1998.

PART V, Chapter 12

1   In a typical story, Tim Judah in the London *Independent* asked 'Has this nation gone mad?' (18 September 1998).

2   *Albania Daily News*, 1 December 1998.

3   See Naumann, Freidrich, *The Mobilisation and Demobilisation of the Kosova Liberation Army* (Stiftung/Bonn Centre for Arms Conversion, Bonn/Skopje, 2001).

4   The Kacaks were Kosova fighters who refused to accept the collaborationist policies of Tirana governments in the Versailles and immediate post-Versailles settlement period after 1922–4, and who fought for Kosova independence.

5   See 'The mysterious Kosovar', *Klan* magazine, Tirana, March 1999.

6   President Bush in 1992 made a direct threat of US military intervention if Milosevic provoked a Kosova crisis.

7   Pettifer, James, *Kosova Express* (C. Hurst & Co., London, Wisconsin University Press, Madison and Liria Books, Prishtina, 2004; Libri, New York, 2006), pp.169 ff.

8   See Sullivan, Stacy, *Be Not Afraid, For You Have Sons in America* (Random House, New York, 2004) for an excellent picture of the KLA recruitment process in the USA.

9   See Pettifer: *Kosova Express*.

10   The Corfu Channel incident in 1948 involved the sinking of Royal Navy shipping off the Albanian coast, and the ending of all contact between Britain and Albania for over 50 years.

11   *Albania Daily News*, Tirana, 1 December 1998.

12   The role of Klosi here is interesting. The *Sunday Times* has traditionally had good relationships with the British Secret Intelligence Service, MI6. The affair was mainly interesting for illustrating the residual influence of the Serb lobby within MI6.

13   In 2002 Klosi was accused of various anti-national offences while head of SHIK and was placed under house arrest for a period while a parliamentary commission investigated his activity.

14   These links were most clearly exposed in 2001 during the visit of Serbian President Kostunica to London. Few realised at the time the major influence on the Foreign and Commonwealth Office in London of the Serbian and Greek Royalist lobbies over post-Milosevic policy. Kostunica visited a secret Windsor conference centre then, as did other British-linked Balkan leaders on occasion, like the late President Trajkovski of Macedonia.

15   This communiqué cannot be identified here without breaching confidentiality.

16   There was still, despite the events of the Bosnian war, an ethnic Greek and Jewish element within US government organs that sought to equate the emergence of Kosova as an independent entity with the advance of 'Islam' within the region.

17   These events laid the foundation for the bitter animosities in and around Peje after the war between FARK supporters and opponents, which led to the assassination of Zemaj in 2002.

18   Reuters, 24 December 1998.

19   Ibid.

20   See Pettifer, James, 'Landmine ban is defied on border', *The Times*, 17 January 1999.

PART V, Chapter 13

1   See Pettifer, James, *Kosova Express* (C. Hurst & Co., London, Wisconsin University Press, Madison and Liria Books, Prishtina, 2004; Libri, New York, 2006) for more on this dimension to the conflict.

2   *Koha Ditore*, Prishtina, 17 January 1999.

3   *Albania*, Tirana, 12 November 1997.

4   In earlier periods in the 1990s the Kosova office in Tirana was alleged to have been used for a variety of illegal activities in the economic field.

5   For further details on French efforts to discredit Racak, see Pettifer: *Kosova Express*.

6   As long ago as the 1950s, the Greek-speaking communities from the south and cities like Vlora had been heavily over-represented in the old Sigurimi. The historical basis for this was the number of very hard-line Greek communist exiles from the post-1949 period who had taken refuge in Albania.

7   See Madeleine Albright's memoirs, *Madam Secretary* (Macmillan, London and New York, 2003) for her own account of this period.

8   See Pettifer: *Kosova Express*, pp. 169 ff. and also Judah, Tim, *Kosova – War and Revenge* (Oxford University Press, London and Yale University Press, New Haven, CT, 2000).

9   ATA News Agency, Tirana, 4 October 1998.

10   See, for example, the distinguished reporting in the London *Sunday Times* by Jon Swain from this region during this period.

11   *Albania Daily News*, 12 January 1999.

12   See Vickers, Miranda, *The Albanians – A Modern History* (I.B.Tauris, London, 2005).

13   Conversations/interview with the authors 1999–2002.

14   See Pettifer, James, *Towards a New Reality – Conversation with Hashim Thaci* (Prishtina, 2002).

15   Thaci was released from jail on the insistence of General Adem Copani of the Albanian Army. James Pettifer's interview with Hashim Thaci, July 2004.

16   For background information on the Cham issue, see Vickers, Miranda, 'The Cham Question – Albanian national and property rights in Greece', G-104, April 2002 at www.csrc.ac.uk.

17   See Pettifer, James, *Blue Guide to Albania and Kosova* (A&C Black, London and Norton, New York, 2001).

18   See, for instance, *Koha Jone* between 12 and 20 January.

19   James Pettifer's interviews with senior RAF officers, 2005, UK.

PART V, Chapter 14

1   See Simms, Brendan, *Britain and the Tragedy of Bosnia* (Penguin, London, 2002), among other volumes.

2   The most readable general account, although naturally with some controversial viewpoints, is Judah, Tim, *Kosova War and Revenge* (Oxford University Press, London and Yale University Press, New Haven, CT, 2000).

3   For an Albanian insider's account, written from a LDK viewpoint, see Tahiri, Edita, *The Rambouillet Conference Negotiating Process and Documents* (Dukagjini, Peje, 2001). See Judah: *Kosova War and Revenge*, pp.198 ff.

4   Ibid., p.197.

5   This was certainly not a universal view in the UK. In the Royal Air Force assessment, Milosevic had determined on 'cleansing' Kosova fully by the late summer of 1998, and intervention plans were made accordingly.

6   In retrospect, it was merely another example of the pro-Serb orientation of the French military.

7   Judah: *Kosova War and Revenge*.

8   See Albright, Madeleine, *Madame Secretary* (Macmillan, London and New York, 2003), pp.394 ff.

9   See Pettifer, James, *Kosova Express* (C. Hurst & Co., London, Wisconsin University Press, Madison and Liria Books, Prishtina, 2004; Libri, New York, 2006).

10   *Klan*, Tirana, 22 March 2000.

11   Albright: *Madame Secretary*, p.398.

12   For more detail and the associated FYROM dimension, see Pettifer: *Kosova Express*.

13   Author's interview with Adem Demaci, Prishtina, October 2004.

14   *Financial Times*, London, 23 November 2001.

15   See Shala, Blerim, *Vitet e Kosoves 1998–1999* (Zeri, Prishtina, 2000).

16   Albright: *Madame Secretary*, p. 406.

17   See Randjelovic, S. (ed.), *The Army of Yugoslavia* (Bojcka, Belgrade, 1999).

18   Zejnullahu, Safet, *War for Kosova (Commander Remi Speaks)* (Zeri, Prishtina, 2001), pp.99 ff.

19   Amery, Julian, *Sons of the Eagle – A Study in Guerilla War* (London,1948), p.1.

20   For Enver Hoxha's views, see his book *The Anglo-American threat to Albania* (Tirana, 1953).

21   For general information on the whole refugee crises, see OSCE, *Kosovo/Kosova: The Human Rights findings of the OSCE Kosovo Verification Mission* (Warsaw, 2000); also

Albanian Non-Governmental Organisations Forum (ANOF), *Albania the Great Shelter* (Tirana, 1999). The best study in English of the effects of the refugee crisis on a single town (Peje) is in McAllester, Matthew, *Beyond the Mountains of the Damned* (New York University Press, New York, 2002).

22   See Pettifer: *Kosova Express.*

23   For a detailed discussion of these issues, see Lambert, Ben, *NATO Air War for Kosova* (RAND Corporation, Santa Monica, CA, 2001).

24   Ibid., pp. 409 ff.

25   See Ignatief, Michael, *Virtual War* (London, 2000).

26   Albright: *Madame Secretary*, p.408.

27   James Pettifer's interview with Hashim Thaci, May 2001.

PART V, Chapter 15

1   Elvira Objina, quoted in Refugee Council, *My Name Came Up* (London, 2000).

2   For the UNHCR's own view of the refugee crisis, see Caux, H. (ed.), *Journey Home – The Humanitarian Challenge in Kosovo* (UNHCR, Geneva, 2002).

3   Fatmir Kocmezi, quoted in Refugee Council: *My Name Came Up.*

4   Interview with Marion Hoffman, post-emergency head of UNHCR Albania, Tirana, 2000. We are also grateful to the staff of CARE Albania, CARE USA and CARE Austria for sharing their memories of this period, and particularly to Karen Moore, CARE International Balkan Director in 2000–1.

5   James Pettifer interview with Julia Pettifer, ex-camp supervisor, January 2005.

6   See Lambert, Ben, *NATO's Air War for Kosova* (RAND Corporation, Santa Monica, 2001).

7   James Pettifer, interview with senior RAF officials, October 2005, Britain.

8   A displaced LDK leader from Prizren, and sometime British agent in the LDK.

9   In Albanian culture, the Gheg Albanians live in the north and Kosova and Montenegro, while Tosks live generally south of the Shkumbini River in southern Albania.

10   Author's interview with aid officials and journalists, Kukes, April 1999.

11   *Albania Daily News*, 29 April 1999.

12   This problem was not confined to the north. For instance, Labinot Fushe camp near Elbasan had to employ armed guards to protect the inhabitants from foraging gangs. Author's interview with Julia Pettifer, September 2004.

13   Author's interview with Albanian officials, Tirana, April 1999.

14   Ibid.

15   See coverage by Stephen Farrell in *The Times*, London, from 2 April 1999.

16   See Pettifer, James, *Kosova Express* (C. Hurst & Co., London, Wisconsin University Press, Madison and Liria Books, Prishtina, 2004; Libri, New York, 2006).

17   In 1998 Gligorov had called for internationally supervised corridors for refugees in the event of a major Kosova crisis, to channel them directly into Albania.

18   See Pettifer, James (ed.), *The New Macedonian Question* (Palgrave, London and New York, 2001); Poulton, Hugh, *Who are the Macedonians?* (C. Hurst & Co., London, 1998); and Phillips, John, *Macedonia – Warlords and Rebels in the Balkans* (I.B.Tauris, London, 2004) for further material on post-communist developments.

19   See Pettifer: *The New Macedonian Question.*

20   The LPK, the Kosova People's Movement, had a coherent and sophisticated underground operation in western Macedonia for several years before the Kosova war.

21   See Halberstam, David, *War in a Time of Peace: Bush, Clinton and the Generals* (Washington DC, 2002).

22   Quoted in Refugee Council: *My Number Came Up.*

PART VI, Chapter 16

1   For information on how the UNMIK saw its post-July 1999 task, see issues of UNMIK magazine *Focus on Kosova*, Prishtina, from 2000.

2   That is, in 1998, when in practice only LDK and allied parties' candidates were contesting the election.

3   The same kind of planning errors seem to have affected the current Iraq war. Local states do not survive major international military operations intact. This is well explored by Anne Holohan in *Networks of Democracy: Lessons from Kosovo for Afghanistan, Iraq, and Beyond* (Stanford University Press, Stanford, CA, 2005).

4   See Andjelkovic, Z., S. Scepanovic and G. Prlinevic, *Days of Terror (in the presence of the international forces)* (Centre for Peace and Tolerance, Belgrade, 2000). For information of the destruction of mosques and Islamic monuments by the Serbs, see Bajgora, S. (ed.), *Serbian Barbarities against Islamic Monuments in Kosova (February '98–June '99)* (Bashksia Islame e Kosoves (Union of Kosova Mosques), Prishtina, 2000). See also Rohde, David, 'Kosovo Seething', *Foreign Affairs*, 79/3 (2000), pp.65–79.

5   *Napi Magyarorszag*, Budapest, 21 May 1999.

6   James Pettifer's interview with ex-NATO official, June 2005.

7   *Albania Daily News*, 28 May 1999.

8   See Norris, John, *Collision Course: NATO, Russia and Kosovo* (Westport, CT, 2005) for our analysis of the diplomacy. Also see various International Crisis Group reports from the period, at www.crisisgroup.org.

9   They had been in position as liaison officers with the KLA during the bombing campaign, through a diplomat, John Duncan, who had been acting as a contact man with the KLA. James Pettifer interview with Lt Col Philip Cox, Tirana, April 2005.

10   See John Norris's interesting but poorly sourced and pro-Russian study of the negotiations for more on this subject (see Note 8, above).

11   Nazarko, Mentor (ed.), *President Rexhep Meidani dhe Kosova* (Toena, Tirana, 2000), pp. 48 ff.

12   See Vickers, Miranda, 'The Cham Question – Albanian national and property rights in Greece', CSRC paper, at www.csrc.mod.ac.uk.

13   From the Albanian word *narta*, meaning 'lagoon'.

14   See Marker, Sherry and James Pettifer, *Blue Guide to Greece* (Somerset, Budapest, 2006).

15   See, for example, Foss, Arthur, *Epirus* (Faber, London, 1971) for interesting comment on the situation of these families from someone who was a right-wing British Hellenist, who had served in northern Greece under C.M. Woodhouse in the Second World War.

16   See Hoxha, Enver, *Two Friendly Peoples* (Tirana, 1985).

17   See, for example, Kotini, Albert, *Chameria Denoncon* (Tirana, 1999) for a pro-Albanian account of the key Second World War period; Meta, Beqir, *Tensioni Greko–Shqiptar (1939–1949)* (Tirana, 2002); for a Greek viewpoint on the issues see Kondis, Vasilis, *Greqia dhe Shqiperia ne Shekulin XX* (Thessaloniki, 1997); also the literary works of Sali Bollati and the US diaspora Chams.

18   In the recent period, since late 2003, this region has been experiencing a strong economic revival owing to the reopening of the Muriqan border crossing south of Lake Shkoder.

PART VI, Chapter 17

1   This document produced by the German Ambassador to Macedonia in 1993 prefigured many of the Ohrid Accords proposals of 2001.

2   See Bashksia Islame e Kosoves (Union of Kosova Mosques), *Serbian Barbarities against Islamic Monuments in Kosova (February '98–June '99)* (Prishtina, 2000).

3   Vickers, Miranda, 'Kosovo: one year later', *Wall Street Journal*, 24 March 2000.

4   This has remained the case in the recent period (i.e. the serious riots in Kosova in March 2004 were centred on the future of Mitrovica).

5   For a good account of this process, see Phillips, John, *Macedonia – Warlords and Rebels in the Balkans* (I.B.Tauris, London, 2004). For an account, from a Serbian point of view, of the post-Milosevic deal over Preshevo that Albanians feared would be a precursor to an imposed settlement in Kosova, see Milo, Gligonjevic (ed.), *Serbia after Milosevic – Programme for the Solution of the Crisis in the Pcinja District* (Liber, Belgrade, 2001). There appears to have been substantial British and US intelligence agency input into this process, and into the document itself – an indication of the adjustment of policy away from the Albanians after the overthrow of Milosevic in 2000.

6   For the early war period, see papers published by the CSRC in Britain (at www.csrc. mod.uk) and Brown, Keith, S. Ordanovski, P. Farsides and A. Fetaku (eds), *Ohrid and Beyond* (IWPR, London, 2003). The leaderships of the UCPMB and the NLA of the Macedonian war were quite separate but there were many links at rank-and-file level.

7   See Goro, Robert, *FYROM: Supermacia e Inferioritetit* (Kurier, Athens, 2001).

8   For background, see Pettifer, James (ed.), *The New Macedonian Question* (Palgrave, London and New York, 2001). The Titoists pioneered many of the techniques of repression later used in Kosova in the Macedonian Socialist Republic, in part because of the wider adherence to Islam there.

9   See Pettifer, James, *Kosova Express* (C. Hurst & Co., London, Wisconsin University Press, Madison and Liria Books, Prishtina, 2004; Libri, New York, 2006) and Tomlinson, Richard, *The Big Breach* (Cutting Edge, Edinburgh, 1999).

10   See Brown et al.: *Ohrid and Beyond*.

11   Like many of his fellow British Serbophiles, he had a wife of Yugoslav origin.

12   See Simms, Brendan, *Britain and the Tragedy of Bosnia* (Penguin, London, 2002).

13   See Pirraku, Muhamet, *Mulla Idris Gjilani dhe Mbrojtja Kombetare e Koseves Lindore 1941–51* (Prishtina, 1995).

14   The circumstances of his removal have since brought much comment.

15   See Churcher, Bob, 'Kosovo Lindore/Preshevo 1999–2002 and the FYROM conflict', G-104, March 2002 and 'Preshevo/Kosovo Lindore – a continuing cause for concern', G-117, March 2003, at www.csrc.ac.uk.

16 See Veliu, Fazli, *LPK dhe UCK: Nje embleme, nje Qellim* (Dritero, Tirana, 2001).

17 See Ostreni, Gezim, *Shpresa dhe Zhgenjimi I Shqiptareve ne Maqedoni gjate dhe pas Luftes se Dyte Boterore* (Prishtina, 2000). Although the book has some scholarly content, its relevance to the 2001 conflict is clear, particularly in the depiction of the Yugoslav army in Macedonia as an army of occupation.

18 See Pettifer: *Kosova Express*.

19 See Churcher: 'Kosovo Lindore/Preshevo 1999–2002' and 'Preshevo/Kosovo Lindore'; also Phillips, John, *Macedonia – Warlords and Rebels in the Balkans* (I.B.Tauris, London, 2004).

20 During interviews in Haracine in January 2000, James Pettifer was told that many Haracine inhabitants had come from Albanian villages near the Macedonia–Serbia border after the defeat of Mullah Gjilane's force in 1949. This indicates the link with the Preshevo crisis.

21 Author's interviews in Tanusche, May 2002, and with Bob Churcher, Robert Curis and Julia Pettifer, all International Crisis Group employees involved in the issue.

22 See Churcher: 'Kosovo Lindore/Preshevo 1999–2002' and 'Preshevo/Kosovo Lindore'.

23 James Pettifer's interview with EU military observer, Skopje, May 2001.

24 Interview with James Pettifer, August 2001, Prishtina.

25 In discussion with James Pettifer, June 2001, Prishtina.

26 Rusi, Iso in Keith Brown, S. Ordanovski, P. Farsides and A. Fetaku (eds), *Beyond Ohrid* (IWPR, London, 2003).

27 Interview with James Pettifer, January 2002, Tetovo.

28 The full extent of the ethnic cleansing ambitions of some of the Macedonian army and political leadership has not been widely realised. Although Robert Frowick was criticised for his early diplomatic activity on behalf of the Albanians, his CIA-origin intelligence was clear on the ambitions of the army. Author's interview with former US State Department official, November 2005.

29 See Ozgur Baklacioglu, Nurcan, 'Devletlerin Dis Politikalari Acisindan Goc Olgusu: Balkanlar' Dan Turkiye'ye Arnaut Gocleri (1920–1990)', unpublished PhD thesis, Istanbul University, 2003.

PART VI, Chapter 18

1 See Nazarko, Mentor (ed.), *Presidenti Meidani dhe Kosova* (Toena, Tirana, 2000).

2 See International Crisis Group report on the Trepce mines, ICG Balkan Report, No. 82, 2000 at www.crisisweb.org.

3 See, for example, the review, 'Ars', published in Shkoder and written in the northern Gheg dialect.

4 For a fuller discussion of these issues, see Pettifer, James, 'Balkan asylum seekers – time for a new approach?', Migration Watch paper, 2003, at www.migrationwatch.org.

5 For a cogent discussion of this and related issues, see Sell, Louis, *Slobodan Milosevic and the Destruction of Yugoslavia* (Duke, NC, 2002); also Adam Le Bor's biographical study *Milosevic* (Bloomsbury, London, 2002).

6 Clearly a major study of the roots of the problem in the Second World War period and the support given to Tito by Churchill and Fitzroy McLean is needed, and its effects on succeeding policy. A start has been made in works such as Carol Hodge's study,

The Serb Lobby in Great Britain (Washington DC, 1999) and in Simms, Brendan, *Britain and the Tragedy of Bosnia* (Penguin, London, 2002). See also memoirs of British diplomats, such as *Dealing with Dictators* by Sir Frank Roberts (Weidenfeld and Nicholson, London, 1979) and Sir Ivor Robert's (former British Ambassador to Belgrade) memoir of the 1993–6 period in Belgrade (forthcoming).

7   LeBor: *Milosevic*, pp.262 ff.

8   See Madeleine Albright's memoirs, *Madam Secretary* (Macmillan, London and New York, 2003).

9   For varied discussions on the pan-Albanian issue see Vickers, Miranda, 'Pan-Albanianism – how big a threat to Balkan stability?', International Crisis Group, February 2004 at www.crisisgroup.org and Jakupi, Ali, *Two Albanian States and National Unification* (Prishtina, 2004).

10   See Vickers, Miranda, *The Albanians – A Modern History* (I.B.Tauris, London, 2005), pp.100–118.

11   See Lane, Col C. Dennison, 'Once upon an army – the crisis in the Albanian army 1995–6', CRSC Document G-114, 2002 (www.csrc.mod.uk).

12   Vickers: 'Pan-Albanianism – how big a threat?'

13   Ibid.

Bibliography

Ademi, Astrit, *Ne Dditet e Shtetit pa Pushtet* (Dardania, Tirana, 1998).

Albright, Madeleine, *Madam Secretary* (Macmillan, London and New York, 2003).

Amery, Julian, *Sons of the Eagle – A Study in Guerilla War* (London,1948).

Andjelkovic, Z., S. Scepanovic and G. Prlinevic, *Days of Terror (in the presence of the international forces)* (Centre for Peace and Tolerance, Belgrade, 2000).

ANOF (Albanian Non-Governmental Organisations Forum), *Albania the Great Shelter* (Tirana, 1999).

Baftiu, Fehmi, *Kosova Krize Nderkombetare* (Clirimi, Prishtina, 2004).

Bajrami, Hakif, *Dosia Demaci* (Shoqata e te Burgoserne Politike, Prishtina, 2004).

Bardha, Ekrem, *Larg Dhe Pranë Shqiperise* (Owufri, Tirana, 2002).

Bashksia Islame e Kosoves (Union of Kosova Mosques), *Serbian Barbarities against Islamic Monuments in Kosova (February '98–June '99)* (Prishtina, 2000).

Baze, Mero, *Shqiperia dhe Lufta ne Kosova* (Koha, Tirana, 1998).

Berisha, Beqir, *Fundi i nje Aventure Politike* (Libri Politike, Tetovo, 1998).

Berisha and Harxhi (eds), 'Komploti Greko Komunist kunder Demokracise Shqiptare 1997-2000', at www.users.erols.com.

Biberaj, Elez, *Albania in Transition* (Westview, CT, 1998).

Binaj, Agim and Beatrice Pollo, *Buxheti dhe Shpenzimet per Mbrojtjen* (Geer, Tirana, 2002).

Bolincaj, G., 'Egoizmat Politike Rrezikonje Qenien Kombetare', *Reviste Ushtarake,* Kosova Ministry of Defence, Geneva, 20 June 1998.

Booth, K. (ed.), *The Kosovo Tragedy – The Human Rights Dimension* (Cass, London, 2001).

Bowden, William, *Epirus Vetus* (Duckworth, London, 2003).

Brown, Keith, S. Ordanovski, P. Farsides and A. Fetaku (eds), *Beyond Ohrid* (Institute of War and Peace Reporting, London, 2003).

Bucpapaj, Muje, *Partia Demokratike dhe Ceshtja Kombetare* (Koha, Tirana, 2000).

Buckley, W.J. (ed.), *Kosovo – Contending Voices on Balkan Interventions* (Cambridge University Press, Cambridge, 2000).

Caux, H. (ed.), *Journey Home – The Humanitarian Challenge in Kosovo* (UNHCR, Geneva, 2002).

Cetta, Muhammet, *Me UCK – ne Ne Koshare* (Prishtina, 2000).

Chandler, David, *Bosnia – Faking Democracy after Dayton* (Pluto Press, London, 1999).

Churcher, Bob, 'Kosovo Lindore/Preshevo 1999–2002 and the FYROM conflict', CSRC paper G-104, March 2002, at www.csrc.ac.uk.

Churcher, Bob, 'Preshevo/Kosovo Lindore – a continuing cause for concern', CSRC paper, G-117, March 2003, at www.csrc.ac.uk.

Clunies Ross, Antony and Peter Sudar (eds), *Albania's Economy in Transition and Turmoil* (Ashgate, Aldershot and Burlington, VT, 1998).

Commission on Security and Cooperation in Europe, *The Elections in Albania March–April 1991*, Washington DC, April 1991.

Council of Ministers, *Republic of Albania, Public Investment Programme 1996–1998* (Tirana, 1996).

Cupi, Frrok, *Vlora '97* (Fan Noli, Tirana, 1998).

Danaj, Koco, *Populli I Tradhtuar* (Java, Tirana, 1998).

Danaj, Koco, *The Clinton Doctrine and the Twenty-First Century* (Erik, Tirana, 2000).

Dobra, Islam, *Lufta e Drenicas 1941–1945 dhe NDSH deri 1947* (Prishtina, 1997).

Favretto, Marcella, 'Anarchy in Albania: the collapse of European collective security', *Basic Papers on International Security*, No. 21, June 1997.

Federal Yugoslav Ministry of Foreign Affairs, *White Book on Terrorism in Kosovo and Metohija and Albania* (Belgrade, 1998).

Fejza, E., Z. Gocaj and I. Miftari, *Vushtria–Viciana me Rrethine* (Vushtrri, 2003).

Foss, Arthur, *Epirus* (Faber, London, 1971).

Friend, Melanie, *No Place Like Home* (Midnight Editions, San Francisco, 2001).

Germenji, Flujurak, *Mbreti ne Atdhe 12 Prill–12 Korrik 1997* (Koha, Tirana, 1998).

Goro, Robert, *FYROM – Supremacia e Inferioritetit* (Kurier, Athens, 2001).

Halberstam, David, *War in a Time of Peace: Bush, Clinton and the Generals* (Washington DC, 2002).

Hamzaj, Bardh, *A Narrative about War and Freedom: Dialogue with Commander Ramush Haradinaj* (Zeri, Prishtina, 2000).

Hodge, Carole, *The Serb Lobby in Great Britain* (Glasgow, 1997).

Holbrooke, Richard, *To End a War* (Random House, New York, 1998).

Holohan, Anne, *Networks of Democracy: Lessons from Kosovo for Afghanistan, Iraq, and Beyond* (Stanford University Press, Stanford, CA, 2005).

Horvat, Branko, *Kosovsko Pitanje* (Globus, Zagreb, 1999).

Hoxha, Enver, *The Anglo-American threat to Albania* (Tirana, 1953).

Hoxha, Enver, *Two Friendly Peoples* (Tirana, 1985).

Ignatieff, Michael, *Virtual War* (HarperCollins, London, 2000).

International Crisis Group, 'The view from Tirana – the Albanian dimension of the Kosova crisis', Balkans Report No. 36, 10 July 1998.

Italian Ministry of Foreign Affairs, 'Italy Supports Albania', Rome, October 1998.

Jakupi, Ali, *Two Albanian States and National Unification* (Prishtina, 2004).

Jennings, Christian, *Midnight in Some Burning Town – British Special Forces Operations from Belgrade to Baghdad* (Weidenfeld Military, London, 2004).

Jerkovic, Nebojsa (ed.), 'Kosovo and Metohija – An Integral Part of the Republic of Serbia and Federal Republic of Yugoslavia', *International Affairs*, Belgrade, 1995.

Jovanovic, Stanoje, *The Army of Yugoslavia* (Vojska, Belgrade, 1999).

Judah, Tim, *Kosovo War and Revenge* (Oxford University Press, London and Yale University Press, New Haven, CT, 2000).

Katana, Halil, *Ringritja e Ushtrise Shqiptare 1997–2000* (Rinia, Tirana, 2004).

Kekezi, Harillaq and Rexhep Hida,, *What the Kosovars Say and Demand* (8 Nentori, Tirana, 1990).

Kondis, Vasilis, *Greqia dhe Shqiperia ne Shekulin XX* (Thessaloniki, 1997).

Korovilas, J., 'The Albanian Economy in Transition: The Role of Remittances and Pyramid Investment Schemes', *Working Papers in Economics* No. 28 (University of the West of England, November 1998).

Kosova Ministry of Defence, 'Reviste Ushtarake,' Geneva, 20 June 1998.

Kotini, Albert, *Chameria Denoncon* (Tirana, 1999).

Kraja, Mehmet, *Mirupafshim ne nje lufte tjeter pub Rozafa* (Prishtina, 2003).

Lama, Kudusi, *Kosova dhe Ushtria Climitare* (Tirana, 2005).

Lambert, Ben, *NATO's Air War in Kosova* (RAND Corporation, Santa Monica, CA, 2002).

Lane, Col C. Dennison, 'Once upon an army – the crisis in the Albanian army 1995–6', CRSC Document G-114, 2002 (www.csrc.mod.uk).

Laska, Ilia, *Zagoria – Historia dhe Tradita* (Albin, Tirana, 2001).

Lebenberger, Ueli and Alain Maillard, *Les Damnés du Troisiéme Cercle – Les Kosovars en Suisse 1965–1999* (Metropolis, Geneva,1999).

LeBor, Adem, *Milosevic* (Bloomsbury, London, 2002).

Leci, Elmas, *Eliminimi I Lidershipit Ushtarak* (Tirana, 2002).

Lemel, H. (ed.), *Rural Property and Economy in Post-Communist Albania* (Berghahn, New York, 2000).

Lushaj, Ramiz, *Po vjen Azem Hajdari* (Tirana, 1998).

Lushi, Uk, *New York–Prishtina–New York Batalioni Atlantiku* (Zeri, Prishtina, 2001).

McAllester, Matthew, *Beyond the Mountains of the Damned* (New York University Press, New York, 2002).

Maliqi, Shkelzen, *Kosova – Separate Worlds* (Dukagjini, Prishtina, 1998).

Meksi, Alexander, *Permes Fjales se Tij* (Luarasi, Tirana, 1997).

Mema, Fatmir, 'Did Albania really need Operation Alba?', *Security Dialogue*, Vol. 29, No. 2, June 1998.

Meta, Beqir, *Tensioni Greko–Shqiptar (1939–1949)* (Tirana, 2002).

Milo, Gligonjevic (ed.), *Serbia after Milosevic – Programme for the Solution of the Crisis in the Pcinja District* (Liber, Belgrade, 2001).

Milo, Paskal, *'Greater Albania'– Between Fiction and Reality* (Tirana, 2001).

Misha, P. (ed.) *Dosja Sekrete e UDB-se-Emigrationi Shqiptare 1944–1953* (Koha, Tirana and Prishtina, 2005).

Mertus, Julie A., *Kosovo – How Myths and Truths Started a War* (Los Angeles, 1999).

Metropolitan Sevastanios of Dryinoupolis, *Northern Epirus Crucified* (Athens, 1986).

Ministria e Mbrojtjes Popullore, *Historia e Artit Ushtarak te Luftes Antifashiste Nacionalclirimitare te Poppulit Shqiptar* (Ministria e Mbrojtjes Popullore, Tirana, 1989).

Nano, Fatos, *Albanian Government Program* (Tirana, July 1997).

Naumann, Freidrich, *The Mobilisation and Demobilisation of the Kosova Liberation Army* (Stiftung/BICC, Bonn/Skopje, 2001).

Nazarko, Mentor (ed.), *Presidenti Meidani dhe Kosova* (Toena, Tirana, 2000).

Neziri, Ibish, *Ahmet Haxhiu nje Jete te Tere ne Levizjen Ilgale* (Ibrezi, Prishtina, 2001).

Norris, John, *Collision Course: NATO, Russia and Kosovo* (Westport, CT, 2005).

Orofino, Giuseppe, *L'Operazione Alba* (Rivista Militare, Rome, 2001).

OSCE (Organization for Security and Cooperation in Europe), *Kosovo/Kosova: The Human Rights findings of the OSCE Kosovo Verification Mission* (Warsaw, 2000).

Ostreni, Gezim, *Shpresa dhe Zhgenjimi I Shqiptareve ne Maqedoni gjate dhe pas Luftes se Dyte Boterore* (Prishtina, 2000).

Ozgur Baklacioglu, Nurcan, 'Devletlerin Dis Politikalari Acisindan Goc Olgusu: Balkanlar' Dan Turkiye'ye Arnaut Gocleri (1920–1990)', unpublished PhD thesis, Istanbul University, 2003.

Petritsch, Wolfgang and Pichler, Robert, *Kosovo-Kosova – Der Lange Weg Zum Frieden* (Weiser Verlag, Klagenfurt, 2005).

Pettifer, James (ed.), *The New Macedonian Question* (Palgrave, London and New York, 2001).

Pettifer, James, 'The Kosova Liberation Army – the myth of origin', in K. Drezov, B. Gokay and D. Kostovicova (eds), *Kosovo: Myths, Conflict and War* (Keele, 1999).

Pettifer, James, *Blue Guide to Albania and Kosova* (A&C Black, London and Norton, New York City, 2001).

Pettifer, James, *Towards a New Reality – Conversation with Hashim Thaci* (Prishtina, 2002).

Pettifer, James, 'Balkan asylum seekers – time for a new approach?', Migration Watch paper, 2003, at www.migrationwatch.org.

Pettifer, James, *Kosova Express* (C. Hurst & Co., London, and Wisconsin University Press, Madison, USA, and Liria Books Prishtina, 2004).

Phillips, John, *Macedonia – Warlords and Rebels in the Balkans* (I.B.Tauris, London, 2004).

Pirraku, Muhamet, *Mulla Idris Gjilani Dhe Mbrojtja Kombetare e Kosoves Lindore 1941–1951* (Dituria Islame, Prishtina, 1995).

Pirraku, Muhamet, *Tivat 1945* (Prishtina, 2004).

Polovina, Ylli, *Kur u Vra Azem Hajdari* (Tirana, 2003).

Poulton, Hugh, *Who are the Macedonians?* (C. Hurst & Co., London, 1998).

Randjelovic, S. (ed.), *The Army of Yugoslavia* (Bojcka, Belgrade, 1999).

Refugee Council, *My Name Came Up* (London, 2000).

Rexhepi, Zeqirja, *Partia Demokratike Shqiptare-Lindja Zhvillimi dhe Verprimtaria* (Tringa, Tetovo, 2004).

Roberts, Sir Frank, *Dealing with Dictators* (Weidenfeld and Nicholson, London, 1979).

Rohde, David, 'Kosovo Seething', *Foreign Affairs*, 79/3 (2000), pp.65–79.

Sell, Louis, *Slobodan Milosevic and the Destruction of Yugoslavia* (Duke, North Carolina, 2002).

Selm, Joanne van (ed.), *Kosovo's Refugees in the European Union* (Continuum, London and New York, 2000).

Shala, Blerim, *Vitet e Kosoves 1998–1999* (Zeri, Prishtina, 2000).

Simms, Brendan, *Britain and the Tragedy of Bosnia* (Penguin, London, 2002).

Smith, M.A., 'Albania: pyramid crisis', CSRC Occasional Brief No. 52, 1997, at www.csrc.mod.uk.

Smith, M.A., 'Albania 1997–1998', CSRC Occasional Brief S-42, 1999, at www.csrc.mod.uk.

Sullivan, Stacy, *Be Not Afraid, For You Have Sons in America* (Random House, New York, 2004).

Tahiri, Edita, *The Rambouillet Conference Negotiating Process and Documents* (Dukagjini, Peje, 2001).

Tito, Josephi Broz, *Tito – Selected Military Works* (Vojnoizdavacki Zavod, Belgrade, 1966).

Tomlinson, Richard, *The Big Breach* (Cutting Edge, Edinburgh, 1999).

Troebst, Stefan, 'Conflict in Kosovo – Failure of Prevention? An Analytical Documentation 1992–1998', ECMI working paper (Flensburg, May 1988).

Unattributed, *Historia e Luftes anti Fashiste Nacionalclirimitare te Popullit Shqiptar (1939–1944)*, 4 Vols (8 Nentori, Tirana, 1994).

Unattributed, *Misioni I Climirit* (Rilindja, Tirana, 1998).

Unattributed, *Ushtria Clirimtare e Kosoves- Dokumente dhe Artikuj* (Zeri I Kosoves, Aarau, 2000).

Unattributed, *Fenikset e Lirise – Deshmoret e Ushtrise Climtare te Kosoves* (Shvluc, Prishtina, 2002).

Unattributed, *Himara Në Shekuj* (Akademi e Skencave e Shqiperise, Tirana, 2004).

United Nations, 'UNHCR in Albania' (Tirana, 1999).

United Nations, 'The Southeastern Europe humanitarian operations' (Geneva, November 1999).

Vaughan-Whitehead, Daniel, *Albania in Crisis* (Edward Elgar, Cheltenham and Northampton, MA, 1999).

Veliu, Fazli, *LPK dhe UCK: Nje Embleme, Nje Qellim* (Dritero, Tirana, 2001).

Verweis, Agnes, *Brave New Kosovo* (Pax Christi, Amsterdam, 2005).

Vickers, Miranda, *Between Serb and Albanian – A History of Kosovo* (C. Hurst & Co., London, 1998).

Vickers, Miranda, 'The view from Tirana', International Crisis Group briefing paper, May 1998, at www.crisisgroup.org.

Vickers, Miranda, *The Cham Issue – Albanian National and Property Claims in Greece,* Conflict Studies Research Centre (CSRC), April 2002, at www.csrc.mod.uk.

Vickers, Miranda, 'Pan-Albanianism – how big a threat to Balkan stability?', International Crisis Group, February 2004, at www.crisisgroup.org.

Vickers, Miranda, *The Albanians – A Modern History* (I.B.Tauris, London, 2005).

Vickers, Miranda and James Pettifer, *Albania – From Anarchy to a Balkan Identity* (C. Hurst & Co., London, second edition, 2000).

Winnifrith, Tom, *Badlands–Borderlands: A History of Southern Albania/Northern Epirus* (Duckworth, London, 2002).

Williams, Abiodun *Preventing War – the United Nations and Macedonia* (Rowman and Littlefield, Lanham, MA, 2000).

World Bank, 'Albania – Country Assistance Review' (Washington DC, 18 June 1998).

Zejnullahu, Safet, *War for Kosova (Commander Remi Speaks)* (Zeri, Prishtina, 2001).

Zogaj, Prec, *Lufte Jocivile – Uncivil War* (Dita, Tirana, 1998).

Zuckoff, Mitchell, *Ponzi's Scheme: The True Story of a Financial Legend* (Random House, New York, 2005).

Index

Page numbers in *italic* indicate a photograph. Subentries are arranged in ascending page order.